THE KAMIKAZE HUNTERS

Will Iredale joined the *Sunday Times* in 1999,
working first on foreign affairs and subsequently the
home news section, where as a staff reporter he specialized
in domestic news and undercover investigations.
He now runs his own consultancy and
lives in London with his wife.

Will Iredale

THE KAMIKAZE HUNTERS

FIGHTING FOR THE PACIFIC, 1945

MACMILLAN

First published 2015 by Macmillan
an imprint of Pan Macmillan, a division of Macmillan Publishers Limited
Pan Macmillan, 20 New Wharf Road, London N1 9RR
Basingstoke and Oxford
Associated companies throughout the world
www.panmacmillan.com

ISBN 978-0-230-76819-2 HB
ISBN 978-1-4472-8471-0 TPB

A CIP catalogue record for this book is available from the British Library.

Map artwork by ML Design
Typeset by Ellipsis Digital Limited, Glasgow
Printed and bound by CPI Group (UK) Ltd, Croydon, CR0 4YY

Visit **www.panmacmillan.com** to read more about all our books
and to buy them. You will also find features, author interviews and
news of any author events, and you can sign up for e-newsletters
so that you're always first to hear about our new releases.

To Martin

Contents

List of Illustrations ix

Maps xi

Prologue 1

Introduction 6

1. Flying sailors 13

2. They were like gods 27

3. Wakey-wakey, rise and shine, show a leg 51

4. Bags of food and lights and girls 70

5. Wings 83

6. They don't know what they want and they won't be happy till they get it 100

7. Flat-hatters 115

8. Blooded 136

9. Flat tops 152

10. An enterprise of the first magnitude 166

11. The balloons go up 184

12. The jitter effect 203

13. The body crashers 223

14. April fools 246

15. A formidable return 261

16. Little yellow baskets 269

17. Breaking point 286

18. The absolute full 303

19. The final onslaught 320

Epilogue 340

Acknowledgements 347

Bibliography 349

Notes and References 353

Index 371

List of Illustrations

Section one

1. Ken Ward takes aim. (Courtesy of Ken Ward)
2. Chris Cartledge sailing on Lake Ontario. (Courtesy of Chris Cartledge)
3. Nancy Parker and Keith Quilter. It was 'quite the wartime romance,' recalls Quilter. (Courtesy of Keith Quilter)
4. Wally Stradwick in Miami. (Courtesy of the Stradwick Family)
5. Keith Quilter in his Corsair. (Courtesy of Keith Quilter)
6. Shooting from the hip. (Courtesy of Roy Beldam)
7. Dickie Reynolds in *Merry Widow*. (© Imperial War Museum)
8. Wally Stradwick poses in his flying gear. (Courtesy of the Stradwick Family)
9. 1842 Squadron. (Courtesy of Keith Quilter)
10. Keith Quilter on the deck of *Formidable*. (Courtesy of Keith Quilter)
11. Flat-hatting sense. (Author's own)
12. Allowances to Make in Deflection Shooting. (Courtesy of Keith Quilter)
13. Gooly chit. (Courtesy of Keith Quilter)
14. HMS *Formidable* in the Pacific in 1945. (Author's Own)
15. Royal Navy Corsairs. (Courtesy of Fleet Air Arm Museum)
16. Chris Cartledge wearing wings. (Courtesy of Chris Cartledge)
17. Physical education on deck. (© Imperial War Museum)
18. Flight deck concert. (© Imperial War Museum)
19. *Flight Deck*. (Author's own)

Section two

20. Seafire landing. (© Imperial War Museum)
21. Corsair landing. (Courtesy of Keith Quilter)
22. Pilots of 1841 and 1842 squadrons. (© Imperial War Museum)
23. The oil tanks at Pladjoe. (Courtesy of Fleet Air Arm Museum)
24. Admiral Ernest J. King and Admiral 'Bull' Halsey. (© AP/Press Association Images)
25. Admiral Bruce Fraser. (© Imperial War Museum)
26. Vice Admiral Sir Bernard Rawlings. (© AP/Press Association Images)
27. Admiral Sir Philip Vian. (© Illustrated London News Ltd / Mary Evans)
28. A US Navy Corsair fires its rockets. (© Mary Evans / The Everett Collection)
29. Mitsubishi Zero. (© Hugh W. Cowin Aviation Collection / Mary Evans Picture Library)
30. A Zero and *Formidable*. (Courtesy of Fleet Air Arm Museum)
31. *Formidable*, 4 May 1945. (© Imperial War Museum)
32. An Avenger flies over HMS *Indomitable*. (© AP/Press Association Images)
33. Target map. (Courtesy of Keith Quilter)
34. A sketch by Wally Stradwick. (Courtesy of Keith Quilter)
35. Admiral Fraser signs the Japanese Instrument of Surrender. (© Imperial War Museum)
36. Liberated prisoners of war. (© AP/Press Association Images)
37. Keith Quilter on a visit to America. (Courtesy of Charlotte Welbourn)
38. Keith Quilter visits a squadron mate's grave. (Author's Own)

Maps

Operation Iceberg: Operations of the British Pacific Fleet
(Task Force 57), March to May, 1945
xii

Final Operations of the British Pacific Fleet and the
American Third Fleet against Japan, July to August, 1945
xiii

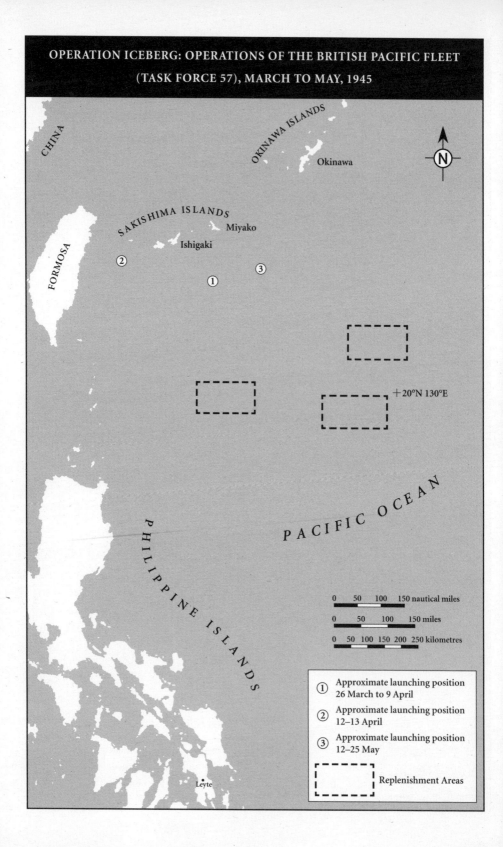

OPERATION ICEBERG: OPERATIONS OF THE BRITISH PACIFIC FLEET
(TASK FORCE 57), MARCH TO MAY, 1945

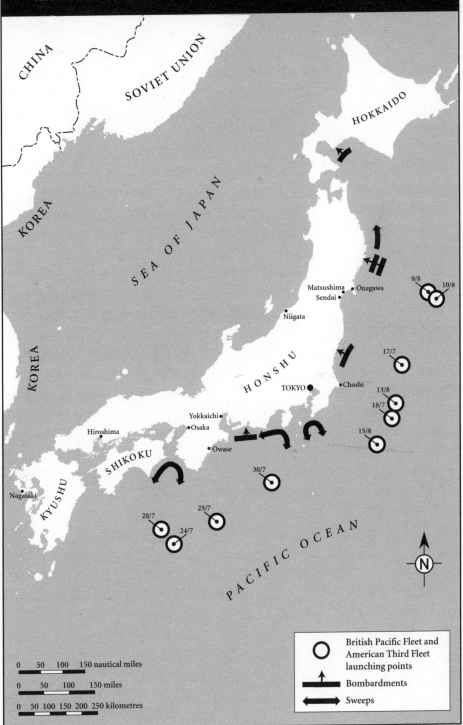

FINAL OPERATIONS OF THE BRITISH PACIFIC FLEET AND THE AMERICAN THIRD FLEET AGAINST JAPAN, JULY TO AUGUST, 1945

CHINA

SOVIET UNION

HOKKAIDO

KOREA

SEA OF JAPAN

9/8   10/8

Matsushima   Onagawa
Sendai

Niigata

17/7

HONSHU

TOKYO   Choshi

13/8

Yokkaichi   18/7
Osaka

15/8

Hiroshima

Owase

30/7

SHIKOKU

25/7

Nagasaki   28/7   24/7

KYUSHU

PACIFIC OCEAN

N

0   50   100   150 nautical miles

0   50   100   150 miles

0   50 100 150 200 250 kilometres

○ British Pacific Fleet and
American Third Fleet
launching points

Bombardments

Sweeps

Prologue

Morning, Wednesday 9 May 1945. It was going to be another beautiful spring day. Not that many would be awake to see it. The previous evening widespread celebrations had erupted across Britain with impromptu parties to mark the end of the Second World War in Europe, and many were nursing sore heads.

The BBC had interrupted a live concert recital on the radio at 7 p.m. on Monday 7 May to announce a two-day public holiday. Within minutes, Union flags were hung from windows and bunting strung across lamp posts. In London crowds gathered in Trafalgar Square, singing and dancing, and bonfires were lit in Piccadilly and Cambridge Circus.

On 8 May – VE Day – church bells pealed up and down the country, and Prime Minister Winston Churchill dined with King George VI at Buckingham Palace before addressing the nation to announce that hostilities with Germany would officially cease at one minute past midnight. With no work the following morning and Britain enjoying a heat wave, celebrations had continued long into the night. For many, savings squirrelled away over the previous six years were now being spent – 'So that on V Day I can get really blind drunk . . . to forget it all for a bit,'[1] said one London window cleaner, reflecting the mood of millions across Britain. The *Daily Mail*'s splash was triumphant: VE-DAY – IT'S ALL OVER. ALL QUIET TILL 9 P.M. – THEN THE LONDON CROWDS WENT MAD IN THE WEST END.[2]

For Dorothy Ward, however, the festivities felt rather hollow. Like thousands of other sweethearts, mothers, wives and daughters, her war was far from over. It lay on the other side of the world. Not in the jungles of Burma, where Allied soldiers who would later dub themselves the 'forgotten army' were still battling against the last elements of the Japanese forces, but further still, on a group of ships gathered in the vast Pacific Ocean which made up the largest fleet the Royal Navy had put together since the days of Nelson, 150 years before.

Dorothy's husband Ken, to whom she had been married for less than a year, was a Seafire fighter pilot with 894 Squadron on board HMS *Indefatigable*, a 750-foot, 30,000-ton aircraft carrier. She had some idea why he was out there of course – to help the Americans take the war to the home islands of Japan and finish the war in the Pacific – but what he couldn't tell her exactly was what he was doing. Perhaps it was just as well. Little did Dorothy realize just what a hornets' nest Ken and rest of the British Pacific Fleet were stirring up that morning. If the Japanese empire was on its knees and nearing the end, then its death rattle was about to reverberate through the Royal Navy in a new and terrifying way.

As his wife contemplated the day ahead, Ken Ward sat up from the bunk in his cabin deep in the humming belly of *Indefatigable*, rubbed his eyes and looked at his watch. It was 16.15, and he'd had a good sleep after lunch, following a routine but physically tiring two-and-a-half-hour morning patrol over the fleet. While *Indefat-igable*'s Avenger bombers and Firefly fighters had taken off for bombing raids on enemy targets, Ward had been on combat air patrol above the fleet, scanning the skies with his flight of Seafires ready to intercept any kamikaze suicide aircraft which might tag on to returning Allied aircraft and sneak in to launch an attack.

Ward jumped out of his bunk and walked to the desk, opened a drawer and picked up the diary he secretly kept. 'May 9, 1945. My flight was airborne at 08.30 for 2 hours and 35 minutes – quite a long time,' he scribbled. 'Nothing appeared on the radar screens, so we had no vector to steer and we saw no bogies [*sic*]. Wonder why?'[3] Looking across to the empty bunks, he idly pondered where his cabin mate was.

At that moment Ken Ward's squadron mates were barrelling their Seafires at 350 mph into the unknown. For four pilots of 894 Squadron, it had been a hot, boring and routine afternoon patrol until a 'flash red' came in on the radio. Five enemy planes, flying very low and fast, had been spotted on the radar, twenty-eight miles to the west and heading towards the fleet. The Seafires were vectored to intercept. Six minutes later they made contact with the Japanese fighters, flying at less than fifty feet above the glassy blue Pacific water. Using classic tactics, the Seafires ploughed into the Mitsubishi Zeros (also known as Zekes) from out of the sun, scattering them in all directions.

At first it seemed the inexperienced Zero pilots were no match for the British flyers. The four Seafires targeted and picked off the weakest, separating him from the pack and chasing down their quarry until, riddled with bullets from their Browning machine guns, the aircraft ploughed into the ocean in a crash of splintering wood and metal. But the Allied airmen had made a schoolboy error by allowing themselves to be drawn away from the other Japanese attackers, who continued towards the British fleet. Seconds later, the remaining Zero pilots pulled gently back on the control sticks of their aircraft and felt the G force push them down into their seats and the blood drain from their heads. Rising to 3,000 feet and levelling out, they looked down at the ships of the British Pacific Fleet below, steaming across the ocean in formation and glinting in the sun like a shoal of fish. Then, checking their bombs were armed, the pilots dropped the noses of their fighters and dived. The kamikaze attacks had begun.

On the Royal Navy aircraft carrier HMS *Formidable*, Petty Officer George Hinkins heard the alarm-to-arms bugle and sat, heart pounding, at his eight-barrelled pom-pom anti-aircraft gun on the edge of the flight deck. There was nothing to do now but watch and wait. Other men on the deck looked up, sweating under their fireproof 'anti-flash' protective clothing, craning their aching necks and ranging their guns skywards for any sign of attack. A dry running commentary was relayed through loudspeakers from the bridge to the ship's crew, as the radar operators tracked the steady approach of the Japanese aircraft. 'They have split up now and are very close.'[4]

Next Hinkins heard the 'anti-hawk' klaxon blast ordering pilots, aircraft mechanics and anyone who wasn't manning a gun or on lookout to take cover and prepare for instant attack. He felt the vast ship make a series of emergency turns as the whole fleet tried to evade the diving kamikazes. Just a few hundred feet away HMS *Victorious* – another British aircraft carrier – had just been hit twice by separate suicide attacks, sending great plumes of acrid black smoke into the sky.

Gunfire from the British ships thundered across the ocean. Little exploding puffs of black smoke from bursting shells peppered the blue sky, and tracers from each ship criss-crossed the flight lines of two suicide planes as they came within range. One began a shallow dive and was shot down in flames before it reached its target. But the other banked to its left, dipped its nose and came tearing towards *Formidable* from dead astern.

Hinkins' gun crew swung the barrels towards the black silhouette of the plane. Under each wing they could see the bulbous growth of a fuel tank, designed to cause maximum carnage when the plane crashed by spewing out flaming petrol. As the Zeke came within range tiny yellow balls of tracer bubbled up from *Formidable*'s guns. Hinkins watched bits splinter off one of its wings, shimmering through the heat of cordite. But the gunfire was ineffective. Despite hitting the aircraft again and again, the Zero kept coming, and a second later it smashed into *Formidable*, exploding in a ball of flame and showering the sea with debris for hundreds of yards. The flight deck was filled with burning aircraft and clouds of thick smoke. At the pom-pom gun nest most of the crew, who had dived behind a protective steel wall before the plane hit, gingerly peeked over to survey the damage.

But not George Hinkins. He had bravely stayed at his gun and been instantly decapitated by an aircraft wheel hurled through the air by the explosion. His headless, charred black body 'sat rigid in his elevated seat, crouched forward in the aiming attitude with hands still grasping the bicycle pedal control in front'.[5]

In less than half an hour the Royal Navy carriers *Formidable* and *Victorious* had been hit by three kamikazes. Five men had been killed with a further twenty-nine wounded, and more than twenty British aircraft on board the ships had been destroyed. These were hardly major losses – operationally at least. The damage was psychological. The attacks had opened the eyes of all serving in the fleet to just how frightening and different the Pacific was compared with anything they had previously experienced in the war.

'As a terror weapon, these kamikazes have a quality of their own,' one officer in *Formidable* later wrote. 'There is [still] something unearthly about an approaching aeroplane whose pilot is hell bent on diving himself right into the ship. Wherever you are he seems to be aiming straight for you personally.'[6]

And it had all happened so quickly. Back in Grantham, Dorothy Ward hadn't even finished her breakfast.

Introduction

The genesis for this book was a chance meeting one sunny summer's afternoon at a village fete in Kent, when I was introduced to a former Royal Navy fighter pilot. I learned he was shot down by anti-aircraft fire during a low-level strafing attack on a Japanese harbour in July 1945, less than a month before the end of the Second World War. After being hit, he managed to glide his crippled fighter with great skill down into the mouth of the harbour, skimming it across the water and coming to a rest 500 feet from the shore. As its hot engine ticked in the sunshine and water lapped over the wings of the slowing sinking plane, he jumped into the sea, inflated the little yellow dinghy stowed onboard, climbed in and desperately began to paddle towards the open ocean.

Because he'd just flown over the rooftops of their town at 300 mph and 'had a go' at their harbour by slamming two 500-pound bombs into an anchored warship, he expected to have quite a few very angry Japanese hot on his tail. He was, to put it mildly, in one hell of a scrape. Or, as he put it, 'up a creek without a paddle'.[1]

But what interested me just as much as how he managed to get out of his scrape was just what he was doing there in the first place. The Pacific was America's turf, after all. It was American blood that turned the blue Pacific waters red as they battled back across the great ocean after the Japanese attacked them at Pearl Harbor on 7 December 1941. It was American carriers off Okinawa that supported the US Marines in their bloody battle to take the island three-and-a-half years later. The pictures of the with the constant knowledge that if they were shot down and captured, torture or execution would almost certainly follow. 'The general sensation of being over Japan was one of foreboding, deep fear. We had heard tales of what the locals did to airmen who got hacked down,'[3] said one airman. Despite being held prisoner for just two weeks, one captured flyer still lost two stone, and it took him over half a century before he could get into a Japanese-made motorcar.

The captains of the Royal Navy carriers were forced to write a steady stream of condolence letters to the families of lost airmen. 'By now you will have heard from the Admiralty the tragic news that your son is missing believed killed,' wrote Philip Ruck-Keene, the captain of *Formidable*, in a letter dated 15 August 1945 – the day the war ended – to the mother of a twenty-two-year-old fighter pilot from London. 'I must prepare you for the fact that there is little hope of his survival as he was shot down over Japan. The tragedy is all the more terrible, as it was so near the end. Please accept the sympathy of myself, his squadron and the ship's company in your grief. Your son had been with me a long time, and was not only one of the best and steadfast of all the pilots, but he was one of the most beloved by all his brother pilots and the ship.'[4] Between 17 July and 15 August, in the final ten days of operations over Japan, thirty-four Royal Navy airmen were killed, a per-head casualty rate nearly 50 per cent higher than those of the Americans flying alongside them.

One of the most abiding features of the British war in the Pacific was American dominance. Three quarters of the British squadrons flew American aircraft leased to the Royal Navy, replacing the antiquated British-built aircraft used earlier in the war, which were largely unsuited to carrier work. The Corsair, a fighter nicknamed 'whistling death' by the Japanese, looked so terrifying with its reptilian wings and long snout, that when one British pilot first set eyes on this 'wicked-looking bastard,'[5] he promptly rushed off to write his last will and testament.

By 1945, almost half of all Royal Navy airmen had been

trained in America. They had a transatlantic twang in their voices, chewed gum and talked of the American sweethearts they'd left behind. 'OK we were British,' one remembers, 'but every instructor was a Yank . . . and you couldn't help but feel part of it. We lapped it up. We were Americanized.'

This book will tell the story of the Pacific battles through the experiences of the airmen. It will follow the flyers from childhood, from the moment they were inspired to fly, to their initial training in Britain and America, through to the last dogfights of the war and the desperate hunt for prisoner-of-war camps in Japan in the days that followed.

I also want to shed light on carrier flying, which shared few similarities with land-based aviation, and needed different skills and techniques. There was no church spire, railway track or river to guide pilots home, no pub or sweetheart to unwind with after missions. Instead, flyers had to locate their ships, often under low cloud or shrouded in fog, in hundreds of square miles of ocean. Landing at fifty feet per second, a pilot had to place his plane on a penny, cutting the throttle and dropping a hook underneath the aircraft to catch one of the steel cables stretched like giant rubber bands horizontally across a moving, greasy deck no wider than the length of a tennis court.

The margin for error was tiny, and accidents were an accepted way of life on carriers. Avoiding being maimed, burned alive or drowned became an obsession. It was an intense, claustrophobic environment, in which tired and 'twitchy' men operated to their absolute limit day after day, flying two or three missions a day which could last up to four-and-a-half hours at a time.

I have also sought to capture the most vivid recollections of Royal Navy sailors who served on carriers struck by kamikazes. To be under attack from a kamikaze is surely one of the most fascinating yet terrifying sensations anyone could experience.

Every year hundreds of books are written about the Second

World War, but there have only been a handful penned about the British Pacific Fleet. When Keith told me his story I wondered why so little had been written. Was his story a one-off? Had the British Pacific Fleet simply been forgotten because it never really deserved to be remembered in the first place? Certainly on the grand strategic level even the most enthusiastic historian of the British Pacific Fleet would struggle to argue that it contributed more than a supporting role in Japan's defeat in the Pacific. Its genesis was political, with the British Chiefs of Staff and, after some initial reluctance, Churchill, believing that a British strike fleet fighting alongside the US Navy would be recognized after the conflict as a contribution to the defeat of Japan.

In other words, the airmen zooming over the paddy fields and green terraces of Japan were at the thick end of a wedge which began in the wood-panelled rooms of Whitehall. And in reality the Pacific *was* America's war. The British contribution was dwarfed by the US fleet – more than four times its size – which was keen to finish the job alone. It could have. However, as the old adage goes, size isn't everything, and despite the operational difficulties of waging a new type of warfare, by the summer of 1945 British and Commonwealth airmen were taking the war to the heart of Japan alongside the Americans, and spilling blood in the process.

Wider ignorance about the British Pacific Fleet is also down to circumstance. Its moment on stage was the fag end of a global catastrophe that killed sixty million people. In the previous five years the carriers of the Royal Navy had seen action across the globe, from the frozen seas of the Arctic to the heat and hell of the Mediterranean and the vast rolling grey seas of the Atlantic. This last act was played out in a theatre far from Britain. Actions in the Pacific that might have made front-page headlines had they been closer to home often made no more than a few column inches down the side of the page. Many people in Britain in 1945 didn't even realize the British were fighting in the backyard of Japan. How can we expect later generations to remember? And despite flying hundreds of missions over Japan in the final weeks of the war, most of the individual stories that might have emerged were swept away by the dropping of the two atomic bombs on Hiroshima and Nagasaki.

But Keith's story is not unique. As one old pilot told me, 'Everybody has a story. Life is like that. But unless somebody writes it down, when they die, the story dies with them.'[6]

I hope this book will go some way to preventing that.

1

Flying sailors

A common reaction during the Second World War when a man dressed in the uniform of the Royal Navy said he was an airman was surprise. 'Don't be silly. Sailors don't *fly*,'[1] one naval aviator was told in disbelief when he answered a question about the gold wings on his sleeve. Yet by the closing months of the war these flying sailors were spearheading the largest fleet the Royal Navy had assembled throughout the entire war, flying hundreds of dangerous daylight missions over the skies of mainland Japan in aircraft marked with the roundels of the Fleet Air Arm (FAA), the air branch of the Royal Navy.

This marked the culmination of events which can be traced back to 1931, when the Japanese seized Manchuria and forged into China six years later to begin the bloody expansion of an empire they perceived to be their right; after all, Western nations including Britain had enjoyed such empires for centuries. Under the rule of Emperor Hirohito, throughout the 1930s Japan became increasingly isolated, withdrawing from the League of Nations in 1933. Its military machinations in China and the subsequent appalling treatment of the Chinese people triggered a series of trade restrictions and sanctions, primarily from the outraged Americans, who banned the export to Japan of aviation fuel, oil and iron, with the failed objective of forcing the Japanese government into a negotiated settlement with China.

In September 1940 Japan signed the Tripartite Pact with Germany and Italy, further worsening relations with the United States. At the same time the shadow of Nazi Germany was falling

over Europe. With Britain's defeat and total German victory imminent, Japanese strategy focused on extending its territory in the
Far East. By July 1941, 80 per cent of Japan's oil supplies had been
cauterized by international sanctions. By sweeping south-west
through east Asia, via Malaya and Singapore, the Japanese top
brass planned to capture the British and Dutch oil and rubber
resources in south-east Asia, securing their left flank by neutraliz-
ing the American fleet at its Pacific headquarters in Pearl Harbor,
4,000 miles from Tokyo, in Hawaii. Tokyo could not afford total
war with America, which annually produced twelve times as much
steel and five times as many ships as Japan, but it believed it would
be able to secure a negotiated settlement.

Britain had opened its vast naval base in Singapore three years
earlier, puffing out its chest and signalling to the world it still had
the most powerful navy and intended to use it to protect its valuable eastern empire. The reality was, however, that by 1938 the
Royal Navy's focus had turned to European waters, where Nazi
Germany was the most immediate threat.

The British hoped that American pressure would keep
Japan in check in the Far East. However, to reassure the Dutch
government-in-exile in London, whose vast East Indies riches of oil
and rubber were vulnerable, and Australia, which was becoming
increasingly anxious, the Admiralty dispatched its new battleship
Prince of Wales and an elderly battlecruiser, *Repulse*, to Singapore.

On 8 December 1941 the predicted Japanese onslaught across
the Far East began, with simultaneous attacks on the Malay Peninsula, Guam, the Philippines, Hong Kong and Singapore. Two days
later Royal Navy Force Z – comprising *Prince of Wales*, *Repulse*
and four destroyers – was attacked by Japanese bombers and torpedo bombers in the South China Sea. The force had been tasked
to disrupt the Japanese landings on the coast of Thailand. In a
little over two hours *Prince of Wales* and *Repulse* were sunk and
almost 1,000 men lost. Britain's naval presence in the Far East lay
in tatters. Humiliated, it would be more than three years before
the guns of the Royal Navy fired in anger again east of Singapore.

By June 1942 Japan had redrawn the map of the Far East. Britain's empire had crumbled – if not always easily and despite individual acts of bravery – after a series of crushing defeats of defenders underprepared and woefully short of decent fighting equipment. The new pop-up empire which replaced it covered almost three million square miles – although much of this was ocean – and included all of Indochina and the present-day countries of Malaysia, Singapore and Indonesia. Despite a determined last stand by the Americans in Luzon's malaria-ridden plains and jungles, the Philippines were taken too. This new empire contained 88 per cent of the world's rubber, more than half of its tin, a third of its rice and the rich oilfields of the East Indies.

The Japanese seemed unstoppable, but the events of 7 December 1941 were to lead to their ultimate defeat. Just before 8 a.m. local time Japan had launched an audacious raid on the American naval base at Pearl Harbor with the objective of crippling the US Pacific Fleet. More than 350 Japanese fighters and torpedo bombers took off from six aircraft carriers and attacked the base, sinking four battleships and damaging four more, killing or wounding more than 3,500 Americans. Until then public opinion in isolationist America had remained opposed to entering the war. No more. President Franklin D. Roosevelt proclaimed the attack 'a date which will live in infamy'. The following day Congress declared war on Japan. Three days later, Germany and Italy declared war on the United States.

But although the attack on Pearl Harbor was militarily spectacular, it failed to achieve its strategic objectives. Japan had underestimated the United States' willingness to fight back and in 1941 couldn't have foreseen the contribution Russia would later make towards Germany's defeat. This meant the United States was able to devote resources to the Pacific over the following years which would otherwise have been tied up in Europe. The Japanese high command also did not anticipate the speed with which America would ramp up its military capabilities.

Unknown to the Japanese, before the Pearl Harbor attack all

three of the US Pacific Fleet's aircraft carriers had put to sea and thus remained untouched. Although carrier warfare was still something of a new art, over the next three years the US Pacific Fleet, initially built around these carriers, became the decisive force in the war against Japan. Remarkably, just six months after Pearl Harbor, the American fleet gained its first victory over the Japanese in the Pacific. By 1945, this mighty machine would be knocking on the door of Japan itself, with British carriers from the Royal Navy's most powerful fleet of the Second World War fighting alongside.

When war broke out in September 1939 the FAA had fewer than 300 front-line aircraft. It was the Cinderella of the services, struggling to be recognized alongside the much larger and more popular Royal Air Force, which had six times the number of aircraft and operated from land bases. RAF fighters and bombers were household names; few people had heard of naval aircraft like the Blackburn Skua or the Fairey Albacore.

This sorry state of affairs had its origins three decades before, with the dawn of flight. The armed forces were slow to recognize the potential of naval aviation. In 1909, six years after their first flight in a powered aircraft, the great American flight pioneers Orville and Wilbur Wright tried to sell a 'machine' to the Admiralty, but received the curt reply, 'Their Lordships are of the opinion that [the aeroplanes] would not be of any practical use to the Naval Service.'[2]

On 10 January 1912 Lieutenant Charles R. Samson became the first Briton to launch an aircraft from a ship, taking off in a Short S.27 biplane from a makeshift ramp on HMS *Africa*, a Royal Navy battleship anchored in the Medway, in Kent. Samson was one of three naval officers and one Royal Marine who had been selected for pilot training in 1911, paying seventy-five pounds each (the equivalent of a labourer's annual salary) for their own instruction and flying aircraft loaned to the Admiralty by the aviator Francis

McClean. Samson commanded the newly formed naval wing of the Royal Flying Corps (RFC), while the other wing, under the control of the army, was responsible for land-based aircraft. Other military air stations soon sprung up across the country, and ships already in service were converted so they could hoist aircraft with folding wings and floats rather than wheels on board with cranes. The planes were stored in makeshift hangars on deck.

One of the first to understand the potential of naval air power was Winston Churchill, who became first lord of the Admiralty in late 1911 and coined the catchier name seaplane to replace 'hydro-aeroplane'. Addressing a packed Guildhall in London during the Lord Mayor's Banquet on 10 November 1913, Churchill acknowledged 'Commander Samson and his band of brilliant pioneers . . . to whose endeavours, to whose enterprise, to whose devotion it is due that in an incredibly short space of time our naval aeroplane service has been raised to that primacy from which it must never be cast down.'[3]

Despite some dyed-in-the-wool Royal Navy traditionalists questioning the place of aircraft in naval warfare, with the dark clouds of war gathering there was a growing realization that aviation would allow fleets literally to expand their horizons. Aircraft could provide reconnaissance and fleet protection, direct ships' gunfire and be used offensively. The navy's burgeoning air branch was brought into the Admiralty fold, becoming the Royal Naval Air Service (RNAS) on 1 July 1914. A month later, when the First World War broke out, the RNAS had 130 officers, 700 petty officers and men and 90 aircraft.

The RNAS initially provided air cover for the British Expeditionary Force, transporting its men and machines across the Channel to the front line in France and Belgium. In September 1914 it assumed responsibility for the air defence of Britain, patrolling large sections of coastline, hunting for German U-boats and Zeppelins. Battles between British and German surface vessels were rare. The German battle fleet was smaller than that of the Royal Navy and was largely kept in harbour. The Germans concentrated instead on tightening the economic noose around Britain firstly by deploying U-boats to attack the British merchant navy, and secondly by using their Zeppelins to monitor and bomb shipping.

In the opening months of the war the RNAS established a large base at Dunkirk in northern France. From here its aircraft operated largely over land, attacking U-boat bases at Zeebrugge and Ostend in Belgium, and cooperating with the RFC over the Western Front. In October 1914 Commander Samson was dispatched by the RNAS to assist with the defence of Antwerp and the retreat of the Belgium army. The front lines were still fluid and the armies had yet to become bogged down in static trench warfare. Supplementing his squadron of aircraft, Samson created an armoured-car section, which roared around the Belgian and French countryside in a Mercedes and a Rolls-Royce reinforced with steel plates and mounted with machine guns.

Samson's panache typified early naval aviators, and he directly influenced not only those who served with him but also boys reading about him in their history books and comics growing up in the 1920s and '30s. Many of these boys were inspired to become naval aviators in the Second World War. In one publicity photograph, taken while he was serving in the Middle East during the First World War, Samson stands in front of his Nieuport Scout biplane loosely holding a revolver by his side, looking more like a Wild West bounty hunter than a naval officer. He has a moustachioed angular face and smiling eyes. A cigarette hangs from his mouth. The Germans even put a bounty on his head.

Accidents were an accepted part of the job, and naval pilots in both wars were obsessed with drowning or burning to death. Letters home are littered with passing references. 'It's all luck,' said one young flyer to his mother, describing how a fellow pilot fell 400 feet and escaped with a sprained ankle, while two Frenchmen stalled their aircraft at 80 feet and 'broke every bone in their bodies'.[4] In most single-engined aircraft at this time the fuel tank was situated next to the engine at the front of the fuselage. If it caught fire, not only did the slipstream blow the flames back into the pilot's face, they also ignited the flimsy wood and canvas structure in a matter of seconds. Many airmen carried revolvers with them, knowing they'd rather put a bullet in their own head than face an agonizing death. Bailing out wasn't an option. Parachutes weren't issued, as the top brass believed that a pilot might be tempted to abandon a damaged aircraft still capable of being landed in one piece.

By 1916 naval aircraft had advanced significantly from the early days of the war, when they had barely exceeded the speed of carthorses. 'Pusher' planes – where the engine and propeller were behind the pilot and literally pushed the aircraft through the air – had been largely replaced by the more familiar tractor layout, with the propeller in front of the pilot, pulling it through the air. But, despite the technological advances, pilots were still open to the elements. For those who had sufficient personal income, returning to duty was often preceded by a shopping trip to Burberry's, Selfridges or Gieve's, the Portsmouth-based military tailors, to pick up leopard-skin gloves, fur-lined boots, gauntlets or other protective clothing the stretched Royal Navy couldn't provide. The most unusual items made their way onto pilots' flying inventories. Whale fat was popular, smeared on faces to protect against the biting wind, while one airman carried pieces of cheese which he nibbled and swallowed to prevent his ears from popping as he gained altitude.

Developments in naval aviation continued, with growing numbers of ships converted to carry seaplanes. On 12 August 1915 a 5,000-ton Turkish merchant ship was sunk in the Gulf of Xeros off the west coast of Turkey, after being hit by a torpedo dropped from an aircraft which had taken off from the British seaplane carrier *Ben-my-Chree*. Such early aircraft carriers were Heath-Robinson affairs. Aircraft lowered into the water to take off or launched off ramps could not land back on the ship, meaning the returning pilot was forced to ditch his aircraft in the sea as near as he could to the carrier and wait for it to be winched back on board. Aircraft fitted without floats simply sank.

As the war progressed, the Admiralty continued to look for answers to the ongoing problem of getting aircraft up in the sky quickly enough to attack Zeppelins. In 1917 the Admiralty acquired the Sopwith Pup. Powered by an 80-horsepower Le Rhône rotary engine, the Pup was an extremely agile biplane with a top speed of 105 mph, armed with a .303-inch Vickers machine gun. In a headwind of 20 knots or more, it only needed a 20-foot platform from which to take off and began to build up a reputation as a Zeppelin-killer. Soon many battlecruisers were fitted with gun turret platforms from which aircraft could be launched at short notice. However, ditching aircraft in the sea after each mission was clearly unsatisfactory. The Grand Fleet Aircraft Committee was therefore set up, which recommended that a large fast ship should be converted so it could carry fighter aircraft. Admiral Beatty, commander-in-chief of the Grand Fleet, commented that 'provision of anti-Zeppelin machines' and 'ships to carry them'[5] was most urgent.

The large dimensions of HMS *Furious* meant it was a prime candidate for conversion. Originally designed as a light battle-cruiser, it was almost 800 feet long. The Admiralty decided that a hangar should replace the forward gun turret, and a slanted flight deck 50 feet wide and 220 feet long be constructed on top of this. The result was hardly elegant. Half aircraft carrier and half battle cruiser, she resembled a waterborne hermaphrodite. To land, a pilot had to fly alongside the moving ship, steer past the bridge, masts and funnel, before sliding his aircraft diagonally across and gently bringing it down onto the deck.

On 2 August 1917, off the north coast of Scotland, twenty-two-year-old Commander Edwin Harris Dunning approached the stern of *Furious* flying his Sopwith Pup at just under 60 mph. With the ship steaming at 26 knots into a 21-knot wind, Dunning's actual speed over the deck was a matter of a few miles per hour. After flying abreast of the bridge and past the funnel, he nudged the control stick to the right until the plane slid over the deck, before cutting the engine, feeling the little plane drop. Men on deck ran over, jumped up and grabbed hold of toggles fitted to the leading edge of the wings. Dunning had become the first man to land an aircraft on a moving ship. Five days later, while attempting another landing on *Furious*, Dunning's aircraft slewed over the side, cartwheeling into the water, and he drowned. Further attempts at carrier landing were banned, but history had already been made.

Dunning's success should have paved the way for a revolution in naval aviation in Britain. But in April 1918, following a series of heavy Zeppelin raids on England which meant demands for aircraft on the Western Front competed with those for home air defence, the British government commissioned General J. C. Smuts to assess the value of the RFC and the RNAS. Smuts concluded there was sufficient overlap for them to be merged, and the newly named Royal Air Force (RAF) was the result. More than 55,000 personnel and 2,500 aircraft were absorbed from the RNAS into the RAF.

It was a decision that had massive ramifications for British naval aviation well into the Second World War. Thanks to severe cuts after the First World War, the RAF feared for its very future and focused on its squadrons of land-based aircraft. As a result, few decent naval aircraft were developed. While there were certainly some champions of aviation within the Royal Navy, backward-thinking 'fish-heads' – the nickname aviators gave some senior figures within the navy – continued to assert the primacy of the battleship, arguing that they alone were capable of fighting off enemy aerial bombing and torpedo attacks, denying the need for naval air power and thus aircraft carriers.

Additionally, aircrew on Royal Navy ships now had RAF rank and uniform, while few former RNAS airmen with naval aviation experience remained. Aviators used to the very different art of flying over land tended to downplay the value of aviation to naval operations. Progress was slow and misjudged. It was a confusing, muddled mess, not helped by the fact that the RAF as a whole had little interest in maritime aviation. In 1923 the Balfour Committee was set up to establish if a more effective structure could be devised, resulting, the following year, in the founding of the Fleet Air Arm with five squadrons. But while the Royal Navy and Royal Marines now – in theory – supplied 70 per cent of the aircrew, the Air Ministry still retained control of training and aircraft procurement. The RAF controlled the purse strings of the FAA and, much to the chagrin of aviation-conscious minds within the Admiralty, focused its energies on developing land-based fighters and bombers in line with the common view that strategic bombing was the key to winning wars.

Inter-service squabbling and arguments about what should be done with the FAA rumbled on through the 1920s and '30s, with regular debates in Parliament. The Admiralty was not oblivious to the important role naval aviation might have and was exploring the benefits of operating multiple carriers together as early as 1930. But like other maritime powers, Britain could not second-guess whether the big guns of the traditional battleship would play the decisive role in future conflicts, or if it would be down to air power provided by the aircraft carrier. The Admiralty complained that it never received the types of aircraft it asked for from the Air Ministry, while it in turn blamed the Admiralty for not being clearer at explaining exactly what it needed. The truth, as always, lay somewhere in between. The Admiralty had indeed been uncertain as to what kind of aircraft it really needed, but who could blame it given the evolving nature of naval aviation? After all, the thinking before the outbreak of the Second World War was that no ship-borne aircraft would be quick enough to intercept an air attack.

As a result, even in the mid-1920s, the Royal Navy's air branch lagged behind naval aviation in America and Japan, whose navies had retained influence over their air arms. In 1921 the US Navy established a Bureau of Aeronautics, ensuring by the outbreak of the Second World War it was marginally ahead of the curve in matters of naval aviation compared to Britain. Only after initial skirmishes with enemy land-based fighters in 1939 and 1940 did the need for high-performance naval aircraft truly become apparent to the British, while the Americans too were in for a shock when their inexperienced aircrews and machines first came up against battle-hardened Japanese forces.

The Japanese journey to naval aviation couldn't have been more different. Japan formed its naval air service in 1912 and used British aircraft including the Sopwith Pup during the First World War. In the early 1920s, eager to secure lucrative arms contracts with Japan, former RNAS aircrew set up a mission in Japan to train pilots of the Imperial Japanese Naval Air Service. Soon the British manufacturers who had hitherto supplied Japan with aircraft were – with the help of British designers – replaced by home-grown firms like Mitsubishi which gained a reputation for copying foreign designs and incorporating them into their own aircraft. This collaboration produced a generation of quality Japanese-built aircraft which would later be used by pilots of the Imperial Japanese Navy with devastating effect against both the British and Americans in the Second World War.

Japan also completed the world's first custom-made carrier, *Hosho*, in October 1922, nine months before the Royal Navy mirrored this feat with HMS *Hermes*. After the carnage of the Great War, the largest nations initially concentrated on mutual disarmament. The Washington Treaty, agreed in 1922, limited aircraft carrier tonnage to a total of 135,000 for Britain and the USA, 81,000 tons for Japan and 60,000 tons for Italy and France. The German navy had no naval air arm, and its later half-hearted plans to build aircraft carriers were overtaken by events in the 1940s. The Admiralty developed a number of aircraft carriers from the foundations established during the First World War, converting elderly cruisers and battleships into somewhat makeshift affairs. Only *Hermes* was designed and built as a carrier, using a 'flat-iron' deck with an 'island' superstructure built on the starboard side, a design which would become standard for all carriers. The first carrier to be commissioned by the American navy was also a conversion, with the former collier *Jupiter* emerging as the USS *Langley* in March 1922.

By the end of the 1920s, both the US and Japanese navies had the same number of carrier-borne aircraft as the Royal Navy. The American carriers *Lexington* and *Saratoga*, which had been converted from battlecruisers, carried 72 planes each, while *Enterprise* and *Yorktown*, laid down in 1934, each operated 80 aircraft. By comparison, *Hermes* carried just 15 aircraft, while the three converted British carriers *Courageous*, *Furious* and *Glorious* each held little over 30 aircraft. Japan initially favoured smaller carriers. *Hosho* was less than 7,500 tons, relatively light for a carrier, but with a 500-foot flight deck it still managed to operate 28 aircraft. However, by the late 1930s, its ships began to exceed the 33,000 ton per ship limit set by the Washington Treaty. The converted battleships *Akagi* and *Kaga* came in at 36,500 and 38,200 tons respectively, and both carried 60 aircraft.[6] The overall tonnage limits laid out in the treaty were also largely ignored by each of the signatory powers. Indeed, by 1941 the Japanese had built up a force of ten aircraft carriers, six of which took part in the attack on Pearl Harbor.

American and Japanese carriers were designed to operate for prolonged periods far from land, with the primary target being the enemy fleet. In the majority of their carriers the Americans built the hangar as a superstructure with open sides so that aircraft could be warmed up before being taken on deck and rolling shutters used to protect them when the weather turned. US carriers relied on having a large number of aircraft on board to ensure the enemy would not get close enough to launch an attack on their vulnerable teak-covered decks. By contrast, British carriers were designed to operate close to home in restricted waters, under threat from both land-based aircraft and surface vessels. The British carrier essentially consisted of an armoured hangar shaped like a shoebox, its roof forming the flight deck, restricting space for stowing and servicing aircraft.

The first of these carriers was *Ark Royal*, completed in November 1938. At 28,000 tons full load and 800 feet long, it carried more than 50 aircraft in two hangars built in the ship's hull. Following *Ark Royal*, a new generation of armoured Illustrious Class carriers was commissioned. *Illustrious*, *Victorious* and *Formidable* were each 740 feet long. The central area of the flight deck was made of 3-inch steel designed to prevent a direct hit from a 500-pound bomb penetrating into the decks below. The hangar, directly underneath, was 450 feet long and 62 feet wide and protected by 16-foot-high steel walls made of specially treated armour plating 4.5 inches thick. Holes cut in each end of the flight deck allowed electrically operated lifts to carry aircraft with folded wings to and from the hangar. The lifts fitted flush with the flight deck when fully raised, securing the hangar. Below the waterline was another 4.5-inch belt of steel, which protected the fuel tanks and ammunition magazines against torpedo attack.

Surrounding the hangar, on six different decks, were cabins, galleys, sickbays, bathrooms and stores, providing a home for more than 2,000 men. Each ship was like a small floating town, powered by oil-fuelled engines turning three massive 37,000-horsepower screws, which thrust the 23,000-ton vessel through the water at 31 knots. Their armoured flight decks restricted the capacity of these ships to 36 aircraft each, and the fourth Illustrious Class carrier, *Indomitable*, was built with thinner armour plate, allowing its designers to squeeze in two hangars and increase aircraft capacity to 45. This double-hangar design was adopted for the Implacable Class carriers, commissioned in 1938, named *Implacable* and *Indefatigable*. The number of aircraft on all the carriers was also boosted by using deck parks.

Despite the construction of these carriers, the failure of the majority within the Admiralty and the Air Ministry to grasp the potential threat that enemy aviation posed to a seaborne fleet was no better illustrated than by the pathetic state of Britain's naval aircraft on the eve of the Second World War. Andrew Cunningham, who would become admiral of the fleet and first sea lord during the war, later wrote of the 'ghastly failure' of naval aviation, so that the Fleet Air Arm 'became a sort of Cinderella, starved, neglected, and nearly forgotten'.[7] It was not until May 1939 that the FAA finally broke away from the Royal Air Force and returned to Royal Navy control, becoming the RN's Air Branch (although it would continue to be commonly known as the Fleet Air Arm) at the recommendation of Sir Thomas Inskip, then minister for coordination of defence.

But it was all too late, and the pitiful state of British naval aviation was ruthlessly exposed in the early years of the Second World War, when hundreds of brave airmen lost their lives flying obsolete aircraft against superior land fighters. Indeed, that the FAA wasn't entirely wiped out was thanks only to a new generation of flyboys who would answer the call to arms.

2

They were like gods

At the outbreak of war in September 1939, the FAA had 232 front-line aircraft and 500 operational aircrew.[1] The men were a mixture of career naval officers who had chosen to fly, naval ratings (enlisted members of the Royal Navy), RAF transfers and a steady flow of civilians who joined up via the Royal Naval Volunteer Reserve (RNVR). It was a small service, and the FAA suffered steady losses in the first three years of combat. Fifty-five men were killed in 1939, jumping to 382 in 1940 and 626 the following year.[2] This was partly due to a series of disastrous actions in Norway and a series of tricky operations in the Far East, the Atlantic, Mediterranean and the seas around Britain. Aircrew joined a ship for the length of its entire commission, but unlike the rest of the ship's company, who might often go for weeks without seeing an enemy plane or ship, they were constantly exposed to the stresses and dangers of flying operations. Despite the highest standards of commitment and courage in combat, countless accidents on flight decks and in operational training compounded the continued loss of men.

While the RAF had prepared for war with 300-mph monoplanes such as the Spitfire and Hurricane, the FAA rumbled along with aircraft like the Fairey Swordfish, a British-built torpedo biplane nicknamed the Stringbag constructed from wood, rope and canvas, in which a crew of three braved all weathers in an open cockpit. Resembling a relic from the Western Front, it had a top speed of just 125 mph, which, the crews joked, was only obtainable downhill. Other front-line aircraft in the FAA's inventory included the Blackburn Skua, a two-seater dive-bomber-cum-fighter and the navy's first monoplane. Although both had their moments – a torpedo from a Swordfish helped disable the mighty German battleship *Bismarck* in May 1941, and a Skua shot down the first enemy aircraft in the entire war on 26 September 1939 – they usually faced an enemy using high-performance land-based fighters which totally outclassed them.

By July 1941 there were 940 pilots across all carrier- and shore-based Royal Navy units.[3] Many of the men who had joined at the beginning of the war had been killed or were exhausted by prolonged operational stress. One officer, who was shot down looking for the *Bismarck* in the Atlantic and rescued after two days in a dinghy, admitted that 'later in the war when we were all that much more tired, I had officers under my command who should never have been allowed near a carrier. I can see two of them now. One eventually blew his brains out with his service revolver and the other crashed on deck, but mercifully stepped out unhurt.'[4] By comparison, the US Navy had just nine front-line squadrons with 200 pilots on 7 December 1941, but by recalling reserve pilots had 6,000 trained pilots and 5,000 more under training just one month after the Japanese attacked Pearl Harbor.

The Japanese Navy Air Force (JNAF) meanwhile had yet to start losing large numbers of its flyers in the Pacific. Despite four years of war with China, by rotating aircrew, most of the pilots manning the 400 fighter aircraft in the carrier groups and the land-based fighter air groups had already gained combat experience. Naval air pilots were chosen from males aged between fourteen and twenty years of age with at least two years' secondary education, and trained using a syllabus created by former British naval air officers, modified by the Japanese navy. It was efficient and thorough, with the wastage rate as much as 40 per cent, ensuring only the best pilots completed the basic and advanced training, gaining at least a hundred hours' flying before joining second-line units to get more experience. Before 1942 five years might pass between a pilot qualifying and joining a carrier squadron. Officer pilots were expected to have an even higher standard of training, with heavy emphasis on tactics. Little wonder they were so well regarded by the Americans in the early naval aerial battles of the Pacific war.

The FAA, however, was in serious need of recruits, and embarked on a push to attract more young men on 'hostilities only' commissions – signing up only for the duration of the war before returning to civilian life afterwards. By the last two years of the war FAA crew rooms were flooded with airmen who wore on their sleeves the wavy gold braid of the RNVR. By 1945 the majority of British naval aircrew had joined up straight from school, college or apprenticeships, and one official report estimated 89 per cent of all Fleet Air Arm flyers on the front line were hostilities only.[5] Most were extremely young, in their late teens or early twenties. 'Twenty-five was ancient, while thirty was as old as Methuselah,' naval historian John Winton later observed.[6]

The FAA was in direct competition with the RAF, which made the most of the national fervour surrounding the Battle of Britain in 1940, attracting new recruits through the Air Training Corps, founded in February 1941 in an effort to make boys aged between sixteen and eighteen 'air minded'. By September 1943, 72,000 cadets had attested for service in the RAF, compared to just 13,000 who had joined the Royal Navy.[7] The navy simply didn't enjoy the same level of publicity as the RAF, while the activities of the carriers and their airmen were out at sea and largely masked from public gaze. When a Royal Navy pamphlet about naval aviation was published in 1943 in an attempt to attract new volunteers, one writer for *Flight* magazine observed the 'apathetic public passes by with carefree indifference the huge piles of the official publication, "The Fleet Air Arm" which stack booksellers' stalls'.[8]

The problem was so bad the Admiralty commissioned Lord Evershed to investigate the organization of the FAA. He found the RAF had been far more effective in using the adventures of its airmen to attract recruitment and give 'courage and enthusiasm' to its personnel. 'There is no escape from the hard fact that the RN and the RAF are in competition with each other in getting the best aviators from British youths,' said Evershed. 'The absence of a "legend" for naval aviators must to some extent have a discouraging effect upon the members of the Naval Air Arm,' he wrote.[9]

In the spring of 1941 the Admiralty launched the Y (Youth) Scheme, which allowed boys from the age of sixteen and a half to join the FAA. The process started with an application letter to one of the recruiting centres in towns across Britain. The candidate would then have a medical and appear in front of a selection board. If successful, he returned to his school or job and waited to be called up on his eighteenth birthday or when the Admiralty was ready for him. The majority of men who served in the Pacific in 1945 were recruited through the Y Scheme.

Since the FAA operated mainly from carriers, its aircraft tended to be single-engined machines and never had a crew of more than three. A recruit could therefore apply to become a pilot, an observer (in the RAF called a navigator) or a rear gunner and radio operator, known as a telegraphist air gunner or TAG. Most wanted to be pilots, and were drawn to the air for a variety of reasons. There was of course the patriotic desire to defend their homeland, but more often, given their youth, it was simply a romantic sense of adventure.

Flying was glamorous. Fighter pilots were like movie stars. The war gave many boys the chance to do in real life something they had only ever dreamed about. Despite many being lured to the RAF by household names like Douglas Bader, the FAA developed a refined veneer to it, helped by the recruitment of famous faces such as the British actors Laurence Olivier and Ralph Richardson. While in reality such stars' roles were confined to training pilots rather than front-line operations, their celebrity certainly helped create the desired impression on teenage boys.

Other recruits were encouraged by propaganda films. *Ship with Wings*, a 1942 box-office hit about an ill-disciplined pilot who is dismissed from the FAA only to redeem himself with heroic feats, was 'the most fascinating wonderful film I had ever seen' one pilot said later. 'It really really took over the whole of my mind. There were these young officers with their wings on their arms, drinking pink gins and surrounded by beautiful girls, and I thought "this is for me without any shadow of a doubt". Landing aeroplanes on ships, the whole thing was just beyond a dream.'[10]

Many of the young men who signed up for the FAA from 1942 were influenced by magazines they had read as teenagers. Like thousands of other boys growing up across Britain in the 1930s, Keith Quilter was mad about aeroplanes. He couldn't wait for the latest edition of *War in the Air* to land on his front-door mat every week. The magazine was a gateway to another world, allowing him to escape the overcast reality of life in a leafy east London suburb and emerge into sunlit skies packed with Zeppelins and Gotha bombers, Sopwith Camels and Hawker Hurricanes. 'There was nothing quite as exciting for schoolboys as the atmosphere generated by aviation,' remembers Quilter, who passed the medical test despite being born with no sense of smell. 'All the forward-thinking chaps were "air minded". Its power and effect can't be emphasized enough. It was the big thing for us, a bit like computer games and the Internet is for today's kids.'[11]

Published over twenty-five weekly editions in 1935–36, *War in the Air* contained articles by a wide variety of authors and covered a range of topics from air battles over the trenches of the Western Front and profiles of the early aviators, to the latest aircraft and tantalizing glimpses of those that would shape the future. Many of the experts writing for the magazine were veteran pilots of the Great War, and its pages were illustrated with dozens of photographs and maps. It was just one of a number of aircraft magazines produced by savvy publishers quick to tap into this new market, capturing the imagination of boys – and the wallets of their parents. But at seven pence per edition, *War in the Air* was a relatively affordable way of helping to satisfy their sons' growing appetite for flight.

Aviation was less than thirty years old, and the excitement was fresh for budding young enthusiasts, who could reel off the major milestones at the drop of a hat. Their pin-ups weren't singers or actors, but pioneering naval aviators like Edwin Dunning and Charles Samson, who sparked teenage imaginations with tales of derring-do, the American flyer Amelia Earhart and 'Britain's hero-ine of the air', the glamorous Amy Johnson. 'All these records were being broken. They were adventurers, and if you had a bit of adventure in your make-up you got into them too,' said Quilter. Many books detailed the workings of aeroplanes, and some boys must have felt if they climbed into a cockpit they'd have already garnered enough knowledge to fly the things. Rifle through the pockets of the average teenage boy in the mid- to late 1930s, and along with the inevitable conker and a marble or two, you were bound to find some well-fingered cigarette cards with pictures of aeroplanes, which would be excitedly swapped among the shouts of the playground or in whispered exchanges at the back of class-rooms.

After-school flying clubs became especially popular, thanks in part to the model-making company Skybird, which teamed up with the Air League aviation society to form the Skybird League. By 1935 more than 300 clubs had been set up around Britain. Model-making classes were given by the Society of Model Aero-nautical Engineers. The Air League believed such schemes to be of 'national importance', helping to spread 'air sense', which could end up 'producing the potential airmen of the future'. It was a canny move by Skybird. Not only did they encourage youngsters to become air minded, they also created a vast demand for their modelling kits.[12]

Born in 1922 and adopted as a baby, Keith Quilter had a happy, loving upbringing and developed an open and enquiring mind. Quilter's parents encouraged and indulged his love of flying. He remembers how 'as a kid I would build aircraft in the back garden by putting step ladders on their side, a chair turned over covered with a rug, two deckchairs on their side and there was my plane'. When he was thirteen, Quilter founded his own Skybird Club, meeting at his parents' house in the middle-class London suburb of Walthamstow. For a few hours a week the conservatory of the Quilter's semi-detached house was filled with the chatter of teenage boys as Quilter and his friends constructed model planes, swapped aviation stories and re-created their heroes' dogfights. Each meeting was carefully minuted, and members were given a Skybird Club badge.

The club soon acquired a sheet of wooden board from Quilter's father. With a lick of green paint it became an airfield. Before long, model hangars and a control tower appeared. The *pièce de résistance* however, carefully placed at the centre of the model before every Skybird Club meeting commenced, was half of a four-blade wooden propeller, salvaged from the remains of a FE2B pusher, a two-seat biplane from the First World War. Designed by Geoffrey de Havilland and built by Farman, a French aviation company, FE2Bs fought dozens of duels with German aircraft over the trenches of the Western Front. The relic was a worthy centre-piece for the budding aviators, creating a direct link between their games and the gritty reality of dogfighting.

Not everyone could get their hands on Skybird models. Roy Beldam, who grew up in the rural hamlet of Eye in Suffolk, fashioned aircraft out of wood and rubber bands. Beldam's father George was a cricketer and photographer, and is credited with capturing one of the first action photographs in sport by developing a shutter quick enough to freeze fast movement. Beldam senior had a unique method of capturing an image of a driving cricketer, setting up five cameras each operated with a piece of string to a finger as he bowled the ball to the batsman. He counted C. B. Fry and W. G. Grace as friends, and took an iconic picture of the Australia batsman Victor Trumper driving the ball, 'which seemed to be hanging in the school cricket pavilions wherever we played', remembers Beldam.[13]

His parents divorced in 1926 when Beldam was just one, and his father died eleven years later. Beldam was subsequently brought up by his mother and stepfather, a retired naval captain who would bring naval customs to the dinner table, toasting 'sweethearts and wives' before the evening meal every Saturday.

Beldam was a strong-willed and independent child. By the time he joined Oundle School aged thirteen, he had developed a love for aircraft and the sea. The seeds had been sown.

But very often the attraction of flight was a more gradual and subtle one. Val Bennett – so named by his parents because he was born on Valentine's Day in 1923 – lived in a cottage at the foot of Hughenden Park, the estate surrounding Hughenden Manor, Benjamin Disraeli's country home. Bennett was the son of a banker who had fought at Gallipoli and on the Western Front. As the youngest of four children – with a nine-year age gap to his nearest sibling – he was a 'fairly solitary' boy who liked to lie in wait in the bushes with his wooden gun and jump out at unsuspecting old ladies walking along the footpath at the bottom of his garden. He spent many of his childhood holidays in Ireland with a somewhat indomitable aunt who lived in a huge country house. There he slowly picked up a love for nature, and became interested in moths and butterflies and 'things that flew. I had a lot of happy times with my butterfly net.'[14]

Soon this evolved into a passionate interest in aeroplanes. 'I remember the earliest biplanes like Avro 504s towing advertising banners over London, with the tag line YOU CAN BE SURE OF SHELL, and I would irritate my father in his workshop to provide materials to make my own models,' said Bennett.

One of the best places to see real aircraft as a boy in the 1930s was at one of the many air displays, often given by veterans of the Great War. The most famous of these was Sir Alan Cobham, a trail-blazing entrepreneur who was supposedly such a natural flyer that on joining the Royal Flying Corps he was made an instructor after only three weeks' training. On being demobbed in 1919, Cobham bought some old Avro machines and set up an aerial taxi service, ferrying 10,000 fee-paying passengers across Europe in its first twelve months alone. Over the following years he pioneered such areas as in-flight refuelling, and set a series of adventuring firsts, including being the first to fly to Rangoon and back, and the first to complete a round trip to Cape Town.

In 1926 Cobham and a mechanic set off in his two-seat open-cabin biplane, attempting to become the first to fly to Australia and back. The trip started without mishap, but cruising forty feet over the desert near Basra in southern Iraq an Arab on the ground took a pot shot at Cobham's aircraft, hitting his mechanic. Mortally wounded but faithful to the end, the mechanic's last words were to remind Cobham to 'turn the oil off' after he'd landed.[15] Cobham was nevertheless encouraged by friends to continue, and on 1 October 1926, after flying a total distance of 28,000 miles, he flew over Westminster Bridge and put down on the Thames in front of the Houses of Parliament, taxiing to the terrace, where a message from the king was read out. It congratulated Cobham 'on the successful conclusion of yet another historical flight'.[16]

Though Cobham's pioneering flights were immortalized in the press, perhaps his most memorable contributions to the growth of interest in aviation were his 'flying circuses' which visited towns across Britain in the 1920s and '30s, wowing crowds with formation displays and offering the opportunity to 'go up' for half a crown. Local papers ran curtain-raising stories about upcoming visits and set up competitions to generate excitement and anticipation. In Leicester readers were offered the chance to win a free flight if they could correctly guess the height of Cobham's plane flying over the city. Hundreds entered and thousands attended his show. While clearly something of a one-man publicity machine, Cobham's enthusiasm for flying convinced hundreds of schoolboys that their destiny was in the air.

Keith Quilter's early love of the air developed into a serious desire to make a career from flying. He had initially wanted to train as an airline pilot or go into the merchant navy, but 'my parents didn't much like the thought of that as an only child, so they talked me into studying aeronautical engineering'. At the beginning of a wet August in 1939 he set off from England with his parents on the P&O ship RMS *Strathmore* for a three-week

cruise to the eastern Mediterranean. The highlight was a call at
Alexandria and a visit to Cairo and the Pyramids. It was to be one
last holiday before he started as a student at de Havilland Aeronautical Technical College in Hatfield, Hertfordshire. Given his
love of the sea, the cruise was a trip of a lifetime, but a few hours
past Gibraltar a signal was received from the Admiralty instructing all non-essential British shipping to leave the Mediterranean.
In the hope that this was only a precautionary measure, P&O
arranged an alternative itinerary for the Quilters' cruise. They
called at Morocco for a shore excursion to the bazaars in the capital Rabat, and then headed west across the Atlantic to spend a few
days among the palm trees and beaches of Bermuda.

Only one day into the passage to Bermuda, Quilter was enjoying the sunshine on deck when 'I spotted the ship's wake completing a very gentle ninety-degree turn to starboard.' This meant
only one thing. Half an hour later an announcement came over
the ship's loudspeakers telling the passengers the ship was returning to Britain. War was imminent. The effects were immediate.
The captain ordered no smoking on the decks after dark and all
passengers with portholes in their cabins were ordered to close the
deadlights. The ship was to be totally blacked-out after dark.
Arriving in Tilbury, they disembarked to a 'complete change'. In
the ten days they had been away 'all the ships already in port had
been painted grey and many of the buildings had been completely
covered in sandbags', said Quilter.

On Friday 1 September 1939, Quilter travelled with his father
to formally sign on as a student at the de Havilland College. All
the buildings had been painted in camouflage. Old cars were
chained together, ready to be pulled across the runway to prevent
enemy aircraft landing. Driving down the A1 back home to
London they stopped for lunch at a pub where the radio was
tuned to the BBC's lunchtime news. 'When they announced the
Germans had walked into Poland we didn't even finish our meal
as we were so worried about Mum, but rushed home only to find
out she didn't even know!' Quilter recalled.

The expectation was that this new war would be dominated by mass bombing of the cities and civilian population. Over the previous year trenches had been dug in parks for people to take cover from falling bombs and bullets raining from the sky. Bomb shelters had been built. Britain was jittery.

Two days later at 11.15 a.m. families across the country gathered around their radio sets to hear Neville Chamberlain's watery voice declare that Britain was at war with Germany. Fifteen minutes after Chamberlain's broadcast, the air raid sirens went off across London for the first time. Quilter hammered on the wall between their house and next door – a signal prearranged with the neighbours if the siren was heard – and together the two families hurried across to an air raid shelter 400 yards away carrying gas masks and a few bits of food to tide them over.

'We all sat timidly inside the shelter for the first ten minutes or so, but when nothing happened most of us came outside to scan the sky and to listen for the sound of approaching aircraft,' said Quilter. The all-clear was sounded after about half an hour. 'I don't think we had another warning in the London area for at least six months,' reckoned Quilter.

In Richmond, south-west London, fifteen-year-old Chris Cartledge also heard Chamberlain's speech and the subsequent air raid siren, and cycled from the family home to the basement flat of a house which had been designated the ARP (Air Raid Precautions) post, where he was a messenger. But the planes didn't come, and through 1939 and early 1940 – the so-called Phoney War – people in Britain tried to get on with their lives as normally as possible. With no bombs falling from the sky, the biggest danger was walking and driving at night without any lights. England was blacked out. Street lights were switched off, vehicle lights and traffic lights were masked, leaving only thin slits clear. Homes were ordered to use blackout curtains and wardens patrolled the streets. The smallest chink of light showing was reason enough for a call. 'We became much more dependent on the moon,' recalls Cartledge.[17] With a good moon people could move and travel about relatively freely, but on moonless or cloudy nights danger lurked from the most innocuous of objects. His father's secretary, Miss Crouch, sustained a 'nasty injury' to her eye when she walked out of their front door and straight into a lamp post on her way to Richmond railway station.

Cartledge had flying in his blood. His father Reginald had been a fighter pilot with the Royal Flying Corps over the trenches of the Western Front, and was shot down in his Sopwith Camel in 1917. Despite excruciating pain from a bullet in his foot, Reginald managed to land his aircraft behind enemy lines but was captured and spent the remainder of the war in a German POW camp. He never talked much to his son about his flying days, and unlike many other teenagers drawn to flying Cartledge wasn't obsessive about it as he was about his music – his ambition was to become an organist.

A pupil of the City of London School, he was relocated away from London when the school moved to Wiltshire to share the facilities of Marlborough College. The London schoolboys used the classrooms and playing fields when they were not occupied by the Marlborough boys, so lessons started before breakfast, followed by games or sports. After lunch they returned to the classrooms while the Marlborough boys used the playing fields, which soon had trenches dug in zigzags around the edges. Each class had its own section to run to in the event of an air raid.

Cartledge left school in the summer of 1940 to join the family's metal business in the City of London. Although he had another year left at school, it was becoming clear the war would not in fact be over by Christmas, and his father felt he would be more use to his family learning the business. By then the Battle of Britain was raging over the south of England. Playing rugby for the Old Citizens in Kent one fine September afternoon, Cartledge looked up and caught glimpses between the clouds of the dog-fighting aircraft and their vapour trails. 'The next day we learned that it had been one of the greatest air battles so far, and a record number of German bombers had been shot down.' As a teenager seeing all the action in the skies, it was increasingly frustrating being stuck on the ground.

At Winchester College Val Bennett and his classmates listened to the reports on the radio of the previous day's air battle and how many aircraft had been shot down. 'It was like being at a football match. The results were broadcast. How many we had knocked down and how many they had knocked down. Except it was deadly important,' he said.

Bennett left Winchester in the summer of 1940, aged seventeen, and entered the de Havilland College – the year below Keith Quilter – to study aircraft engineering. The college was up the road from where the Mosquito bomber was being produced. 'When it flew in 1940 I was in love with it. Beautiful and streamlined. I thought, *I want to be a designer there.*' At de Havilland, Quilter and Bennett were in a reserved occupation, meaning there was no immediate need for them to go to war, but on a dank grey morning on 3 October 1940, the war came to them.

Bennett was with ten other boys in the drawing office preparing for a class when there was a roar. He looked up through the frosted-glass window and saw the shape of an aeroplane flash past. 'I thought, *What the hell was that?* and made a drawing of it on my pad as I knew we'd be discussing it later.'

In the room next door Quilter was busy in the sheet-metal workshop between the technical school and the rest of the assembly building, known as 94 Shop. The air raid sirens had sounded some minutes before, but the boys had learned to carry on working and rely on the school's own spotters, who sounded klaxons if they saw aircraft approaching, warning everyone to take immediate cover. Seconds later the klaxons blasted, sending dozens of boys streaming out of the main buildings towards the shelters at the edge of the airfield. 'The bomber had found himself on top of the factory with no time to bomb, so he did a 180-degree turn and came back,' said Bennett, who sprinted to the relative safety of a nearby shelter.

Quilter, however, had a split-second decision to make. He could use the inside shelters in 94 Shop or evacuate the building via the technical school and use one of the outside shelters. He chose the latter, sprinting for his life towards a shelter fifty yards from the building just as a Junkers 88 twin-engined bomber swooped over the airfield with its forward guns blazing. 'I made it to the shelter and tumbled down the steps, when there were three or four mighty explosions. It was like I had sat on the detonator as the bombs went off,' said Quilter.

In the aftermath Quilter and Bennett gingerly stuck their heads up from their shelters to find the building which had housed the technical school and 94 Shop totally destroyed and the remains burning furiously. The lone Junkers 88 dropped four bombs, killing twenty-one and injuring seventy – mostly boys and young men – before it was shot down by anti-aircraft fire a few miles away. 'The concrete sides of the inside shelters had fallen on the poor devils inside and killed them. I had made a very lucky choice as to which shelter to go for,' added Quilter.

The attack brought home to both boys the enormity of the war. Increasing numbers of students were volunteering for active service rather than staying in their reserved occupations on the home front. 'Various other members of the school felt the war was passing them by, and we got bored at stressing and studying,' said Bennett.

As the war in Europe spread into North Africa, so the Mediterranean became a crucial theatre for the Royal Navy, and the FAA played its part in a series of operations against strong German and Italian air opposition which helped restore its reputation after the disastrous Norwegian campaigns. For three years from 1940 the Allies were denied the Mediterranean as a supply route to and from the Middle and Far East via the Suez Canal, but Churchill was keen to ensure the Royal Navy retained a presence. This resulted in some of the most intense naval actions of the war, many in the convoys which supplied the strategically vital Allied-held island of Malta. Under continuous bombardment from Sicily,

Malta provided a base from which Axis ships transporting vital supplies and reinforcements from Europe to North Africa could be attacked.

Strikes were opportunistic and daring. The most famous single action by the FAA was the night raid on the southern Italian port of Taranto on 11 November 1940, when more than twenty Swordfish flew from the aircraft carrier *Illustrious* and sank three Italian battleships after flying through barrage balloons and enduring horrific flak from shore batteries to drop their torpedoes. Half the capital ships of the Italian navy were destroyed in one night, reducing the Axis threat and giving the Royal Navy more freedom in the region. The Taranto raid gave the Japanese a blueprint for their attack on Pearl Harbor the following year. It also received considerable publicity in Britain and fired the imagination of many youngsters who would later join the FAA.

Keith Quilter read about the Taranto raid but knew he could only get out of his reserved occupation by joining one of the flying services. Like a number of his close friends, he too felt he wanted to get into the action but 'did not fancy having to kill people'. His first attempt to enlist was a visit to the nearest RAF recruitment office, where he applied to join Air Sea Rescue, only to be told that he could not enter this branch of the RAF directly. So after reconsidering, he applied to the Royal Navy to become a pilot in the FAA.

Chris Cartledge also thought that becoming a naval pilot would provide access to the best of both worlds. By 1941 he was still commuting from Richmond to his father's metal business in the City. London was being bombed almost nightly, although in the comparative safety of Richmond most of the noise was from the anti-aircraft batteries blasting into the sky. With his two sisters, Cartledge carried out two-hour shifts at the local ARP station several nights a week. The main hazard was the fragments of shrapnel which rained down from exploding anti-aircraft shells. Cartledge was reading socialist and rationalist literature and becoming increasingly scornful of authority as a result. He didn't feel especially patriotic and was rather 'something of a mixed-up kid buzzing with all these ideas'.[18] In 1942 he decided to volunteer for the FAA. He just couldn't get the image of those dogfight trails in the sky out of his head and thought that 'combining flying with a life at sea' would be 'exciting and romantic'.[19]

Fellow Londoner Wally Stradwick, living in Clapham, south London with his mother and younger sister Sheila, had kept a diary since 1939 when he just sixteen. His entries were those of a typical teenager: school and worry about exams; an obsession with football; irritation at broken mudguards on his bike; enjoying milkshakes and ice cream in milk bars. But by 1940 he was documenting daily life under the German bombing raids. Following a haircut at the local barbers, Stradwick noted in August 1940 that 'in conversation, it came out that they remained open during the air raids. About the only shop that does. It would be a little awkward if they shaved one side of a chap's face, then closed up.'[19]

Uninterrupted sleep was rare. 'Every day now there are about 4 raids usually at mealtimes and then there is usually a long-drawn-out nuisance raid every night lasting until just before dawn,' he wrote on Monday 2 September 1940. Stradwick was more worried about his exams, but 'the raids are so frequent now it is impossible to remember the exact times'.

The raids continued day and night into the autumn of 1940, increasing in length and intensity as the Luftwaffe attempted to step up its pre-invasion softening-up of Britain's cities. On Wednesday 11 1940 Stradwick wrote:

As shelters were full up all round Clapham High St Mum & I went on the common. Managed to get in a shelter. My God! It was terrific. The biggest barrage ever. A message was sent through to the public via the wardens that all the AA guns were going to fire continuously throughout the night without the aid of searchlights, and that the public were not to think they were bombs. The Clapham guns (4 x 4.5s) were only about 100 yards from the shelter and talk about noise and a shaking. Shelter

crammed full. All clear at 5.40 a.m. Didn't get up this morning
until 12. I honestly cannot see how the public are going to stick
this any longer and through the winter. No leisure, sleep, spare
time and maybe no homes – and no lives. Mum and I went out
about 7.15 and found nearly all the shelters full or with crowds
outside them.

A few days later Stradwick experienced the 'worst night so far':
'Terrific damage . . . many people have had to evacuate the streets
around us . . . Mum thought we would try the Tube so when the
warning went we rushed out to Clapham North Station. It was
awful down there. Just a compressed mass of sweating humanity.'
On Monday 8 December 1940: 'It was hell! Planes were coming
over about 5 a minute. Flares were dropping like sparks from a
fire. Loads of shrapnel fell: just as if some giant was shovelling
coke on London.' But out of this came another spark. In his diary
Stradwick made numerous references to the dogfights above
London, and seeing the little fighters defending the capital captured his imagination. Like many other young men, he wanted to
be part of it and decided to enlist in the FAA.

Although the demographic of volunteer recruits for the FAA
was mainly middle class and grammar- or public-school-educated
like Stradwick, a small number were sailors from the lower decks
who applied as 'fleet entries'. One sailor was first drawn to flying
while serving on the ancient aircraft carrier HMS *Eagle* in the
Mediterranean in 1940. 'I was washing decks and I thought these
young fellows were like Gods flying the Swordfish.'[20] Also, as the
war dragged on, the Royal Navy increasingly looked around the
world for volunteers, drawing heavily on the empire dominions.
By 1945 there were more than 1,000 New Zealand and Canadian
airmen in the FAA, the majority being Kiwis.

The Royal Navy used a curiously archaic recruitment process
called the impression method. Assuming they had passed the
medical and had the School Certificate, FAA candidates were
assessed on the impression they made in an interview with a

selection board; the RAF, by contrast, used a much more formal series of tests. A 1943 Admiralty guide, published as publicity for recruitment, gives an insight into the RN process. Unsurprisingly perhaps, *When a Sailor Learns to Fly* compared the interview to a cricket match: 'Peters wants to be a pilot. He is alert, intelligent, with plenty of initiative. He is a hard-hitting batsman and a dashing three-quarter. He can drive a car and is fond of tinkering with its engine. He is a sound shot . . .'

Arriving for the interview, we're told Peters is ushered into a room containing a panel of senior naval figures.

> He takes the chair opposite the President and awaits the attack. He does not find the ordeal so terrifying as he expected. It seems that the Board is not trying to bowl him out, but is sending down an over that will enable him to display his form. He answers the President's friendly queries about himself frankly and without trying to show off. Then the Instructor-Captain takes a hand. By a few shrewd questions, he is able to assess just how much trigonometry and maths Peters really knows: no chance of stealing a quick run here. But the Instructor-Captain seems satisfied and then the President hands him a list of HM [Royal Navy] ships.
>
> 'Just tell me what you think they were called after,' he says. 'Take this one – Kenya.'
>
> 'A British colony in Africa, sir.'
>
> 'Right. And this one – Benbow?'
>
> 'A British Admiral, sir.'
>
> 'Good,' says the President. 'We had someone in just now who said it was a public house.'

Peters is asked why he wants to join the navy and why he wants to be a pilot. Does he know anything about motor cars and their engines? What are the main types of naval aircraft?

'What would you do if you were flying from London to Liverpool and your observer gave you a north-easterly course?'
is the next question.

'I should tell him to think again, sir.'

'I should hope so!'

Peters is then asked to withdraw. After a few apprehensive moments, he is recalled. 'It's all right,' the President tells
him. 'We've decided to recommend you to be trained as a
pilot.'[21]

In hindsight, the impression method seems an odd way to determine whether someone could cut the mustard in the air. When in
late 1943 there was an increase in the number of FAA trainee
pilots being thrown off flying courses because they simply weren't
up to the job, the FAA director of flying training in the US wrote
to the Admiralty asking why the impression method was still
being used, when 'this is known to be useless'.[22] But the Admiralty
persisted, and it was only in the final months of the war that it
allowed the FAA to grade new recruits.

When Wally Stradwick was invited to appear for an interview
with the selection board on Friday 16 January 1942, he was unsure
what to expect. 'I shall take togs along, in case they keep me there
over the weekend. Honestly, I hardly slept last night. If I have ever
been nervous and dubious of my chances before an exam or a
race, it was only mild compared to what I shall be like until I get
over this stunt. Still I'm afraid I shall always find something to
worry about,' he wrote in his diary.

On the morning of the 16th Stradwick reported forty-five
minutes early to the office in Cockspur Street, just off Trafalgar
Square in central London, 'outwardly calm, but inwardly feeling as
if I was fainting in church'. Along with seven other hopeful candidates, Stradwick learned there were three hurdles to clear: the
selection board, a medical and an eye test. It didn't matter what
order you took them in; 'if you failed one, you failed the lot'. Afterwards, he jotted the experience down in his diary:

The three 'fates' were on different floors and all going at the same time. It wouldn't have been so nerve-racking if we had had any encouragement as we obviated some of the jitters by talking about the daftest tripe. But my hat! First one, then the second fellow came down from the Selection Board, after what seemed like hours only to tell us they had failed on mechanical and trigonometry. Then the third fellow who had been up to the MO [medical officer] came down. His heart was not strong enough. It was about 11.30 by this time and I was the next on the list – MO as it happened. I was in there 1 hr and 20 mins. They must have examined every part of my body; blood pressure tests, holding up the 'mercury' [to test lung capacity], testing with musical forks. I passed and was told to report at the Selection Board after lunch. When I got back the fellows left told me that another fellow had failed the MO and another chap had come and failed the Selection Board. Cheering messages.

After being grilled by the three-man selection board for forty-five minutes, answering questions on mathematics, plane recognition and general knowledge, Stradwick was recommended as a pilot. All that remained was the eye test, which lasted an hour and a half. 'What with coloured lights, dark goggles and red lines all around the shop I wasn't sure what I was seeing at the end.' Waiting outside while the experts conferred, Stradwick 'never prayed so feverishly in all my life'. Of the candidates interviewed that day, only three got through, including Stradwick.

Many who applied to become pilots were disappointed. Val Bennett was told they had enough pilots but with his qualifications he'd be ideal as an observer. 'So I thought about it and thought I better be a bloody observer, even though I had always liked the idea of driving the thing . . . I wasn't going to fight with the Board in front of me. As a 19-year-old you say "OK".'

Each new recruit was sent a certificate of fine waxed paper bearing their rank and serial number. This would accompany them throughout their service, being updated as necessary. Then it was a case of waiting to be called up for training. For Keith Quilter, that meant going back to his studies at de Havilland in Hatfield. At weekends he jumped on his motorcycle and rode over to his parents' home in Maidenhead, to where his father's paint company had relocated from London because of the Blitz. He joined the Upper Thames River Patrol, 'a sort of floating version of the Home Guard', covering a beautiful stretch of water between Maidenhead and Bray.

The unit comprised men too old to fight and a smattering of youngsters like Quilter who were either waiting to be called up or in a reserved occupation. Knowing they were highly unlikely to be ambushed by Nazis leaping out from the reeds, it was an idyllic way to spend the weekends. Evening patrols invariably found chinks of light showing through the blackout curtains in the windows of riverside pubs, which Quilter was obliged, 'as a matter of duty, to land and have these corrected over a pint or two'. But his favourite time was the dawn patrols during the summer months 'with the river very quiet and a low mist hanging over the water as we quietly and slowly made our way along while all was dead quiet and asleep ashore'. At last, in November 1942, three months after he had passed the selection process, Quilter received his joining instructions for the Fleet Air Arm.

After recovering from his gruelling selection board, Wally Stradwick joined the Clapham Squadron of the Air Training Corps, where other deferred airmen waiting to be called up were encouraged to learn more about the basics of flight and a few lucky ones occasionally got to 'go up' at Gatwick Aerodrome. All the other men were down to join the RAF, and Stradwick found them 'rather a snobby crowd' especially when they heard he was joining the FAA. But armed with a charming and mischievous manner, a good sense of humour and a strong, fine-looking face topped with a mop of black curly hair, he was difficult not to like. He also had a quiet vulnerability and, as the oldest of three children growing up without a father, an inbuilt sense of responsibility.

This was all underpinned by a solid Catholic faith. Stradwick couldn't understand why the Admiralty was delaying his call-up. 'There's a beauty of a tussle going on in the Coral [Sea],' he wrote in his diary in May 1942. 'The US and Jap naval arms are having a real good plaster at each other. A good few boats are going down as well.'

This four-day 'tussle' was a historic one. By the summer of 1942 the US had assumed strategic responsibility for the Pacific. Their main objective, bearing in mind the Allies' first priority was the war against Germany, was to contain further Japanese gains wherever possible until a more favourable situation in Europe enabled the Allies to take the offensive in the Pacific. To the Japanese, anything still seemed possible, but in a move they later characterized as a 'victory disease', they overreached themselves.

The Battle of the Coral Sea was the first battle in history in which two major fleets fought one another with carrier aircraft without the fleets making visual contact or firing on each other. The Japanese had captured Rabaul on New Britain, and were eager to use this new air and naval base as a springboard from which to extend their gains into the South Pacific. One of their main objectives was to cut the supply routes from America to Australia, which had become the Allies' main base for the war in the Far East. With this in mind, the Japanese decided to take Port Moresby in south-east New Guinea, from where they could dominate the Coral Sea and launch attacks on Australia, just 200 miles to the south.

Allied codebreakers then learned the Japanese had sent a force to seize Port Moresby, and as a result this came under attack from carrier planes from an American task force commanded by Rear Admiral Frank J. Fletcher assembled in the Coral Sea. Over the following hours there were a number of missed opportunities as the carrier fleets of both sides groped to find each other in bad weather. American dive-bombers from the carriers *Lexington* and *Yorktown* struck first, attacking and sinking the light carrier *Shoho*. When the main forces traded air strikes, *Lexington* was fatally hit – and later scuttled by the Americans – and *Yorktown* damaged, while the Japanese carrier *Shokaku* suffered damage, and air groups from the carrier *Zuikaku* were also badly depleted.

On paper American losses were greater, and the Japanese may well have succeeded if they had pushed on towards Port Moresby. But with reduced air cover, the Japanese invasion force turned back, conceding a strategic victory to the Allies. The Americans had been let off the hook, but the Japanese losses had a major impact upon their ability to perform in the Battle of Midway a month later, when a much larger Japanese fleet led by the 64,000-ton monster battleship *Yamato* tried to lure two task forces into a direct fight, with the intention of crushing the American Pacific Fleet and suing for a negotiated peace.

At Midway the Japanese failure to destroy the American carriers at Pearl Harbor came back to haunt them. Unaware of the American carriers *Enterprise*, *Hornet* and *Yorktown*, on the morning of 4 June 1942 the Japanese carriers *Akagi*, *Soryu* and *Kaga* were attacked by dive-bombers from *Yorktown* and *Enterprise* just when their flight decks were packed with aircraft being prepared to launch strikes against the American fleet. All three carriers were sunk, and the following day the Japanese fleet was in retreat. The war in the Pacific was turning. Never again would Japanese forces enjoy their previous domination in the air or on the waves.

Stradwick was clear in his mind. 'As a result of this scrap, which hasn't finished yet, Archie Sinclair [Archibald Sinclair, minister for air] mentioned in the House that this country must build up its Fleet Air Arm, and never let it go short of the best of planes and men. Nice work. About time the powers that be started action in that sphere. It's a great pity they don't hasten call-ups.' By August 1942 five Royal Navy carriers had been sunk, including *Ark Royal*, but the four Illustrious Class armoured carriers were now in service and two more Implacable Class were under construction. Sinclair's call to arms was slowly becoming a reality. While the FAA would never have the same number of hopeful recruits banging on its door as the RAF, there were now more than

1,600 pilots with naval wings, and many more who would play a significant role in the last year of the war were flooding through flying schools.

3

Wakey-wakey, rise and shine, show a leg

'Much jubilation!' wrote Wally Stradwick in his diary after receiving a letter from the Admiralty ordering him to report to its aviation training headquarters in Portsmouth.[1] 'I immediately experienced the urge to perform something in the line of cartwheels.' Two weeks later, in the late-summer sunshine of 1942, he made the stomach-churning journey familiar to many hostilities-only naval airmen in the Second World War. Catching a train from London's Waterloo railway station to Portsmouth, he took a quick ferry crossing to Gosport and a short bus ride and reported at HMS *Daedalus*, an onshore Royal Navy airbase in Lee-on-Solent. Life as a naval cadet had begun.

At the end of the first week Stradwick scribbled down his impressions.

> Well I've now been in the Royal Navy a few days. It seems longer . . . 'Charlie' sounds at 6.30 and it's almost a possibility to get a wash as there are about ten handbasins between nearly 200 of us . . . meals, liberty boats, and divisions are notified on the loudspeakers by bugle calls. These dashed loudspeakers get on our nerves. All the time from 6.30 a.m. to 10 p.m. lights out or rather 'darken ship', apart from the time we are receiving instruction, etc. the ordinary programme is relayed. It gets noisily and gratingly monotonous.

Stradwick's shock at his new surroundings was echoed by many civilian recruits. After two weeks at HMS *Daedalus* the cadets made the short journey from Lee-on-Solent to Gosport to another 'stone frigate' – slang for a Royal Navy shore base – HMS *St Vincent*, where all new pilots and observers took a two-month course studying basic seamanship. To the frustration of the young men, who were understandably champing at the bit to get into the air, there was no flying yet. Instead, the course at *St Vincent* covered a plethora of subjects, from Morse code, to ship recognition, navigation, knots and plenty of square-bashing. It was a boot camp where the Royal Navy could stamp its mark by knocking tradition and discipline into new recruits.

'It doesn't matter a fish's tit whether you can fly like Alan Cobham, if you are not, first, a bloody good seaman and fit material to become a bloody good officer,' one instructor bullishly told the recruits.[2] Stradwick noted, 'the things that are invariably stressed at most lectures are 1) We are in the Royal Navy. The Fleet Air Arm is a specialist branch and not a separate service or even one closely united to the RN. 2) One day, if lucky, we will be officers and that entails terrific responsibilities and understanding.'

Each potential pilot and observer was now an officer cadet naval airman 2 class. Immediately after arriving they reported to the clothing store, known in the navy as 'slops', to be issued with their 'matelot' uniform. This comprised a seemingly endless list of items, including two black handkerchiefs – to be worn around the neck as a sign of respect for Lord Nelson – a 'ditty box' to carry everything in, oilskins, an overcoat and a kitbag. Finally, when the overloaded and somewhat bemused recruits thought that was it, they were also given a copy of the *Admiralty Manual of Seamanship (Volume One)* and two wooden stencils to stamp their names into every item of clothing using black and white paint.

The matelot uniform wasn't as practical as army fatigues. Most cadets found it impossible to put on without a daily wrestle. The jumpers, made of serge, were invariably too tight. The trousers were cut in traditional navy style with a square flap instead of flies, which deterred any temptation for a quick leak. But the uniform wasn't meant to be practical. Never was there a more graphic illustration of rank, tradition and culture than the bell-bottoms and visorless cap, a way for the Admiralty to brand its identity onto every man. The cadets were now part of a giant machine. If there was any doubt when they arrived, by the end of the first week the navy had made it clear to the trainee flyers who they served.

Following yet more medicals, and stripping naked for the obligatory FFI (free from infestation of nits, lice and scabies) examination, they were given a painful injection against tetanus and typhoid, prompting some to 'pass out there and then, others later'.

St Vincent resembled a smaller version of London's Holloway prison with gloomy eighteenth-century red-brick barrack blocks surrounding a vast tarmac parade ground. The cadets were split into fifty-strong numbered groups, with three new courses (two pilots' and one observers') starting every two months. It was a conveyor belt. New recruits arrived; the navy cut the wheat from the chaff, and two months later those who hadn't been 'dipped' (thrown off the course) progressed to the flying stage of training.

Most cadets were in their late teens or early twenties, but their backgrounds were varied. Just a year before, one pupil had been chauffeured every morning to University College School in Hampstead, north London, in his father's Rolls-Royce. Another was the son of a builder and admitted 'we were poor with pocket money out of the question'.[3] Others had been plucked from their civilian careers – from the police to the civil service, engineering to teaching – all joined together by a desire to fly. They were plunged into a strange new world of navy-speak and endless traditions. Royal Navy bases on land were still called ships, rooms were known as cabins and lavatories heads. Leaving the base was going ashore. Meals were served in mess decks, from where the chosen cook of the mess – the man on duty that day – collected the food before serving it to his cabin mates. After arriving in January 1942 Chris Cartledge wrote to his parents describing his new life.

I am now at *St Vincent*. It's a permanent place and used to be a training ship for boys. Now it is taken up mainly by pilots and observers of the Fleet Air Arm . . . There is a very strong school atmosphere which is rather restricting to say the least of it. We have got a lot of work to get through during our seven weeks, followed by a week of exams. One doesn't have to be brilliant to pass but must be capable of absorbing hundreds of facts. Mostly strange to the majority of us. Our subjects are navigation, flash and semaphore, flags, machine gun, aircraft recognition, seamanship, practical, i.e. tying knots, etc., tradition and ranks, flags, etc. *St Vincent* certainly is a great stepping stone and it will pay us to work really hard while we are here. I shall have to cut out any other reading. When I get to EFTS [Elementary Flying Training School] I shall have more time to practise becoming a future Harold Laski. They have roughly sorted us out into grades of quickness . . . the 150 or so of us divided into 6 classes – A B C D E F. I am in B. Each day a man from the class is appointed as class instructor and has to look after his class for that day. It is for these infrequent and probably shocking exhibitions that they will try and tell whether we contain their damned officer-like qualities. Fortunately my experience as prefect will help me a lot in this. The food here is good and doesn't quite equal the extraordinary good food of Lee-on-Solent. There is no need for you to send me any extra. It is the quality that is inclined sometimes to go down not the quantity. The messing arrangements are different here and we have to do a lot more washing-up, polishing floors, etc., ourselves. We have fire-watching nights too. Every other night I sleep in another bed and someone else sleeps in mine and by this method throughout the ship the captain considers we're quite secure from any fire attack that the cowardly Hun may make. The worst parts of this place are the CPOs. These correspond with the army's sergeant majors. They will let fly at you at any possible excuse. This is called 'getting a bottle' and 'bottling down'. Of course you never pronounce the double t's in the bottle, and so the word becomes bo'ull. Most expressive. I don't think I'll say any more . . .'[4]

The petty officers and chief petty officers ran *St Vincent*. They were feared by some cadets, scoffed at by others, but regarded with curiosity by the majority. In reality their bark was worse than their bite. They were salt-of-the-earth naval men, career sailors – mostly from working-class backgrounds – who had risen through the ranks in the Great War or the 1920s and '30s. Most were too old to serve in the front line and had been given the task of knocking 300 years of tradition into the heads of the young volunteers.

As Stradwick put it, 'When you get CPOs telling you that it took [them] 22 years to learn what we have in 8 weeks, the stiffness of the course comes home to us. The lads have agreed that the whole damned stuff – there's just too much of it. Especially with all the day's manual labour thrown in.' Every morning blinking, bleary-eyed recruits were woken by the tinny bark of a CPO's voice piped through the loudspeakers: 'Wakey-wakey, rise and shine, show a leg.' The day revolved around classes interspersed with parades or drill, when the piercing commands of the CPOs echoed across the vast quadrangle.

The cadets were set menial tasks to perform between breakfast and morning parade, such as 'clean block' sessions – scrubbing the floors on their hands and knees – or picking up matchsticks and cigarettes ends from the parade yard. The cushiest job was lighting the fire in the hearth of the captain's house on the edge of the base, where a steaming cup of tea was usually offered by his wife and cadets could waste a few minutes in the warmth with small talk.

The men slept in dormitories, with about a dozen beds each side of the room, port on the left, starboard on the right. These were subjected to rigorous daily inspections to ensure spotless beds and equipment. Punishments varied, but even minor misdemeanours such as losing a paybook could result in two weeks confined to barracks. Chris Cartledge cynically summed up the regime in a letter home: 'the genuine impression I get is that the more irrational the custom the most doggedly is it adhered to.' Still, Cartledge reassured his parents, 'every time I feel I am getting unbalanced, I plough into *Europe, Russia and the Future* [by G. D. H. Cole].'[5] Nowhere was safe from the sharp eyes and tongues of the petty officers. Walking into church one Sunday morning a cadet absentmindedly left his cap on. Just as he was about to sit down for the service to begin, a CPO whispered in his ear, 'Fleet Air Arm officers do not keep their 'ats on in the 'ouse of God. You cunt.'[6]

When Stradwick got weekend leave at home in Clapham after just a week of 'unadulterated hell' at *St Vincent*, his relief was palpable: 'I am now enjoying the unbelievable and until now unknown comforts of home sweet home. Free! No chance of a CPO jumping out at you. No need to fall in at 5 o'clock, or double all over the place. Good food, served up well, and a good sleep tonight . . .'

For almost every man who went through *St Vincent*, one petty officer's name still resonates. CPO Wilmott was a small wiry man in his late forties with a craggy face, and 'with his red and purple complexion he appeared about to have a heart attack at any moment'. He had thin lips and narrow eyes that stared out from behind little round glasses. Wilmott was a product of the gunnery school on Whale Island. One cadet, who was on 41 Pilots' Course in 1942, remembers typical exchanges were brief.

'Am I 'urting you?'

'No, Chief.'

'I should be, I'm standing on your 'air. Get it cut!'

'Yes, Chief.'[7]

Wilmott's bluff and bluster highlights the contrast between the education and background of the CPOs and their charges, who in a year or eighteen months would be commissioned officers and outrank them. It was an unusual situation, which could have led to entrenched acrimony or mutual resentment. On the whole, however, there was little genuine resentment from the petty officers towards the recruits. Rank did not bow to class. With a war raging, and cadets churning through the school, there was little time for bitterness to develop, although class differences sometimes led to confusion. On parade one morning CPO Wilmott ordered, 'Them with those funny names with things in the middle, fall out.'[8] He wasn't being facetious. Frank Stolvin-Bradford and five other boys with double-barrelled surnames gingerly stepped forward.

Despite or perhaps because of his eccentricity, Wilmott had developed something of a legendary status at *St Vincent*, and the myth was magnified by reputation and hearsay handed down from course to course. The dormitories fizzed with unsubstanti-ated rumours, the chief one being that during an air raid on Portsmouth one night he looked up and heard the drone of an approaching enemy aircraft. Flicking his cigarette away, Wilmott huffed and puffed up the stairs to the roof of the barracks and singlehandedly shot down a lone low-level Heinkel bomber with a Lewis gun.

Wilmott was blessed with a razor-sharp wit, softened by un-intentional comic turns only adding to his status with recruits. He had a habit of riding an upright ladies' bicycle around the parade ground. One afternoon, distracted after dishing out a particularly acerbic verbal assault littered with obscenities, Wilmott proceeded to cycle straight into some bushes, drawing 'cheers from the crowd' which prompted the old sailor to break into a gummy smile, revealing a mouth half full of tobacco-stained teeth like the keys of an aged, broken piano.[9] The affection was not universal. Another airman remembered him as 'an arsehole . . . a terrible man . . . we had to obey him to a tee'.[10] But Val Bennett seems to have reflected most men's opinions, reckoning he was 'actually very human'. Men like Wilmott were the backbone of the Royal Navy. They *lived* for it.

Differences in opinion about *St Vincent* reflected the individ-ual but were also down to education and upbringing. Most cadets had some grounding in military discipline by virtue of the war, which had meant compulsory service of some sort, whether at school, in the Home Guard or in the officer cadets. Homesickness was common, at least in the first weeks, especially for cadets barely out of their teens. Other hangovers from childhood persisted. One of the unusual extra duties on night-time fire-watching was dubbed 'piss the bed party'.[11] This involved prodding men who couldn't hold their bladders all night and encouraging them to visit the heads. On his first night in the dormitory at *St Vincent* in 1942 one New Zealand cadet looked across at the next bed, where a young man who 'looked like a schoolboy' was kneeling down with his head bowed. Thinking at first he was ill, the Kiwi then realized he was actually saying his prayers. 'He immediately went way up in my estimation. It must have taken courage in a room full of older sailors he had only met that day.'[12]

With so many men sleeping and living in such close proximity, illness spread like wildfire. Some developed maddening coughs at night caused by blanket dust, making it difficult to get to sleep. But the syllabus of the course was so dense that missing just a few days meant having to be kept back another month and joining the next course, as Cartledge explained in a letter home.

> Dear Folks, Bonjour! There is a wild scare on around the dormitory as an epidemic of mumps is sweeping into us. It struck the other end of the dorm first and knocked two out, it then took a vicious turn and caught the bloke Bassett next to me. Its latest victim is Davy. A most interesting person, who absolutely lives for his hobby of birdwatching. It's most annoying because he used to play the pedal part on the harmonium in exchange for which I promised to go birdwatching with him one day. Anyway, he will have to join the next course. Same with Bassett . . .[13]

To keep the men fit and healthy, sport and exercise were encouraged, with heavy emphasis on boxing and squash. Regular football matches were organized between sides from different courses. But sport, like all other activities, could be interrupted by air raids. For those on the early courses in the first two years of the war German raids on nearby Portsmouth were frequent. Each morning cadets dreaded being chosen for the worst fatigue duty of all – the 'pick and shovel' party, which had the grim job of clearing nearby bombed buildings of any bodies from the night before. By 1942, while raids were less frequent, recruits still reported for duty watch every other night. If the air raid sirens sounded, they had to get dressed, don their oilskins and gas masks and charge across the parade ground to man water pumps. *St Vincent* escaped with only superficial damage, but the anti-aircraft guns around Portsmouth 'put on a mighty show'.

Evening trips ashore gave some respite, and were announced by a bugle call piped through the speakers. Those wanting to take a liberty boat reported to the front gate for inspection by the officer of the watch, before being allowed out if they passed muster. There were two watches, port and starboard, with only one allowed ashore at a time. Once they escaped the walls of *St Vincent* for the reality of wartime suburbia, entertainment wasn't exactly bursting at the seams. For a shilling cadets could buy a seat at a music hall in Portsmouth, which, together with fish and chips and a couple of pints, pretty much used up their pay of two shillings a day. But without the restraints of family and school, many discovered alcohol in serious quantity for the first time, and booze-ups in the pubs of Lee were a popular way to break the monotony of camp life.

Intimate experiences with the opposite sex – or for that matter the same sex – were the exception rather than the rule beyond a drunken fumble or the odd kiss. Although one or two of the older men were married, and some might claim to have a 'casual skirt' or sweetheart back home, most cadets were pretty innocent. Those more experienced regaled their cabin mates with stories of their conquests in language that was a 'revelation of blasphemy and obscenity'.[14] The course included a lecture on sexual hygiene, which featured outrageous and ribald examples and threw in warnings and medical advice.

Life was basic and boisterous, and a casual reconnoitre of dormitory life would have made the concept that these men would soon be spearheading the Royal Navy's most powerful airborne strike force a hard one to grasp. After arriving at *St Vincent* in June 1942, one future pilot was preparing for bed when a large crowd gathered in his dormitory around two boys sitting in their pyjamas with a box of matches. Beans had been served in the canteen for tea, which, combined with a group of bored teenage boys, created the perfect conditions. 'I was amazed because not only did they manage to make the necessary noise and blue flame . . . it was just like turning on a gas cooker,' said the bemused onlooker, who was baffled at the 'very sight of two of these chaps competing against each other and somebody else holding a ruler out so they could get an approximate measurement'.[15]

More constructive recreation was encouraged. At the chapel's Sunday service Chris Cartledge played the organ, with mixed results. In one letter home he told his parents, 'the chaplain had me completely scuttled last Sunday. He jumped over the creed and about 5 responses without giving me the slightest warning: the result was a sensational breakdown from the organist, the congregation clawing for the note which wasn't forthcoming.'[16] Despite such distractions, the intensity of the course and the cadets' desire to take to the skies meant that most recruits were preoccupied with their final exams. The pressure increased further when they were given flying kit, including 'beautiful sheepskin boots with inches of fur lining and a suit which feels like a luxurious sleeping bag'.[17]

Cadet pilots were asked to state their preference as to where they would like to carry out their flying training. They had two choices: stay in the UK for the first part of their training before completing it in Canada, or do their entire flying course in the US, the latter option being open from before the US entered the war. Although the final decision was up to the divisional officer, most pupils generally got what they requested. Whether they chose to train in the UK and Canada, or the US, the course was scheduled to take about a year. But from joining *St Vincent* to becoming a member of an operational squadron, the process could take eighteen months, depending on flying weather, numbers of training aircraft and capacity in the schools. Bottlenecks causing new pilots to hang about at dispatch centres for days or even weeks at a time were common.

After finishing at *St Vincent* trainee observers were sent to Arbroath in Scotland, or Trinidad, where the warm weather and clear skies well away from the war meant uninterrupted navigation training until they received their commission in around seven months. Following basic training at HMS *Royal Arthur* – a former Butlins holiday camp in Skegness – TAGs received intensive training in Morse and radio, with gunnery and radio training at Worthy Down in Hampshire, or in Canada.

On results day at *St Vincent* emotions were mixed. Wally Stradwick received a first-class pass and like other successful cadets spent the next few evenings celebrating at the pub. But he was sorry for those who failed, who had to return their flying kit and 'crawl away somewhere while we danced and sang and cheerfully commence to sew on our killicks'.[18] Those who failed to pass first time could retake, but this meant being kept back to join the next course, separating from their friends. The course ended with a passing-out dance and a parade in the main quadrant in front of a senior naval officer.

While both Stradwick and Keith Quilter looked forward to training across the Atlantic in the States, many, such as Chris Cartledge, began their instruction at the RAF's 14 Elementary Flying Training School in Elmdon, which had been requisitioned by the Air Ministry from Birmingham Council. Although the FAA had come back under Admiralty control before the war, in Britain the RAF was still responsible for training all FAA pilots. Now classed as (temporary) acting leading naval airmen but still dressed in their traditional matelot's uniform, graduates from *St Vincent* were issued with their flying logbook, a service bible in which was recorded every single hour's flight made until they stopped flying – either because they left the Royal Navy or because they were killed.

For eight weeks the elementary course at Elmdon was split between flying and ground school, with lectures ranging from the secrets of the internal combustion engine to air navigation. Pilots had to complete a maiden solo flight around the airfield after a period of dual instruction in an open tandem cockpit. Occupying the rear seat of the primary trainer – usually a Tiger Moth biplane or a Miles Magister monoplane – the RAF instructor could tell if new recruits sitting in the seat in front had 'air-experience' within the first week. It was flying for beginners. If a pupil hadn't managed his fifteen-minute solo flight within ten to twelve hours' flying time – normally about two to three weeks depending on the weather – he just wasn't cut out for it and was dipped. The most common reasons for failure were airsickness or lack of coordination.

Before their first flight with an instructor rookie pilots were walked around the aircraft to check for faults and ensure the chocks firmly secured the wheels. Although the Tiger Moth was a forgiving little plane in the air, it didn't have brakes, and it was not unknown to see one careering across the airfield with a hapless student flapping his arms from the cockpit. Pupils were shown how to put on a parachute – which since the First World War had sensibly been introduced – and climb into the cockpit of the aircraft without putting their feet through the delicate fabric of the wing.

The Tiger Moth was the RAF's default basic trainer, with more than 4000 built during the war. Designed in the 1930s and made from wood and canvas, it was painted in green and brown camouflage with a yellow belly, and had basic instruments and a fixed undercarriage with a metal sled under the tail for use on grass airstrips. It was powered by a 145-horsepower Gipsy Major engine, started by a mechanic on the ground who called out, 'Contact!' to tell the pilot to switch on the magneto – a sort of ignition – before swinging the two-blade wooden propeller until the four cylinders burst into life in a puff of white smoke.

With the cadet pilot sitting in front, the instructor taxied to the end of the airfield, turned into the wind and opened the throttle to pick up speed. As the tail rose, the fuselage levelled out onto the two wheels, immediately improving the view ahead. The roar of the engine and the vibration from the airframe increased, and the grass below was soon whizzing past in a blur of green. Then the vibrations abruptly ceased as the airflow increased just enough over the wing surfaces for the plane to climb unsteadily into the air. With every second that passed the view improved, to reveal more of the countryside as it slipped underneath like an enlarged map.

For many new pilots it was the first time they had ever flown and a hugely exciting experience. A few days after joining the course at Elmdon in May 1942 a buzzing Cartledge wrote home in confident mood, telling his parents,

> Flying is a complete cinch! I enjoy it more every time I go up. It's wonderful what unshakable faith we put in our flimsy little machines; here are we up here, the ground down there and no apparent reason why we shouldn't crash down to meet it at all. When we do a turn the machine seems to pivot round on the bottom wing tip, how we stay up I don't know . . . We hope to be doing our solo before we have been here a fortnight, if the weather is OK.[19]

One of the first things young pilots were taught was that the attitude of the plane was crucial. In level flight the horizon coincided with the nose of the aircraft and the wings either side. The instructor communicated with the pupil through a Gosport Tube, speaking into a mouthpiece attached to a rubber tube, with headphones on the other end. 'Put your right hand on the stick and your feet on the pedals. You have control.'

The pupil learned that pushing the pedals – called the rudder bar – would swing the nose of the aircraft to the left or right, while gently pulling the stick back or pushing it forward controlled the elevators and forced its nose up or down. Moving the stick to the left or right dropped each corresponding wing by moving the ailerons – the hinged sections on the trailing edges of the wings. By combining all these controls, the pupil had the basic building blocks of flight. With practice, he was armed with enough knowledge to attempt his first solo. The first mistake many pupils made was to grip the control stick too tightly. Pupil pilots were told to 'treat is as if it was a gentle lady. Just stroke it.'[20]

Taking off in a Tiger Moth was relatively simple – reaching 50 mph and pulling gently back on the stick it rose into the sky – but what goes up must come down, and coming down in one piece wasn't so easy. For the perfect landing, the pilot approached the airfield at around 60 mph, gently losing height and speed by throttling back, until the plane was about five feet above the ground and he could distinguish individual blades of grass. Then by pulling the stick gently back and shutting off the throttle, the aircraft dropped the final few feet and thumped onto the airstrip. That was the theory at least. However, a few miles per hour under the correct speed and the Tiger Moth stalled, dropping like a stone.

Instructors were given guidance on spotting the telltale expressions and body language of those pupils who struggled. A natural pilot enjoying the experience would be relaxed and comfortable, looking around and taking things in. On the other hand, if the pupil was 'closing his eyes, clenching the teeth, gasping, holding the breath, apprehensive looking around, or [had] a set, strained or anxious expression' it was safe to assume he might not be suited to flying. 'A man may show nervousness in his posture and movements, shrinking into the cockpit, holding himself away from a spin, or actually holding on to the side of the aircraft,' instructors were told.[21]

Occasionally onlookers were treated to the sight of an instructor's knuckles gripping the side of the fuselage as his determined pupil attempted yet another ham-fisted landing. With dual controls the instructor could take over at any stage should anything go wrong, but he knew the pilot would never learn from his mistakes if he did so too early. Instructors knew not to write off pupils prematurely, because once they got the knack it became more natural every time they flew, and most achieved their first solo flight after eight hours.

Following his first solo the pupil progressed to learning about wind and air pressure, getting used to the balance and feel of the machine, how the airflow over the wings affected its flight through the air and the ways it reacted to combinations of the different controls. He grew to understand more about the character of the sky, and how easily air pockets – fluctuations in atmospheric temperature – could seize the aeroplane without warning and throw it around. Flying in open cockpits, pupils soon discovered the air temperature dropped as they climbed, even in summer. Flying kit, which included double-layer white silk gloves worn under leather gauntlets, a leather helmet and goggles, wasn't so much a fashion statement as life-saving equipment.

It was a different world in the sky, and the most innocuous-looking features seen from the ground could be sinister in the air. In one of his earliest solo flights Chris Cartledge flew into a cloud for the first time and was immediately submerged in a thick white fog. 'I could feel the aircraft going all over the place and the altimeter raced so fast I could not tell if I was climbing or diving. I was in a fearful panic and I heard myself crying out with wails of fear,' he said. As quickly as he had entered it he shot out of the base of the cloud and into clear sky, heading for the ground at great speed, but luckily still had plenty of height to level the wings and pull out of the dive. But he 'was very wary of clouds for quite a while afterwards'.[22]

Unlike the aviators of the Great War, pilots were told not to believe in their own senses but rely on their instruments. The airspeed indicator and altimeter were critical: they gave the pilot vital information on the attitude of the aircraft in cloud or at night, when he could not see the horizon or the ground. Many hours were spent practising instrument flying – commonly known as IF – in the Link Trainer, a sort of early version of the modern flight simulator. The pilot sat in a wooden box mocked up as a cockpit, which had instruments and controls and mimicked the basic principles of flight by using a series of pumps, valves and bellows, which allowed horizontal and vertical movements corresponding to the pilot's controls. The instructor set different conditions, such as a course at certain speeds and heights, and observed the pilot's responses. The course he steered was traced onto a piece of paper, so the pupil could see how his attempt compared to what he should have actually done. Although it wasn't like flying the real thing, it gave pilots the preparation they needed and saved lives.

Pupils then progressed to the real thing, practising IF in dual-control aircraft using only the dim glow of the instruments as a guide in an otherwise pitch-black cockpit over which a hood was strapped. Training included at least two hours of night flying, during which the pilot had to disregard all his senses and trust the instruments to guide him through the night sky and safely down to the airfield, which was lit only by flares. Death could come at any time. After breathing a sigh of relief at successfully landing in the dark, one pilot on Chris Cartledge's course strolled happily back to the hangar and walked straight into the revolving propeller of a taxiing aircraft.

Perhaps the most frightening phenomenon was the spin, when the aeroplane became a gyrating object devoid of any aerodynamic properties, plummeting to earth in a sickening spiral with the doomed pilot trapped inside. Aviation pioneers had encountered the spin quite by accident, turning their aeroplane or banking too sharply (sometimes when 'stunting'), which reduced the machine's speed so much that the airflow over the wings diminished too much or vanished, causing it to stall. Friendly landmarks below became a swirling blur of land and sky, as the pilot wrestled with the throttle, stick and rudder bar to regain control before the plane smashed into the ground. But just as quickly, and not really knowing how, one or two of the early pilots did regain control and lived to tell the tale.

By the 1940s aviators had mastered techniques for exiting

spins and would stall their aircraft so they could practise again and again how to get out of one. 'My instructor put me into a spin yesterday, it didn't terrify me half as much as I had expected, he told me to get her out, which is quite simple as no doubt Daddy knows,' Chris Cartledge told his parents.[23] With confidence and practice, pilots would deliberately spin their aircraft and try to outdo each other with the number of rotations they could achieve, before centring the rudder bar and pushing the stick forward, which returned the aircraft to normal flight. But it was highly dangerous, and such high jinks regularly caused deaths in training.

After about twenty hours' flying time – a third of the way through the elementary flying course – around a quarter of pupils had been dipped. Those remaining started aerobatics, which 'absolutely terrified' Cartledge, whose 'instructor showed me stall turns and looping the loops and roll off the loop; I enjoyed it immensely with him but this morning he sent me up to do stall turns on my own, as well as spins. I don't mind spins, but it took me about three stall turns in each direction before I could approach them without my heart pounding away ten to the dozen.'[24]

Pupils began to enjoy themselves as their instincts sharpened, but the flying was intense and there was little time for leave. On the odd occasion the men did escape it tended to be for a few pints in Chester or Birmingham or a weekend visit back home. One weekend Cartledge scooped two tickets to see a Birmingham production of *Macbeth* starring John Gielgud and Gwen Ffrangcon-Davies. 'It was an absolute godsend,' he wrote home. 'I have never been so appreciative of Shakespeare before. I had the feeling that I get from listening to great music. I really felt like letting out a yell. Lady Macbeth was acted perfectly, I've forgotten her name but I think she was Welsh.'[25]

After around thirty hours dual flying and the same amount of solo practice, pupils faced their ground exams and a final flying test with the chief flying instructor. A myriad of skills learned over the sixty-odd hours of flying was condensed into a forty-five-minute test, including aerobatics, instrument flying, navigation, spins, taking off and landing, and various turns and stalls.

For Cartledge and other successful pupils, a new adventure then beckoned at the Service Flying Training School (SFTS) in Canada, where they would undergo the next part of their training, learning to fly more powerful aircraft with the chance to win their wings. Early in the war the main SFTS station was at Netheravon, an RAF base in Wiltshire. However, in January 1941 the first FAA pilots arrived at the newly opened 31 SFTS in Kingston on the northern edge of Lake Ontario. The move to Canada was in many ways a no-brainer for the Admiralty. Immunity from enemy action meant pupils could train in peace, and by November 1943 2,400 pilots a year were being sent to Canada for elementary and service training. The following year a second base was set up at St Eugene in Quebec.

But the training in Canada was not an unqualified success. The wastage rate was huge, with up to 60 per cent of pupils being sent home because they failed to make the grade. One problem identified by the Air Ministry was the lack of basic flying training in the syllabus at *St Vincent*. Trainee pilots, the Air Ministry argued, should arrive for the start of their flying course already armed with a rudimentary theoretical knowledge of flight and engines. By March 1945 the EFTS had been increased from eight to ten weeks and the initial training course at *St Vincent* revised to include more airmanship and air navigation.[26]

But pressure on the FAA and the RAF meant additional capacity was required to meet the growing demand for quality pilots. In June 1941 Admiral John H. Towers, chief of the US Navy's Bureau of Aeronautics, proposed that a percentage of British pilots destined for the FAA and the RAF Coastal Command should train at bases in America. Over the next three years the Royal Navy was loaned thousands of American aircraft, parts, ammunition and ships. Just as vitally, this closer cooperation – stimulated by Japan's attack on Pearl Harbor – ensured a rapid increase in the number of FAA pilots training in the USA. The intake of students doubled, and the Towers Scheme was soon providing 44 per cent of all FAA pilots.[27]

This lessened friction between the RAF and Royal Navy. FAA trainees were taught carrier-based warfare by Americans with recent combat experience in the Pacific theatre. An experienced US Navy or Marine carrier pilot could provide more pertinent instruction than an RAF pilot who had no such experience and was used to land-based aviation in the European theatre. But transatlantic training also had a huge personal impact on British student pilots. Leaving a war-torn country dulled by years of blackouts and rationing for the land of milk and honey changed their lives. For them, the Second World War would be bathed in technicolour.

4

Bags of food and lights and girls

Wally Stradwick was assigned to the Towers Scheme at the end of 1942 and set sail for the States on board *Andes*, a former Royal Mail passenger ship requisitioned for the war as a troop carrier. Around fifty ships were used during the war to transport mainly British, Commonwealth and American servicemen. Some, such as *Andes*, the *Queen Elizabeth* and the *Queen Mary*, operated an unescorted shuttle service back and forth across the Atlantic. With their powerful engines, the journey was made in four or five days, their speed putting them out of reach of the hunting packs of German U-boats. But space was limited, and the slower troopships needed military convoy protection and took up to two weeks.

Life on board was basic; the ships were required to carry far more passengers than they had been designed for and lacked stewards. The luxuries of peacetime cruising were distant memories. The ornate veneered walls of the ballrooms were carefully boarded over and public areas filled with bunks; hammocks were hung in every spare space.

During the North Atlantic winter months snow, sleet and spray formed a thick covering of ice on deck, causing the great ships to roll and pitch as they cut through waves as high as a two-storey house. Keith Quilter, also travelling on *Andes* just after new year in 1943, experienced 'the roughest seas I ever saw in my entire time in the Royal Navy. North Atlantic in January was quite incredible. I'd be up on the deck quite high off the sea level and you'd look up at these hills of waves.'[1]

Men below deck, passing the time by playing bridge, poker or chess, would occasionally feel a horrible vibration as the ship's powerful screws rose out of the water. 'We are on the lowest deck and well forward. It's fun!' wrote Stradwick a few days into the sail.

> Five or six of us seated below the swinging hammocks and playing cards . . . suddenly an extra strong roller will lift and hit her keel under the hull and she will shudder violently. The next instant, mugs, plates, cutlery and all sorts of odds and ends will rain from the kit racks above . . . last night was the best. It was really rough and the tub rocks like mad in the swell. A terrific percentage of the troops including our lads have been hit badly by seasickness.

Most struggled with seasickness, and the lavatories were awash with faeces and vomit. For the lucky few who did not suffer, Stradwick among them, the canteens were empty at mealtimes. 'Boy did we feed!' he exclaimed.[2]

One morning Keith Quilter woke up to find the constant hum of the moving ship had stopped. He had arrived in Halifax, Nova Scotia. Walking up onto the deck it was as though he was in a 'fairyland' with the ice-covered ship bathed in floodlights. 'After three years of blackouts, we felt as if we were in a Hollywood film set. North America had bags of food and lights and girls. It was a new world.' The impact could be equally strong for those arriving down the coast in New York. As the *Queen Mary* slipped past the Statue of Liberty in March 1943 one British trainee pilot was moved by the transformation from a 'hungry, rather drab, blacked out and bombed Britain. To gaze at the myriad of twinkling lights of Manhattan and the never-ending flow of traffic from the prow of the great liner was magical.'[3]

All cadets arriving in Halifax or New York were immediately transported by train to the Personnel Dispatch Centre in Moncton, New Brunswick, a holding centre sleeping 800 men which allowed the RAF to regulate the flow of men to and from the flying schools in both Canada and the USA, depending on capacity. Moncton was a typical little Canadian town: small wooden houses perched on neat lawns framed by manicured trees. Shiny American cars sat in every driveway. Some cadets stayed in Moncton for a day or two, others for up to two months, depending on the weather and the demand from the flying schools. Arriving in the snowy winter could mean weeks without moving, but that had its advantages. Wally Stradwick observed how they 'behaved like young schoolboys. In the grills which are everywhere we could indulge in anything we fancied: eggs, chicken, oranges, ice cream, milkshakes . . .'

When they finally left, those men destined for the USA settled down for the long, winding train journey from Moncton to Detroit, smoking cigars, drinking Coca-Cola and eating ice cream, before starting their primary flying training at the US Navy airbase in Grosse Ile, Michigan. (In April 1944 training was transferred to St Louis, Missouri.) Over three months the cadets would learn the basics of flying, with the overall objective no different to the training at the British Elementary Flying Training School. If they passed, the cadets progressed to three to four months of intermediate and advanced training in Pensacola, Florida. This was equivalent to the Service Flying Training School in Canada. Success would mean the ultimate reward – their wings and an officer's commission.

Grosse Ile was a sprawling American naval air station housing 3,000 personnel, located on the southern end of a small flat island in the Detroit River set in a patchwork of open fields and woodland. The countryside so closely resembled England 3,500 miles away that one cadet from Lancing, near Brighton, wrote that it was 'very pretty in its way – much like the Thames at Walton or Windsor . . . it is very difficult to imagine I am so far from you all at home'. This cadet, like nearly all the men who had emerged from the monotonous diet of war-weary Britain, enthused about the food: 'Our meals consist of various fruits and salads e.g. peaches, strawberries, pears, apple pies, ice cream + cream cake – very little potato – cereals, we have corn flakes or puffed rice in bowls of milk! and two eggs or sausages + tomatoes or beans + ham or liver – anyway the diet is so varied that it is impossible to remember everything we eat . . .'[4] A few weeks after he arrived, he admitted, 'now that we can get all these things in plenty we ignore them for the most part. I guess it's that feeling that you can't get 'em that makes you want 'em,' adding, 'I'd give a lot for a cup of Mum's tea – I haven't had a decent cup since I left England.'

In the first few weeks after the arrival of each new Towers draft, doctors reported a rise in stomach complaints from cadets whose rationed-conditioned stomachs rebelled. According to an internal Admiralty assessment, they were 'inclined to indulge rather much' in ice cream, milkshakes and Coca-Cola.[5]

The base boasted recreational buildings housing bowling alleys, a cinema, badminton courts and two gyms. Onsite shops sold medicines and clothes. The facilities were far superior to training schools back in Britain but the training programme was intense. Cadets flew every day of the week except Sunday, and were issued with US Navy khaki shirts, trousers and black socks, replacing their somewhat tatty square-rig uniform, which nevertheless still had to be worn when they were on shore leave.

FAA cadets shared classes with RAF cadets learning how to pilot flying boats and US Navy Air Corps personnel. They were all taught a flight syllabus developed by the US Navy, updated throughout the war to accommodate the requirements of the Royal Navy and to take into account the latest theories and skills gleaned from combat. The course started with the basics – circuits, landings, spins, various acrobatics and formation flying. Exams in ground-school subjects, which included gunnery, navigation, aerodynamics, and aircraft and ship recognition, were taken every week. Heavy emphasis was also placed on physical training, including hand-to-hand combat, which, according to the official Grosse Ile airbase magazine, aided 'self-preservation in case one is forced down over enemy territory'. Assuming they were still in some sort of condition worth preserving, aircrew were reassured their training was 'stressed for defense against ju jitsu trickery'.[6]

Training also included boxing bouts, with students matched according to weight, fighting three one-minute rounds. Keith Quilter was put in the ring against a fellow pupil who asserted he had stolen his girlfriend. Quilter was promptly knocked out, following which the now satisfied cadet never mentioned it again. In the swimming pool cadets were taught to tread water and swim fully clothed while exposed to the hazards of cold, oil and fire.

The flying course at Grosse Ile was divided into six parts – initial dual instruction, the primary solo, the advanced solo, formation flying, night flying and the final exams. The course included a total of about a hundred flying hours in all. Leave ashore was allowed on Wednesday nights between six and nine and every other Saturday. Evening classes occupied the rest of the week. If cadets failed a ground exam, they had to revise until they passed, otherwise they were forbidden leave.

The day began at 5.30 or 6 a.m., when, according to Wally Stradwick,

> work began in earnest . . . By request I have to wake Doug, Stan and the three others every morning – and after a shower and a shave, I manage to make my bed and finish breakfast or chow as they call all meals here. We muster at 07.45 and proceed to ground school which lasts until 11.40 a.m. Chow again, and muster with flying kit at 12.30. This week we have been on flying in the afternoon which lasts until 5.30 p.m. Then to top everything there is night school from 7.30 p.m. to 9 . . . one certainly doesn't get a lot of time for writing in this place.

Students were designated a main flying instructor with regular 'checks' by other trainers. They came to dread the big blackboard in the hangar, which showed the up and down checks chalked in big arrows next to their names. Instructors with a propensity for giving down checks were dubbed down men. Sugar daddies gave up checks. One up check signified progress to the next stage, but if they were given two down checks in succession, cadets were dipped and sent home or, in a few cases, allowed to try again in Canada or train as observers. Instructors might occasionally allow a cadet more time if they believed their deficiency was a minor fault which could be ironed out with practice.

'You took a fearful look at the flight board when you came down to see if the arrow had been chalked up or down,' said one British airman. 'They would consider giving you a bit of extra tuition but did not waste much extra time on you. You were out. I was surprised to see how many were quickly dipped for things like airsickness, lacking depth perception or were disorientated, things they could easily have found out in the UK.'[7]

It was found that the British lacked mechanical knowledge of engines in comparison to American students, leading to 'hamhandedness, clumsiness and lack of coordination'. This was primarily because the typical American cadet had been 'tinkering with cars from his earliest years'. FAA cadets were strong on ground-school subjects, however, and according to the flight school librarian at St Louis, 'British boys on the whole tend to read more intelligent books on world affairs than their American counterparts, who mainly read detective stories . . .'[8]

The most common reasons for failure were airsickness and an inability to judge the height of the ground when landing. Many FAA students, including Wally Stradwick, had never even been up in an aeroplane – even as passengers – until they had their first orientation flight with an instructor at Grosse Ile. Stradwick wrote he was neither 'over thrilled or nervous, but took it as a matter of course. It's great fun however, and doesn't seem unduly hard.' But others didn't share his enthusiasm. One student at Grosse Ile was dropped at his own request after just four hours' flying, admitting to instructors that his fear originated in a one-off flight back in the UK; he nevertheless thought it necessary to travel to America to confirm his first impression. With hindsight it seems crazy that the students on the Towers Scheme weren't given some sort of flying test or grading before travelling 5,000 miles at great expense to the taxpayer. Such a test would have made even more sense for the New Zealand candidates, who could travel 18,000 miles before going up for their first flight.

Out of the 709 FAA students on the course at Grosse Ile between July 1942 and December 1943, 34 per cent were eliminated, compared to 24 per cent for RAF trainees and 12–16 per cent for US Navy students. An official report concluded the twelve hours' flying instruction RAF cadets received before leaving Britain reduced washout rates by 15 per cent, while US Navy students underwent more thorough physical and psychological tests prior to reaching this stage. But almost two thirds of the cadets who failed the course were still recommended for a commission, suggesting selection boards in the UK chose cadets for flight training on their officer qualities rather than their aviation skills.[9]

This shows the frailty of the impression method of recruitment at its starkest and contributed to the Admiralty's decision to introduce grading in the final months of the war. A Royal Navy doctor sent to investigate failure rates recommended introducing twelve-hour flying courses in England to reduce the attrition rate, concluding, 'It certainly appears to be most wasteful to send so many students across the Atlantic, only to be rejected in large numbers in the early stages of training.'[10]

Towers cadets got their first taste of flying in the Spartan NP-1 or the N3N, a dual-control biplane designed and built by the American government-owned Naval Air Factory. Like the Tiger Moth it had an open cockpit, but possessed a more powerful 235-horsepower radial engine. Trainees soon moved on to the Boeing Stearman, a similar-sized aircraft nicknamed the yellow peril, since its bright colour warned everyone nearby a learner flyer was at the controls. Keith Quilter thought the Stearman a 'super little aeroplane. You could really throw it around in the air.'

Apart from the airspeed indicator and the compass, the crucial instruments to watch were the turn and bank indicator – known in American parlance as the needle and ball – and the altimeter. Cadets fell asleep at night with the words 'needle, ball, altimeter, needle, ball, altimeter' ringing in their ears from the instructors

constantly repeating the words hour after hour. Most students
training in the US achieved their solo at around ten to fifteen
hours of flying time with the instructor – longer than the average
eight hours in Britain. Following their solo flight, they ploughed
on through the rest of the course at a rate of knots to meet the
demands of intensive wartime training.

Flying was good fun but death was just one silly mistake away.
While practising a low-level attack one pupil pulled back on his
stick too sharply and fatally plunged to the ground from 200 feet.
On another occasion an instructor was demonstrating spins to a
pupil who had forgotten to fasten his safety belt. As the aircraft
inverted, the trainee slipped from his seat, hitting his head against
the rudder and being knocked unconscious before he had a
chance to open his parachute.

Students were trained by US Navy instructors overseen by
Royal Navy airmen like Lieutenant Commander P. B. Jackson, a
Swordfish veteran who had helped sink the *Bismarck* in 1941. His
job was not to teach flying but to provide support and advice for
the pupils. Cadets sometimes struggled to understand the American drawl of the instructors as they barked orders down the
Gosport Tube in the noisy aircraft, protesting that instructions
couldn't be clarified because there was no way to respond. In the
last few months of the war the Admiralty sent a senior officer to
investigate the high washout rate. Some instructors admitted
being 'fed up' with the young pilots finding it hard to understand
what they were being told to do. A gripe for the cadets was the
rigid demerit system, in which points were issued for a variety of
breaches of regulations such as not making beds properly, having
dirty kit or damaging an aircraft. Many felt it was childish and
unnecessary.[11]

It's no surprise then that when the FAA trainees were allowed
out, the bright lights of Detroit were the big draw. Mixing with the
local population wearing their traditional Royal Navy uniform,
they largely experienced genuine hospitality from the American
public, who realized these young men were not so different from

their own. The American way of life seeped into every pore. After a flight, rather than chatting over a cup of tea as they would in England, instructors and cadets debriefed swigging bottles of ice-cold Coca-Cola bought for a nickel from vending machines in the hangar. Each morning they marched the few hundred feet from their barracks to the airfield accompanied by a US Navy band of black musicians – a spin-off from the large number of African Americans migrating to Detroit from the southern American states, attracted by the work opportunities. Keith Quilter loved the big band dance tunes, and reckoned the marching music had quite a swing to it. 'I always felt if we gave them a little nudge they would have happily burst into jazz. They played the marches in a jazzy fashion,' he said.

By 1943 America's industrial machine of war was in full swing. But the war didn't manifest itself in civilian life as starkly as it did in Britain. One student reported in a letter to his sister that Detroit was

> a wonderful city in many ways, yet somehow unlike our own towns it lacks personality. Nobody cares a damn for Tom, Dick or Harry – everyone seems to be rolling in money, and believe me it speaks in a loud voice in Detroit, and all out for a good time. People dress quite smartly sometimes with good taste but apart from war industry, which is certainly colossal, there is little to indicate a major war with terrible stakes is raging in Europe – it made me think a bit when I first visited the place.[12]

His views were echoed by Keith Quilter, who recalled 'the thing that struck in Detroit was how ignorant they were about Europe. We got used to the fact that the US was isolated and they imagined we still had hansom cabs back in England.' One New Zealand pupil remembered, 'generally speaking the Americans treated us generously' but his 'origins and nationality were a mystery to many, confused with Nova Scotia, New Caledonia and other New Places'.[13] The confusion worked both ways, as Wally Stradwick found out when he tried to cross the road. 'I still haven't accustomed myself to right-side driving in this country. I always step off the kerb looking the wrong way. Over here one <u>always</u> crosses at the lights. I didn't in Woodward Avenue and caused several women to scream.'

Although most students initially struggled with the new diet, climate, customs and habits, by and large most eventually adapted to the American way of life and milked it for all they could. Training in America provided them with experiences most of their generation could only dream about: 'The lights of Detroit on a Saturday night are well worth seeing – people just don't seem to go to bed all night long. Shops don't close until midnight and all bars about 2 a.m. – the nightclubs remain open until about 6 a.m. You'd never think there was a war on or that there was such a place as Europe.'[14]

Before hitting the town it was normal practice to book a hotel room in downtown Detroit to get some sleep once it was time to call it a night. A typical evening on leave started with a few drinks and supper in a grill or with a local family who had volunteered to act as hosts. This was followed by more drinks and dancing in one of the many nightclubs. The Brass Rail was particularly popular, claiming to possess 'the longest bar in Michigan'.

Wally Stradwick's first taste of leave was at a masked Valentine's dance where he was handed a numbered mask and a 'love note' which had to be read out to the girl wearing the corresponding-number mask. 'I was lucky,' he wrote later, that 'a very nice cultured girl [called] Joan Stringer was my Valentine and we got along fine.' The following morning, back in the barracks at Grosse Ile, Stradwick observed 'the lads are all sleeping in various positions. Perhaps it's a good thing we only have this once a fortnight.' Stradwick embraced the nightlife of Detroit with an infectious zest for life and an undoubted talent to party hard. 'The bars over here are really good, and it gives you a terrific kick to enter the comfortable splashes of light and colour and see the absolutely amazing variety of bottles on the glass shelves,' he wrote when he first arrived.

One Saturday night Stradwick left the group of cadets he was drinking with to spend a few hours with Betty, a local girl he had started seeing. After failing to find them a few hours later, he decided to spend the rest of the night 'going solo', touring the bars and clubs of the city, and ended up 'absolutely pickled' in an all-night cinema talking to a German-born US Army fighter pilot who was 'one of the most interesting chaps I have ever met. 24 years of age, he has shot down 4 Japs and 1 Gerry.' As dawn broke the two men sobered up over coffee in a juke joint before attending Mass in the local Catholic church.

With his charming personality and film-star looks, Stradwick found it easy to make new friends. But he also got into scrapes with the opposite sex. A few weeks later, while waiting to meet Betty and her friend Beverly, Stradwick and a few other cadets were in the Brass Rail 'knocking back straight double whiskies with a pint of beer between each . . . we were soon rolling tight and feeling merry as hell'. The evening was going well until Stradwick's friends Dick and Arnold 'walked in with a girl. While I was pretty caned a fortnight back she had made me promise to meet her at the English Tavern at 7.30. Naturally I had forgotten all about it and immediately at this moment, thought of Betty and Beverly arriving.'

Facing imminent embarrassment and a lot of explaining, Stradwick and his friend Stan wisely chose to make a hasty exit through the side door. After meeting Betty and Beverly elsewhere to watch a 'double-feature horror' – during which he endured the real horror of having to help an inebriated Stan down to the heads to be sick – they carried on the party at the girls' house until 3 a.m. Then Stradwick returned into town to an all-night diner, where he 'had a good feed while Stan would only drink tea'. The night finished in the apartment of West Cox, the manager of the English Tavern, who they bumped into leaving the diner. 'I nearly burst out laughing at the look of mute appeal on Stan's face when

West handed us each a large glass with about four or five fingers of neat Scotch inside,' recalled Stradwick. Despite this, he was still up at 9 a.m. the following morning for a flying lesson. In the hangar 'fellows were lying on chairs, stairs, and the deck, trying to make up for sleep. It was funny. Everyone completely buggered!'

On another occasion Stradwick's antics almost turned sour when he and a friend met two girls for dinner. The evening took its familiar course, and after a few more drinks at the Van Dyke Club ('quite a cosy little place, plenty of music and songs, and plenty of drink. What a time we had!') they left at 2 a.m. Stradwick wrote later,

> We got out to the car and after putting the hood down we were feeling in a very merry mood and decided to have a procession down Jefferson [the main street in downtown Detroit]. We both had huge cigars and Derek drove while I stood up in the back, puffing like a furnace. However, when Derek suddenly slammed on the brakes, I nearly spread my face over the windscreen. Then a police car roared after us and wanted to see Derek's licence. We thought we had 'had it', but he didn't take Derek's name and just made Derek and Cynthia change over.

They were lucky. Had the police decided to report them, they could have been on the next ship back to Britain. But despite escapades like these, by and large there were few clashes between FAA personnel and locals. Cadets were issued with guidelines and warned not to antagonize Americans through behaviour which might cause their hosts to question if Britain was worth fighting for. Besides, Detroit had bigger problems to worry about. In June 1943 race riots confined the cadets to barracks for six weeks. Federal troops were called in to restore order, but the tensions remained. A few drunken British sailors were small fry by comparison and they were usually on the base flying. And flying hard. Stradwick, who had only just turned twenty, was turning into a first-class pilot. It didn't really matter how drunk a cadet got on leave, how many girls he took to bed or whether the police stopped him for speeding, as long as he became a good flyer.

At the beginning of June 1943 Stradwick became the first pupil on his course to pass primary training, flying a total of 92 hours without, according to his logbook, a single down check. The average on his course was about 105 hours, with 20 cadets – 40 per cent – dipped. Stradwick was in no doubt that the training was the best around: 'As Commander Rose remarks, they don't want pilots here. Nothing but aces. One thing is definite. Anyone who gets through this course can knock spots off most other pilots.' But he wasn't quite there yet. For Stradwick and the other pilots on the Towers Scheme the final hurdle before joining a squadron was still to come. In late summer 1943 one British cadet wrote home,

> By the time this reaches you many leaves will be on the ground and winter will be just around the corner. I can scarcely believe the time has gone so fast. Anyway where I am going it will be like spending winter on the Mediterranean coast so I don't expect any of the usual winter colds this year. As it happens I have timed things nicely as the weather during the summer months reaches about 100–110 in the shade whereas in the winter it drops about 20 – just nice.'[15]

Their destination was Florida.

5

Wings

To have passed primary training in England or at Grosse Ile proved a cadet was already a decent pilot. But, strenuous as the courses were, they only taught the basics. To get his wings, a cadet would have to master powerful monoplanes.

For those on the Towers Scheme in America, the main advanced training centre for most of the war was at the US Naval Air Station in Pensacola, Florida, where cadets could spend over six months undergoing intensive flying training. Most travelled down from Grosse Ile on a hot and cramped train which took three days to snake its way through the states of Michigan, Ohio, Kentucky, Tennessee, Alabama and Florida, 'each of which is nearly as big as England', wrote a British cadet in a letter home to his sister in October 1943.[1] The heat became increasingly intense as the train travelled south, rolling through endless cotton and maize fields, and woods packed with scented conifers and pines.

Located on a peninsula south of Pensacola city, hugging the shoreline of the Gulf of Mexico under the hot Florida sunshine, the base sprawled over more than 5,000 acres along Pensacola Bay. It was built as a shipyard by Spanish colonists in the late seventeenth century and had become America's primary naval aviation training centre by the end of the First World War. Here aviation training became an efficient production line with the express objective of turning large numbers of cadets into polished pilots. The airbase reached its peak in 1944, when 12,000 men passed through its doors, flying almost two million hours. Conditions for flying were usually perfect, but during the rainy season in

July and August huge electrical storms formed from nowhere, creating violent turbulence which threw aircraft around like wooden toys, making them potential deathtraps.

Pensacola was made up of a series of large satellite airfields – each dedicated to a particular skill – through which pupils progressed. The sky was filled with planes day and night. The main base was dominated by red-brick and white-clapboard buildings, with attractively landscaped gardens, manicured lawns, flower beds and palm trees which swayed gently in the warm sea breeze. Like Grosse Ile, Pensacola's facilities were second to none and superior to many of the Royal Navy's British establishments.

Men relaxed in the base's cafes over coffee or fresh juice, browsed in its shoperamas and spent time in the bowling alleys. Food was abundant, with plenty of fresh fruit, 'man-sized' steaks, seafood, curries and salads. One flyer wrote to his family, 'As you can see I'm safely here now. I am having a wonderful time bathing in sea that is lukewarm and beautiful sunshine. The sands here are a dazzling white and lovely to walk on . . . I should imagine that the French Riviera at Cannes or Montecarlo would be very similar to this.'[2] He went on to paint a picture that must have been hard for his family to visualize shivering back in autumnal Britain.

> Sunshine is rife down here and although it is 9 p.m. and dark outside I am sitting writing this by open window in my shirtsleeves and still I'm perspiring . . . this evening the crickets are chirping away in the darkness – thousands of them – remember the jungle scenes on the films – with the buzzing noises in the atmosphere – well they are just like that . . . still one becomes acclimatized very quickly and I spend about an hour a day in the swimming pool so I feel very fit.

A few weeks later he received a letter back from his sister, who wrote, 'When I woke this morning there was a lovely thick frost on the lawn outside and quite a thick fog – I thought of you in your shirtsleeves in Pensacola, and still perspiring and couldn't help envying you just a wee bit.'

The whole place seemed something of a dream, with the warm waters of the Gulf of Mexico a short walk away, past a large outdoor swimming pool and red-clay tennis courts. It 'leaves us flabbergasted', admitted Wally Stradwick. 'Any time of the day after noon, everyone seems to be on their way to the beach clad only in trunks. Just the life!'[3]

The FAA cadets wore standard American flying cadet gear – khaki shirt and trousers with a white T-shirt – but coupled with their Royal Navy hats presented a somewhat peculiar sight. When flying they wore a simple zip-up khaki overall with a khaki helmet. A full set of sports clothes, shorts, shirts, tracksuit and 'sneakers' was also issued. As they progressed, fur-lined jackets and aviator sunglasses were distributed.

While he couldn't ask for better conditions, the reality of the situation hit home when Stradwick and his fellow cadets were asked to fill out a next-of-kin form. 'Cheerful business all this,' he scribbled in his diary. 'Last week there were five deaths in three days at one of the fields. I've suddenly got a great desire to live through this course and the war. I posted about 11 pages off to Betty. I hope she can read it all because on the train I had to write in pencil. As far as I can see, any chap who gets right through this course is a really hot flyer and deserves to live.'

All new arrivals underwent written and verbal tests in a decompression chamber, simulating the effects of thinning oxygen at altitudes of 18,000 feet or above. Flying training began on the Vultee Valiant, a 450-horsepower monoplane with more advanced controls than they had hitherto experienced, such as variable flaps to keep the aircraft under control with less speed – a vital ingredient for landing on a carrier. This part of the course also introduced basic flying formations, including the standard V made up of three aircraft, and the echelon, in which aircraft flew tight behind each other on the diagonal at an angle of forty-five degrees.

Once they had mastered the Vultee Valiant, trainees moved on to the Harvard or SNJ, the standard naval training aircraft used by schools in both America and Canada. The Harvard was a

200-mph monoplane powered by a 600-horsepower Pratt & Whitney Wasp radial engine. While it had only a third of the power of American front-line fighters, it shared many characteristics with them, such as a retractable undercarriage and greater control of the aircraft's power, including the ability to vary the fuel mixture into the engine and the pitch of the propeller, features which act rather like gears in a car. It was renowned for the tearing noise caused by its propeller tips reaching the speed of sound. Anyone standing at right angles to the take-off run would receive the full, ear-splitting benefit, while the pilot sat behind the engine remained happily unaware.

Rising at 05.30 each morning, pupils would alternate between spending hours in the Link Trainer and flying solo or with their instructor in the air, familiarizing themselves with instrument flying in bad weather or darkness. All manner of aerobatics, stalls and manoeuvres were practised until the pilots became at one with their machines and could land using their instruments alone. In one of the most challenging sections flying in a dual trainer in the air, pupils were taught how to interpret the sounds of a radio beam through headphones and use this information and their instruments to home in on the airfield at precisely the right speed and height. When they thought the airfield was dead ahead, the instructor in the seat behind snapped up the hood to reveal how close they actually were. Such intense concentration would be critical when trying to locate a moving carrier at sea or an airfield in bad weather.

Up at the Service Flying Training School in Kingston on the north-eastern corner of Lake Ontario Chris Cartledge had also started his second stage of training after making the journey across the Atlantic from Elmdon, where he'd successfully negotiated the basics. The flying school in Kingston was run by the Royal Canadian Air Force. Unlike their fellows down in Florida, cadets still slept in bunks in large dormitories, and although food and drink was abundant, it wasn't up to US standards. This didn't stop Chris Cartledge admitting in a letter home that 'money disappears in no time in this land of ice creams, chocolate and milk'.[4] He embarked on a fitness campaign after sending a photograph home and receiving a reply noting with slight disapproval that he had put on weight.

Cadets were free to leave the base once the day's schedule had been completed. Some enjoyed watching Duke Ellington play in Kingston, and in the summer they could wander down through the pretty wooded paths to the rocky beaches of Lake Ontario for evening swims or to explore islands in little sailing dinghies. 'We see the most marvellous sunsets over the lake, and brilliant moon scenes, and if it weren't for the wretched war I should be perfectly happy,' wrote Cartledge to his sister Jo in late August 1942. Cartledge and his friends Bill and Dick pooled their money and bought a clapped-out 1926 Chevrolet for seventy-five dollars, which they christened Horatio, visiting Toronto and Niagara Falls in the late-summer sunshine of August and enjoying the rich colours of the fall.

However, rules and regulations continued to bug the eighteen-year-old, who told his sister, 'there is rather a lot of being kept in one's place here, e.g. I was leaving the camp the other evening and was accosted by the corporal MP at the gate who said he wouldn't let me out as I was. He said I was definitely scruffy! He said my shoes were dirty, my trousers filthy and uncreased, my shirt grimy and without a tie and my cap was a total wreck. Perhaps he was justified, but JO! . . .' In one sense, one could hardly blame Cartledge. Flying now consumed them day and night – they were training to be honed fighter pilots – yet still they were pulled up for what must have felt like petty infractions.

Kingston's bucolic and remote location made the war seem particularly distant and sapped motivation. 'If Joseph Stalin took a walk through Canada he would have a pink fit. Everyone appears to be on holiday . . . War seems miles away. Everything seems miles away, and yet I don't really feel very far from home,' wrote

Cartledge. But for Cartledge and his fellow cadets in both Canada and America the most intense part of their training was now under way. Until this point they had merely been learning how to fly. Now they would turn their aircraft into effective killing machines.

Instructors raised the pressure accordingly. Cartledge admitted in a letter home that 'my vagueness is not appreciated by my instructor, and he doesn't shrink from telling me so in the strongest terms. He is proving to be my bugbear. When instrument flying under the hood I hear a screech – "If I tell you to lose height by 500 feet per minute at 120 mph on 080 degrees, why the hell do you gain height by 300 feet per minute at 110 mph on 130 degrees? You silly little fool!" Well, as you may imagine, there is not much time for casualness.'

In Pensacola the cadets moved to Barin airfield, twenty miles to the west in Alabama. Otherwise known as Bloody Barin or simply the graveyard, the airfield justified its reputation. Instructors showed students graphs highlighting when the most crashes and fatalities would happen. This was one of the most dangerous times for the young flyers. Their increasing confidence masked the fact that they still didn't have enough experience to avoid mistakes if the Harvard wasn't given the respect it deserved.

Up in Kingston, Ken Ward had been one of the first in his course to go solo on the Harvard, in six hours and twenty minutes. However, one day while executing a loop the Harvard suddenly went into a spin at 4,000 feet. 'She would not come out of it either, no matter what I did,' said Ward, 'and I was losing height rapidly. I almost gave up trying to regain control and thought of bailing out. Instead, I let go of everything, the aircraft shuddered once or twice and then came out of the spin in a lovely dive, so I pulled out at 1,500 feet, very much relieved.'[5]

Despite not yet being at war, death was a constant spectre and stress took its toll. Three months into the course in Kingston, Cartledge wrote home to his sister, 'as I fly there seems nothing frightening or dangerous about it but my nerves and I think most of the others in my course are definitely more shaky now than [they] used to be. My stuttering is worse and my fingers tremble when I hold them out.'[6] Serious 'crack-ups' and stress-related illnesses were not uncommon. A study commissioned in 1945 which investigated wartime incidences of flying stress in the Fleet Air Arm concluded that 'large number of breakdowns' occurred during training. The report recorded that, officially, there had been 160 such cases throughout the war.[7] However, many more went unnoticed, despite attempts by instructors to look out for symptoms, such as drinking too much or being overly irritable, sensitive or morose.

New words entered the pilots' vocabulary. 'Twitch' was an aviators' condition in which a healthy concern for one's safety turned morbid. The word had numerous shades of meaning. A pilot could be a bit twitchy after a few ropey carrier landings but then be fine. At the other end of the scale, severe twitch, often built up over time exposed to the pressure of combat, could render a pilot literally a dribbling mess and unable to fly, demoted to a menial ground job in some far-flung windswept airfield or released by the FAA completely. Twitch was often triggered by a 'prang' – a seemingly innocuous word describing anything from a harmless bump from which the pilot walked away without a scratch, to a horrific accident and a horrible death by burning or mutilation. More often than not twitch was kept in check by not dwelling on accidents and keeping busy, or through the panacea of alcohol. But it could grow like a cancer, an anxious mental state eating away at the nerves until it overwhelmed everything else.

In the final weeks before they received their wings, pilots learned basic fighter tactics, attacking enemy aircraft and evading attack, advanced formation flying, navigation and gunnery. The skies above Kingston and Pensacola were filled with the vapour trails of mock dogfights. Tactics were discussed and practised, with one flight of two aircraft acting as the enemy while the others attempted such moves as 'high side S's', coming out of the sun and getting behind the enemy or trying to turn inside him.

'The most nerve-racking was approaching each other head to head,' said one pilot who trained in Pensacola, 'with closing speeds of some 400 mph you hoped your opponent remembered to turn the correct way at the last moment.'[8] Pilots honed their gunnery skills by diving and strafing dummy enemy airfields and rocky outcrops at sea. This was far easier said than done. 'It was very hit and miss,' said another, who trained in Kingston, but 'it was great fun because you really felt you were being a hot pilot when you actually fired a gun at something.'[9]

Cadets also spent many sessions on clay-pigeon ranges under expert tuition, the theory being that this would improve their air gunnery. By acquiring an instinctive feel for the deflection or 'aim off' needed to hit a clay pigeon, it was thought the student more easily acquired the more complex skills needed to hit one moving aircraft from another. These skills were transferred to the sky, where pupils flew Harvards fitted with a single .300-inch machine gun mounted on the fuselage. Attacks were made from all angles on drogues towed through the sky, with each student using bullets dipped in different coloured paint so that hits could be identified. Some aircraft were fitted with 16-mm gun cameras. Depending on the angle of attack and how far away the target was, the pilot had to work out what aim off was needed to compensate for its speed. Just as a clay getting nearer the shooter and flying overhead requires less lead, so as an attacking aircraft falls directly behind the target, the amount of deflection reduces with every second. The objective was the same in both – for the rounds fired from the guns to arrive at exactly the same time and place as the moving target.

Getting it right was down to instinct and practice – and mastering the gunsight. American aircraft used a reflector gunsight, with a reticle (or graticule) comprising a dot and two concentric rings projected onto a forty-five-degree glass panel. As the pilot looked through the glass and focused on the target, the reticle appeared as though it was distant in space without him having to change his focus or close one eye. Depending on the speed and angle of attack to the target, he could then use the rings to work out the lead and when he should press the trigger. British aircraft used gyro gunsights, which worked out the lead for the pilot and were generally more accurate.

Margins were tiny. Certainly for the cadets, hitting a small target like a drogue with a single gun was very difficult and sorted out the good shots from the rest. In Pensacola one pilot got twelve out of thirty-nine shots on target – the top score and good enough to win him a night out in New Orleans, with a pilot thrown in so he didn't have to fly himself back the following morning nursing a hangover.

For those on the Towers Scheme in Florida nights out on the town tended to be in Mobile or Pensacola, where bars like the San Carlos Hotel were particularly popular. Neither town had the same variety of clubs or bars as Detroit or New Orleans, but men learned to find their fun where they could. Although trainees were technically only allowed ashore one night a week, by swapping passes they could go out any night they wanted, the only drawback being the lack of sleep before flying the next day.

Stradwick, for one, continued to embrace the few precious hours he had ashore like they were his last. 'I will now account [*sic*] the story of two men in a car (with due respects to Jerome K. Jerome),' he wrote in his diary in August 1943.

Last Wednesday night Johnnie Wells and I were on leave together. I was due back at 11 a.m. on Friday and with the help of some ink eradicator we fixed Johnnie's pass. Well, we hired a car on some RAF chap's licence and first went to the San Carlos, where we waxed rather merry, and then started off for Mobile. Just outside Pensacola we picked up four Yank sailors and between the lot of us we made some noise. Johnnie and I were both feeling very merry and when I took over the wheel halfway and mopped into Mobile I naturally wasn't worried about speed. Going through the Bankhead Tunnel I was doing about 45 and blowing the car horn like mad to the amusement of some girls in the car behind us. Suddenly a policeman dashed out and stopped us. He wanted to run me in, but I talked him out of it while Johnnie was trying to stuff the licence into my pocket.

After unloading the sailors, Stradwick and Wells bowled into the Hollywood Club for more drinks, where they danced with some local girls before dropping them home. Getting lost in the unfamiliar streets of Mobile, they turned down a one-way street where 'two cops bristling with guns charged out and stopped us'. Once again Stradwick managed to charm their way out of being arrested, but a few minutes later they had only just passed back through the Bankhead Tunnel 'when a speed cop rode past us and waved us to a standstill'.

Their luck had run out. Charged with speeding, Stradwick and Wells were taken to the local jail, put up in front of the judge and fined twelve dollars each. Stradwick was unrepentant and 'didn't see justice in the whole thing and after going to swipe the cop who was a really thorny piece of work, I was told that soon I'd be in jail for three days without bail. Poor Johnnie was punching me in the back because he'd forgotten his identity (alias) on the driving licence.' Forking out their fines, they were allowed to leave and returned to Pensacola in the early hours, where they sobered up by holding each other under a cold shower. Fighting dreadful hangovers, Wells suggested they go sailing the following morning, but knocked Stradwick stone-cold with the boom while attempting an overenthusiastic tack.

Such heavy nights were rare given the relentless pace of the training schedule. In September 1943 alone, for example, Stradwick flew seventy-three hours and forty-five minutes. More often men would escape for a few hours, perhaps hiring a car to take a date to the open-air cinema or catching a bus into Pensacola.

The shift to Florida and exposure to a new and unfamiliar culture could cause embarrassment and confusion. Catching an empty bus outside the air station one morning, Keith Quilter settled in the back and planned how he would spend his few hours on leave. As he got closer to town he looked up. 'The black people looked daggers at me as if to say "What are you doing back here?" and the white people sitting up front were doing the same.' It was his first introduction to the colour segregation of the American South. 'No one said anything – looks were quite enough,' remembered Quilter.[10]

Another British pilot was invited to a local dance, which 'was a bit rustic but done with great gusto. All the local people and the girls were pretty and gaily dressed. It reminded me of a scene from the *Oklahoma* musical,' he said, and he found the women 'most curious in a very open manner' and their 'slow Southern accent very beguiling'.[11] To American women the Royal Navy pilots seemed polite and glamorous, while the cadets found them confident and exotic. In the hot sticky heat of the South dances could be sexually charged affairs, but as they were often held on the air station, any initial sparks had to be fanned at a later date to coincide with leave, away from the prying eyes of the military police. 'You had to watch it,' said one pilot. 'I got caught once with a girl outside the dance hall. The ruddy MPs would clobber you. They were very strict.'[12]

Bearing in mind the years of rationing and shortages in wartorn Britain, it was little wonder American women appeared sophisticated. For female friends and family members of nearly every Royal Navy airman training in America, envy of the warmer climate or better food was overshadowed by the cadets' access to items simply not available back home. Everything from silk stockings to hats was requested. Following one young airman's offer in a letter to his sister in England to send home 'stockings or perfume', she wrote back setting her brother a more challenging mission.

By the way, Pete, do you remember asking me to find out if Mother was in need of anything in the way of clothes a month or so ago. Well, if you can pluck up courage, she needs some underwear – it's no good getting her French knickers or such like as she won't wear them (if you'll pardon my frankness), but should you have the nerve to go into a Ladies underwear shop, then if you tell the assistant that you want underwear for your Mother, then she'll know what to give you. I hope you won't mind this long explanation – good job you're my brother. Mother would probably pass out if she knew what I was writing to you. Anyway, I know you won't mind.[13]

Such warm and personal letters illustrate just how vital regular correspondence was. The use of telephones was forbidden, and mail was the only way the men could keep in touch with their families. Letters might arrive only two weeks after being posted, but parcels could take up to two months. Details of the training had to be left out for security, and the same pilot alluded to the frustration of writing 'empty letters' – without being able to say anything of substance. But when he wrote home revealing he had finally gained his wings and had led the cadets' parade, the pride in his mother's words in her letter back was heart-warming: 'We are so glad you got your wings dear and we feel so proud for you. How I wish I could have seen you leading the parade. It gave me a great thrill I can assure you . . . I shall be so glad when you come home dear. I shake out the old tweeds and tell myself it won't be long now. We're all longing to see you but you're in the best place for the time being.'[14]

Following an average of 200 hours of flying and after passing their final exams and a solo flight assessed by the chief flying instructor, successful cadets in Canada gained their wings. Towers graduates got their wings after around 250 hours. It had been intensive, tough work. In Pensacola pupils were presented by the air station captain with a diploma indicating they had won their US Navy wings in addition to having their logbook stamped and authenticated with FAA wings. Pilots crowded into the tiny office of the Royal Navy representative, who 'proceeded to pull open a drawer and said "Help yourself, boys." The drawer contained beautiful cloth, gold-threaded Fleet Air Arm Wings.'[15]

Cadets were awarded their commissions soon after, becoming temporary sub-lieutenants (A) in the Royal Navy Volunteer Reserve (the RNZNVR for New Zealanders); those under twenty were commissioned temporary midshipmen. In Canada most would have to wait until they got back to Britain before they received their commissions and could trade in their bell-bottoms for smart new officers' uniforms. Their new wings were proudly sewn on the left sleeve, along with the wavy gold braid signalling they were hostilities-only servicemen. Tailors on both sides of the Atlantic did a roaring trade kitting out the newly commissioned pilots.

Most airmen shared four ambitions: to be awarded their wings, receive their commission, join an operational squadron and see action. The first box could be ticked. Now they could reflect at last on the future and what part in the war they might play.

Stradwick had spent a year in America and had loved it. But, as with many, his new life had created even more uncertainties and questions about his future. 'Firstly, I want to be in this country and be near Betty; secondly I'd like to go home and see Mother, Sheila, Gerald and the folks. Finally, the one thing I've always wanted and that's to have a damned good crack in action before the war's over. One thing! I'll certainly be able to fly,' he wrote in his diary. He was not alone in being seduced by the American way of life, and he was seriously considering putting his roots down there once the war was over.

'Oh how I wish I knew how I was going to get on after the war. At school I was going to be a schoolteacher but the war broke that up and somehow I don't fancy going to swot again. Starting in a country other than my own will certainly be an experience,' he wrote. But now he would shortly be joining an operational squadron and then returning to England. To . . . who knew? But he was certain about one thing. 'This should all work out unless some imbecile decides that we should fly west to pick up a carrier and then go into the blasted Pacific. I don't think I'd fancy that some-how,' he scribbled in his diary on New Year's Eve 1943. 'A bad thing about life here, is that there is far too much time available for serious thought. I often wonder about the future, how everything will wind up, and where I shall settle down. What a life we lead!'

On the eve of the fifth year of the war Stradwick's reluctance to receive a long posting to the tough, bitter battleground of the Pacific was understandable. The American training culture was very much focused on the carrier war in the Pacific, which took place over long distances, with fleets away from land for months on end fighting against the feared Japanese, whereas the naval campaigns in the Mediterranean and the Atlantic saw carriers away from their bases for shorter lengths of time.

Unlike the Royal Navy, the US Navy had no operational shore-based fighter squadrons. Instead, newly qualified pilots with up to 450 hours' flying time were sent straight to Pacific carrier fleets. Many pilots with action under their belts were then posted back to the US as instructors. Stradwick heard first-hand battle stories from American pilots returning from their tours of duty. While it was hugely exciting knowing they might soon have a 'crack at action', for the Royal Naval airmen the Pacific was a completely different type of war and one that the British had yet to experi-ence. And although Stradwick and his fellow aviators didn't yet know for sure where they'd end up, events throughout 1943 had made it clear the tide was turning towards the east.

In the freezing waters of the Arctic British carriers were busy supporting convoys carrying vital war materials to Russia, turning the screw on the Germans on the Eastern Front. The FAA also continued to play a vital role in escorting merchant convoys across the Atlantic and patrolling British home waters. But perhaps most crucially Royal Navy planes had supported the Malta convoys and the successful Allied amphibious landings in Africa and Italy via Sicily, and after three years of bloody fighting the Mediterranean had been all but secured.

Although D-Day was still to come, the narrowness of the Channel meant much of the airborne support would be provided by land-based aircraft. Any landings in the south of France would more than likely meet little air opposition from a hard-hit German Luftwaffe fully occupied to the north and east. With the temporary crippling of the mighty German battleship *Tirpitz* by midget submarines in the autumn of 1943, Royal Navy ships and aircraft were freed up, and the British finally had the luxury of thinking how its carriers could participate in the war in the east.

In August 1943, in the Canadian late-summer sunshine, Winston Churchill and American President Franklin D. Roosevelt and their Chiefs of Staff gathered inside the picturesque seventeenth-century ramparts of the Citadel of Quebec for the first Quadrant Conference. On the agenda was the war's grand strategy. In addition to discussing plans for D-Day and the bombing campaign of Germany, the Combined Chiefs of Staff also agreed that, while ensuring the Allies stuck to the principle of defeating Germany first, greater priority should be given to the Pacific campaign. Crushing Japan arguably roused stronger feelings in America than the campaign against the Germans.

For the best part of the next year Churchill argued with his Chiefs of Staff about what form a British contribution to the Allies' strategy in the Far East should take. One alternative option to direct participation in the Pacific was an amphibious invasion via the Indian Ocean of northern Sumatra, from which the Allies would retake Malaya, reasserting some of Britain's influence in its former colonies and redeeming its defeats earlier in the war. The Chiefs of Staff, however, were mindful that fighting alongside the Americans in the Pacific itself would illustrate to the world that Britain was in the thick of it at the Japanese defeat. Either way, by the time the leaders met again just over a year later, the speed of the US Navy's advance through the Pacific to the doorstep of Japan had made nearly all other options obsolete.

The central Pacific had been relatively quiet throughout 1943 as the US Navy beefed up its forces. By autumn, however, the

Central Pacific Force, which later became the US Fifth Fleet, the largest and most powerful in naval history, had been born. With six new heavy carriers, five light carriers, twelve battleships and an armada of supporting cruisers and destroyers, the Fifth Fleet went on the offensive with a series of operations that aimed to take strategically important Pacific atolls in the Marshall, Caroline and Mariana Islands.

Over the next four months US Marines experienced some of the bitterest fighting of the war as they winkled out fanatical Japanese opposition on islands and atolls of coral and rock just a few miles wide. On 23 November the Americans captured the equatorial Pacific atoll of Tarawa with more than 1,000 marines killed and 2,000 wounded over just three days of fighting. The carrier USS *Liscome Bay* was torpedoed by a Japanese submarine, killing almost 700 men. Little wonder Stradwick seemed uneasy about joining the Pacific war. But by spring 1944 the Americans had captured atolls in the Gilbert and Marshall Islands on which they could establish airbases for the next thrust west. Spearheaded by Task Force 58, a fast carrier force which was split into two groups of four carriers, each supported by its own battleships, cruisers and destroyers, the Fifth Fleet maintained constant pressure on the Japanese as it pushed across thousands of miles of Pacific water, operating either together or in groups, allowing units to refuel and resupply without diluting its potency.

Each part of the fleet had its brief. Task Force 58's carrier aircraft would target islands to prevent the Japanese bringing up reinforcements, allowing marines and US Army assault troops from V Amphibious Corps to assault the beaches. There were no permanent bases. Every single item needed by the Americans – from the bullets for the aircraft to the flour that made the bread for the men aboard the ships – had to be transported to the 'battlefield' by a vast number of supporting craft. By gaining command of the sea and the air, the Americans could bypass smaller atolls held by Japanese forces with no danger of being attacked from the rear. Such Japanese outposts were cut off and left to wither until the end of the war. Meanwhile, in the south-west, the other arm of the Allies' Pacific offensive – led by General Douglas MacArthur – was pushing Japanese forces back across New Guinea. The Japanese High Command was forced to abandon its outer defensive ring and establish a new line, 1,000 miles to the west, stretching from the Mariana Islands in the central Pacific down to western New Guinea. The American net was closing in.

But the part that Britain would play in the Pacific when the time came depended not just on the international politics that Churchill was debating with his Chiefs of Staff, but also resources. In March 1943 Edgar Granville, independent MP for Eye, had stood up in the House of Commons and asked A. V. Alexander, the first lord of the Admiralty, what assurances could be given 'that when the Fleet Air Arm have to go out and fight, as the Americans are having to fight now, in the Pacific, they will be given adequate, efficient and effective aircraft to enable them to undertake their responsibility'.[16] It was a fair question, because what had emerged was that the aircraft currently used by the Royal Navy would need to be replaced by something a lot better if the FAA was to have any chance in the Pacific.

6

They don't know what they want and they won't be happy till they get it

It was a typically gloomy February day. Londoners walking across Parliament Square bowed their heads against the icy wind and driving rain. Deep inside the Palace of Westminster another heated debate about the state of Britain's naval air power was firing up. This particular discussion was taking place in the Robing Room, the Lords' temporary wartime home due to bomb damage to the chamber of the House. It was just the latest in a stream of parliamentary debates, with both MPs and Lords trading blows on an almost monthly basis over the shortcomings of naval aviation. In a parliamentary sketch a few days later the political correspondent for *Flight* magazine suggested that 'were it not for the fact that the subject is serious, one would be tempted to apply to the debate in the House of Lords last week the familiar paraphrasing of a famous soap advertisement that was current many years ago. As applied to the Irish, the paraphrase ran "They don't know what they want and they won't be happy till they get it."'[1]

By 1943 there were two main types of naval aircraft used by the Royal Navy. Bombers, otherwise known as TBRs (torpedo, bomber, reconnaissance), carried a pilot, an observer and, in some types, a telegraphist air gunner. They were used to drop torpedoes or bombs and to carry out reconnaissance. Fighters, meanwhile, escorted the bombers to their targets, protected the fleet and acted as ground-attack aircraft. At first they too often had two seats, with the observer tasked with navigating and spotting enemy ships or aircraft. But as the war progressed it became clear that lighter, more manoeuvrable single-seaters were more effective against land-based single-seat enemy fighters.

To be successful, both types of carrier plane had to combine a number of important traits. For a pilot to feel confident against enemy aircraft in the air, to intercept fast fighters and to bomb well-defended positions, carrier-borne aircraft needed to be powerful and nimble. But dexterity couldn't come at the expense of clout. Aircraft had to be tough enough to take punishment from enemy gunfire and strong enough to carry a few decent guns of their own. A reliable engine was equally crucial. Because of the limited size of carriers, there were no twin-engined aircraft in the FAA. Flying over miles of sea or enemy terrain, the crew therefore needed to have complete faith that their single engine would get them home.

The pilot had to be able to control the aircraft at relatively low speed when landing on the small confines of a flight deck. As this speed was normally just above that at which the aircraft stalled, pilots preferred planes with mild stalling characteristics such as a gentle shudder – rather like a motor car – instead of, for example, one wing suddenly dropping like a stone. An effective carrier plane also required a reasonably clear view ahead so that the pilot could see the deck when he landed, and its undercarriage needed to be strong enough to withstand the pressure of slamming down onto an unstable deck at up to sixteen feet per second without crumpling. In addition the fuselage had to support a rear arrester hook that wouldn't be ripped out with the force of catching the wire slung across the flight deck at 50 mph. Finally, the plane had to be small enough to land safely and be stowed away in the hangar below, but large enough to carry an observer and a rear gunner if required.

All in all, the requirements were complex: the FAA needed a jack-of-all trades multi-role aircraft, but what it had, in the early years of the war, were obsolete masters of none. According to Eric Brown, a legendary naval aviator who has flown more types of aircraft than anyone else in history, this sorry state of affairs was a direct result of the pedantic approach of the naval staff to the operational requirements of the FAA. Their 'lack of boldness and imagination [was] hardly calculated to inspire British naval air-craft designers of the day', he reckoned.[2] But while Brown makes a fair point, he doesn't quite tell the full story. The Air Ministry had asserted before the war that if the fleet came up against superior land-based fighters, then RAF protection would be provided. But it was not, and the result was exposed cruelly in action, time and time again.

Take the Blackburn Skua. When it was conceived in 1935, it was state-of-the-art. A two-seater monoplane with an all-metal fuselage and a retracting undercarriage, the Skua was designed as a dive-bomber-cum-fighter. In the former role it was quite effec-tive, with some success early in the war including the sinking of the German cruiser *Königsberg* off Norway in April 1940. It also had the honour of dispatching the first FAA kill of the air cam-paign, shooting down a German Dornier 18 flying boat over the North Sea. But knocking down a slow-moving flying boat could be done with a pea-shooter. A flying boat wasn't exactly a Messer-schmitt Bf 109. And that's where the problems began.

The Skua had a top speed of 225 mph and when fully loaded with a 500-pound bomb, its 900-horsepower Bristol Perseus engine took over 20 minutes to drag it up to 15,000 feet. Like many FAA aircraft, it had a second seat for an observer, whose jobs were reconnaissance and navigation over the sea and, later in the war, operating the radar. The crew was enclosed by a rectangu-lar panelled canopy, giving the impression they were pottering about in a greenhouse. It didn't exactly strike fear into the enemy. As the war progressed it became clear that the plane was no match for German land-based fighters, and many Skuas along with their brave crews were shot down. This model was soon relegated to towing drogues for rookie FAA pilots to practise target shooting, in which capacity it arguably made a greater contribution to the war than in action.

Other fighters came and went, including the single-seat

Gloster Sea Gladiator – yet another biplane – and the Fairey Fulmar, introduced in May 1940. Both had their moments, but weren't big hits. Desperate times called for desperate measures, and it was decided to convert land fighters. The Hawker Sea Hurricane performed its most notable feats in the Mediterranean, protecting convoys supplying Malta. It also escorted the convoys to Russia and across the Atlantic. But while compared to previous British naval fighters it was a dream to fly and a decent dogfighter, the Sea Hurricane was soon pitted against more powerful, better armed aircraft with greater range. It was a stop-gap. The simple fact is that converting land planes for carrier use generally didn't work. There was, though, perhaps one exception.

'Many moments live on in one's memory,' says Ken Ward, 'but it was my first flight in the Seafire IB, No. 906, which I recall most vividly.'[3] The carrier version of the Supermarine Spitfire, the Seafire shared the graceful lines of its more famous cousin. Eyes were drawn towards the sky as the velvety Merlin engine purred overhead. Following tests with arrester hooks and wings that could be folded for easy stowage, the first Seafires entered service with the Royal Navy in 1942 and took part in countless operations over the next three years.

When Ward arrived back in Britain in early 1944 after getting his wings in Canada, he was posted to Yeovilton in Somerset, home to the Fleet Air Arm's fighter school. On his first flight in the Seafire he was struck by the 'amazing speed of take-off from the solid runway and the way she leaped into the air almost without any action on my part. The airspeed seemed unbelievably fast and I was exhilarated by the ease of control and the rapid response to any movement of the control column . . . I tried a few aerobatics, two slow rolls, one each way, and a loop, gradually using up my allotted time of thirty minutes.'

The Seafire produced a number of Royal Navy aces, and finally the British had a naval fighter they could be somewhat proud of. With a top speed of more than 350 mph, armed with two 20-mm cannons and four .303-inch machine guns, its handling and firepower gave pilots the confidence to take on most land fighters. However, for all its strengths in the sky, the Seafire still had serious faults as a naval aircraft. It was too elegant for the rough and tumble environment of a carrier deck. More Seafires would be written off in deck landing accidents than against enemy fire, with the main culprit being an undercarriage that would crumple in rough put-downs.

This problem was not confined to the Seafire. Most British aircraft used by the FAA were originally designed to cater for a vertical landing speed of ten feet per second. During 1943 this meant one failure for every 200 landings for British naval aircraft, compared with one for every 700 for American naval aircraft, and one failure for every 1,200 landings by land-based planes.[4] Watching returning aircraft come in to land on a carrier became something of a spectator sport for off-duty pilots and other members of the crew, who would crowd the small walkway overlooking the flight deck, dubbed goofers' gallery. Indeed the Seafire gained such a reputation for accidents, it was given its very own verse in the pilots' unofficial drinking song, 'A25', named after the form which had to be filled in by the pilot if an aircraft was damaged:

> When the batsman gives 'Lower' I always go higher,
> I drift off to starboard and prang my Seafire,
> The boys in the goofers all think that I'm green,
> But I get my commission from Supermarine.
> Cracking show, I'm alive, but I still had to render my A25.[5]

British naval aviation wasn't in a much better state on the TBR front. The much-maligned Swordfish was actually one of the FAA's most successful performers with almost continuous action throughout the war and a decent record hunting submarines. It was friendly to fly and easy to land on a carrier, and it was responsible for two dramatic successes for the FAA in the early years of the war – the torpedo attack on the Italian port of Taranto in November 1940, and helping to sink the mighty German battleship *Bismarck* in May 1941, the latter attack led by Lieutenant Commander Eugene Esmonde.

Although these two events earned the Swordfish a legendary status, their success was something of a fig leaf. This was graphically revealed on a cold February afternoon in 1942, when Esmonde commanded six Swordfish in a Charge-of-the-Light-Brigade-style attack on the German battlecruisers *Scharnhorst* and *Gneisenau*, which were making their way from the French port of Brest, through the English Channel and back to Wilhelmshaven and Kiel in Germany. Without fighter cover, pounded by heavy anti-aircraft fire from the ships and under constant attack by faster and better-armed German fighters, all six Swordfish were shot down before they could launch an effective attack. Only five of the eighteen crew were rescued. Esmonde's body was found floating in the Thames Estuary. Before taking off he had spent a few minutes with the padre. As he left, Esmonde smiled and quoted words from an eighteenth-century cleric: 'Are you so ready that if death should come tonight, you would not be afraid to die?' Then he laughed and said, 'Joke over.'[6]

There was little to laugh about. While there is no doubting the heroism, which earned Esmonde a posthumous Victoria Cross, the deaths highlighted just how vulnerable the Swordfish was becoming as aviation technology advanced. A few weeks earlier Esmonde had visited new recruits at *St Vincent* to deliver a lecture. On hearing the news of his death, Chris Cartledge wrote home to his parents describing the 'air of depression' which hung over the school. 'We all liked him very much. He was one of the best and certainly the most experienced pilots in the Fleet Air Arm. I think it's pretty disgusting the way they provide such good pilots with such antiquated machines,' he lamented.[7] The rookie pilots of the future knew they might end up flying the same plane. If they had to use machines like the Swordfish in the Pacific against the likes of the Japanese Zero, they would be mincemeat.

This view was echoed in the debating chambers in Westminster. Challenging First Lord of the Admiralty A. V. Alexander during a Commons debate in March 1943, Edgar Granville referred to the ill-fated attack on the *Scharnhorst* and *Gneisenau*, in which 'the young naval pilots went out literally to certain death in those antiquated crates'. Granville mocked Alexander, finishing with the barbed observation that 'it is not so much a question of production capacity as of Ministerial capacity'.[8]

The FAA's desperate need to find decent naval aircraft was no better illustrated than by the fact that in December 1943 it was operating sixty-two different types of plane. An Admiralty report noted wryly, 'a comb-out of obsolete types is now at hand, but we shall still have to make do with many of these cuckoo eggs'. In a memo Churchill noted the importance of having an adequate number of modern naval fighters, but he also recognized the necessity of making the best use of budget-hit cash reserves. A heavy programme of rearming had begun in autumn 1942, with front-line aircraft numbers rising above 500, but that was not enough. The reality was that if the FAA wanted to reach the Admiralty target of almost 2,000 aircraft by mid-1944, it would need to turn to America.[9] Thus in December 1942 Oliver Lyttelton, the minister for production, signed a deal with the US government to supply American aircraft to the FAA under the Lend-Lease agreement.

The US Navy and Air Force had always remained separate, meaning that those at the top of the navy could be influenced by naval aviators who had a grasp of what was needed to make a good carrier plane. When the RNAS and the RFC merged at the end of the First World War with such dreadful results for British naval aviation, specialist areas were diluted. In other words, experts on land aviation tried to assert their authority over carrier aviation, which they knew little about. By keeping their services separate, to some degree the US avoided this problem. After a slow start, the US began to produce highly effective carrier-based fighters and bombers. By the time the planes were required in great numbers in 1944, not only did American aircraft possess the all-round capabilities British models lacked, but the Royal Navy finally had the platforms, confidence and personnel to launch carrier strikes against heavily defended land targets and take on enemy fighters.

The American aircraft which made the single biggest impact on Royal Navy aviation in the Second World War was the Chance Vought Corsair. Everything about the Corsair oozed power. It was the first fighter plane to be pulled through the air by a 2,000-horsepower Pratt & Whitney Double Wasp engine powered by eighteen cylinders arranged in two banks of nine, which turned the largest three-bladed propeller ever used in a fighter, with a circumference of over thirteen feet – more than two feet greater than a Spitfire. To ensure this massive screw cleared the ground, the Vought engineers could have fitted a six-foot undercarriage to the fuselage but knew this would snap off in the rough and tumble of carrier flying, so they came up with an ingenious solution, designing a wing with a downward kink to which was attached a more robust undercarriage. The wing then swept up four feet to join the fuselage, with the extra height ensuring the propeller remained clear of the ground. The wings folded hydraulically, saving valuable time on deck and space in the ship's hangar. In flight the under-carriage rotated ninety degrees and folded up neatly into the wings. As a result, the Corsair was the first American fighter to exceed 400 mph in level flight. This was achieved at the expense of its appearance, however, giving it a distinctive inverted seagull shape which made it seem more at home among the dinosaurs.

The Corsair's firepower was anything but prehistoric. It was armed with six 0.5-inch Colt-Browning machine guns – three in each wing – with 400 rounds each in the two inner guns and 375 rounds in the outer gun. A hydraulically charged mechanism fired 800 rounds per minute, giving the pilot less than 30 seconds trigger time but plenty of bang for his buck. The Corsair could also carry a 1,000-pound bomb on a bracket underneath the starboard wing or one 500-pounder under each wing, and, by lowering the undercarriage, two flat panels on the front of the wheel struts acted as dive brakes, making accurate dive-bombing possible without a great deal of practice or experience.

Pilots dropped their bombs in a steep dive directly above a target, or 'skipped' them along the ground or water in a low, fast, horizontal attack with their wheels up in 'clean' position. This latter technique was especially effective for attacking ships in harbour or against aircraft hangars. The fuel tank, windscreen, seat and cockpit sides were all armoured, and it could carry enough fuel to fly for four hours at 35,000 feet. The wings were folded from the cockpit, saving valuable time on deck. In dogfights, Corsair pilots learned to use the plane's powerful engine to counter its weight – it had a rate of climb of around 2,500 feet a minute. The trick was to dive before 'zoom' climbing to make attacks from underneath or launching another attack from above.

Later models of the Corsair had the equivalent of a jockey's whip, a water-injected turbocharger. Already flying at full speed, if the pilot gave the throttle handle a sharp smack with the palm of his hand, he would feel a kick from behind as the aircraft leaped forward, immediately increasing its speed by about 50 mph. This only lasted a matter of a few minutes, but it was a great asset if he needed to close down a fleeing enemy aircraft or get the hell out of a sticky situation.

Most experts and pilots seem to agree that if the Corsair was not the best all-round naval fighter of the war, then it was certainly up there among the best. 'Widow maker, brutal monster, you loved and hated it,' said one British pilot, who was lucky to escape two nasty accidents during training in the Corsair. 'With its dreadful reputation and maybe due to the accidents I was somewhat wary.' Nevertheless, he motored on and 'with experience, my confidence grew and I realized what a wonderful plane it was'.[10] Keith Quilter felt from the start 'it was something special. It was like getting into a very hot sports car as opposed to an ordinary car'.[11] 'She was an awkward plane to fly,' countered another British pilot. 'It was ages before I felt I was in control of her, and you felt like you were in a racing car . . . She looked ominous, and when you looked at all the dials in the cockpit, you thought, *Christ!* But the power! Once you got to know her she was lovely. I had an affinity.'[12]

Such vignettes illustrate just what a challenge the Corsair was. Like a petulant teen, it went through a difficult adolescence. Early models had a bouncy undercarriage, making landing on a carrier deck dangerous. Its large wing area meant it had a tendency to float in the air, even once the throttle had been cut. On a confined carrier both these traits could lead to nasty accidents. The Corsair also had a grim habit of stalling as it approached landing speed at around 80 mph, causing the port wing to suddenly drop. With its powerful engine and torque, rookie pilots opening the throttle to try and counter the stall could end up with the fuselage actually spinning around the propeller – not surprising given it had ten times as much power as the aircraft they had been training on. Pilots' handling notes were clear that no spins should be attempted in a Corsair. Recovery was said to be almost impossible.

The Corsair had a tremendous range of around 1,000 miles thanks to the large fuel tank between the propeller and the cockpit. A removable belly tank gave the option to go even further. However, as a tail-first landing was required to catch one of the arrester wires, pilots – who sat thirteen feet back from the nose – found it extremely difficult to see the deck as they landed. So after a number of accidents – during which it was dubbed the Ensign Eliminator because of its unforgiving nature with their rookie pilots – the US Navy concluded most would not have the necessary skill to carrier-land the Corsair.

Assigned to land-based duties with the US Marines in the Far East, by the end of 1943 Corsairs had claimed more than 580 kills flying from Pacific islands. In other words, it was a damned good fighter but just needed to be tamed for carrier use. Undeterred by the US Navy's experience and desperate for a potent carrier fighter, the Royal Navy pressed ahead and formed its first Corsair unit, 1830 Squadron, on 1 June 1943 under the direction of Casper John, its Washington-based assistant naval air attaché.

By luck, the FAA discovered that clipping the Corsair's wingtips the eight inches needed to fit in the smaller hangars of the Royal Navy carriers also had the side effect of reducing its float on landing. Other difficulties were ironed out. A small spoiler fitted on the leading edge of the starboard wing prevented the lopsided plummet when it stalled. A modified undercarriage removed the bounce, and early models with a 'birdcage' canopy were replaced with smooth perspex canopies. The pilot's seat was also raised by seven inches, improving visibility.

The biggest hurdle, however, was making the Corsair an easier aircraft to land on a carrier. In July 1943 Mike Tritton – an Old Etonian who joined up as a volunteer and had gained his wings three years before – was sent to command 1830 Squadron, one of the first FAA units re-equipping with the new Corsair at Quonset Point on the east coast of America. A veteran of the siege of Malta, flying off the carrier *Furious* in a Fairey Fulmar – an inferior but reliable fighter – Tritton had just the experience needed.

Tritton helped devise a new technique for landing. On their downwind approach pilots would fly parallel with the carrier in the opposite direction to which it was steaming. As they passed abeam of the island of the ship, they started a 180-degree banking turn to port, which meant the moving carrier remained in constant view over the dip of the left wing as the pilot came in behind it to land just as he was straightening out. Tritton and his squadron successfully completed a series of trials both ashore and on board the American aircraft carrier USS *Charger*. It was not all plain sailing. One pilot remembered sheltering in a hangar as shards of broken propeller scythed across the airfield.

The Royal Navy soon set up a system for forming and working up squadrons in America and shipping their pilots and 'cabs' across the Atlantic ready to go into action. By the end of 1943 it had more than 500 Corsairs in service, and throughout the following year FAA Corsair squadrons were being formed, worked up to operational standard and shipped over to Britain at the rate of almost one a month. At the end of the war almost 2,000 Corsairs had been sent over to the UK, with nineteen first-line Corsair naval squadrons equipped by VJ Day. Between the US Navy, Royal Navy and RNZAF, 2,410 enemy aircraft were destroyed by the Corsair for a loss of just 189 – a ratio of 11:1 – making it one of the most successful all-round fighters of the Second World War.[13] The Corsair earned itself a number of sobriquets, including the Bent Wing Bastard from Connecticut, Old Hog Nose and the Whistling Death because of the whining sound it made when diving. But as an out-and-out fighting machine, with its rugged shape, firepower, speed and range, it was widely admired by both the Allies and the Japanese.

The Corsair was just one of a new wave of naval fighters and bombers developed by the Americans which were mass-produced. Under Lend-Lease, the Royal Navy also used the Wildcat (which it initially called the Martlet) and the Grumman Hellcat. The latter was not flown by as many FAA pilots, but proved such an effective carrier aircraft that the US Navy adopted it as its standard carrier fighter after snubbing the Corsair, only moving back to the latter in the closing months of the war. The Hellcat was certainly easier to land, with the pilot perched in his cockpit high on the fuselage, and with a more forgiving stall. Like the Corsair, the Hellcat was powered by a 2,000-horsepower engine and armed with six 0.5-inch machine guns, but chunkier armour made it 25–30 mph slower than the Corsair. Nevertheless, two Hellcat squadrons saw frontline service with the FAA in the Far East, and even in their limited role they were to prove highly effective in the Pacific, especially as night fighters.

Britain also turned to American engineering to replace that old plodder, the Swordfish. The Grumman Avenger gave the Royal Navy an insight into how bigger aircraft specifically designed for carriers could perform. Designed for a three-man crew, it had a tubby forty-foot fuselage, due to its large bomb bay, which could accommodate a thirteen-foot-long 22-inch torpedo, or either four

500-pound bombs or two 1000-pound bombs. It was powered by a 1,700-horsepower Double Cyclone radial engine, which shook a carrier deck during take-off and gave it a top speed of 270 mph.

Ian Paterson remembers sitting in the cockpit in a chair with armrests: 'you felt like the lord of the manor. It had very gentle landing characteristics, but it also had power.'[14] Its excellent view of the flight deck made it an ideal carrier plane. In true American style it had a larger-than-life cockpit. A urine receptacle was even provided. Another pilot said the Avenger was 'rugged, robust, huge . . . Sitting in the Avenger was just like sitting in the boss's big chair in an office. You felt in control, even if you weren't. I was so thankful so many times for the absolute steadiness. I used to fly with my feet crossed up on the cockpit bar, sitting back, swigging lime juice.'[15]

Separated by armour plate, the observer sat in the cockpit directly behind the pilot, where he could pull out a wooden desk to place his charts and navigation maps. If enemy fighters approached the observer was also able to operate a 0.3-inch rear gun below the tail fin by sliding down through a small chute into a tunnel along the belly of the aircraft, although this left him horribly exposed to fire from enemy aircraft attacking from underneath. The crew was completed by the telegraphist air gunner, who sat crouched in an electrically rotating glass turret on its dorsal, armed with a 0.5-inch machine gun. Extra firepower was provided by two more machine guns in the wings fired by the pilot, which meant that the crew were all armed.

The Avenger was a big aircraft for a carrier to hold. In a picture of the aircrew and ground crew of one squadron, no less than sixty-five men in rows of three all happily fit under its wings, which spanned fifty-five feet. Like the Corsair, the wings were hydraulically folded from a lever in the cockpit, but pivoted back through ninety degrees to tuck in snugly against the fuselage, giving the plane an insect-like appearance. No better is this is illustrated than in a painting by Leonard Rosoman, who was commissioned by the War Artists' Advisory Committee as an official war artist, and served aboard *Formidable* in the Pacific. Entitled *Angry Aeroplanes*, in the picture two Avengers squat on a flight deck, resembling huge brown moths.[16]

As with all American carrier aircraft, Avengers were built to last. Paterson reckons that although he 'loved the old Swordfish', in which he flew many more hours than in the Avenger, the latter could take a 'heck of a beating and a tremendous amount of damage'. It was not officially cleared for aerobatics, but for Roy Hawkes it was 'robust and a real joy to fly'.[17]

By the end of 1943 fourteen FAA front-line squadrons had received Avengers, and by VJ Day it was operating 1,000 models. Initially serving from escort carriers or land bases, Avenger squadrons saw action on Russian convoys, off Norway and helping to keep the English Channel clear in the build-up to D-Day. But by far their biggest contribution would be in Far East in the last nine months of the war. Although the Avenger was technically a torpedo plane, by 1945 the Royal Navy rarely used it for this purpose, instead using it in action as a low-level 'glide bomber', diving in at an angle of forty-five degrees to drop bombs on land targets.

Most of the Avenger squadrons were formed in the east-coast US Navy bases of Norfolk, Quonset and Squantum, with pilots either joining straight after getting their wings or after spending some time on operations in other aircraft. But what determined whether pilots went on to fly fighters or bombers? According to the FAA's own figures, 90 per cent wanted to be fighter pilots, but where they ended up was driven by demand. In 1944 the Admiralty ordered that 60 per cent of candidates should be trained for fighters, with 30 per cent for monoplane dive-bombers and just 3 per cent for biplanes. The remaining 7 per cent were trained for other duties, such as flying search and rescue aircraft.[18]

Sometimes a pilot's allocation was simply down to fate. One British pilot, for example, had returned from getting his wings in Canada and was posted to Scotland for a few weeks before starting operational training at the FAA fighter school in Yeovilton. But on the last day in Scotland one of his colleagues was killed flying into the sea. 'So I was hauled up to the CO, and he said, "You're going on the next TBR course, because that's where this chap was going and we've got to fill it."'[19] Generally, however, instructors watching their pupils would spot whether someone was cut out to be a fighter pilot. One pilot admitted he didn't have 'the feeling' for aerobatics when his instructor, a former Battle of Britain pilot, insisted he carry them out in a Harvard after he had eaten a Hershey Bar. 'It was the only time I was airsick,' he said, confirming his view that he was more suited to bombers.[20]

Ian Paterson reckons a bomber pilot was 'somebody reliable and . . . not given to taking undue risks. Somebody who would cooperate with other people in the back seats . . . I was never one of those dashing upfront follow-me-type chaps. I think they were looking for those kind for fighter pilots. The adventurous type. I was more the steady-as-she-goes type.' He believes he was destined for TBRs from the very beginning. 'Aerobatics didn't appeal to me at all and I wasn't particularly efficient in them. If I had been a fighter pilot I think I would have been cold meat.'

He was spot on. Naval fighter pilots were a different breed altogether.

1. Ken Ward takes aim during his training at *St Vincent*, November 1942.

2. Chris Cartledge sailing on Lake Ontario, off the coast of Kingston, September 1942. While Britain was being bombed, Canada was an ideal location for FAA flying training.

3. Nancy Parker and Keith Quilter fishing in Tuxedo Park, New York, spring 1944. It was 'quite the wartime romance,' recalls Quilter.

4. Wally Stradwick relaxes in Miami in late 1943, soon after receiving his wings. He was just one of thousands of FAA pilots who learned to fly in the US. By 1945, the Towers Scheme provided 44 per cent of all FAA pilots.

5. Keith Quilter in his Corsair, autumn 1944. 'Widow maker, brutal monster, you loved and hated it,' said one British pilot.

6. Shooting from the hip: Roy Beldam, far left, larks with friends during pistol practice while briefly ashore in North Africa in January 1945, before *Formidable* continued its journey east to the Pacific.

7. Dickie Reynolds was the highest-scoring Royal Navy Seafire ace in the Second World War, and shot down two kamikazes in one mission in his plane, *Merry Widow*.

8. Wally Stradwick poses in his flying gear. The Londoner was one of the first to qualify on his course, and wrote in his diary how eager he was for a 'damned good crack in action' before the war ended.

9. 1842 Squadron, pictured soon after it had formed up in April 1944. By the time the war ended half were dead.

10. Keith Quilter on the deck of *Formidable* with his Corsair mechanics.

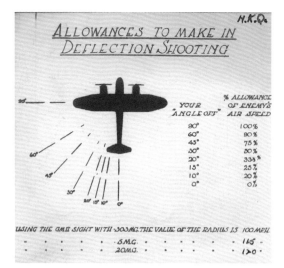

11. British airmen training in America were issued with myriad US Navy training manuals, including one which tried to discourage low-level stunting, known as flat-hatting.

12. Hitting a moving target was extremely difficult. Depending on the angle of attack and how far away an enemy plane was, the pilot had to work out what 'aim off' was needed to compensate for the target's speed.

13. British pilots carried US-manufactured 'gooly chits' in case they landed in occupied territory. It reads: I am an American airman. My plane is destroyed. I cannot speak your language. I am the enemy of the Japanese. Please give me food and take me to the nearest Allied military post. You will be rewarded.

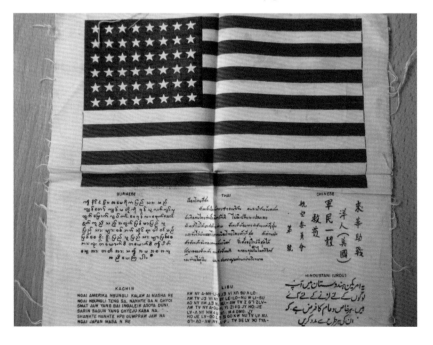

14. HMS *Formidable* in the Pacific in 1945. 'Formy' joined the British Pacific Fleet in May 1945 and was almost immediately plunged into action against the kamikazes.

15. Royal Navy Corsairs, marked with the distinctive British Pacific Fleet roundels, take off from the flight deck of a British carrier for their next mission.

16. Chris Cartledge, with his newly won wings sown on his left sleeve, reads in his cabin under the watchful gaze of Stalin and Lenin, spring 1943.

17. Regular physical education classes were organized on the flight deck for the ship's company, their routines led by a Royal Marine standing on the platform at the far end.

18. Away from front-line operations the flight deck could be used for a variety of other purposes, including deck hockey, boxing matches, film screenings and concerts in the lift wells.

FLIGHT DECK

September, 1944

19. *Flight Deck* was a monthly magazine popular with aircrew. Published by the Admiralty, it featured serious articles as well as irreverent gossip and cartoons.

7

Flat-hatters

For a naval fighter pilot fast reactions were essential. Soon after Ken Ward graduated from Canada with his wings and returned to Britain, he was practising take-offs and landings in Seafires at the FAA station in Eglinton, Northern Ireland. As he touched down on the right-hand side of the runway, his port tyre burst, throwing the aircraft sharply to the left and into the path of Richard Reynolds, another recent graduate, who was landing in his Seafire alongside. 'His reaction must have been immediate,' said Ward later, 'for with a loud roar from his Merlin engine he pushed the throttle through the gate and leapfrogged over my Seafire. His wheels could have caught my plane, and the result would have been catastrophic for us both. No other pilot I know could have done that – for the distance and time interval were so short.'[1]

What Ward had witnessed was the reaction of a natural. Reynolds, always known as Dickie, was born in 1923 and went to school in Cambridge. Commissioned as a sub-lieutenant in the RNVR in March 1944, one fellow Seafire colleague noted he was 'way above average' as a pilot, going solo at Sealand after only six hours.[2] Good-looking and fresh-faced, Reynolds was welcoming and reassuring to raw young recruits. Another friend recalled, 'everything about Dickie was exciting and turbulent . . . yet he was also very kind and tolerant and helpful'.[3] In the air Reynolds missed nothing and soon gained the nickname Deadeye Dick, 'yet he was in his own way curiously modest, and certainly never flaunted his towering reputation as a pilot', added the friend.[4]

By November 1943, after gaining his wings in Pensacola, Wally

Stradwick had been chosen to become a fighter pilot and followed the route of hundreds of fellow Towers' airmen, taking a short conversion course to a more powerful plane at the US Naval air station in Miami before joining his first operating squadron. 'I have never seen anything like it!' he wrote of Miami. 'The white buildings which are all shapes and sizes remind me of some film shots I've seen of Rome and Malta. Downtown Miami beach there are rows and rows of beautiful hotels, private homes, pretty canals and the Miami river.'[5]

The air station had comfortable living quarters and wide roads bordered with flowers and palm trees. Here pilots flew the North American Texan or sometimes got to practise in the more powerful Brewster Buffaloes, honing their aerobatics and gunnery skills. Both aircraft were great fun for pilots who wanted to follow their natural instincts. In another diary entry Stradwick described how 'we were intercepting bandits all over the place and all screaming "whoopie" whenever one of us got on the tail . . . at the end of the period we were rather bottled on the way home by the chase pilot [an instructor] because we started doing slow rolls in formation over downtown Miami.' Other aerobatic favourites included ground strafing and dive-bombing, but these were also only meant to be attempted under specific conditions and when instructors were monitoring in chase aircraft.

The pilots trained so hard and regularly that a sort of muscle memory developed. It 'became like riding a bicycle', reckons Keith Quilter, who also moved on to Miami after gaining his wings at Pensacola.[6] More than forty-five years after the war ended, flying back from Exeter and crossing the Severn Estuary, another former Corsair pilot was invited by a friend to have a stint at the controls and spotted a small tanker chugging away in the estuary below. 'My first instinct was to put the nose down and shoot it up,' he said.[7]

Instructors aimed to channel and hone these urges during training, but pilots had plenty of time in the air without being monitored, and this was when the fun began. Flying low and fast across the countryside, under bridges in towns or skimming a few feet over a lake at 300 mph was the best way to get an adrenaline fix. It was also one of the easiest ways to die. Recovering from a spin at 150 feet was impossible, while flying into a telegraph pole or trees had the same effect as being hit by anti-aircraft fire.

Low-level stunting was even given its own name – flat-hatting – supposedly after a pre-war incident in America when the wheels of a low-flying plane clipped a pedestrian on the head and crushed his new top hat. FAA fighter pilots were given a US Navy manual entitled *Flat-Hatting Sense*, which warned them of the perils of grandstanding, showing off, flying foolishly or carelessly. 'Flat-Hatting is a no-good way to fly. In other words, don't do it. Not only will it get you nowhere, it will get you killed.'[8] One of the most frequent reasons for flat-hatting, according to the manual, was the presence of women. 'To show off for a girl, of course, it is necessary to fly very low to see who you are. This is the PRIME CAUSE of accidents of this sort . . . girls and women, incidentally, have no conception of what constitutes dangerous low flying.'

By way of support for this last assertion, the guide cited evidence from a genuine court martial, during which it emerged that one pilot's girlfriend and her mother were in an American city hotel room when the suitor came to call, by aeroplane. The complaint of a large group of people was that the young man flew around the hotel 'like a pigeon, disturbing practically everybody and scaring several into mild shock'. When the court asked the girl's mother if, in her opinion, the accused had been flying low, she replied heatedly, 'Certainly *not*! That boy never once got below the fifth floor!'

So there it was: if one thing above all was forbidden to naval fighter pilots, it was flat-hatting. The problem was, they loved doing it. 'Johnnie Wells was up in the same period and as it was the last flight we decided to have some fun,' wrote Wally Stradwick. 'After flying in formation down towards Monroe [a county on the south-west tip of Florida], I did three snap rolls at 800 feet. Then we flew in formation down the main street of Monroe at

300 feet and worked our way to the house of some girls Johnnie knows.' Stradwick and Wells peeled off and dived, only to be spotted by an instructor flying nearby. They were both reported but escaped severe punishment. A few months later Stradwick wrote how he 'had some fun flat-hatting, particularly when coming in over a small village I saw a train coming through, and made a pass at it'. On another cross-country flight he had to keep his height below a hundred feet 'but that suited us down to the ground – literally . . . Wizard hop all around especially the last 80 miles or so when we knew we had enough gas, banged open the gate and up with the revs, and really flew low the whole way back. We are hoping that we don't have to have these planes on ops with us, because they'll be rather tired out by the time we've finished here!'

Other forbidden games included 'chasing tails' or 'rat-racing' in which pilots flew at high speed while weaving around electricity pylons. While such acrobatics were prohibited, throwing off an enemy fighter in a dogfight could be the difference between living and dying. After Chris Cartledge received his wings in Canada he returned to Britain and was introduced to the Hawker Hurricane at the FAA's fighter school in Yeovilton. He 'had to learn to throw it about to its limits. Our instructor would do just that, and our job was to hang on to his tail. Then it was our turn to manoeuvre as violently and unpredictably as possible in order to throw him off our tail.'[9]

One warm May afternoon while leading another new pilot, Cartledge's instructor dived low over Downside School, fifteen miles west of Yeovilton, pulling up a few hundred feet from the ground. The rookie following close behind ploughed straight into the school cricket pitch, killing himself and nine other people, including some Downside boys in the middle of a match. He had succumbed to the phenomenon known as the squashing effect or mushing, when the trajectory of the plane continues falling for a second or two after the pilot has pulled back his stick to level off and climb.

'Hedge-hopping' was also popular, but with trees and high-tension wires strung across the countryside pilots often returned trailing debris from their aircraft like cans from the back of a newly-weds' car. In Florida one pilot on an unauthorized flight to 'take a look at the Bahamas and visit Key West' returned with 'a telephone wire wrapped in with the undercarriage'.[10] On another occasion Wally Stradwick was 'beefing along' at low level when he felt contact with something 'and spent the next five minutes throwing tree branches out of the cockpit'. According to Stradwick, pilots were forbidden from flying so low 'as so many people have had their windows and crockery smashed'. When he landed, the mechanics were horrified to discover the engine was 'absolutely stuffed' with pine cones and branches.

Pilots were warned particularly against flying low over water as it was difficult to assess accurately how far the aircraft was from the surface. Despite this, Keith Quilter admitted, 'we did a lot of low flying over the lakes . . . it was pilots' forbidden fruit but we were trained to fly and strafe.' For fighter pilots like Quilter, 'low flying is the most enjoyable bit. You have a sense of speed you can't get in the air.' Indeed, the British approach to strafing specifically encouraged low fast flying.

One of the key figures at the air station in Miami was Lieutenant Commander Donald Gibson. After joining the Royal Navy as a seventeen-year-old midshipman in 1933, Gibson volunteered for flying and won his wings just before war broke out. He experienced first-hand the FAA's ill-fated Norwegian campaign in 1940, taking part in the disastrous daylight attack on the German battlecruisers *Scharnhorst* and *Gneisenau* in Trondheim harbour, when eight of fifteen Skuas were shot down and their crews killed or captured. Gibson compared the raid to the Charge of the Light Brigade and said later, 'In future all admirals should ideally be shot at in an aeroplane while they are still young.' In 1943 Gibson was appointed senior British naval officer at Miami, passing on his experience to 'sprogs' – newly qualified aviators. Although there was still some involvement with US Navy instructors, the trainees would learn to attack and strafe the FAA way.

Gibson distributed a thirty-two-page booklet on fighter operations entitled *Straight from the Horse's Mouth*, which he had authored with other instructors. Based on 'experience, sometimes bitter', its purpose was to give young flyers a reference on the important elements of their training after they went into action. Gibson explained, 'the art of being a fighter pilot consists of thirty per cent knowledge and seventy per cent horse sense, neither being any use without the other'.[11] Chapters included 'General Advice to the Fighter Pilot', 'Strafing', 'Formation and Escort', 'Harmonizing of Guns' and 'Deflection Shooting'.

There were often clear differences between US and British tactics.[12] On ground strafing, for example, US Navy doctrine called for fighters to come in high on an attack and employ a steep dive in order to suppress flak. However, according to one Canadian Royal Navy pilot who started the Miami course in late May 1943, Gibson 'advised us to disregard the USN strafing techniques and concentrate our efforts on a very low-level high-speed approach to the target which was only to be attacked once'. In his chapter on strafing Gibson said pilots should keep low, and 'when I say low I do not mean keep at about fifty feet, I mean five. Let your airscrew be just above the ground . . . never do more than one run on the target. It is highly wasteful and it is likely that a further run would not be effectual, but merely costly in the pilots of your squadron.'

'British strafing' and other tactics taught by Gibson would become widespread in action, although strafing tactics were far from uniform throughout the FAA. Approaches varied between squadrons, fighter wings and task groups depending on the whims and experience of leaders. This meant that pilots sometimes had to follow tactics that went against what they had been taught, although most pilots had to work bloody hard just to make sure they mastered the new aircraft they were given and could actually fly the thing.

By the time Towers Scheme fighter pilots joined an operational squadron most had flown as much as 300 hours. By comparison, RAF pilots joining squadrons in the Battle of Britain and going into action had often flown around half of this, and sometimes far less. But even with 300 hours the demands the more powerful new high-performance fighters, such as the Wildcat or the Corsair, made were huge. Wally Stradwick was a typical case, progressing straight from flying the 600-horsepower Harvard to the Wildcat with more than 1,000 horsepower, and after just six 'hops' moving on to the Corsair, which had a 2,000-horsepower engine. Although for him the Wildcat was 'a lovely kite and you can just twist all over the sky', the Corsair impressed immediately, and Stradwick admitted, 'we've been doing little but sit in its cockpit, checking ourselves out. The thing has switches and gadgets for everything.'

Pilots were punished for crashes and there were also threats of being booted off a squadron or a 'good recommendation for the infantry'. But 'restrictions and dire threats will never stop prangs', concluded Stradwick. 'Anyone would think we always fly with the one intention of pranging.' One of the severest penalties to discourage stunting and flat-hatting was the removal of rank. A British Corsair pilot who flew an aircraft under a bridge in a town in Maine lost three months' seniority.

Before his operational training at Yeovilton Chris Cartledge was posted to various FAA stations around the UK, flying Blackburn Skuas towing drogues for target shooting, until he himself was posted to a front-line squadron. One day, at Errol air station near Dundee, Cartledge landed heavily and put the station's only operational Hurricane out of action. He wasn't injured but admitted that the prang changed his whole attitude towards personal safety and survival. 'Up till that time I had possessed that youthful illusion that it won't happen to me,' he said.[13]

A few months later, taxiing an unfamiliar Skua at Inskip, a small Royal Navy airfield in Lancashire, Cartledge temporarily lost control, veered off the airstrip and was horrified to see his port wing collide with the rudder of a Seafire being warmed up for take-off. 'At that moment all sense of responsibility left me,' said Cartledge. Having extricated his undamaged wing from the

Seafire, he took off for Speke, failing to report the accident but leaving behind a speechless and highly indignant Seafire pilot. Cartledge's only concern was to get back in time for a date arranged with a Wren in Liverpool. On landing he was greeted by a 'very concerned and angry CO who ordered me straight back to Inskip to report to the Station Commander'.

Cartledge was put on a charge for failing to report an accident, taking off without permission and causing the accident in the first place. He was court-martialled. Luckily, there was no precedent and the court had to drop the main charge, but the charge of 'negligence in piloting His Majesty's aircraft' remained. His CO thought it was daft to lose a first-class pilot for a moment of madness and spoke up for him at the hearing in front of an impressive row of senior naval officers. Cartledge's defence was that the camouflage on the Seafire was so effective that it was virtually invisible against the background of the dismal muddy airfield. But it didn't wash. When he returned to the court the sword was on the table pointing straight at him, signifying a guilty verdict. His punishment was to lose two months' seniority as a midshipman, which was actually pretty lenient.

Writing home to his parents later, Cartledge made clear his disrespect for authority, mimicking the pidgin German of a contemporary humour book: 'Dis morn I did submit mineself to the disciplinary Kourt. Triviality was predominant and ik was condemt guilty! . . . All were stern and very, very imposing, and ick was small, very small . . . Much pointing of swords . . . Ick wass lost 2 months of mine seniority and wass reprimanded. What ignominy! How very small vass ick? But dem swords – how lordships do play! But ick was BAD, he will reform; as the Latin says – Disparagus Notus.'[14]

By the time they joined their squadrons, many FAA fighter pilots had been training together since the days of *St Vincent* and close friendships had been formed. One of Wally Stradwick's best friends was twenty-year-old Sylvester 'Syl' Rabey. At the beginning of 1944 Stradwick and Rabey had joined other newly qualified pilots for a New Year's Eve dance in Brunswick, Maine, where FAA squadrons flying American aircraft had been established. The party had, noted Stradwick later, rather a 'stuffy and formal atmosphere . . . still, by ordering four rounds at a time we did quite well for ourselves. In a couple of hours the whole show went the way of all Fleet Air Arm dances. Everyone from the CO down was absolutely rolling tight, and on the stroke of midnight, all bedlam broke loose.' Most of the men didn't get to bed until 4.30 and missed flying the next day, 'hangovers universal' with compulsory parade as a punishment. On another night out in nearby Boston Stradwick found himself with a 'glamorous creature named Marjorie', while 'Syl and I both got very merry and kept things right on the ball' before going bed at 4 a.m.

A few days later Stradwick and Rabey were together in the air on a training exercise, flying Wildcats in formation over the Maine countryside, which was covered in a blanket of snow. As the light began to fade in the late afternoon so the conditions rapidly deteriorated, with the cloud base forming at 1,000 feet and visibility worsening. Just as they decided to head back to base, Stradwick noticed smoke appearing from under Rabey's propeller and watched on helplessly as his friend lost height and speed and began to look for somewhere to crash-land.

'I told him to keep calm and open his hood. He didn't reply, so I told him again to open his hood and he screamed something about "forced landing" and I noticed he had dumped his flaps,' said Stradwick. By now Rabey was panicking and flying dangerously low, but instead of putting his aircraft down on Little Sebago, a frozen lake with two-foot-thick ice, he continued to circle over the trees. Then, about thirty feet from the ground, Rabey's plane 'appeared to jerk sharply to the right, and plonked down, right way up. Flames burst up around the nose, but appeared to subside, and I went over low three times but was unable to discern any movement,' wrote Stradwick.

Stradwick tried to land at Lewiston, the nearest FAA airfield, but bad weather forced him back to Brunswick, where he immediately rushed off with the officer in charge of the crash party, which consisted of an ambulance and a crash-recovery truck. It was now pitch black. Arriving near the crash site, Stradwick met the local police before leading the party with a torch through the knee-deep snow into the woods. There he found his friend. The plane had almost totally burned out, and 'poor Syl was just a black featureless shape – like a dwarf. His left arm was held upwards!'

A few days later at the naval cemetery in the nearby town of Portsmouth, Stradwick and five other fellow pilots carried their friend's coffin and buried him with full military honours. 'It was bitterly cold and everyone was shivering; and down by the water's edge with the girls crying, it wasn't so happy!' said Stradwick. Rabey's belongings were packed up by his colleagues, who went through his mail to get the addresses of his parents and girlfriend. 'Writing to them will be a delicate business to which I don't look forward . . . Poor Syl – I think he went into a panic – and went the one way we all fear – burning to death.' Rabey's accident had a powerful effect on the young pilots. 'Since his death, we have as usual made arrangements with each other with added requests which we hadn't noticed until now, as to what we'd like done if we get it,' wrote Stradwick.

Brushes with death were treated with morbid celebrations. When another member of Stradwick's flight, Derek Wheway, came into land in his Corsair without putting his wheels down, its propeller and wing elbows scraped along the runway sending up huge sheets of flame. The aircraft – all $75,000 worth – around a million pounds in today's money – was written off, but Wheway was safe. A few days later Stradwick and his colleagues had a binge in the mess in honour of 'Wheels-up Wheway', with 'the price of admission for ourselves of 6 bottles of beer at least. We all took a dozen each for a start.' After an 'intermission to reload' with another crate of 24 beers, the night ended with a fire-extinguisher fight, bottles smashed, doors broken and everything drenched so 'the lounge looked as if a tornado had kissed it'. The next day the chief steward went 'off his rocker' and the men had to fork out for the damage. 'Boy! But it was worth it!' wrote Stradwick.

By the spring of 1944, the conveyor belt of FAA Corsair squadrons working up before crossing back to the UK was well under way. Some were assigned service in home waters, while others were sent out to the Indian Ocean. Meanwhile the US Fifth Fleet and the American marines had successfully captured the Marshall Islands in February 1944, and the march across the Pacific to Japan rolled on. The new FAA pilots suspected it was only a matter of time before they went into action, and 'from newspaper reports from home and the fact that five [squadrons] will work up at the same time, it'll probably be the Pacific for us. I'd like to see England again before going on ops!' observed Stradwick, who, together with Wheway joined 1842 Squadron, which formed at the beginning of April 1944.

This was the tenth FAA Corsair squadron to form, and its make-up was pretty typical of most FAA fighter squadrons flying American aircraft that would serve in the Pacific. The squadron comprised eighteen pilots. The commanding officer (CO), senior pilot and senior sub-lieutenant – all of whom had already completed a tour with operational squadrons in Europe – came over from England, together with four pilots who had recently finished their training in Canada and gone back to England. The remaining eleven in the squadron had been trained by the US Navy under the Towers Scheme, and came straight from Miami via the base at Lewiston, where they had been flying Wildcats. All eighteen were volunteers, and they would spend the next twelve weeks together learning to fly the Corsair. By the time they sailed for England to join a carrier, they would have flown a further 150 hours each. Eighteen months later, by VJ Day, half the squadron would be dead and just three of the original eighteen would still be flying.

One of the airmen to join 1842 Squadron from England was Chris Cartledge, who described in a letter home how his life was

> one prolonged flight at present with stops for eating and sleeping . . . With such exhausting days I have little energy to fall back on in the evenings therefore my painting suffers. Nevertheless our cabin seems still to attract the casual loafer and if it no longer assumes the character of an atelier, it becomes the smoky den of gossiping pilots. This alas prevents me from reading too much and I have to tolerate plenty of shop talk, but it is pleasing to think that our cabin has more appeal for them than their own.'[15]

In addition to honing flying skills, gunnery, dive-bombing and navigation, working-up periods also allowed squadrons to develop their identity and for individuals to scope each other out. With so many alpha males and egos under one roof, a solid and charismatic CO was essential. Cartledge was excited to see that Tony Garland, a fellow former pupil of the City of London School, had been chosen to command 1842 Squadron. 'He was four or five years older but something of a golden hero for me. Very good at sports, swimming and cricket. He was a great guy and a good leader,' remembers Cartledge.[16] Writing home, Cartledge recorded, 'The squadron grouses but it is wonderful to see what can be done by a CO who realizes that the Fleet Air Arm wasn't formed merely for the convenience and pleasure of its members. I am rejuvenated in spirit by the driving force of the Commanding Officer who transmits his own keenness to us.'[17]

By all accounts, Cartledge's approval of Tony Garland was shared by his fellow pilots. Garland was avuncular but firm, and always willing to lead by example. He was soon given the affectionate moniker Judy by his pilots and took his new squadron through weeks of intense flying, often three or four hours a day, so that handling of the controls became automatic. 'We became like birds,' said Cartledge. But Garland also went the extra mile to ensure his young pilots were as well prepared as possible for the action ahead.

One Sunday, with flying seemingly out because of terrible weather and the cloud base at only 800 feet, he seized the chance to take Stradwick up as his wingman and practise formation flying in thick cloud. 'It was the first time I had done cloud flying for such long periods . . . You almost sweat blood at times when the cloud gets very dense and you have no idea of your altitude,' wrote Stradwick. Later Garland decided the whole squadron should do low flying in formation 'so down we went and what a riot. Everyone trying to watch each other besides things like tree tops, telegraph poles and village town halls – all with bags of slipstream!'

No. 1842's sister squadron, 1841, founded just a month before, also worked its new pilots hard, and they had already flown more than 1,000 hours together by mid-April. Its CO was twenty-six-year-old Richard 'Biggy' Bigg-Wither, who had joined up just before the outbreak of the war. After winning his wings in 1940, Bigg-Wither flew anti-submarine patrols in a Walrus, before transferring to 805 Squadron flying Martlet fighters, in which he attacked Afrika Korps transport and bases in the Egyptian desert. The squadron were soon wowing the American public at an air show in Concord, New Hampshire. A local newspaper reported:

BRITISH NAVY PLANES STUNT AT AIRSHOW

A squadron of young British Royal Navy pilots flying one of the world's fastest fighter planes, the Corsair, brought aerial warfare close to home for thousands of spectators at Concord's first air show yesterday . . . Flying in an inverted T formation, 12 of the 20 powerful fighters landed on the runway at 20-second intervals while the other eight, which had provided the Top Cover 'peeled off', and under orders, returned to the base after an impressive demonstration of combat formations . . . As the Corsairs rolled to a rest, their wings folded automatically, reminding spectators that these fighters are designed for operations from carriers . . . Personnel of the squadron under Commander Bigg-Wither has been trained in this country, is for combat duty and scheduled to go overseas soon. So the tall, youngish leader told the crowd when he was introduced over the loud-speaker . . .[18]

'The crowd gaped in wide-mouthed wonder,' wrote a fellow pilot in 1841, who was responsible for keeping an account of its daily activities in the squadron diary. Recounting the squadron's air display at Concord, he painted a somewhat less sanitized picture than that of the newspaper: 'The types landed in a fairly orthodox manner . . . everyone folded their wings as they crossed onto the grass strip just in front of the spectators . . . The crowd were very impressed. But this was easy to do for they didn't seem exactly air minded & certainly not Corsair minded. One individual remarked to the CO that he supposed the gunners were located inside the wings!' After the pilots landed and 'rushed to the nearest Coke machine, which promptly ran out', they spent an hour with the crowd. The Corsairs were then started up again and 'stones, dust, shit and derision was hurled at the spectators who stood 30 odd yards astern!'[19]

The pilots had been busy signing autographs with excited Americans eager to have their pictures taken. They were treated more like film stars than naval pilots and, knowing soon enough this would all come to an end, they lapped it up. Indeed, for their last few months in America there were 'parties all over the place'. From Brunswick it was only a two-hour train ride down to New York City, where the Americans had requisitioned the Barbican Plaza Hotel for the Royal Navy, which used it as a base for the Fleet Air Arm. Popular venues included Nick's Bar in Greenwich Village, where jazz musicians such as Miff Mole, Muggsy Spanier and Pee Wee Russell knocked out hot jazz tunes. Dances were held at the Ritz Carlton Hotel and the La Rue Club, resulting in the most unlikely liaisons. One evening Stradwick claimed he 'suddenly found myself at the corner tabling talking to the film actress,

Margaret Sullavan. What a life!' On another night out in New York he watched Count Basie play at the Lincoln Lounge, and celebrated his twenty-first birthday in March 1944 with two days' frantic partying, which included an evening at Café Society Downtown, a jazz bar featuring many of the greatest musicians of the day. After two late nights getting to bed, Stradwick and a female friend found themselves drinking 'Brandy Milk punches after brekkie'.

Staying at the Barbican Plaza Hotel, Chris Cartledge visited the city's art galleries and heard Bruno Walter conducting Bruckner's Te Deum and Beethoven's Choral Symphony. He wrote home to tell his family of the 'whirl of excitement I am living . . . every day I venture out into Manhattan and experience the wonders of New York, for wonders they are, their extravagance contrasting even more vividly with war weary London.'[20]

Another new member of 1842 Squadron was Keith Quilter, who, like Stradwick, joined after a conversion course on Wildcats. 'We worked very hard, flew very hard, and in order to make the most of our last few weeks in the bright lights of the USA, we played very hard,' he remembers. Arriving in Brunswick after their brief conversion course in Miami, Quilter and Ted Portman, a close friend since the Pensacola part of the training course, were given three weeks' leave when heavy snow stopped all flying. This meant a trip to New York was on the cards, and the duo wangled an invitation for a New Year's Eve party with a family in Tuxedo Park, an exclusive gated development forty miles from Manhattan. Built in 1886 by Pierre Lorillard, a tobacco heir, as a hunting and fishing retreat for his wealthy New York friends, Tuxedo Park is a series of vast mansions set in 2,000 acres, and considered one of the finest examples of pre-First World War architecture in the United States. It was an escape for the rich and powerful. Mark Twain was said to have summered among its cool lakes and shady green conifers.

The Parker family were typical residents. Raeburn Hughes Parker, a New York businessman, his wife Alice and their three children lived in a mock-Tudor mansion on the shores of Lake

Wee-Wah. A huge bust of Winston Churchill occupied the sitting room, a nod to a family connection: Jenny Jerome, Winston Churchill's vivacious American mother, was first cousin to Alice's mother. They were something of an Anglophile family – Parker liked riding with the hounds in Tuxedo Park and bought his shirts and shoes from England. Like many Americans during the war, they wanted to 'do their bit' by hosting British servicemen on leave, and informed the English-Speaking Union in New York they'd happily accept two officers at a loose end. This also suited nineteen-year-old Nancy and her friend Allie. A couple of dashing British fighter pilots might just liven up their holiday.

On a snowy New Year's Eve Quilter and Portman were greeted off the train from New York by Nancy and Allie. 'As soon as they stepped off I poked Allie and said, "Dibs the tall one,"' remembered Nancy later. 'I took one look at him and said, "That's for me."'[21] Nancy Parker was an indomitable, long-legged and attractive embodiment of the all-American girl. The Parkers' oldest child, she was fiercely intelligent, and had finished her second year at college, majoring in secretarial training. With tumbling brown hair, she was sporty and athletic, but at five feet nine inches in heels tended to tower over boys on nights out. She preferred instead to sit at home in front of a roaring fire, go for long walks or ice-skate on the lakes in Tuxedo Park. 'I was such a country girl, I didn't like NYC or nightclubs,' she said.

The attraction was instant. 'I fell in love with him the first night . . . he was such a wonderful dancer and we just got along so well it was no strain at all, his being a Brit didn't make a difference to me. He charmed me with who he is and his looks . . . and that uniform.' Over the following months their relationship blossomed, and Quilter admits he fell 'very passionately in love' with Nancy. 'It was my first love and quite the wartime romance.' When they were apart, the young couple communicated through almost daily letters. 'He loved to draw planes doing all kinds of antics. For years I saved those letters,' said Nancy. On his few precious days of leave Quilter, sometimes accompanied by Portman, would travel down to Tuxedo Park at weekends, to ice-skate or play tennis with Nancy and her friends and family.

But opportunities for romance became less frequent as training intensified. Preparations for operational flying on the front line were coming to a climax. Quilter and his fellow pilots had come far, but they still had to master the most crucial skill of naval aviation – the deck landing.

Most newly qualified pilots looked forward to their first carrier landing with immense trepidation. To prepare they carried out dozens of aerodrome dummy deck landings (Addls) with their squadrons on dry land. Addls used white lines representing arrester wires painted on a runway marked out to mimic the length of a flight deck. Pilots would come in, touch down and then open the throttle to do another circuit. And so it went on. But repeated practice allowed them to master the correct speed and curved approach, and finesse the vital three-point landing within the confines of a small deck.

A month after starting, the 1841 Squadron diary noted, 'never in the history of 1841 Squadron have so many Addls been done, in so short a time, by such a weary crowd of types', adding the pilots 'are gradually improving and people are coming round the turn at speeds that would have given many of us the twitch a month ago!'[22] But the first landing on an actual deck could be a fraught affair, no matter the amount of practice. In the UK deck landings were made on smaller carriers, such as HMS *Argus*, in the Firth of Clyde. At only 400 feet long with six arrester wires strung across the deck to stop the aircraft, pilots were asked to complete four to eight landings.

After three aborted attempts on *Argus* for his first ever deck landing, Chris Cartledge went round for a fourth attempt but failed to keep a straight course over the centre of the flight deck. He veered to the right and watched in horror as the ship's radio mast sliced three feet off his starboard wing, upon which 'my

Hurricane then made a graceful curved descent into the Clyde Estuary beside the carrier'.[23] Cartledge scrambled out of the sinking plane, was picked up by a rescue boat and taken aboard a nearby destroyer, where he was given some dry clothes and 'filled up with gin, none the worse for the dip'. A month later he returned to make his successful landings.

After a total of 122 Addls, Ken Ward took his Seafire to the Isle of Arran, where he was told to do six approaches onto HMS *Ravager*, a small escort carrier. The plan was that he would not actually land, but almost touch down and after a thumbs up from the bridge, open his throttle and go round again. Following two successful runs, however, in driving rain and thick cloud his Seafire hit one of the ship's guns on the flight deck, which sliced off a chunk of its tail rudder. Struggling for control, Ward managed to limp to a nearby airfield, where the Seafire ran off the runway and ended up in a Scottish bog. He smashed his head against the gunsight but was 'very thankful to be alive'.[24] Landings were generally easier for Avenger pilots, perched high up in their glass-covered 'offices'. With a good view ahead and no curve approach required, the Avenger was a more stable aircraft 'very docile and strong. Like driving a bus,' said one pilot.[25]

For those training in America, deck landings were made on various carriers, normally in Chesapeake Bay, near Washington DC. Leading a flight of four Corsairs in hazy weather, Keith Quilter identified what he thought was the USS *Charger*, a small escort carrier. Calling to ask permission to join the circuit for deck landings, however, he was horrified to be told that he was in fact looking at the USS *Essex* – one of the US Navy's largest carriers. 'When we saw *Charger* it looked like a matchbox!'

The good fortunes of one squadron could contrast sharply with those of another. Just one month before the pilots of 1842 had all safely completed their first deck landings, its sister squadron 1841 experienced a miserable few days, with only a handful of pilots successfully completing their four landings. In a typical incident one Corsair came in too low, snapped its hook off on the rounded-down aft of the flight deck and rolled over the wires. It smashed into the barrier and finished on its nose, with the pilot, typically English, 'apologizing profusely to all spectators'.[26]

With his deck landings safely negotiated Keith Quilter could concentrate on other matters. By June 1944 he and Nancy Parker were head over heels in love. One evening, with Nancy's parents in bed upstairs, she and Quilter curled up on the sofa together and listened to the radio playing Frank Sinatra songs. Abruptly, a voice broke in to announce Allied forces had landed on the beaches of Normandy. It was 6 June 1944. 'I've always had a slight guilty conscious when people mention D-Day and ask me about the war,' says Quilter, 'and I think back to that evening and where I was and reply, "Yes it was very tough."'

The next day 1842 Squadron was back flying hard off the New England coast when Ted Portman and another squadron member were killed smashing into each other in mid-air practising barrel rolls. Each Corsair had a wing torn off and plummeted straight into the sea. It 'shook the whole squadron as well as the pilots', wrote Wally Stradwick. Keith Quilter was 'devastated' by his friend's death, remembered Nancy. 'They all thought it would never happen to them. You expected to maybe be shot down by a Japanese, but a training accident?' Quilter made his mind up. He was due to leave soon for England. Early one summer's evening, knowing Nancy's father would have arrived home from work and soon be tucking into his first martini, he nervously picked up the receiver. The English boy from Woodside Park was going to ask Mr Parker for his blessing to marry his daughter.

In the still twilight the phones at the Parkers' house in Tuxedo Park shrilled. 'We heard Daddy say, "Hello, Keith," and we all raced to whatever phone we could find,' recalled Nancy, with her mother and younger brother and sister excitedly wrestling with the other phones in the house to listen in. Ted Portman and Quilter had become like members of the family, and after the tragedy of Ted's death this would be a happy moment to cherish. But there would be no fairy-tale ending. Parker reluctantly refused to give his permission, which Quilter accepted with good grace. Nancy burst into tears. 'We were all just distraught because we were so upset about Ted and with Daddy saying no I couldn't marry Keith, that was it. We were furious with Daddy,' said Nancy.

But Parker's decision was understandable. 'I'm sure Ted's death made it more real to Daddy,' Nancy said. 'He was very fond of Ted as well as Keith, but Daddy was very fierce and controlling and he did not want me to end up being a widow of an Englishman. He had made up his mind that I was too young and with the war on life was too uncertain. I think Ted's death just brought it home. We had talked about marriage but it hadn't occurred to us we weren't in control of the decision. He definitely had my interest at heart.'

This experience was typical of many other relationships thrown together and ultimately torn apart by war. And for Quilter and Nancy Parker time was running out. At the beginning of July 1842 Squadron was ordered back to Britain. At last the pilots would be going into action. With her parents' blessing, Keith and Nancy managed to spend a few final snatched weekends together up in Brunswick or at the Parkers' bolt-hole in New York. During their last evening in Brunswick Quilter unclasped a small fabric brooch and handed it to Nancy. He was giving the woman he loved a fighter pilot's most cherished possession – his wings. 'It just did me in. I wore them night and day,' said Nancy. 'I think he felt he wanted to give me something to remind me of him. I remember crying all the way home from Maine. I knew I wasn't going to see him for heaven knows how long, and I don't remember saying, "See you again," and I don't remember us making any promises.'

At 5 a.m. on 30 June the aircraft carrier HMS *Rajah* quietly slipped out of Brooklyn Navy Yard, New York. It was part of a convoy of more than forty ships heading for England, with the young pilots of 1842 Squadron and their aircraft aboard. As the skyscrapers of Manhattan slowly dipped below the horizon, Keith Quilter sat in the wardroom thinking of Nancy and wondered if he'd ever see her again. Playing on the ship's radio was 'I'll be seeing you', a song made popular by Bing Crosby in the recent Hollywood film of the same name. 'It was one of our favourites. I have always remembered it', said Quilter.

8

Blooded

Chris Cartledge, Wally Stradwick, Keith Quilter and the rest of 1842 Squadron arrived in Liverpool in early July 1944, a week after leaving New York on HMS *Rajah*. After spending a year and a half in America, some of the pilots had developed a transatlantic twang in their voices. 'Everyone thought we were Canadian,' remembers Quilter.[1]

Immediately granted two weeks' leave, the three men headed for London, which was under daily attack from V-1 'doodlebug' flying bombs. Stradwick felt 'almost like a stranger at first and was grieved to see how grim the city looks and to think of how tired the people must be although even now with the blasted radio bombs there is no excessive griping'. He took his mother and sister away for a few days together in the Dorset seaside town of Swanage. Walking along the pretty coastal path to Studland Bay, Stradwick reflected that 'lying up there on the grass and gazing into the sunny blue, even when Floats [floatplanes] and Lightnings were droning across the sky, I just couldn't believe that I was in the Navy, had been for two years and flew Corsairs'.[2]

At the end of July the squadron was ordered to Eglinton Royal Naval Air Station in Northern Ireland to pick up new Corsairs recently shipped over from America. But tragedy struck when one of the pilots crashed at high speed. As 1842 Squadron armaments officer, Keith Quilter was one of the first on the scene. Confronted by an enormous crater filled with smoking wreckage, he was tasked with identifying the pilot's remains. 'It was just like looking in a butcher's shop. Lumps of raw meat here and there,' said

Quilter, who grimly confirmed the pilot was his squadron-mate Derek Wheway. 'He had very wavy hair and his complete scalp was about thirty yards away. It was the most gory thing I had seen.' Once again, Wally Stradwick had to go through a close friend's personal property. 'The whole squadron were shaken by his death. The best guys seems to go,' he wrote after the funeral.

But there was little time to mourn. Just after lunch on 18 August 1944 HMS *Formidable* slipped out of Scapa Flow, the Royal Navy's Orkney base, into the open sea and headed for the Norwegian coast. In her hangar and on the flight deck, thirty Corsairs of 1841 and 1842 Squadrons, and twenty-four Barracudas of 826 and 828 Squadrons were lashed down securely. Gales battered the ship. Flying was impossible. The bows plunged into the huge waves, drenching the aircraft on the flight deck.

Although *Formidable* was a veteran of the war with a distinguished record and action around the world, this was her first operation since a six-month refit at the Harland and Wolff dockyard in Belfast. Once safely at sea, Philip Ruck-Keene, a submariner and *Formidable*'s new captain, used the PA system to tell his ship's crew what most knew already. Their mission was to destroy the German battleship *Tirpitz*. Several strikes would probably be made. 'He expected that we would be away about two weeks, which is definitely the FULL!' said an entry in the 1841 Squadron diary, using a common informal shorthand for 'the full works'.[3]

The destruction of *Tirpitz* had become a personal obsession of Winston Churchill. In December 1942, anxious that the pride of the German navy might break out into the waters of the Arctic or the North Atlantic and wreak havoc on Allied shipping, he sent a memo to First Sea Lord Sir Dudley Pound, asking simply, 'Where is *Tirpitz*?'[4] The answer seemed reassuring. Apart from the odd foray to sea, Hitler's 42,500-ton battleship sat in one Norwegian fjord after another for most of the war, pursuing a life of masterly inactivity. Indeed *Tirpitz* never sank a single ship and only once fired her main armament at sea. But roosting in her fortified lair as a 'fleet-in-being', she was arguably more influential than out at sea, and she played a crucial role by occupying major units of the Home Fleet in the North Sea when they were desperately needed for other theatres of war around the world.

Tirpitz was armed with eight 15-inch and twelve 5.9-inch guns, giving her – on paper – terrifyingly potent firepower. Her design was balanced, clean and easy on the eye, creating a shock-and-awe beauty. For Hitler, *Tirpitz* encapsulated everything that Nazi Germany stood for. The ship had gained an almost legendary status. Just the very mention of her name caused beads of sweat to form on the foreheads of Allied naval staff. The genesis for this fear can in no small way be traced to the success of her smaller sister ship *Bismarck*, which had dispatched the ageing Royal Navy battlecruiser *Hood* and damaged the battleship *Prince of Wales* earlier in the war. Although *Bismarck* was eventually hunted down and sunk by the Royal Navy, it took an almighty effort to do so. It was the perception of power that gave *Tirpitz* her formidable reputation.

This was tragically illustrated in July 1942 when Pound had ordered a Russian-bound convoy to scatter, following incorrect reports that *Tirpitz* had left Norway and was en route to launch a possible strike. Without armed protection, three quarters of PQ17's thirty-five merchant ships were sunk by German U-boats and the Luftwaffe. *Tirpitz* had actually slunk back to port after learning the carrier *Victorious* was at sea, worried about a torpedo attack. But Pound hadn't believed such a ship would flee. Until she was destroyed, *Tirpitz* would affect the Royal Navy's whole strategy in the North Atlantic and cast a shadow over the Russian convoys. To crush such a symbol of Nazi prestige would also be a monumental political coup for Churchill, and he bullied and cajoled both the Air Ministry and the Admiralty to do something.

The RAF and the FAA had tried and failed on a number of occasions to cripple *Tirpitz* through air strikes and torpedo attacks. Off the coast of Norway in March 1942 an attack by twelve Albacore torpedo aircraft from *Victorious* had failed to score a hit. Some success was finally achieved in September 1943 when in a daring raid by midget submarines in Kåfjord mines were laid under her hull, but by March 1944 intelligence sources indicated *Tirpitz* was almost fully repaired and might take to the sea once again. The FAA launched a campaign of strikes throughout the spring and summer of that year. Operation Tungsten, the largest operation the FAA had so far undertaken, commenced on the clear dawn morning of 3 April 1944, when two waves of aircraft took off from the decks of *Victorious* and *Furious* off the Norwegian coast. Taken by surprise, *Tirpitz* was hit more than a dozen times, over 100 men were killed and 300 wounded. But despite initial hopes, the damage to the ship was repaired. The British would need to try again.

Following Tungsten, aircrews were replaced in preparation for what would be the biggest naval attack on *Tirpitz* of the entire war, Operation Goodwood. Some squadrons, including 1842, were fresh off the boat from America. Others, such as 887 and 894, equipped with Seafires, had already experienced action during the Allied invasion of Italy the previous autumn but had since been diluted with newly qualified RNVR pilots. For many aircrew Operation Goodwood was their first taste of action. They would be blooded. For these pilots, though they didn't know it yet, Operation Goodwood would also be something of a dress rehearsal for what would come in the Pacific, with a fleet of carriers and escort ships spending weeks at a time away from port, launching a series of strikes in quick succession and refuelling at sea.

The Germans had learned from Tungsten and had positioned spotters on the mountains around the fjord where *Tirpitz* was anchored. Their job was to provide advance warning so that the dozens of gun positions on the steep black sides of the fjord and the guns of *Tirpitz* herself would welcome attacking aircraft with a lethal tunnel of lead. Little wonder that one Royal Navy admiral thought *Tirpitz* 'probably the most heavily defended target of any attacked in the war'.[5]

The bomber of choice for the strikes was the Fairey Barracuda, a British-designed torpedo-cum-dive-bomber which had entered service in 1943. Intended as a replacement for the Swordfish, pilots quipped it was the typical result of a design put together by committee. It certainly wasn't pretty. The three-man crew sat in tandem under a long continuous glazed canopy, while the navigator also had a window on either of the fuselage under the high wings, which had to be folded manually by the deck-handling parties. With its various aerials, flaps and radar displays, the Barracuda resembled a flying television set. For its weight it was under-powered and had a nasty early safety record. Little wonder it was soon replaced in the Pacific by the superior Avenger.

A key finding from earlier strikes was that once the Barracudas had crossed the Norwegian coast, they took too long to arrive at the target, which meant the Germans were able to ignite their smoke generators. These created an effective screen, covering *Tirpitz* within ten minutes so to the attacking pilots above the fjord looked like a 'bath filled with cotton wool'. To try and maintain an element of surprise, it was decided also to arm some of the faster Corsairs with 1,000-pound bombs.

This was Ruck-Keene's first command of a carrier. As the ship sailed north towards the Arctic, he ordered the squadrons' ratings – the fitters, riggers, electricians and armourers on whom the aircrews depended for serviceable aircraft – to work eighteen hours a day if necessary to get the aircraft into fighting shape. It was no less intense for the aircrews, who studied models of the fjord and received a series of briefings about the target and how the raids would be executed.

Each flyer was issued with a watertight pack containing Norwegian money, a map and a miniature compass disguised as a button. Passport photos were taken so that if contact was established with the Norwegian resistance after being shot down, fake passports could be forged for escape to neutral Sweden. A lecture was given by Lieutenant David James, a former gunboat commander who had escaped from a German POW camp in 1943. He had headed for the coast in his Royal Navy uniform and foxed the German authorities by carrying the forged pass of a fictitious Bulgarian naval officer with the delicious name I. Bagerov. James was finally captured in the German port of Lübeck, but escaped again a few months later after fellow inmates held up a life-size dummy dubbed Albert RN at the daily roll call to ensure he wasn't missed. Now an intelligence officer, James passed on his experiences evading enemy capture and escaping POW camps.

On 20 August the fleet gathered sixty miles off the north-west coast of Norway. *Formidable* was joined by the Royal Navy's newest carrier *Indefatigable*, which had made its debut in the July attacks against *Tirpitz* and was carrying Barracudas, Hellcats and Seafires. It also carried another new British aircraft, the Firefly – a two-man ship-launched fighter-cum-dive-bomber, which would be used to strafe flak positions. The old faithful *Furious* made up the carrier triumvirate. Carrying a mix of Seafires and Barracudas, this would be her last operation before retirement. The three fleet carriers were supported by the smaller carriers *Nabob* and *Trumpeter* and a fleet of frigates and destroyers, all commanded by Admiral Moore, from his flagship *Duke of York*.

The first strike on 21 August was postponed due to bad weather, and when the strike finally launched at 11 a.m. the following morning, the Barracudas and Corsairs were recalled because of thick cloud over *Tirpitz*. 'Why the thundering blazes the fighters couldn't go in, we just don't know. The bally square-heads must have known everything by the time we started our climb,' cursed Stradwick. A number of Hellcats did find a gap in the clouds but had little effect. Enemy reaction was largely light, although *Nabob* was hit by a U-boat torpedo which blew a thirty-foot hole in her stern, but she managed to limp back to Scapa Flow. The Seafires of 894 Squadron were scrambled from *Indefatigable*, and almost immediately 'Tally-ho' came over the radio, with Dickie Reynolds sharing one of a pair of Blohm & Voss 138 reconnaissance aircraft. 'Of all the pilots that might have been busy finding aircraft to shoot down, he actually found one,' said one fellow pilot.[6]

Flying operations were cancelled on 23 August because of fog, and despite the aircrews being woken at 06.00 on 24 August, by mid-morning squally showers and low cloud made another post-ponement likely. In *Formidable*, two decks down directly under the hangar, Wally Stradwick was settling down in his comfortable double cabin with Eddie Thornberry, the twenty-one-year-old son of a schoolteacher from Northern Ireland. Next door, Keith Quilter and his cabin mate Chris Cartledge tried to keep them-selves occupied. With pictures of Lenin and Marx on the wall and surrounded by books about art, music, socialism and philosophy, Cartledge couldn't have been more different from the technical flyer Quilter, who was more pragmatic in his outlook on life. But the two men got on well, and in those empty hours waiting for the mission to start 'I learned stuff about all these artists who I'd never even heard of until then,' said Quilter.

Cartledge wrote to his parents providing a glimpse of life on an operational carrier.

> Although the actual flying time is not so impressive, the strain is greater because the procedure entailed in operating from a carrier is rather complicated. No one really seems to know what is going on, least of all the pilots, and the slightest breakdown holds up the whole organization. Every single detail has to be carried out in a pre-arranged way and if a mistake is made, about five different people see it and the poor mistaken culprit knows all about their annoyance. Ah me! There can be no vagueness about flying Corsairs from carriers.[7]

They were all trying to keep their minds off the mission ahead. Over in *Indefatigable* Barracuda pilot Roy Hawkes admitted,

> one had slightly mixed feelings about beginning a fighting career against such a powerful adversary. Thoughts had to be disciplined as never before and all sorts of little private deci-sions were made. Did one leave a letter for home? Did one tidy the personal effects to save the padre a possible problem . . . or did one just carry on as usual, putting all one's energies

into the success of the venture by maintaining and improving professionalism?[8]

At 13.30 all pilots and observers were called to the briefing rooms. The weather over the target was fine. The mission was on. After taking off and forming up 60 miles off the coast, a force of 33 Barracudas armed with 1,600-pound bombs and 10 Hellcats with 500-pounders, escorted by 19 Corsairs and 10 Fireflies, would fly south over the western end of Langfjord. The flight path would then sweep around 180 degrees to approach from the south to attack *Tirpitz*, anchored at the head of Kåfjord, which was four miles long and surrounded by steep black mountains. This time, however, even if the Barracudas turned back, the Corsairs and Hellcats were to press home their attacks. Eleven Corsairs from 1841 Squadron and eight Corsairs from 1842 Squadron were tasked with strafing AA nests and flak ships in the fjord before the Barracudas started their bombing runs. Five other Corsairs had been fitted with bomb racks under their starboard wings to which were attached 1,000-pound bombs. Utilizing their greater speed, these Corsairs would overtake the main strike force en route and dive-bomb *Tirpitz* before the smokescreen was fully effective, providing the element of surprise the attacks had previously lacked.

Weighed down with the 1,000-pounders and belly tanks of extra fuel, there was every chance the Corsairs might not even clear the water after taking off. Volunteers were called for. As CO of 1842, Tony Garland led from the front, and as his wingman Keith Quilter stepped up to the plate. Chris Cartledge volunteered to carry the third bomb, and would be accompanied by his wingman John French. The fifth bomb was carried by Lachlan Mackinnon, a Scotsman in 1841 Squadron.

At 14.30, following final briefings and umpteen 'final' visits to the loo, the fleet turned into the bitter Nordic wind and the pilots sitting in their aircraft were given the order to start engines and begin their pre-flight checks. With a volley of mechanical coughs, engines creating thousands of horsepower soon throbbed in unison. Dozens of men scurried about on the windswept decks, each with his own jobs to do – removing the chocks from under the wheels; locking hoods in place with a final thumbs up and an encouraging grin to the pilot; checking bombs were secured – all the while avoiding the lethal blades of thirty-four propellers spinning fifty times a second.

Even with their belly tanks, the nineteen escort Corsairs on *Formidable* were able to accelerate more quickly than the Barracudas, so they were positioned nearer the front of the deck. As the carriers turned into the wind, the leading aircraft was marshalled to the centre line, and following an energetic wave of the deck control officer's green flag, the first Corsair accelerated down the flight deck and off the end, followed by the other Corsairs and then the Barracudas. Once each aircraft had cleared the bow, it veered to starboard before straightening out to prevent its slipstream affecting the next plane taking off.

As the five dive-bombing Corsairs with the 1,000-pounders needed the whole 750 feet of flight deck to provide the best chance of getting airborne, they too had started their engines to warm up on deck, but were then taken below in the forward lift before the Barracudas took off then moved back along the hangar underneath to emerge up the stern lift. With a totally empty flight deck in front of them, they now restarted their engines and used its full length to take off.

In bright sunshine it took almost an hour for the main strike force to form up above the fleet, giving plenty of time for the five Corsairs, accompanied by a flight of Hellcats, to make good speed and get a head start. Visibility was fine and the snow-covered peaks of the Norwegian mountains could be seen clearly. 'The view was magnificent,' remembered Cartledge, flying his dark green and gunmetal-grey Corsair just fifty feet above the white-capped sea to keep under the German radar.[9] Once past the coastline the aircraft climbed over the mountains towards the western end of Langfjord.

For those who had never been in action there was a chill of

excitement. *How would the enemy react? When would the shooting start?* Tucked behind Tony Garland's wing, Keith Quilter looked down through the perspex of his cockpit into the dark blue waters of Langfjord, admiring three or four beautiful-looking ships 'which were a lovely shape' from about 10,000 feet. Quilter noticed one ship flashing its signal light. 'My first thought was that they must have mistaken us for German aircraft and were asking for a recognition signal,' he remembers. But almost immediately black puffs started exploding immediately behind him. 'This was my first experience being fired at by the enemy and they were firing their AA at us, not signalling.'

But the German flak was inaccurate, and the Corsairs continued through the azure sky. Less than five minutes later *Tirpitz* came into sight, sitting in Kåfjord just like the model had shown she would be, her clean black outline visible against the dark blue water. Tony Garland ordered the flight into a line-astern formation before he peeled off in a forty-five-degree dive, followed closely by his squadron mates. Although a thin white blanket of smoke had already spread across the fjord and over the *Tirpitz*, black smoke from the cordite of her blazing guns hung above the ship and her huge unmistakable outline could still just be made out by the pilots. One by one, they fell through the sky like swooping birds. Third in line behind Garland and Quilter, Cartledge turned, pushed his stick forward, his eyes squinting in the hazy sunshine to focus on the target ahead. Breaking through the 300-mph mark, he spotted Quilter's bomb burst alongside *Tirpitz* a few hundred feet ahead, sending up a vast funnel of frothing white water. A near miss. The air was now thick with black bursts of flak, and yellow balls of tracer from the blazing anti-aircraft guns on the side of the fjord and from *Tirpitz* herself slid past Cartledge's head.

'There was a lot of flak coming up from all directions as I released my bomb and pulled away hard almost blacking myself out due to the speed and momentum I had reached,' said Cartledge, who spotted a gunnery position on the side of a hill, so attacked it before turning and diving down to sea level to escape back along the fjord.[10] The water in front of his Corsair was kicked up by bullets from a machine gun firing from the hill behind, but he managed to escape unscathed.

However, his wingman John French had not been so lucky, blasted out of the sky as he began his attack. The gunners in the AA batteries had clearly got their eye in, and 1842 Squadron had lost its first pilot in anger. By 16.00 much of the fjord was filled with thick smoke up to around 800 feet, and the Barracudas had little success hitting the *Tirpitz* as they dived through heavy flak. For the rest of the Corsair pilots from 1841 and 1842 Squadrons, however, there were rich pickings for those willing to stick their necks out.

At least half a dozen flak ships were destroyed, while others were left blazing or sinking. The Corsairs flew low over Altagaard airfield, shooting up pillboxes, hangars and the control tower. Wally Stradwick was particularly enjoying his first taste of action, finding it

> wizard pranging trawlers, flak posts and anything that fired at us. One gang on a trawler were amazingly accurate and started to give us the full dose just as we were flying peaceably down this fjord. Jinking like mad right on the water, we spotted his position and then went round the cliffs and came down against the dark background. Simply gave him the full nausea – the bally thing started to blow up when I was closing at about fifty yards and I just missed it. That close shave technique seemed to be adopted by me every time.

As Stradwick pulled away from the fjord 'a smart joker suddenly opened up at us from a wood and put my radio out of action' but luckily didn't hit any vital controls.

After expending their ammunition, the aircraft made their way back to the fleet in ones and twos. They had not encountered any enemy aircraft but fuel was now getting dangerously low. Stradwick landed back on *Formidable* with less than 10 per cent left in his tanks, while another pilot approached the round down with flames pouring from under his Corsair, crashing into the icy water to be rescued by a cruiser before hypothermia could set in. Most of the Corsairs had suffered damage of some kind – testament to the heavy AA fire they had come up against – but even with holes punched in wings, tail fins and engines, their rugged frames got the majority safely home.

Although none of the Barracudas had been shot down, one air gunner lost a leg and two planes hit the barrier on *Formidable*, causing a backlog of aircraft to stack up in the sky above, stretching dwindling fuel further. Fire crews, doctors and deck handlers rushed out to drag burned and bloodied aircrew away and below decks for treatment. With *Formidable*'s deck temporarily out of action, four Corsairs, including Keith Quilter's, were ordered to land on *Indefatigable*.

Back in the intelligence rooms the aircrew drew breath and assessed results. On *Formidable* 1841 Squadron had lost one pilot, while in addition to John French, 1842 had lost Eddie Thornberry, whose Corsair burst into flames and turned on its back as he tried to crash-land on a fjord after being hit, igniting his drop tank still half full of petrol. Unknown to the *Formidable*'s crew a family tragedy was unfolding. Below decks one of the naval surgeons treating the wounded pilots was Thornberry's twenty-six-year-old brother Joe. 'Although we didn't tell him at the time, I think he sensed it. He was so fond and so proud of the youngster,' one officer told a newspaper later, while Thornberry's mother confirmed 'this was my younger son's first big operation' and clung on to the hope that he 'may have been taken prisoner'.[11]

In his diary Stradwick wrote later, 'Another good cabin mate gone. My God it all seems just a matter of time waiting your turn.' It was a heavy price to pay given the raid was a failure, with *Tirpitz* largely unmolested. However, German naval reports afterwards described the attack as 'the heaviest and most determined so far. The English showed great skill and dexterity in flying. For the first time they dived with heavy bombs. During the dive-bombing fighter planes attacked the land batteries, which, in comparison with earlier attacks, suffered heavy losses.' It could have been so different. Although one 500-pounder hit a turret, causing minor damage, another 1,600-pound armour-piercing bomb dropped by a Barracuda had penetrated a number of decks before lodging in an electrical room in the belly of the ship. But it failed to explode, which the German report 'considered an exceptional stroke of luck, as the effects of that explosion would have been immeasurable'.[12]

That evening fog enveloped the fleet. In *Indefatigable* Quilter and the other pilots waited for it to clear to make the short hop across to *Formidable*. The following evening, when there was still no change, they assumed another night would be spent where they were and got stuck into a drinking session at the wardroom bar, swapping stories with the other pilots. However, they'd forgotten summer Arctic nights never close in. At 22.00 the weather cleared and they were ordered to fly back to *Formidable* in the watery light 'with more beers under our skin than we could admit', said Quilter. Although they all landed on safely, the usually impeccable Quilter burst a tyre as he touched down. 'The sun was very low and dead ahead. Whether it was me being over the limit or not I don't know.'

The fleet remained off the coast of Norway for the next few days, waiting for a break in the bad weather. On the afternoon of 29 August sixty aircraft carried out the Fleet Air Arm's final strike on *Tirpitz*. The mission got off to the worst possible start when the Barracudas flew to the wrong fjord and arrived over *Tirpitz* fifteen minutes later than planned, by which time the inevitable smoke-screen was impenetrable. The Corsairs once again concentrated on aggressive low-level strafing runs against ships and flak positions and took the brunt of the enemy anti-aircraft fire. Another of Wally Stradwick's close friends and Pensacola drinking buddies, Gordon 'Doc' Walker, was shot down during a strafing run, while Tony Garland's aircraft was hit although he managed to limp back and land safely on *Formidable*.

Keith Quilter's aircraft was also hit in the leading edge of the port wing, and he could only keep the plane level with both his hands on the stick. Quilter's mechanic later found the bullet had gone completely through the first and second ammunition boxes behind the machine guns and come to a rest in the third. 'If it had been an incendiary bullet I doubt if I would have survived,' reckons Quilter. Most aircraft in 1841 Squadron took nasty hits, and its new senior pilot, a Canadian called Hammy Gray, impressed the others by leading an aggressive attack on a German destroyer before nursing his aircraft back to the carrier with a large hole punched through its rudder and patiently circling *Formidable* for thirty minutes until it was his turn to land.

Later, the pilots sat down together to study the film from the cameras fitted to all aircraft. The camera was triggered when the pilot fired his guns, allowing an accurate assessment of what targets had been hit. Reviewing the shaky black and white film from Gray's camera, they were amazed to see an extreme close-up of the destroyer he had attacked at point-blank range, with the entire screen filled with flak bursts from its AA guns. The cherubic-looking Gray joked he was a 'dumb Canadian who needs a good talking-to', but he had earned the respect of his junior pilots in what was his first action and was later nominated for a mention in dispatches.[13]

The fleet dispersed and headed home. 'After losing three of the twelve pilots we took, Scapa resembled paradise on our return,' said Stradwick, who was still shocked at the loss of his good friend Doc Walker. 'If ever a chap was really fired with a zest for life it was Doc. Just before taking off Charlie and I were talking with him just outside the wardroom. "If there's one guy who gets back," he said, "it's me. I wanna live." He meant "live" too!'

Those who had survived their first action looked at the world afresh. Roy Hawkes caught a train south to visit his parents at the family home overlooking Weymouth Bay in Dorset. 'Although only twenty-one, I was old enough to appreciate that experience was of pure magic . . . after surviving the enemy's fire, I was alive, carefree, on holiday and singing my way home,' he said.[14]

For his part in the attacks Chris Cartledge was one of three Corsair pilots including Tony Garland awarded the Distinguished Service Cross. But he was puzzled to be one of those singled out. 'I never knew what I got mine for. I just think they decided to give a few sprinkled about for that operation.' He also couldn't help but compare himself to RAF pilots in Bomber Command, remembering one pilot who was given a DFC for flying more than sixty missions over Germany. 'I thought his was worth about a hundred of my DSCs,' said Cartledge.[15] It was difficult to assess the meaning of such awards. Clearly they provided recognition and were morale-boosting, but unless they were awarded for an obvious single action, most aircrew received them with the unsaid understanding that they were symbolically accepting them on behalf of their squadron.

Cartledge thought there was a general feeling among 1842 Squadron that they were not a powerful enough force to attack such a large and heavily armed and armoured warship like *Tirpitz*, saying the mission was 'something of a reckless waste'. Keith Quilter agreed later that 'it was suicidal really but one doesn't ask questions and just gets on with it'. The newspapers disagreed. CARRIER PLANES 'BLASTED HELL OUT OF *TIRPITZ*' announced the *Daily Sketch* on 6 September, just one of a number of dramatic headlines written by the editors of Fleet Street. But the reality was it would take a lot more than a few 1,000-pound bombs to take *Tirpitz* off the map.[16]

Nine days later the RAF whistled up a force of twenty-seven Lancasters operating from a forward base in Russia, twenty-one of which carried 12,000-pound Tallboy bombs. One of these bombs struck *Tirpitz*, going straight through her decks and keel before exploding on the seabed, tearing a forty-foot hole in her hull. *Tirpitz* was moved to another fjord further south, but two more Lancaster squadrons finished the job, and on 12 November 1944 the giant ship lay capsized in an icy Norwegian fjord, a useless lump of steel. Although the FAA may not have actually sunk *Tirpitz*, her demise at the hands of Bomber Command was in fact highly significant for the carriers and their aircrews. The navy's flyboys were now free to head east.

9

Flat tops

In a letter home to his parents Chris Cartledge reported that 'probing my way about this floating maze I have succeeded in avoiding any more vicious wallops on my poor bruised skull; but still, after making the journey some fifteen times, do I continue to find a new route that I travel from the back to the front. I am seriously thinking of draughting [*sic*] out a plan for the installation of a comprehensive system of escalators and tube trains for the internal communications of this over-heated labyrinth.'[1] Cartledge's experience during his first weeks in an aircraft carrier was shared by many other men. Aircrews joked they were simply the visiting tenants and the carrier was their landlord. For a new lodger it was certainly a daunting place to be.

A Royal Navy carrier was like a floating town, with around 2,000 men living a cramped and difficult life within its steel walls. Everything revolved around flying. The flight deck on most of the principal Royal Navy carriers was around 750 feet long and 90 feet wide. The actual landing area, however, was much smaller, covering just the rear third of the deck. This section was equipped with between eight and ten arrester wires made of strong steel hawsers the thickness of a forearm, stretched horizontally across the deck, with a mechanical system for raising them by some six inches. The aim was for the pilot to approach the carrier from the rear of the ship as it steamed through the water, bringing his aircraft down in the landing area so the arrester hook protruding from under the fuselage caught one of the wires, bringing the aircraft to a halt.

The commander of flying, known as Wings, was in overall

control of all aircraft and men both on deck and in the air, barking orders through a microphone via loudspeakers fitted up and down the long deck to help the pilots achieve safe landings. The deck landing control officer or batsman – always an experienced pilot himself – stood at the side of the flight deck on a platform, holding two paddles shaped like large ping-pong bats. Next to him was a net he could leap into if a pilot made a botched landing and he was faced with being wiped out by several tons of aircraft. The thinking was that the batsman standing on the deck could feel the movement of the ship better than a pilot sitting behind a large engine who was also concentrating on getting his hook and undercarriage down, lowering the aircraft's flaps and adjusting the pitch of the propeller.

Using a series of agreed signals, the batsman instructed the incoming pilot during his final approach to adjust his height, speed or line, right up to the point when he crossed the bats in front of his legs, indicating the pilot should 'chop' the throttle to cut the engine, thereby bringing his aircraft safely down to catch a wire. Some 'personality' batsman couldn't help introducing little flourishes to their signals.

The first arrester wire was rigged anywhere between 40 and 75 feet from the stern of the deck – known as the round down – with the remaining wires then spaced along the deck at intervals of about 26 feet. The pilot therefore had around 230 feet of flight deck in which to land his aircraft and pick up an arrester wire. Although the breadth of the deck at its fullest was 95 feet, in reality the pilot had about half this width to make a safe landing. Either side of the flight deck was a 40-foot vertical drop to the sea. Many landings were misjudged, leaving aircraft hanging precariously on a wire as the sea boiled away below. A large aircraft carrier also creates a wash of turbulent air extending from the stern of the ship, through which any aircraft has to approach. This affects its aerodynamics and handling. Losing height and crashing head first into the round down was always a danger.

For an aircraft to be kept under control it needed to remain *above* its stalling speed through the air but be moving as slowly as possible to make a safe landing. The carrier therefore had to steam into the prevailing wind to reduce the speed of the aircraft relative to the deck it was landing on. The less wind, the faster the carrier needed to be travelling, to increase the wind speed over the deck. The large carriers could reach speeds of up to 30 knots. The essential ingredient was for the aircraft to land *into* the wind. Keith Quilter reckons he approached the flight deck in his Corsair at an average speed of about 72 knots (around 80 mph) – just above stalling speed – while the ship steamed directly into the prevailing wind at whatever speed was necessary to give a 'wind down the deck' – normally between 20 to 30 knots, depending on sea conditions. The final speed his aircraft was doing relative to the flight deck, and from which the arrester wire had to bring the Corsair to a stop, would have been around 30 mph. This meant Quilter had about a five-second margin over the eight arrester wires to make contact.

If a pilot was 'in the groove' – in other words travelling at the right speed and at the right height above the deck – when the batsman gave the cut, which was usually as he was just crossing the round down, he hit the deck in about two or three seconds and caught the second, third or fourth wire. Each wire disappeared around pulleys through the 3-inch steel flight deck into the hangar below, where it wound around hydraulically pressured spools on which tensions of varying strength could be imposed, depending on the size and weight of the aircraft. As the wire was snagged by the arrester hook, it was pulled from the spools, decelerating the aircraft to a standstill in 160 feet or less. The G force exerted on the pilot was between two and three – about twice the pressure felt when breaking hard in a sports car – depending upon which wire was engaged.

The pilot and the batsman also had to take into account the vertical pitch and the horizontal roll of the ship caused by the swell of the sea. These could catch the pilot out by either dipping the flight deck just as he cut the throttle, leaving him too high to catch a wire, or raising it rapidly, resulting in a heavy touchdown, bouncing the aircraft over the wires. If the batsman felt the pilot was not making a satisfactory approach, he crossed the bats above his head, signalling the pilot to open his throttle and fly around for another attempt.

For those aircraft that did land, the dozen men of the flight deck handling party rushed out from walkways at the side of the deck to uncouple the hook from the wire and, on some aircraft, fold the wings. This was an unenviable job. 'A flight deck must be one of the most dangerous places on earth,' said one airman. 'Not so much for the aviators because all we had to do was get from the operations room in the superstructure across to our aircraft, and that was comparatively easy. But for the guys working on the flight deck. They were tough by any standards and it was a very hazardous, very uncomfortable, very dangerous job. They could easily be knocked over the side or be knocked over by an aircraft landing.'[2]

Some sixty feet forward of the last wire were two eight-foot-high steel nets stretched across the width of the deck. They were officially called the safety barriers but universally referred to as the crash barriers, and comprised hinged steel stanchions at both sides of the deck connected by two steel hawsers of enormous strength, about three feet apart, linked by three or four vertical hawsers. Raised as each approaching aircraft came in to land, the crash barriers were designed to stop a six-ton aircraft which failed to catch a wire from hurtling into previously landed aircraft parked at the forward end of the flight deck. If the aircraft did safely catch a wire, however, the barriers were hydraulically lowered to allow its passage into the forward area, where it could be taken via a lift to the hangar below or stowed safely on the deck. The barrier was then raised again as the next aircraft approached to land.

Norman Hanson, CO of 1833 Corsair Squadron, reckoned, 'If the pilot didn't catch a wire on his first contact with the deck, the odds were he would finish up in the barrier. This happened to far too many pilots; and how you fared in the barriers was sheer conjecture. Some boys were burned to death; some [. . .] were thrown over the side; others didn't need even an aspirin. It was all a matter of luck.'[3]

While the carrier was landing its aircraft on in operations, the whole fleet accompanying it had to turn and take the same course, even if it was towards an enemy coastline or force. This was because, where enemy submarine or air attack was a threat, carriers were required to be escorted at all times – it was essential they had the protective guns of their accompanying destroyers and battleships. So carrier commanders were under a great deal of pressure to land their aircraft safely on as quickly as possible.

Taking all this into account, it's surprising there weren't more accidents. A total of 24 pilots were killed in deck landing accidents in 1945. On average, one pilot could expect to die in every 31 accidents on the deck, or 6 in every 10,000 deck landings. Over-shooting the wires and ending up in the barrier or the deck park accounted for a third of all accidents. Seafires – with their fragile undercarriages – were most accident-prone, with 292 accidents for every 10,000 deck landings, compared with 132 accidents for the Corsair, 126 accidents for the Hellcat and 86 accidents for the Avenger over the same period.[4]

Despite dozens of successful landings, 'the relief was palpable, every time. Every landing was a personal triumph,' remembered one pilot. 'Confidence was the overall secret, control was impera-tive.'[5] In other words it was psychological, and mind over matter was at the heart of all successful deck landings. All it took was a nasty landing or a few near misses, and a pilot risked losing his nerve. Once that happened, it was very difficult to recover. One pilot in 1841 Squadron finished up with his Corsair hanging over the edge of the deck. 'I was pretty twitched coming into my next deck landing and, had it happened again, I suspect it may have finished me as a navy pilot, at least as far as landing on the deck is concerned. Fortunately I got on safely without any drama,' he said.[6]

An unpublished report written after the war investigating the effects of flying strain on FAA pilots identified one of the reasons pilots broke down was the 'anxiety state accentuated by deck landing phobia'.[7] But, more often than not, a bad landing on deck was just plain embarrassing, and would simply lead to much ribbing and leg-pulling from squadron mates over a few drinks in the wardroom. It might look easy, but everyone knew it was bloody difficult.[8] Little surprise then that the perils of deck landing were recounted in the black humour of some of the verses in the naval pilot's pub anthem, 'A25'.

> They say in the Air Force a landing's OK,
> If the pilot gets out and can still walk away,
> But in the Fleet Air Arm the prospects are dim,
> If the landing's piss poor and the pilot can't swim.
>
> I thought I was coming in low enough but,
> I was fifty up when the batsman gave 'Cut,'
> And loud in my ear'oles the sweet angels sang,
> Float, float, float, float, float, float . . . barrier . . . PRANG!
>
> Whenever I land on I haven't a care,
> I float over wires with my head bowed in prayer,
> And while evil goofers chant 'High tiddly high ty,'
> I know my redeemer is Christ the Almighty.
>
> If you come o'er the round down and see Wings frown,
> You can safely assume that your hook isn't down,
> A bloody great barrier looms up in front,
> And you hear Wing's shout, 'Cut your engine – you cunt.'[9]

On the starboard side of the flight deck rose the fifty-foot-tall four-storey 'brain' of the ship called the island. This was the air control tower and ship's bridge rolled into one. A warren of almost forty little rooms filled with machinery, chart tables, telegraphs and compasses competed for space with miles of cabling and voice pipes fitted for quick communication through its steel walls. The captain sat at the compass platform three decks up, protected by a semicircle of reinforced windows providing a 180-degree forward view. The next deck down were the air operations room and the flight direction office – a mini air command centre – where information received from the ship's radar was interpreted and radio instructions were transmitted to the aircraft. Aircrews made their final nervous checks in 'ready rooms' at deck level before running out across the flight deck to their fighters and bombers. Showers, heads, sickbays, mess rooms and offices filled the other spaces, and a tiny six-foot-square cabin with a folding bed, washstand and writing desk was provided for the captain.

Sprouting from two masts was a canopy of aerials and radar dishes – the eyes of the ship. All this valuable equipment made the island a prime target for the enemy. To protect it, various platforms surrounding the island mounted 20-mm Oerlikon cannon and smaller-calibre machine guns.

Sleeping accommodation for most officers was in the ship's main hull, and the quality of their space was based on seniority, luck and sometimes bartering skills. Squadron commanders, senior pilots and the lucky few were given single or double cabins with a folding top bunk, a bed, wardrobe, drawers, a writing desk and an unplumbed washstand. If they were really lucky the cabin might also have a tiny scuttle, letting in a splash of natural light – a rare commodity inside a carrier. The less fortunate made their home towards the rear of the ship in smaller, stuffier berths measuring just six feet wide. These windowless wedge-shaped recesses below the waterline constantly throbbed from the huge propeller blades powering the mighty ship through the water. Most furnished their cabins with a few mementos to try and make them more homely, sticking up photos of sweethearts and pin-ups – or in Chris Cartledge's case Lenin and Stalin. But the vibration and heavy seas sent photo frames and travelling clocks crashing onto the deck. After a morning shake and a cup of tea, a steward supplied warm water for shaving before making the bunks and tidying the cabin. He also took dirty washing away to the onboard laundry and later returned it washed and ironed.

When air squadrons were aboard, the ships were so crowded

that the most junior pilots sometimes had no cabin at all. Instead, they were allocated bunks folding down from the walls – bulk-heads – in the main passages. Although it was almost impossible on an aircraft carrier to get privacy, men did what they could to find ways of passing spare time. Cartledge told his parents, 'I think quite a lot about painting but conditions do their best to prevent me from acting on these thoughts.'[10] Nevertheless, he tried to find a quiet spot on the deck to paint and draw, or buried his head in books like Lin Yutang's *The Importance of Living*, Tolstoy's *War and Peace*, and *Down and Out in Paris and London* by George Orwell.

Most ships set a room aside as a Church of England chapel, and when the ship was in harbour a compulsory Sunday service was held on the flight deck (Roman Catholics were excused). Such services were impractical when the ship was at sea. In *Formidable* the padre offered an open room as well as hosting prayer meetings and gramophone recitals. His value was as much pastoral as spiritual, and he proved popular with aircrew before missions.

Norman Hanson maintained that while he found life on *Illustrious* leading 1833 Squadron 'infinitely happy and enjoyable' he couldn't help drawing comparisons with shore-based aviators, who

> could at least go off to the nearest town and see a film; or find a few civvies with whom to have a drink and forget 'shop' for a while. One could take out one's wife or girlfriend. But in a carrier we were *there*. There was no escape from it. Your Corsair was in the hangar, one deck up. The flight deck, that torrid arena of the grim game of life and death, was only two short ladders beyond that. Life was lived, utterly and com-pletely, within a space of something like 10,000 square yards. Within that area we ate, slept, drank, chatted with our friends, attended church, watched films, took our exercise – and flew, landed or crashed our aircraft. Friendships became, if anything, too close, and the hurt was all the more painful for that very reason.[11]

But compared to ratings, whose living quarters hadn't altered that much since the days of Nelson, officers had little to complain about. Just as in the eighteenth century ratings still slept in hammocks or camp beds and lived in cramped mess decks dotted about the lower levels of the ship. They each had living space of around nineteen square feet. The messes were defined by their strong smell of sweat, the fug of tobacco smoke, humidity and temperatures often exceeding 30 degrees Celsius. Here the men ate, slept, played darts and cards or wrote letters home to their families and sweethearts. Its wooden tables and benches were the focal point of each mess. Ratings had four meals a day. Breakfast, dinner, tea and supper. Tea, sugar and milk were issued by the dry provisions store, and hot meals collected from a central galley by two ratings designated the 'cooks of the mess'.

For a few days after the ship set sail, the cooks in the central galley had an abundance of fresh vegetables, fruit and meat, but after a week at sea dehydrated potatoes, meat and dried vegetables became the staple diet. Common dishes included kippers, kidneys on fried bread and bacon smothered in tinned tomatoes – nicknamed train smash because of its visceral appearance. The heads were below decks, built in long rows without doors so that 'it looked like a stable with horses' heads sticking out'. In *Indefatigable* each cubicle had tiny saloon-bar-style swinging doors. 'I never knew anybody's face but I recognized the knees,' the captain of the heads, an old seaman, joked.[12]

Every rating was issued with a regular ration of tobacco. It was generous in size but not particularly good quality and was available either in cigarette form or loose. Ratings over the age of twenty were also entitled to an eighth of a pint of rum, collected daily from the sweet-smelling spirit store in the bowels of the ship. With each measure the equivalent of a modern pub triple at 54 per cent alcohol by volume, it was watered down 2:1 for all ratings, and issued daily just before dinner at midday under the supervision of the officer of the day. Those who didn't drink claimed three pence per day in lieu, paid quarterly. Petty officers received their tot of rum neat and some men illegally saved up their tots in bottles for a decent drinking session.

The ratings were divided into branches. Some were non-specialist able seamen, while others took further training in specialist areas like gunnery and signals. There was always routine work to be carried out: cleaning and polishing brass fittings or wooden decks, and constantly repainting the ship to protect against corrosion. Ratings were not soldiers; with little action against the enemy for days, weeks or even months at a time, their jobs were more akin to factory workers, working in teams to ensure the ship operated efficiently.

Underpinned by years of tradition, the daily routine was split into seven watches, allowing the various duties to be shared among the crew. When the ship was in operations or at risk from enemy attack, it went into action stations. This was the highest alert. All watertight scuttles and internal doors were closed. Ratings manned their posts. Men on the morning or middle watches would attach pieces of paper to their hammocks asking to be woken in the small hours by mess mates coming off duty. One popular message, typifying mess-room banter, read, 'Shake hard. If hard, shake well.'[13]

The messes nearest the hangars were occupied by the squadrons' highly skilled non-flying ratings. They included fitters, who looked after the planes' engines, riggers, responsible for the airframes, and electricians and armourers. In *Indefatigable*, for example, 479 maintenance crew were needed for an air group of 73 aircraft. Maintaining the aircraft was one of the toughest and most responsible jobs on the carrier. Naval aircraft operated under great stress. Aircraft lashed on deck were exposed to salt spray and heavy rain showers. Flying long operations over the sea or enemy territory in single-engined planes, reliability was paramount. Each aircraft had its own team who nursed and mothered it, strike after strike.

In the tropics hangars became hellish dungeons, with temperatures reaching over 50 degrees Celsius. Men toiled and perspired for hours into the night in stifling heat to ensure their steeds were airworthy the following morning. Friendly faces were transformed into unrecognizable and macabre black masks of oil and grime. The hangar was a tough no-frills environment which left little to the imagination. As duty hangar officer of the watch inspecting aircraft in *Indefatigable* late one night, Ken Ward recalled to his wife later, 'I must tell you this, darling. Walking through the hangar just now with ratings sleeping all over the place, I came across one wearing only a pair of pants. He had got a terrific Joe! There it was sticking out – most embarrassing. I wonder of what he was dreaming! I can't imagine.'[14]

If the hull of the ship was the body of the carrier and the island its brain, then, for the aircrews at least, the wardroom was its soul. All officers took their meals in the wardroom. When they were flying, breakfast and lunch were irregular, but once it was dark and if there was little flying, supper was a simple three-course meal. Operations were discussed but the worst thing was to 'line-shoot' by boasting about individual acts of skill or perceived acts of bravery. Writing it down in a private diary was one thing. Boasting to your friends was another, and would result in a swift rebuke and leg-pulling.

Most squadrons kept 'line books' – scrapbooks recording irreverent observations wrapped around a chronological narrative of events. They were supplemented with photos and cartoons of amusing incidents, anecdotes, and thumbnail sketches of characters. Leafing through their pages gives a far more accurate picture of the life of a squadron than any official record.

The wardroom was used for briefings, aircrew meetings and for more formal dinners when the ship was in harbour. But it was at the end of a long day's flying that it really came alive. The bar was the beating heart of squadron life and was situated either in the wardroom or across a central passageway in an anteroom. Officers could buy duty-free beer or spirits, drawn against a monthly allowance which varied depending on rank. 'As a subby you had three pounds a month. With gin at tuppence and whisky at threepence. Beer was sixpence, so if you were offered a drink the worst thing you could do was to ask for a beer,' said Val Bennett, who was in *Indefatigable*.[15] The most popular drink was gin and lime juice, known as a gimlet.

Alcohol was the fabric which bound squadrons together against the backdrop of an intense environment in which men spent months in each others' pockets without being able to escape home or to the pub between ops. 'We were like a rugby team on tour,' said Quilter. Drinking bouts would often end with 'teams' scrummaging down in the wardroom, resulting in broken glasses and bruised bodies.[16] Wally Stradwick recorded one particular 1842 Squadron drinking session in the ship's bar, during which he and his friends

> bought out all the beer, so switched to gin. When the bar closed, we hung on to our glasses and trotted down to our cabin, unearthed a bottle of Bacardi, and continued. During the evening sing-song and bedlam, another bottle of rum was consumed, also a half of gin. Poor old Judy had really been game trying to stick with us, and while Charlie and I carried him up to his cabin and forcibly plonked him in bed, we could hear the boys yelling as they smashed the bottles and glasses. We were all rather tight.

Stradwick returned to his cabin to try and get some sleep, but found that 'staying in my bunk reminded me more of aerobatics so I got out went up the ladder and found Charlie in the wardroom. We were sober enough to discuss flying tactics until 2.30 a.m. and then we went or rather sneaked up to the flight deck in our dressing gowns to get some fresh air. It was a clear night and almost a full moon shining. Wonderful!'[17] But not everyone chose to drink. Chris Cartledge could not absorb very much alcohol without 'noticeable results and possibly loss of judgment while flying next day'.[18]

The ships' captains tended to turn a blind eye to most drinking sessions, knowing they were a necessary release for pilots in carrier combat. The captain set the tone of a ship and his attitude filtered down. Carriers may have looked similar, but they were very different in their spirit and character. Although he'd spent much of his naval career commanding submarines, Philip Ruck-Keene, the captain of *Formidable*, understood that carriers were now the capital ships of the fleet. He was well liked by the aircrews, whom he referred to affectionately as 'my boys', and they in turn, among themselves, dubbed him Ruckers.

Mutual respect was not always universal. Naval aircrews, especially those made up largely of civilian volunteers, considered themselves a breed apart from ship-based Royal Navy officers, most of whom had little experience or understanding of flying. Comradeship in wartime was about identifying shared experiences, yet there was little common ground between an airman who spent hours in the air flying hundreds of miles being shot at over enemy territory and a ship-bound officer. Bearing in mind the vast majority of aircrew were hostilities-only volunteers – who would be returning to civilian life after the war – while they wore the uniform, took the pay and were proud to fly in the FAA, many cared little for what they considered to be the often-stuffy attitudes of Royal Navy officers, who they dubbed RN bastards or fish-heads.

This rivalry was generally dressed up in light-hearted banter, but hinted at a more deep-set belief that reservists – especially 'air branch types' – didn't always live up to the high standards the Royal Navy expected. Regular officers often saw aircrew as rabble who had gained their commissions with undue haste, and appeared to have a somewhat low regard for tradition. The exceptions were those few RN aviators who recognized that RNVR officers were never going to be bound by the same formalities. In return, these men were generally liked and respected by the 'wavy navy' flyers. 'We FAA types were a complete mystery to the RN officers, and we used to play on it and exaggerate our complete lack of seamanlike knowledge and attitudes so as to wind them up,' said Keith Quilter.

A light-hearted letter written by a number of RNVR flyers to *Flight Deck*, the wartime Fleet Air Arm magazine, in February

1945, outlined how a typical airman had 'an eye for a figure, a taste for the gin and a capacity for beer [and] manages to combine with these, efficiency in the air, and the ability, enforced as far as figures are concerned, to lay off all three when at sea'.[19] But their spirit of defiance was perhaps best celebrated in the FAA drinking songs belted out around the wardroom piano. 'Balls-Up', a pastiche of a popular song of the time entitled 'The Hut-Sut Song', mocked a Royal Navy 'straight A' regular airman observing hostilities-only pilots landing.

> A solitary straight 'A' watched
> As the first one hit the barrier.
> 'My God! These HO's may wear wings,
> But they're fuck all use in a carrier.'
>
> There's a balls up on the flight deck,
> And the Wavy Navy done it.
> There's a balls up on the gangway,
> And they don't know who to blame.[20]

10

An enterprise of the first magnitude

On the same day Operation Goodwood began, 6,000 miles away in the Indian Ocean Royal Navy aircraft launched daring raids against various targets on the south-west coast of Sumatra. They attacked Japanese shipping in the large port of Emmahaven and a cement works in Padang which produced 200,000 tons of cement a year and was the primary supplier outside the home islands to the Japanese forces, which used the cement to beef up its fortifications.

As with the *Tirpitz* raids, the principal strike aircraft was the Barracuda, supported by American-built Hellcat fighters from *Indomitable* and Corsairs from *Victorious*. The two carriers, escorted by the battleship *Howe* and a small force of cruisers and destroyers, sailed deep into Japanese-controlled waters, risking attack from submarines, ships and enemy aircraft. These were the first Allied aircraft to fly over south-eastern Sumatra for more than two years, and to the surprise of all they met very little opposition from the Japanese. One FAA New Zealand flyer later commented to a newspaper, 'It was only a matter of lobbing a few bombs on specified targets and having the satisfaction of cementing the works up a little.'[1]

The raids were the latest in a series of operations by the Royal Navy's Eastern Fleet, based in Ceylon, which had been gradually growing in size since early 1944 as reinforcements arrived from all around the world. Naval aircraft from the carriers *Illustrious*, *Indomitable* and *Victorious* had conducted a series of limited air raids against Japanese targets in the Bay of Bengal and Sumatra, often at the request of the Americans to divert Japanese strength away from their own operations. While damage to the Japanese was relatively light, such strikes proved invaluable in allowing the new FAA squadrons to gain experience and acclimatize to the heat, humidity and isolation of the vast oceans.

By the summer of 1944 the Americans were producing so many ships and aircraft that they were able to commit greater forces to the Pacific, increasing the pressure on Japan through their dominance of the ocean and a series of critical battles. Perhaps the most significant of these took place in June 1944, when fifteen of Admiral Spruance's carriers from Task Force 58 carrying more than 950 aircraft faced nine carriers of the Japanese fleet under the command of Admiral Jizaburo Ozawa.

At 08.30 on 19 June 1944 the Japanese located Spruance's fleet and launched 373 planes, hoping to make the crucial decisive strike. However, the aircraft were picked up by American radar more than 125 miles away from their target, allowing the US fleet to launch its entire fleet of fighters. Hellcats ploughed into the Japanese Zeros and Yokosuka dive-bombers. For the first three years of the war the highly manoeuvrable Zeke had been a devastating weapon flown by experienced pilots, but most of these pilots had been killed and replaced by airmen who were rushed through aviation schools and inadequately trained. The Zero now showed its age, and was outgunned and outpowered by the Hellcat. In just eight hours more than 300 Japanese aircraft were shot down for the loss of just two dozen Hellcats. Some American pilots made up to six kills in one mission, and the battle was dubbed the Great Marianas Turkey Shoot after one pilot said it was just like shooting 'turkeys back home'.

Fifty Japanese aircraft still broke through to cause significant damage to two American battleships and two carriers. However, sent out by Japanese navy superiors obsessed with a decisive encounter, the inexperienced airmen at the sharp end were never going to have a serious impact on the American fleet. Against overwhelming opposition, there were individual acts of bravery by

Japanese pilots. One had just taken off when he spotted a torpedo fired from an American submarine sliding through the water towards the carrier *Taiho*. He immediately changed course and crashed his aircraft into the sea, sacrificing his life to save the carrier. By the end of the following day, however, Japanese air power in the Pacific had been decimated. They had lost over 600 of their aircraft and three carriers had been sunk. More than 400 Japanese aircrew died. What was left of the fleet withdrew to the north-west.

With victory in the Battle of the Philippine Sea, the Americans were free to invade Saipan, which they secured on 9 July 1944 after fanatical resistance from the Japanese military. Brainwashed into thinking they would suffer a horrible fate at the hands of the American marines, dozens of civilians, including women and children, threw themselves off cliffs in mass suicides. The neighbouring islands of Tinian and Guam were secured by the middle of August, despite isolated pockets of Japanese soldiers holding out in the jungle – the last of whom did not surrender until the 1970s.

By the autumn of 1944 General MacArthur's army was advancing through New Guinea, and, just 1,000 miles away, Nimitz's Pacific Fleet was pushing west, boxing in the Japanese. MacArthur and Nimitz would soon join forces to land at Leyte, and the recapture of the Philippines would cut the Japanese home islands off from the precious oil and rubber resources of the Dutch East Indies and Malaya. Now Nimitz's mighty fleet could drive north towards the Japanese home islands.

With *Indefatigable* and *Formidable* on their way to join *Illustrious*, *Victorious* and *Indomitable*, the Royal Navy was assembling a powerful carrier force of its own in the Indian Ocean. But where they would then be deployed was by no means certain, a fact of which Churchill was well aware when he arrived once again in Quebec for the Octagon Conference with President Roosevelt on Wednesday 13 September 1944. Somewhat acrimonious discussions between Churchill and his Chiefs of Staff as to how any British military force in the Far East should be used had rumbled on.

Churchill still favoured an amphibious campaign through Sumatra and Malaya, which might go some way towards erasing the humiliation of Britain's early defeats in the Far East. But the Chiefs of Staff continued to insist that an amphibious war using ground forces was impractical. Manpower and cost were serious constraints. A major amphibious war in the Far East could only begin if the war with Germany was wrapped up, and it was becoming clear this would not happen until the spring of 1945 at the earliest.

Additionally, given America's successful thrust back across the Pacific over the previous two years, it was only a matter of time before there was a final showdown in the central Pacific, even if the final shape of the assault on Japan had not been decided. An invasion – code-named Operation Downfall – had already been tentatively approved in July 1944 by the Americans, with a projected five million mainly American ground troops supported by a vast air and sea force. Timetabled for the autumn of 1945, this would dwarf the Normandy D-Day operations, and would definitively showcase the US military's prowess.

While an invasion would be overwhelmingly American, by hook or by crook Britain needed to be seen alongside its old ally for the final defeat of Japan. Not participating would leave Churchill open to American accusations that Britain's main concern was restoring its rule in its old colonies while the Americans bore the brunt of the final battles. It would be politically damaging if a British fleet stewed on the sidelines like some impotent second eleven while America took centre stage and lifted the trophy. The British had to think about the post-war world. Britain had vast colonial interests in the Far East. Retaining influence was crucial. It had also borrowed huge amounts from America over the course of the war. Supporting the Americans to the bitter end could make negotiating the payback of these loans an easier task.

As Churchill sat down with Roosevelt and their chief military advisers at 11.45 on that late-summer morning, he knew that, in the short term, the only realistic and affordable military option open to the British was to offer a naval force. The meeting started brightly enough, with Churchill summarizing the various military successes in Europe of the previous weeks, enthusing that 'everything we had touched had turned to gold'.[2] After reviewing the ongoing bloody campaign in Burma, Churchill moved on to the Pacific and didn't beat around the bush. There were, he said, certain people who were 'inimical' to good Anglo-American relations and were 'putting it about' that Great Britain would take no part in the war against Japan once Germany had been defeated.

If one of the chairs around the table creaked at that very moment, observers could have been forgiven for assuming this was due to Admiral Ernest J. King shifting uneasily in his seat. King was commander-in-chief, United States Fleet. Many thought him to be something of an Anglophobe. He certainly had a short fuse and was described as a 'formidable old crustacean', with one myth maintaining that he 'shaved every morning using a blowtorch'.[3] His perceived dislike of the Royal Navy may partly have been caused by resentment; the British had, after all, dominated the world's oceans for hundreds of years. But by late 1944 that order had well and truly been turned on its head. However, King was actually against the British contributing to the Pacific war because he believed a Royal Navy Pacific fleet would struggle to operate on its own without help from his own far more experienced forces. The Limeys had never fought in the Pacific, where the conditions demanded an entirely new type of warfare. King might also have seen the political machinations behind the British position. Given the US Navy's increasing dominance over the course of the war, it's easy to sympathize with King's reluctance to share the laurels.

However, Churchill insisted that the empire was 'eager to play the greatest possible part' in defeating Japan, adding that 'grievous losses' had been suffered in defending British territory. Turning to address Roosevelt directly, Churchill said a British fleet would be happy to take part in the main operations against Japan 'under United States Supreme Command'. The president immediately replied that Churchill's offer was 'accepted on the largest possible scale'. Churchill fleshed out some detail, promising a 'powerful and well-balanced force', but King was still not convinced and attempted to pour cold water on proceedings by indicating a paper had been written about the level of involvement of the British, which was being studied.[4] By mentioning it King was trying to delay a British contribution. This riled Churchill, who retorted that surely it was better to replace 'battle-worn' vessels of the US Navy with new British ships. The temperature rising, King snapped back that the matter was under examination.

'The offer of the British Fleet has been made,' growled Churchill. 'Is it accepted?'

'Yes,' replied Roosevelt. 'I should like to see the British Fleet wherever and whenever possible.'

Looking on, Admiral Nimitz, commander-in-chief of the Pacific Fleet, believed Churchill had been offended. He later said, 'to him it was inconceivable that an offer of the fleet of Drake and Hawke and St Vincent and Nelson should not be instantly and gratefully embraced'. King meanwhile was 'visibly shaken', as Roosevelt had pulled rank by accepting the prime minister's offer of a British fleet without first discussing it.[5] But Churchill's volte-face over the whole issue delighted his own chief of staff. It was a significant moment. The balance of power might have changed since the early days of the war, and the once-powerful Royal Navy would now be the junior partner to the Americans, but Churchill had got his way. For now.

Why did Roosevelt accept the British fleet so willingly? The interventions of Harry Hopkins, one of Roosevelt's closest advisers, and Cordell Hull, the US secretary of state, may have contributed to his decision. On 4 September Hopkins replied to a signal from John Winant, the American ambassador in London, who had warned three days before that allowing Britain's war against Japan to be limited to the recapture of its previous territories as opposed to 'smashing Japan' would create 'a hatred for Great Britain [in the US] that will make for schism in the post-war years'. Hopkins replied, 'We simply must find a way to have Great

Britain take her full and proper place in the war against Japan.'[6] On 8 September, in a memo to Roosevelt, Hull noted that it was crucial that Britain was involved in the Far East war 'to the greatest possible extent', adding that if this did not happen there would be 'immediate and hostile public reaction in the United States'. It seems Roosevelt's views may have chimed with those of the British Chiefs of Staff. Both had their eyes on post-war cooperation in the Far East.[7]

The day after the first Octagon meeting, the Combined Chiefs of Staff met again in the main conference room of the impressive Château Frontenac Hotel perched high on the north bank of the St Lawrence River. This time they were without their two leaders. Admiral King made it clear he still objected to British involvement in the main operations against the Japanese, even suggesting at one stage that it 'was not his recollection that the President had agreed to this'. Outgunned by his colleagues, however, King eventually recanted, and by the conclusion of the meeting the Chiefs of Staff had agreed that a British fleet should participate in final operations against Japan in the Pacific, probably in the spring of 1945. Such an involvement could only take place, however, with an assurance from the British that its force would be self-supporting, and would not drain the resources of the larger, more experienced US Fleet. 'The method of employment,' said the Chiefs of Staff, 'will be decided from time to time in accordance with prevailing circumstances.' In other words, the operations of the British force depended on the location and progress of the US Fifth Fleet.

Churchill returned to London and on 28 September relayed the outcome of his meeting with President Roosevelt to the House of Commons. 'On behalf of His Majesty's Government, nearly two years ago, I assured the President that Great Britain would pursue the war against Japan with all her strength and resources to the very end,' he began. 'As I explained to Congress when I last addressed them, we have losses to repair and injuries to repay on the Japanese account at least equal to, if not indeed greater than, those suffered by the United States. Accordingly, we offered to the United States the fine, modern British Fleet, and we asked that it should be employed in the major operations against Japan. This offer was at once cordially accepted.'[8] Churchill warned that a feature of the war against Japan 'will be the severe, intense, prolonged and ever-increasing air bombardment to which the Japanese mainland installations and munitions centres will be subjected . . . The huge distances, the tropical conditions and other physical facts, added to the desperate resistance of the enemy, make the war against Japan an enterprise of the first magnitude.'

Thus, on 22 November 1944, the British Pacific Fleet was officially born in the sticky warmth of Trincomalee, the Royal Navy's main base on the north-east coast of Ceylon, as its commander-in-chief Admiral Bruce Fraser hoisted his flag on the gunboat *Tarantula*. Once *Indefatigable* and *Formidable* arrived to join *Victorious*, *Illustrious* and *Indomitable* in early 1945, the carrier fleet would then sail from Ceylon to its new main base in Sydney, which was still being constructed. From there it would join the vast American fleet up in the Pacific wherever the front line might be. At this point it was estimated this lay some 2,000 miles north of Sydney; however, by March 1945, thanks to the speed of the American advance across the Pacific, it was double that distance away.

Fraser, at fifty-six years old, was a popular choice for the job. He had joined the Royal Navy as a fourteen-year-old cadet in 1902, served as a gunnery officer in the First World War, captained the aircraft carrier *Glorious* in the 1930s and, after holding various other senior naval positions, was appointed commander-in-chief of the Home Fleet in May 1943. Commanding a force from the battleship *Duke of York*, Fraser had sunk the German battlecruiser *Scharnhorst* on Boxing Day that year, in gales and rough seas off the North Cape of Norway. Just 36 German sailors were plucked from the icy waters from a complement of 1,803. Although never one to gloat, it was just vengeance for Fraser – *Scharnhorst* had destroyed his old ship *Glorious* three years earlier

– and cemented his stature as a fighting admiral. According to one of his admiring staff officers, Fraser 'combined the best leadership qualities of Alexander and Montgomery, the diplomatic skill of Eisenhower and the indomitable spirit and stubbornness of Churchill'. The silver-haired, blue-eyed Fraser clearly inspired loyalty in his immediate staff, and he was 'literally adored by all those who served him'.[9]

As commander of the British Pacific Fleet, his gift for diplomacy would be particularly useful. Although accountable to the Admiralty in London, he would also need to deal directly with the Australian government, which had agreed to provide the headquarters, dockyards, airfields and storage depots for the British Pacific fleet's main base. Many in Australia were sceptical about the fleet's arrival, remembering that it was the Americans, not the British, who had come to their rescue earlier in the war when Japanese forces had swept south across the Pacific and carried out raids on Australia's northern shores. Relations would need to be handled with care. Fraser embarked on a campaign to get the Australian press onside; making an enemy of them could be as damaging to the health of the fleet as any Japanese kamikaze.

BRITAIN'S NAVAL MIGHT TURNS TO THE PACIFIC declared the headline on page two of the *Sydney Morning Herald* on 12 December over a piece reporting that Britain's navy, 'the mightiest in her history', was turning its eyes towards the Pacific, joining 'the great fleets of the United States in battering Japanese naval power from the seas'. The paper approved of the 'bluff, hearty, energetic' Fraser, with his 'imagination, daring and drive' to lead 'one of the greatest battle fleets' ever mustered by the Royal Navy, and predicted, 'the combination of these vast fleets . . . spells final and inescapable doom for Japan'.[10] The paper opined that the 'news that such a fleet has been formed will thrill the Empire. It is the answer to critics who complained, foolishly or maliciously, that Britain intended to shirk her obligations in the war against Japan . . . For this country the advent of a powerful British fleet will be of the deepest Imperial significance.' Such appreciation from the foremost newspaper in the country was music to Fraser's ears.

The backbone of the battle fleet would be the Royal Navy's Illustrious and Implacable Class armoured carriers. Four would be in action at any one time, and they would be reinforced by dozens of other ships, from battleships to cruisers and destroyers. Some of the ships were in Ceylon while others would make their way from Europe over the coming months as the war with Germany came to an end. With so many ships still tied up around Europe, Fraser had to appeal to the navy boards of Australia, New Zealand and Canada to help assemble his task force and its fleet train. Connecting the fighting ships over thousands of miles with their base in Sydney, the fleet train would supply food and fresh water, replacement aircraft, ammunition, fuel and floating hospitals. After each operation, the task force would rendezvous with the fleet train at an agreed point a few hundred miles back from the combat zone, and within forty-eight hours would be fully operational again. The carriers and the main task force were like a nest of hungry chicks, and to keep them nourished Fraser would need to use resources from the Commonwealth and beyond.

Although some ships had been making their way east since the spring of 1944, allowing the beginnings of a fleet train to assemble, the rump would have to be assembled in just weeks, and combined with the assortment of ships already available from Australia. This in itself was a huge task. It had taken the Americans two years to hone the highly complicated logistics of supporting its vast fleet operating far from home for months on end. No wonder Admiral King questioned if the British fleet could remain self-sustaining. Fraser knew that the size of his fighting fleet would depend on the ability of the fleet train to support it, not the other way around. Positive press from the Australians about Commonwealth cooperation was vital.

Fraser's relationship with the Americans and specifically with Nimitz, his operational commander, was also of crucial importance. Although it had been agreed that the British Pacific Fleet would operate alongside the Americans against the Japanese home islands, this was by no means assured. Fraser knew just how easy it would be for Admiral King to arrange for the British fleet to end up in the south-west Pacific under the command of General MacArthur, to assist as his campaigns in the Philippines and Borneo came to a climax.

In December 1944 Fraser flew to Hawaii to meet Nimitz in person, and received a warm reception further brightened by the flash bulbs of the press and the garlands of flowers presented by girls in hula skirts. They had first met a decade before and, renewing their acquaintance, hit it off immediately. One commander who accompanied Fraser commented, 'there was no doubt that the US command in the Pacific wanted the BPF, and from the moment of the arrival of the party at Pearl Harbor we had the maximum co-operation from Admiral Nimitz'.[11] While Nimitz did not rule out the possibility of the British fleet operating in the south-west Pacific, Fraser left Hawaii confident that he had done all he could for now to ensure his fleet would be where it mattered when it mattered, in the thick of the action against Japan.

It was during these meetings that Nimitz asked Fraser if his fledgling fleet would make a detour en route from Ceylon to Australia to attack two important oil refineries near Palembang in the Sumatran jungle, which provided Japan with much of its aviation fuel. American Army Air Force bombers had attacked the plants the previous August but failed to score significant hits. Now it was the turn of the Royal Navy flyboys. It would be the first time a British fleet had ever launched an airborne attack using four of its main carriers. With more than 100 aircraft and 200 aircrew, Palembang would be the FAA's biggest operation so far in the Second World War.

Operations were to be led by Major Ronnie Hay, one of the most experienced pilots in the FAA. Hay joined the Royal Marines in 1934 aged eighteen, volunteered for the FAA and embarked in *Ark Royal* in April 1940, and shot down a Heinkel bomber near Aalesund, Norway on his first operational sortie. Over the next three years he was never far from the action, supporting the Dunkirk evacuation, serving on the Malta convoys, in the Battle of Britain and against *Bismarck*. After surviving the sinking of *Ark Royal* in November 1941 in the Mediterranean, he was awarded a DSC. By his own admission, Hay wanted 'more rank and more gongs'. Following stints as a staff officer in Ceylon and India, he secured a return to operational flying, first by leading the air defence of southern India, and then as the commander of 47 Naval Fighter Wing on *Victorious*. Now he had been asked to take on his most important job yet, as airborne coordinator for the British Pacific Fleet's maiden mission.

Hay described himself as an 'air admiral', but the job was more akin to that of a conductor. He would circle above the main strike force as it attacked the target, passing on instructions over the radio to the fighter and bomber crews as the mission unfolded, allowing effective real-time analysis of the attacks from more than a hundred Royal Navy aircraft at a time. This crucial role had been adopted by the US Navy for some time but was new to the Royal Navy.

Although his opinionated views grated on some – one fellow pilot described Hay as a 'queer fish who kept to himself and was hard to get to know' – to others the Scotsman was debonair and unflappable, his diminutive frame at odds with his towering personality.[12] His superiors counted on his experience, skill and lucidity in operations, while those he led were attracted by his ballsy attitude and no-nonsense manner both on the ground and in the air. He had a razor-sharp mind and would give his instructions in a conversational manner, firing out his clipped words as rapidly as the Browning machine guns mounted on the wings of his Corsair fired out 0.5-inch bullets.

Hay gained his squadrons' trust and respect. They also admired his mischievous capacity for fun. Before the fleet left Ceylon, Hay had flown 400 miles north to Ulundurpet in southern India to pick up a four-gallon jar of Perry's Navy Strength Gin, which he bought for 'some ridiculous sum' and carried back in his

cockpit wedged between the seat and control column. Little
wonder he wanted to get it back in one piece – the jar was the
equivalent of more than 700 single pub measures, or twenty-four
months' ration. A few days later Hay asked his girlfriend, a Wren
he had met in Ceylon, what they should do with it all. They agreed
on a party, but for what? 'We could celebrate our engagement?'
she suggested. It was an unusual proposal, but entirely fitting,
and the couple were married in Colombo in October 1944, four
days after Hay had done a 'very rotten slow roll' in his Corsair
over *Victorious*, following an all-night session 'getting fearfully
plastered with all my squadron mates'.[13]

The FAA and RAF shared the airfields across the island. The
largest was at the former racecourse in Colombo, where the men
slept in the grandstand. Most were simpler affairs – clearings cut
out of the jungle with a strip of interlocking steel plates forming
the runway. These plates made a loud clatter when aircraft landed,
'which was fine until some clot came down with his hook on', said
one pilot.[14] During tropical storms the sky seemed to split and the
rain fell in torrents, transforming the airfields into quagmires.
At Puttalam, sixty miles north of Colombo, elephants – including
one called Fifi – were used to tow Corsairs around the water-
logged airfield.

Life was often primitive. Officers lived in wooden-framed
cabins with thatched roofs and other ranks in dormitories, though
there was usually a petty officers' mess and an officers' wardroom.
Food was strictly rationed, and the usual tinned and powdered
offerings were reduced to a warm sludge by the heat. Hot curries,
fresh juices and exotic fruits including paw-paw, mango and
watermelon broke the mealtime monotony. While everyday life
was basic, it was also beautiful. One pilot arriving in Ceylon wrote
home, 'The people are so well disposed and good looking. Their
clothes blend with the countryside; they have a natural instinct for
harmonious colours . . . I am only irritated by those who treat
them automatically as inferiors. They only do it as a matter of
form because they see other people doing it.' But he was struck

too by the poverty. 'Of course there are so many sordid scenes. Elephantitis, Rickets, etc., turn their victims into pathetic and revolting creatures, who exhibit themselves in the public streets and squirm begging in the gutter.'[15]

At night scented woodsmoke hung in the air, fireflies twinkled in the jungle blackness, frogs and insects croaked and chirruped. The humidity made it impossible to sleep under anything more than a mosquito net, which would thud intermittently as a flying insect lost its way. Morning habits were adapted to include a careful examination of sweat-soaked flying gear hung up at the end of the previous day, as nocturnal visitors were common. One officer claimed to have found four scorpions inside his overalls in the morning. Shoes made a perfect den for snakes. Six-foot-long land monitor lizards patrolled the wooden verandas looking for scraps of food thrown out by the kitchen staff. Monkeys chattered in the trees.

Where possible, most units operated under tropical routine, flying hard from dawn with lighter work or 'make do and mend' in the afternoon, meaning they were free to do as they wished when the fierce sun reached its zenith. At the end of a hot day officers showered, donned their smart white tropical rig and visited the mess or went into Colombo, sipping cool drinks on the terrace of the Galle Face Hotel while watching the golden sun sink into the slate-grey Indian Ocean. After dinner the fun often continued at the Silver Fawn nightclub – nicknamed the Silver Prawn – perhaps ending with an early-hours skinny-dip in a secluded bay. From the hotel bars of Colombo to the steamy verandas of the tea plantations of Kandy in the north, and at the vast naval base at Trincomalee to the east, courtships between Wrens and airmen blossomed.

At the *Indefatigable* mess Christmas party on 19 December 1944 Ken Ward recorded in his diary how 'as the boys got drunker, so did the Wrens. I remember one type sitting on the floor with his hand up the skirt of one of these Wrens, and apart from a few wriggles she didn't object. She merely stood there with her legs open, apparently enjoying it. Horrible! I was fed up with the whole thing.' Ward and a few others then watched a 'battle-royal begin, as the drinks gave out. Glasses were flashing all over, and pineapples rolling around – what a sight! Someone falling over a Wren officer and lying on top of her in a very suggestive attitude! That was enough – we went to bed.'[16]

But as fun as these evenings were, the pilots were focused on the job ahead. On either side of Christmas, oilfields at Pangkalan Brandan in north-east Sumatra were attacked with carrier strikes involving almost one hundred aircraft from *Victorious*, *Indomitable* and the newly arrived *Indefatigable*. Just as with Operation Goodwood, although opposition and casualties were light, these raids allowed new pilots to accumulate vital combat experience. Hellcats and Corsairs from *Indomitable* and *Victorious* shot down five Japanese fighters and were so excited finally to get into a dogfight they abandoned the Avengers they were meant to escort after they had finished their bombing runs. 'What always seems to happen is that someone sees a bogey, makes a hasty report, and chases off, followed by anyone else who is anywhere near,' said one Corsair pilot later, admitting it was not 'every month of the year that you see a Zero in the Fleet Air Arm, so you can hardly blame a fighter pilot for making the most of his opportunities.'[17] Luckily the bombers reached and returned from their targets largely unscathed, but the mission had exposed weaknesses which would need to be dealt with.

These operations were merely the hors d'oeuvre. Throughout January 1945 the vast harbour at Trincomalee steadily filled up with new ships arriving from Britain. Battleships, heavy and light cruisers, destroyers, submarines and every variety of escort ship and supply vessel occupied every spare jetty, wharf and mooring. Moored at the heart of Trincomalee harbour was the 1st Aircraft Carrier Squadron – *Indefatigable*, *Indomitable*, *Illustrious* and *Victorious* – which carried a total of 238 aircraft and was escorted by the battleship *King George V*, four cruisers and ten destroyers.

It was the largest airborne force the Fleet Air Arm had ever assembled.

Formidable had also been due to arrive, but was delayed at Gibraltar while a new gear wheel was fitted. She was soon nicknamed HMS *Immoveable*, a sarcastic swipe by her frustrated aircrew – including Wally Stradwick, Keith Quilter and Chris Cartledge. Stuck in Gibraltar, *Formidable*'s airmen continued intensive flying practice over the Rock and North Africa. With the war in the Mediterranean now nearing its end, the biggest dangers were largely self-inflicted. A quarter of the squadron was almost wiped out one night driving along the coast road from Oran to Las Senia when the driver took on a corner too enthusiastically. The jeep ended up in a ditch, while its passengers – including Stradwick, Cartledge and Tony Garland – ended up in hospital, bruised but not badly injured.

Life in Gibraltar wasn't without its more pleasant distractions, however. Some of the men made the most of a nearby Women's Auxiliary Air Force (WAAF) station, and casual relationships blossomed. Stradwick and fellow 1842 flyboy Quilter enjoyed double dates with two WAAFs, taking the ferry across the bay to Algeciras. Under the control of neutral Spain, Algeciras was a hotbed of German and Italian spies monitoring Allied shipping movements, and social events were often attended by both German and Allied officers, with all parties in civilian clothes. 'It was a bit weird to be at a tea dance in the middle of the war with Germans sitting at the next table,' remembers Quilter, who soon became adept at scaling the roof of the WAAF station for illicit nocturnal liaisons.[18]

Fitted with a new gear wheel, *Formidable* continued its journey east through the Mediterranean but it would not join the rest of the carriers in the Pacific until the following March.

The man chosen to command the 1st Aircraft Carrier Squadron was Admiral Sir Philip Vian, otherwise known as Vian of *Cossack* fame. Like Bruce Fraser, this six-foot-tall forty-nine-year-old had a reputation as a battle-hardened fighting admiral, never far from the action. In February 1940, while commanding the destroyer HMS *Cossack*, Vian masterminded the dramatic boarding of the German prison ship *Altmark* in a Norwegian fjord. After vicious hand-to-hand fighting with bayonets and the last known use of a cutlass by the Royal Navy, almost 300 British merchant seamen locked away in the lower decks were freed. The first they had known about the unfolding drama was hearing hatches being removed above, then a shout in the dark: 'Any British seamen below?' Receiving replies in the affirmative, the boarding party responded, 'The Navy's here.'

Vian was a force of nature. However, on the surface at least, he lacked Bruce Fraser's charm and tact. After interviewing him in 1945, one reporter revealed, 'If he doesn't like the question he brusquely dismisses it.'[19] This manner was accompanied by an unforgettable physical presence. 'He had very beetling blue eyes with huge bushy eyebrows and hair coming out of his ears,' said Ronnie Hay, who felt his new boss was a 'pretty terrifying-looking chap . . . he had a very intense way of speaking'.[20] Opinion was divided. Some, especially within the ranks of the flyboys, regarded him as a fish-head who knew little about carrier flying or the pressures aircrews were under. Others reckoned he was just the man needed to get the British Pacific Fleet quickly up to fighting weight and who went out of his way to protect his aircrews. Regardless of the opinions of the flyers, by appointing Vian Fraser had signalled to the Americans that the British were taking their participation in the Pacific war seriously. Vian was a heavyweight player you wanted in your corner. He would also stand up to the Americans and didn't care what they thought of him.

Those working closely with Vian saw a softer side to his public face. Ronnie Hay admits he was initially 'all in fear and trembling' when Vian arrived. 'We thought he was going to do another Altmark, say, "The Navy's here," and steam his bloody carriers straight up the old spout.' But Hay soon discovered his new boss had intelligence and was willing to learn. 'I got on very well and respected him. You always detected kindness.'

Vian had an immense challenge. This was a new type of warfare for the Royal Navy, with multiple carriers flying off hundreds of aircraft for daylight attacks against heavily defended targets many miles away. He had to get it right. In Trincomalee harbour little launches motored about between the ships, carrying commanders and senior staff between various planning conferences. The imminence of the fleet's departure was confirmed when Louis Mountbatten, supreme Allied commander in south-east Asia, visited the fleet and made a series of morale-boosting speeches, and on the wet and grey afternoon of 16 January 1945 Ken Ward recorded in his diary how 'a terrific vibration shook the ship as her screws started, and we quietly slipped out of the harbour'. The British Pacific Fleet was going to war.

The stakes could not have been higher. Fraser knew his force had the chance to demonstrate it was an effective fighting unit. Success against Palembang would help convince the Americans his fleet should be there in the final battle with Japan. But the Sumatran oilfields were well defended by anti-aircraft guns and surrounded by Japanese airfields from which they could launch swarms of fighters. Not only was it likely his young, largely inexperienced aircrews would sustain heavy losses, Fraser also knew that failure to deliver the required result might just render the British Pacific Fleet a white elephant before it even reached the Pacific.

11

The balloons go up

At 16.00 on Tuesday 16 January 1945, as the hilly rainforest surrounding Trincomalee slipped out of sight, the carrier captains revealed the details of their mission to the aircrews. Their objective was to attack the two most important oil refineries in the Far East and put them out of action. The refineries lay on the T-junction of the River Musi and the River Komerine, five miles downstream from the town of Palembang and forty miles inland from the eastern coast of Sumatra. Captured from the British by Japanese paratroopers in February 1942, the plants produced 90,000 barrels of oil a day, enough to supply 75 per cent of the aviation fuel required by the Japanese for their war in south-east Asia. Cutting off this supply would dent Japan's war effort at the very moment it was being squeezed right across the Far East.

Admiral Vian knew a successful strike would be a feather in the cap of his new fleet. Perhaps there was a twinge of *Schadenfreude* too. The previous August more than two dozen B-29 Superfortress heavy bombers, the jewel in the crown of the USAAF, had flown for almost twenty hours in a 4,000-mile round trip from Ceylon to Palembang. But their night-time raid – one of the longest flown to carry out a single air raid in the entire war – halted production for just a week.

Precision attacks were required in order to destroy key buildings and installations to ensure production was interrupted. The only way to achieve that, according to Admiral Fraser, was through the 'rapier thrust of light but accurate carrier-borne aircraft bombing'[1] – at low level, in daylight, against two of the most heavily defended oil refineries in the world. For an inaugural strike by a new carrier force, this was about as tough as it got.

Commanders briefed aircrew for the first attack. After replenishing oil and aviation fuel at sea on 20 January, the four fleet carriers and the rest of Task Force 63, the code name for Vian's fleet, would head for their flying-off position, 30 miles off the west coast of Sumatra. On 22 January 48 Avengers each armed with four 500-pound bombs would take off and fly 180 miles across Sumatra to dive-bomb the target. Twelve Fireflies would escort the main strike force, breaking off to attack individual targets. A cover of 48 Corsairs and Hellcats would also escort the main strike, and, flying ahead in a separate strike, 24 Corsairs flown by the most skilful ground-strafing pilots from 1833 and 1830 Squadrons in *Illustrious* and 1834 and 1836 Squadrons in *Victorious* would make aggressive low-level sweeps, called ramrods, hitting three enemy airfields to prevent Japanese fighters taking off to attack the Avengers.

Palembang was a training centre for the Japanese, and some of the defending enemy fighters would be flown by instructors there. The standard of flying was expected to be high. It was the job of the Seafires and the remaining Hellcats to stay behind to defend the fleet from any Japanese attack. Although intelligence showed there was likely to be little in the way of naval opposition, an enemy assault from the air was a very real threat.

The first mission, code-named Meridian I, was to target Pladjoe, the largest and most important oil refinery in the Far East, built on a roughly square site stretching a mile and a half along the southern bank of the Musi. After the strike the fleet would withdraw to refuel before repeating the process a few days later by attacking the smaller refinery at Soengei, on the opposite bank of the Komerine. If required, a third strike following Meridian II would mop up any remaining targets.

As the fleet steamed south, tension grew. On each carrier aircrews attended countless briefings on topics ranging from tactics to be deployed in actual attacks, through to survival in hostile terrain if they were shot down. Following one intelligence briefing, Seafire pilot Ken Ward in *Indefatigable* jotted in his diary that dangers included 'various natives, friendly and otherwise . . . one tribe go around completely naked, Joes and Jills exposed fully to the sun or what-have-you. The women are very passionate.'[2]

A tongue-in-cheek guide on how to deal with 'natives' was included in an edition of *Flight Deck* published in early 1945. Entitled 'Jungle Manners', it considered that 'proper treatment of the natives' was just as important as a good escape kit and a supply of food and water, if a downed airman was to stand a chance of successfully escaping from enemy territory. But the reader was warned against any 'Hollywoodian notions' that the average native wanted to eat him, when in fact 'he is likely to be far more frightened of you' and may even speak pidgin English, 'so if you find the average native smelly, obnoxious or both, try not to show it'. The article recommended that tricks such as making a cat's cradle with string could be used to win favour with difficult locals and gain their confidence, but only by the practised – 'A muddled cat's cradle only makes you look silly and entails considerable loss of "face".'[3]

This light-hearted article was well intentioned and in fact did have some merit. A number of airmen who landed in hostile terrain throughout the war survived after initiating contact with local communities. And although the Dutch colonization of Sumatra meant it was unlikely aircrews would end up in the supper pot of the cannibals they had heard so much about, there were plenty of anti-European militia groups all too willing to hand them over to the Japanese – an equally grim proposition. The flyboys were all too aware of how they might be treated if they became prisoners of the Japanese. In January 1944 Anthony Eden, the foreign secretary, had given a speech in the House of Commons which included graphic examples of what happened to POWs, including one man who was tortured until 'he was practically out of his mind' and a number of Indian soldiers captured in Burma who were tied up and 'systematically bayoneted from behind in turn'.[4]

One Hellcat pilot in *Indomitable* said later, 'We were given practice interrogations of what to do and say if made a POW, which made one realize how easy it was to make a slip which would mean so much to the Jap.'[5] Evasion was the only hope. Pilots were taught how to live and eat in the rainforest without human contact. Native animal life to avoid included the Sumatran tiger, the rhinoceros and a variety of poisonous snakes and saltwater crocodiles. Worse still were the unseen threats. Malaria was rife.

Every flyer wore a life jacket – called by Allied airmen across the world a Mae West because some wag had once joked it resembled the generous bosom of the American actress. In this and in pockets all over their overalls was stuffed an array of survival items, including matches, a mirror, a mosquito net, anti-malaria pills, anti-burn lotion, morphine ampoules, bandages, water purification pills, insect repellent, chewing gum and chocolate. A rubber cushion containing fresh water was packed tightly over each parachute. Some crews also carried belts of twenty gold sovereigns to bribe locals. Unlike during the *Tirpitz* operations, it was pointless to carry passport photographs. 'None of us resembled Malays, Chinese or least of all Japanese,' said one pilot.[6]

The flyers were given locations, dates and recognition signals to memorize for rendezvous with rescue submarines. Walrus rescue aircraft flown from *Victorious* were on hand to pick up ditched aircraft if they could make it to Lake Ranau, a freshwater lake twelve miles inland from the western coast.

Refresher courses reminded crews of Japanese aircraft they might expect to encounter. Instead of struggling to remember makes and models, the FAA had adopted the American system in which Japanese fighters were given boys' names, and the bombers named after girls. Radio communications, reports, squadron diaries and briefings were littered with references to various harmless-sounding appellations, including Betty, Dinah and Judy; Oscar, Tojo and Zeke.

In the early years of the war, the Oscar – or the Nakajima Ki-43 Hayabusa – was a formidable foe, produced in greater numbers than any other land-based Japanese fighter. A single-seater, it was lightweight and manoeuvrable, with a large wing area allowing a small turning radius and high rate of climb. However, armed with just two 7.7-mm machine guns, it lacked the speed, firepower and ruggedness of the new generation of Allied fighters such as the Corsair and Hellcat, whose pilots knew they had a good chance of seeing an Oscar's fragile frame disintegrate if they could get close enough to get off a decent 'squirt' with their own 0.50-inch machine guns. Its replacement, the Tojo – the Nakajima Ki-44 Shoki – sacrificed dexterity for speed and rate of climb, and was better armed with four 12.7-mm machine guns or two 12.7-mm guns and two 20-mm cannon. Superior to the Oscar, it would prove a sterner test for the fleet's fighters.

Most of the Japanese planes operated within forty miles of Palembang, where at least four airfields, which were really no more than dusty airstrips cut into the jungle with wooden hangars and huts, were defended by batteries of heavy- and light-calibre anti-aircraft guns. The Japanese air defences included six fighter squadrons and one reconnaissance squadron, equipped with a variety of aircraft including at least fifty Tojos and thirty Oscars. FAA aircrew were told to expect a vigorous response from Japanese fighters, which 'should be able to give a good account of themselves but much will depend on how much warning they get and how good their individual pilots are'.[7]

Civilian engineers who had worked on the refineries before the war helped Royal Navy intelligence experts build exact models of the installations for the flyers to study. For the Avenger and Firefly crews in particular, it was essential they knew the position of their individual targets to work out the best angles of attack. Pilots on the American raid had reported 'intense and accurate' anti-aircraft fire at 10,000 feet, and intelligence photos indicated some AA positions. But the Japanese camouflaged gun positions with bamboo frameworks and creepers, leaving just the gun barrels clear to elevate and depress, so it was hard to assess exactly where all the guns were.

The flyers didn't know it yet but both refineries bristled with firepower. According to post-war British analysis, the Japanese devoted greater resources to the defence of Palembang than even Singapore – not surprising given its output of oil and vulnerability to air attack from carrier planes. The Palembang Defence Corps was responsible for the 270-odd anti-aircraft guns dotted about the two refineries, and coordinated with the fighter defence squadrons via a central plotting and control centre. These included one hundred heavy AA guns, fifty lighter anti-aircraft guns, and banks of anti-aircraft mortars sited on likely lines of approach to the refineries. The mortars fired canisters to a height of 1,500– 2,000 feet, which each ejected seven explosive charges attached to paper parachutes that detonated if the parachute or its cords were fouled by aircraft. With somewhat grim irony, some of both the 20-mm and 40-mm guns around the refineries were British made, captured by the Japanese.[8]

Palembang was surrounded by an effective early-warning radar screen with a radius of a hundred miles, allowing the Japanese around half an hour to prepare and apportion targets for the battery commanders before the strike arrived. In their reports from the August raid the American B-29 pilots had also suggested the existence of barrage balloons. Intelligence photos taken five weeks later indicated there might be up to twenty-five sites from which balloons could be launched. The British were understandably concerned. It was bad enough to be faced with enemy fighters and a barrage of hot lead at various altitudes. They didn't relish having to dive through numbers of balloons attached to great steel hawsers which would chop straight through an aircraft's fuselage. However, in the final briefings the aircrew were told, based on the available photographic intelligence, that it was unlikely any balloons would be flying. 'This was, to our horror, to prove very wrong in the event,' said a senior pilot later.[9]

After refuelling, Force 63 steamed towards its flying-off position for the planned dawn strike on Monday 22 January, but mist and heavy rain delayed the strike for forty-eight hours. Nervous crews passed the days as best they could. In *Indefatigable*, *The Canterville Ghost*, starring Charles Laughton, was screened in the wardroom. Flyers played impromptu games of deck hockey. A sack full of mail was delivered by a cruiser.

Finally, on the 24th, as dawn broke, the skies cleared and the order 'Hands to flying stations' was piped over the tannoys. The ships' crews manned their designated positions, while the flyboys quietly dressed in their flying overalls, tried to gulp some tea and force down a little breakfast, although few had the stomach for it. One squadron CO admitted later he was 'pretty tensed up with apprehension . . . fear for the opposition we should certainly meet and scared stiff at the thought of falling into the hands of this particular enemy'.[10]

The airmen removed all badges of rank in case they were captured, the thinking being that higher-ranked prisoners would be assumed to possess more valuable information. Notes sewn into the back of flying overalls detailed in Malay how much the men were worth if returned safely to the UK government. Airmen nicknamed these gooly chits because of rumours of what hostile locals or the Japanese might do if they caught downed crew.

The Corsairs over in *Illustrious* were assigned the ramrod strikes on airfields. A thrilling but dangerous job. Pilots wrote 'death letters' to be sent to their families if they didn't return. One New Zealand Corsair pilot in 1833 Squadron was shaken when his best friend and fellow Kiwi handed over a letter and said, '"Ben, I won't be coming back this time. You'll post this letter for me, won't you?" My reaction was, "Balls you silly bastard!" . . . However he was adamant in a calm, calculating way . . .' The pilot was indeed shot down and never seen again.[11]

At least the Avenger pilots and observers going into their first action could prepare for battle together. But the TAGs – the vital third member of each crew – were not commissioned officers so slept and messed separately, only joining their crew mates for briefings and missions. Some believed this created a gulf between the crew and a handicap in the air, but gunners required less training and were therefore cheaper and easier to replace.

Armed and fuelled, the aircraft emerged from the hangars to be 'ranged' on the flight decks, packed so tightly together that their folded wings almost touched. Over the tannoy Wings ordered the crews to their aircraft. In *Indefatigable* Roy Hawkes climbed up onto his Avenger, while his TAG and observer opened the hatch in the rear of the plane and settled into their positions. Nervous energy led to mistakes. One observer slipped climbing onto a wing and broke his elbow on the steel flight deck.

Each Avenger had its own team on the deck, including the rigger and engine mechanic. 'It was like nursing a child. They were indispensable,' said Hawkes, who needed help from his rigger getting into the tight confines of his cockpit.[12] Like all pilots, his parachute fitted snugly into the bucket seat, above the dinghy and his water cushion. With various charts and maps strapped to his legs, there was little room to manoeuvre, even in the relatively comfortable confines of the Avenger.

Hawkes was armed to the teeth. To one leg was strapped a machete and to the other a 'wicked hunting dagger'. Each man had a .38-inch revolver. 'In addition I carried my own semi-automatic pistol . . . a little monstrosity which had been purchased from a gunsmith in Winchester,' said Hawkes. Most importantly, Hawkes remembered to pack Mickey – a teddy bear which accompanied him on every mission. Many men carried lucky charms or talismans of some sort – mascots, coins, family mementos or presents from sweethearts. It was not unknown to see an airman rush below after realizing he'd left his charm in his cabin.

Hawkes' faithful rigger patted him on the shoulder and gave the thumbs up. Putting the oxygen mask over his mouth and sucking in a mouthful of sickly-sweet air, he was ready.

Over in *Illustrious* Norman Hanson, the CO of 1833, waited in his Corsair on the flight deck at the head of the ranged aircraft. The day was not yet warm and occasional squalls showered the flight deck. Hanson was 'cold and shivering with the usual butterflies doing circuits and bumps in my tummy'. In the half-light of dawn two deck officers moved about with Lucite torches, 'blue and theatrical, in their hands. I was nervous, like a racehorse ready to go,' said Hanson.[13]

Hanson spotted a hiccup of oily black smoke puff from *Illustrious*' funnel as the stokers down in the boiler room flashed up more burner to increase the ship's speed to 30 knots. 'Fighters, start up,' came the voice over the tannoy. One by one the Corsairs coughed into life, each emitting little puffs of blue smoke, until the whole flight deck was throbbing in rhythmic unison.

Hanson was first to fly off, with his squadron of Corsairs followed by the Avengers. He felt his aircraft lean slightly to the left on its springy undercarriage as the great carrier began its sweeping starboard turn into the wind with the rest of the fleet. One final look down at the instruments as the breeze strengthened over the flight deck, and prompted by a whirling gesture from the flight deck officer's torch, he released the brakes, pushed forward the throttle and accelerated 400 feet along the deck. Flying off over the bow, he felt the usual momentary sink before slowly gaining altitude and jinking to starboard, thankful for another safe take-off.

The rest of the carriers echoed the process. One by one the planes took off, gaining height and joining the growing swirling circular mass of aircraft, flying in an anti-clockwise direction in the grey sky above. A handful of aircraft wouldn't start or had to return with faulty engines, but at around 7.10 a.m. – fifty-five minutes after the first aircraft had launched – the main strike force had formed up, and the great vortex of aircraft unravelled into a long stream. Admiral Vian watched from *Indomitable* as dozens of little dots headed for the mountain range of the Sumatran coast, its serrated crest silhouetted faintly against the brightening eastern sky.

Ten minutes later, Force X-Ray, the ramrod wing of twenty-four Corsairs, took off and set off across the sea. Its departure had been delayed by faulty aircraft from the main launch making emergency landings back on. Playing catch-up, it was vital it reached the airfields before the Japanese fighters could get into the air and attack the Avengers heading for Palembang. But time was running out.

The four Avenger squadrons were split into two wings. No. 1 Bomber Wing comprised 857 Squadron from *Indomitable* and 849 from *Victorious*, while No. 2 was made up of *Illustrious'* 854 Squadron and 820 from *Indefatigable*. Carrying four 500-pound bombs each, the Avengers crossed the coast at 07.18, steadily climbing at 400 feet a minute to a height of around 7,000 feet to clear the mountain range. By now it was turning into a fine morning, the bright sky with a thin layer of high cloud contrasting with the sea of green below.

In the humming cockpit of his Avenger Roy Hawkes looked down at the mountains and the jungle spreading out as far as the eye could see. The bombers flew in flights of six, line astern in a stepped-down formation. 'The underside always felt naked so it was nice to have company and guard each other,' said Hawkes.[14] He looked up and saw his Corsairs weaving above him, partly so they could stay with the slower bombers flying at 180 knots, but also to spot enemy fighters.

Observing them all was Ronnie Hay in his Corsair, poised like a conductor at the start of a symphony. But as the air group crossed the coast, it had been picked up by Japanese radar. One hundred miles away the Japanese had been alerted and they hoped to strike a discordant note in proceedings. In a well-practised drill, the 350 men of the Palembang Balloon Corps rushed to their positions while the gunners prepared the anti-aircraft batteries. The cylindrical balloons, each carefully hidden inside its own individual thatched wooden hangar, were dusted off and the order was given to release them. Dozens of dirty brown bubbles attached to steel cables glinting in the sunshine like spiders' silk covered in morning dew began to rise over the refineries and from barges moored in the river.

Now it was just a matter of watching and waiting.

*

The twenty-four Royal Navy Corsairs of Force X-Ray barrelled across Sumatra at 220 mph, their faded green and grey camouflage rendering them almost indistinguishable against the jungle canopy just fifty feet below. The ground-attack ramrod aircraft comprised three groups of eight assigned the call signs Whippet I, II and III.[15] The plan was to hit three airfields with the objective of destroying as many Japanese fighters as possible. At each airfield one or two groups would go down and strafe while the third circled at 4,000 feet to watch for enemy fighters and to destroy any aircraft that succeeded in taking off.

As they approached the first airfield, two groups were ordered to sweep around to attack line abreast from different angles to confuse the Japanese gunners. But as they zoomed towards the airfield, the most exciting target was a solitary steamroller repairing the runway. The construction gang toiling away on the morning shift got the fright of their lives as the hunched silhouettes of seven Corsairs screamed towards them. They barely had time to drop their spades before being on the business end of forty-two 0.5-inch Browning machine guns, a brutal death. As the Corsairs raced across the dusty red strip there was little in the way of anti-aircraft fire, but two collided, sending chunks of metal flying and one aircraft into the ground, where it skidded across the airfield and blew up. The other pilot had a wingtip of his Corsair sheered clean off by the collision but managed to limp back to the carrier force and land safely.

Four minutes later Force X-Ray swept over the second airfield. Against furious point-blank AA fire the planes shot up various Japanese aircraft parked on the runway and in canvas hangars covered in foliage. One Corsair was hit, crashing upside down and cartwheeling in flames through a line of parked aircraft. Another pilot skimmed the ground and released his belly tank full of fuel straight through the doors of a hangar, which exploded in a ball of orange fire, destroying six aircraft. With the airfield covered in burning aircraft and hangars, the flights rendezvoused to race to the final target, the airfield at Talangbetoetoe, ten miles north-west of Palembang.

As the air-raid sirens droned across Talangbetoetoe airfield, Hideaki Inayama and the other pilots of the 87th Squadron of the Imperial Japanese Army Air Force grabbed their parachutes and flying helmets and climbed into their fighters. The 1,500-horsepower radial engine of Inayama's Nakajima Ki-44 Shoki grumbled into life, sending clouds of red dust flying. Opening the throttle and hurtling down the runway, 'suddenly, the sun was momentarily blotted out. A stream of small bright lights flashed past my starboard wingtip. I was being strafed!' said Inayama later. Glancing up, he caught the momentary flash of two Corsairs.

> Jerking back the stick, I jumped my Shoki into the air, retracted my undercarriage and simultaneously jabbed at the button operating the flaps, skimming along the tops of the coconut trees. No smell of burning! No unnerving knocking! My engine roaring smoothly! How those British pilots could have missed such a sitting duck I could not imagine, but I could thank my lucky stars that I was not already buried in the funeral pyre of my faithful Shoki.[16]

Safely in the air and heading towards the refineries, Inayama was airborne in the nick of time. Eight attacking Corsairs of Whippet II now made determined attacks from different directions against 'accurate and intense' anti-aircraft fire, dodging the AA mortars' explosive charges floating down on their little parachutes. The airfield was surrounded by heavy jungle. Sight lines were extremely short and pilots had only seconds to pinpoint a target and press home their attack, all the time trying to avoid colliding with their squadron mates. One Corsair was brought down as it prepared to shoot up the control tower. The remains of a decapitated body were found later by the Japanese.

The three ramrod attacks were a baptism of fire for the British

Pacific Fleet flyers. Four Corsairs had been shot down in an hour. And as thrilling as low-level attacks could be, they were also snap-shots of extreme violence against an enemy who knew how to create attractive targets on the ground and lure attacking aircraft into lethal tunnels of lead. Ronnie Hay had previously warned pilots about 'returning to a hornets' nest once it has been well stirred up' and pilots were learning that attempting more than one or two sweeps against Japanese airfields was deadly.

'Palembang was big time. It was death or glory stuff,' said one pilot.[17] But as they headed west back towards the fleet, they'd left a trail of destruction at all three airfields and done a good job of destroying what targets were available, including thirty-four air-craft on the ground. Eight aircraft from 1830 Squadron alone fired a total of 7,450 rounds. However, they couldn't help wondering how many more Japanese fighters could have been prevented from getting into the air if they'd not been delayed at the start of the mission. The question now was, just how costly had that delay been to the main strike force, which was now bombing the refinery?

As the fighters of Force X-Ray began their sweeps, the forty-odd Avengers of the main bombing strike force, protected all round by their escort of almost fifty fighters and twelve Fireflies, were fast approaching Palembang. In the hazy sunshine the crews could just make out the silvery river and the great expanse of the oil refinery. Blue, grey and white storage tanks striped with red were framed against the dark green jungle. The bombers increased their speed to 180 knots and began to lose height from 12,000 feet. They were just fifteen miles away. So far so good. And best of all, there was no sign of the expected fighters. Perhaps the ramrod boys had managed to get them all on the ground.

Then everything seemed to happen at once.

The radio silence was broken by the call of 'Rats!' as the force was ambushed by around twenty Tojos and Kawasaki Ki-45 Nicks orbiting the skies south-west of Palembang at heights between 15,000 and 30,000 feet. Using classic tactics, the Japanese fighters dived out of the morning sun and broke straight through the top and middle cover of Corsairs and Hellcats. They weren't interested in dogfights; the Japanese pilots had been briefed to attack the Avengers.

Leading one of the covering flights in his Corsair, Norman Hanson heard the air come 'alive with warning shouts, orders to close up and all the natter that excitement generates. And then I could see them. Over to the north, pinpricks were hurtling down-hill from a great height and contrails streaming out of the azure sky as our fighters pulled tight corners to get at them.'[18] Pilots' radios filled with panicked shouts. An excited voice bawled, 'Rats 10 o'clock up,' then the babble became unintelligible, 'like turning on the wireless at full blast with three radio stations on or near the same wavelength', said one Avenger pilot.[19]

The Avenger crews then watched in horror as at least forty balloons, the existence of which had been almost dismissed in their briefing, rose over the target. Initially ordered to release the balloons to just 2,500 feet, the Japanese now unwound them to varying heights of between 4,000 and 6,000 feet. The same thoughts went through all the pilots' minds. 'Balloons were the kiss of death to a dive-bombing squadron,' said one.[20] Ronnie Hay ordered the Fireflies to carve out a passage for the bombers by shooting down the balloons, but their 20-mm cannon failed to ignite the balloons and only three were shot down. With the radio full of excited chatter, shouts and warnings, most of the Firefly pilots didn't even hear Hay's order.

Each of the four Avenger squadrons circled the refinery using landmarks on the ground as reference points to locate its desig-nated targets. The individual commanding officers followed by their squadrons would then 'push over' at about 7,000 feet, diving in to release their bombs, ideally between 3,500 and 2,500 feet above the ground. Each bomb had a twenty-five-second delay and was fused by a wind vane in the nose after falling 1,000 feet.

The first to attack was 857 Squadron, whose CO was just putting his flight into a line-astern formation when a fierce box barrage of light and heavy anti-aircraft fire opened up. The guns tracked the Avengers using widely spaced bursts of flak which shook the aircraft with violent bangs that could be clearly heard by the crews over the radio chatter and engines. Although the Fire-flies had been unable to destroy the balloons, the first Avengers now started their dives.

A furious battle now covered the sky, with almost thirty Corsairs and Hellcats engaged in dogfights with Japanese fighters over an area roughly the size of central London. Encounters were frightening, confused and random. An Oscar appeared in Norman Hanson's rear-view mirror, its wing guns flashing. Hanson braced himself, expecting to be hit. Instead, the Japanese aircraft vanished and just as quickly reappeared a split second later 'pulling up in front of us, the length of two cricket pitches away. We all heaved back on our sticks and gave it the works; no need for gunsights. The silly bastard was half stalled, sitting there like a broken-down old whore,' said Hanson.[21]

A Hellcat pilot in 1844 Squadron on the outside of his flight peeled off to engage a Tojo in a dogfight, but 'when I turned back there wasn't an aircraft in sight, not one. I thought, "Jesus what happens now?".'[22] Fighting over such a large area, and with planes coming at them from all angles, fighter pilots travelling at high speed often found themselves one second engaged in a melee, and the next suddenly quite alone. Watching on, Ronnie Hay made notes and took photographs. 'Fights were raging all over the target area. It was almost funny to see the aircraft scrapping and all the while the AA bursting at all heights up to 15,000 feet,' he said.[23]

Back on his bombing run, however, Roy Hawkes wasn't find-ing life particularly funny. 'Aircraft were everywhere . . . One felt naked and vulnerable,' he said. There were now dozens of fighters producing 'a spectacular boiling cauldron' while all the time the bombers flew resolutely through the centre of a 'massive, uncon-trolled air display'. At one stage Hawkes looked to his right to see a Japanese fighter slipping up underneath him on his wing. 'The enemy fighter and I exchanged glances over our oxygen masks. Then he peeled off to starboard and was gone.'[24]

While the bomber pilots concentrated on hitting their targets, the gunners at the rear crouching in their little glass turrets desperately tried to keep the enemy fighters at bay. The metallic rattle of the turret guns rang through the aircraft. 'You were hammering away at your guns hoping you'd hit them. You didn't have time to be scared,' said one.[25] The flak was so intense many crews thought they could smell it, but it was cordite from the firing of their own guns.

By now the Avengers of 857 and 849 Squadrons had almost completed their attacks. Although some released their bombs above the balloons, others risked hitting the cables by diving through to bomb at the optimum height of around 2,500 feet. One pilot below the balloons had a fright when he saw four bombs whizz by just in front of his nose from the Avenger above him. Dropping his own bombs, and pulling hard on the stick to climb out of the dive, the pilot heard his observer yell over the intercom, 'You've hit it – a real beauty right on the nail.'[26]

With No. 1 Bomber Wing leaving the sky over the refinery, four miles south of the target the Avengers of No. 2 Wing, comprising 854 and 820 Squadrons, were preparing to start their attacks. The AA fire had intensified and thick black smoke obscured large parts of the target. At six-second intervals, the Avengers of 854 began their dives. Pilots watched as the balloon cables flashed by only feet away, before dropping their bombs at just 2,000 feet.

Finally, it was the turn of Hawkes' squadron. He was 'tail-end Charlie' – the last aircraft of the whole strike. Wincing at the carpet of intense flak below, Hawkes' mind flicked back five years to a very different place. As a seventeen-year-old boy he would jump on his bike and rush home from Dorchester Grammar School to the family cottage overlooking Weymouth Bay to watch screaming German dive-bombers attack the little ships in the harbour. 'I was scared stiff at the thought of flying through this barrage, but I remember thinking that if all those Stukas I saw diving through the flak in Weymouth Harbour weren't hit, then it would be unfair if I was, and that's what got me through,' he said.[27]

As they approached the refinery, the Avengers disappeared and reappeared through the patchy cloud. Hawkes' attention was focused on his instruments and keeping in formation with the other aircraft. Japanese fighters continued to do their best to prevent the Avengers from maintaining their height and direction. In the final seconds before diving the squadron opened its formation and the pilots located their pre-designated targets. By luck there was little cloud over the actual refinery. Hawkes flicked the switches to open the bomb doors, before looking down at his target – a catalytic cracking plant.

Hawkes radioed his crew to let them know he was about to dive. Gently pushing the stick down, his shoulders strained against the seat straps as the aircraft fell through the sky. For the next ten seconds he focused on nothing but the cylindrical building ahead. Hawkes felt his fear vanish and his training kick in: 'the speed builds up – the target gets bigger and bigger and you know by instinct when you need to raise the nose slightly and press the tit'. There was no bombsight. The pilots aimed the nose of the aircraft at the target and released the bombs at around 2,000 feet. 'It was like darts,' said Hawkes.[28] The aircraft jolted as the bombs dropped away and Hawkes heaved back on the stick, levelling out at 1,000 feet before climbing again.

Just six minutes after the first aircraft had started its dive, the attack was over. Avengers emerged from the swirling smoke in a straggling procession, flying on their own or in pairs to an agreed rendezvous point ten miles north-west of Palembang town above an island in the Musi River. It was crucial that the bombers gathered as quickly as possible for protection in numbers before heading back to the fleet before their fuel tanks ran dry. None of the Avengers had hit a balloon or cable, but the intense anti-aircraft fire continued. Although the Fireflies and a handful of fighters were patrolling the route from the target to the rendez-vous, they could not cover the full fifty square miles, and most of the fighters were still in dogfights thirty miles away, meaning the Avengers were sitting ducks just as another wave of Japanese fighters began a fresh attack.

After taking part in the main battle over the refinery, Japanese fighter pilot Hideaki Inayama was running low on fuel and was about to head back to Talangbetoetoe airfield when he spotted a lone Avenger on its way to the rendezvous point. Its bomb doors were still open and it was trailing smoke. As Inayama dived and closed to just 500 feet, tracer bubbled up from the Avenger's ball turret and slid by Inayama's cockpit. But he pressed on and could soon make out the head and face of the young British gunner. Holding his fire until his aircraft was bouncing around in the Avenger's slipstream, Inayama opened fire at point-blank range: 'the bullets from my four 13-mm. guns ripped into the Avenger, its "greenhouse" canopy bursting into fragments like leaves in a gale. Flames seared back from the port wing root, and the Avenger rolled over onto its back, and then fell away into the jungle below.'[29] Inayama lined up his sights on a second damaged Avenger, but it flew into scattered cloud just as he was positioning to attack. With his fuel level critical, he headed back to base.

Black smoke belched from the refinery in a column reaching 10,000 feet as the final few Avengers formed up with most of their fighter escort and set a course for the coast. At about 09.15 – three hours after they had taken off – the strike force returned to the fleet. The majority were able to make it back to their own carriers, returning like tired birds after a great migration. The crews were just pleased to still be in one piece. 'I felt a relief that I had been and done it and had come away unscathed and also finding that I hadn't been shit scared,' said one pilot.[30]

Landing on did not pass without drama. Norman Hanson's Corsair had been hit in a dogfight. He made it back to the fleet but, approaching *Illustrious* and rapidly losing height and speed, he was forced to ditch. He was pulled from the water by a destroyer after almost drowning. For the next hour and a half, exhausted, cold and sodden, Hanson coughed and vomited seawater through his nose and mouth. A few hours later he retired to his cabin. On his little desk was a glass filled to the brim with neat rum, next to which was a card from his squadron's ratings. It read, 'Jolly good luck, sir. May you *always* come back.'[31]

But some had not. Thirteen airmen were missing or killed, including six crew from two Avengers in 820 and 857 Squadrons. In the wardroom of *Illustrious* the losses were keenly felt. Its squadrons had shown aggressive spirit but had lost four Corsair flyboys. In *Indomitable* all fingers were crossed for one of the FAA's Maori pilots, twenty-five-year-old Jack Haberfield, who was last seen in his Hellcat chasing an enemy fighter. The odds were stacked against the missing, but as the fleet slid away from the coast to refuel there was still a hope they might still be alive. The British Pacific Fleet had been blooded. Five days later they would have to come back and do it all over again.

12

The jitter effect

In the evening after the Palembang strike the gin and beer flowed in the smoky wardrooms of the carriers as young crews grateful to be alive raised a glass or ten to lost colleagues. Stories were shared and experiences swapped. The Avengers had pressed home their attacks with skill and courage, hitting three quarters of their targets, while the fighter boys had shot down thirteen enemy aircraft – including two Tojos Ronnie Hay had dispatched after they had pounced on him while he'd been taking photos of the bombing strike. He later admitted, 'You'd only got to look at a Japanese and he'd burst into flames . . . one squirt and they'd blow up.'[1]

The weaknesses of the Japanese aircraft – little armour, no self-sealing fuel tanks and inadequate armament – had been exposed. Also by 1945 the most experienced Japanese pilots had been killed and replaced by novices, and the Royal Navy's aircrews had got away more lightly than if they'd been up against seasoned opposition. Nevertheless, in his action report Hay concluded it was 'one of the better strikes the Fleet Air Arm has ever accomplished'.[2]

The following afternoon Admiral Vian signalled the rest of the carriers from *Indomitable*, his flagship, to congratulate their crews' 'resolution, skill and team work' in giving the refinery a 'crippling blow'.[3] But the hornets' nest had been well and truly poked. With the other refinery as yet untouched and the chance that some of the airmen shot down may have been captured and revealed British intentions under interrogation, the crews knew the Japanese would be expecting a second strike within days. Opposition in the air and on the ground might be even more intense and lessons must be learned.

One Avenger CO was scathing at the lack of cover his aircraft received from the Hellcats, noting, 'it appears the signal for bombing is also the signal for some [British] fighters to go and find a target'.[4] Norman Hanson felt that fighter pilots needed to learn that bringing the bombers home safely was infinitely more important than 'bagging a few enemy fighters'. Radio discipline was also a problem and 'would not be tolerated at a training school . . . people were thinking aloud far too much', added Hanson.[5] In the maelstrom of a major mission many of the escorting fighters had showed fine offensive spirit, but in their enthusiasm to get stuck into a dogfight, a good number of Corsair and Hellcat pilots forgot the bombers. At the same time the bomber crews had to learn it was not always in their best interests for the escort to stick too closely. And considering that for many this had been their first action, it's not surprising radio discipline had been breached. Nervous energy in action had eclipsed months of training.

A more serious worry for the bomber crews was the balloons. Over the following days the flyers were once again briefed. This time the target was the smaller refinery of Soengei Gerong. At a conference of wing leaders one of *Illustrious'* COs stated his belief that it was essential for the Corsairs, Hellcats and Fireflies to go on ahead in order to blast a way through the balloons, believing that 'their unforeseen presence on this occasion [had] jeopardized the whole operation'.[6] But when the final battle orders were distributed mention of the balloons was conspicuously absent. The signal lamp in *Illustrious* blinked furiously across the water as its commander signalled Hay on *Victorious* for clarification. Out of the gloom flashed back the reply. No action would be taken against the balloons.

The squadron leaders faced a conundrum. They could either go for the safer option and bomb above the balloons, or dive through them knowing their squadrons would follow faithfully with both a better chance of hitting their targets and of being killed. One Avenger pilot recounted how a CO on *Illustrious* told his aircrews that Meridian II was a suicide mission. The squadron leader made it clear he planned to fly through the balloons but told his men, 'I consider this strike to be so dangerous that if anyone would prefer not to fly, I shall respect his wishes and not think any the less of him for so doing.'

'I could hardly believe my ears,' said the pilot 'Nobody spoke. "Right, thank you, gentlemen," said the CO. "Tomorrow morning then."'[7]

This scene was repeated in all the carriers as the airmen were briefed. The plan was much the same as for Meridian I. The main bombing strike would be escorted by fighters to and from the target. However, the fighter escort was to be reduced by eight Corsairs in order to reinforce the Seafires covering the fleet in case the Japanese launched a counter-attack. Even with the Fireflies acting as close escort, this probably explains why Vian and Hay felt they couldn't spare any fighters to fly ahead and knock out the balloons. The route of the strike itself was also modified so the Avengers would swing south after the attack to avoid the intense anti-aircraft fire over the north of Palembang town. The separate fighter ramrod attack was split into two forces code-named X-Ray and Yoke and timed to arrive simultaneously over the two most formidable airfields, Lembak and Talangbetoetoe, before the main strike.

As some Avenger squadrons had more crews than aircraft, the men drew straws to decide who would fly again. The lucky ones were replaced by the handful of crews who had not flown in the first strikes. For the majority flying again, 'the glamour has gone. The spirit of adventure has gone. You have been highly trained to do a job and you knew you had to do it.'[8] Crews once again prepared themselves and looked for distractions to take their minds off the following day. In *Indefatigable*, *Hers to Hold*, starring Deanna Durbin, was screened in the wardroom. Others listened to the gramophone, enjoying the jungle-like tom toms of American jazz drummer Gene Krupa bashing out the hit tune 'Sing Sing

Sing'. In *Indefatigable* Ken Ward recorded how 'the atmosphere in the Wardroom was stifling tonight as the boys had a good round of drinks before the strike'.[9]

Early the next wet, squally morning, 29 January 1945, dozens of aircraft took off once again, launching Meridian II. Forming up in dreadful conditions and only narrowly avoiding a number of mid-air collisions, forty-two Avengers and almost fifty Corsairs, Hellcats and Fireflies headed for Sumatra. The rain eased over the mountains, revealing a ceiling of white cloud hanging at 13,000 feet.

Ian Paterson, flying an Avenger in 849 Squadron from *Victorious*, checked his various dials and instruments yet again. Sitting behind the bulletproof partition in the middle of the aircraft, his observer Tommy Gunn was busy with his maps and charts, plotting the route to the target and monitoring the VHF radio set. Up in the turret, TAG Bob Taylor was squeezed behind his gun, eyes narrowed and darting around the sky on the lookout for enemy fighters. Like many bomber crews, the trio had got to know each other well since first flying together in a Swordfish squadron in November 1943. But, after fourteen months of mundane operational flying, this was their first taste of action. 'It was a very happy relationship,' said Paterson.

> Both of those chaps are exceptionally fine people, and I think it is fair to say Bob and I were rather quiet types, and our association was always one of more reservation but respect for the other's personality and ability. But invariably the pilot and observer would strike up a friendship and they would do a lot of things together, and I found myself with Tommy in the same position. We virtually went around together and did everything together, and we had a very close relationship.[10]

Tommy Gunn was twenty-one and had grown up in the little Norfolk village of Mundesley on the East Anglian coast. 'We used to tease him about Mundesley being a bit of a backwater,' said Paterson. 'He was one of these very quiet laddies. Never had too much to say but never had an unkind word for anybody. Everybody who knew him loved him. He was gentle and helpful. Anything anybody could want as a friend.'

Twenty minutes into the journey Gunn reported to Paterson he could smell burning coming from his VHF set, so they decided to turn it off. This was a vital piece of kit which enabled them to locate the fleet after strikes. However, as they were with other Avengers they hoped they'd be able to get back without it. Now Gunn's main focus was to assist Taylor in defending the aircraft. They had agreed before the flight that if they were attacked by fighters Gunn would leave his observation cockpit and crawl down along the passage in the belly of the plane to man the rear-facing stinger gun under the tail.

Almost two hours after taking off, the refinery appeared on the horizon and loomed ever larger through the haze in the distance as the strike rumbled on. Its anti-aircraft defences had been beefed up since the first strike, and opened up with fierce fire when the bombers began to deploy for their attack runs.

'As we got nearer we could see the flak in the box barrage. It was like a carpet,' said Paterson. One pilot was seen to disappear down into his cockpit and reappeared a few seconds later with a tin helmet carefully perched on top of his flying helmet. The dreaded balloons were there once more, glinting in the sunshine. Upon seeing them, Ronnie Hay decided after all to order the Fireflies in. Three balloons were successfully shot down, but it was too little too late. Fifteen minutes before, the ramrod sweeps had attacked the airfields as planned, but had found few targets on the ground and had only shot down a handful of aircraft taking off. Most of the Japanese fighters were already airborne and ambushed the main strike as it prepared to attack. Dogfights broke out as the covering fighters tried to cut the enemy off before they could penetrate the Avenger formations.

The flak was far more accurate than on the first strike, and the Avengers started to take a pounding, rocking and jolting as though flying through severe turbulence, with black and brown puffs of

smoke exploding around them. 857 Squadron was once again the
first to dive. One Avenger was hit repeatedly with flak and left
with holes in the wings, a stump hanging down where a wheel had
been shot clean off from the undercarriage, and its bomb bay
doors stuck open. But still it flew on. Directly behind, enemy
fighters ripped through 849 Squadron just as its CO gave the order
to deploy for attack. Both his wingmen were shot down.

Diving at 300 mph and trying not to black out but beginning
to ease out of his dive, Ian Paterson was just closing the bomb
doors when 'there was a double crack like a stockman's whip
behind me. Almost immediately, there was another loud crack.'[11]
A shell had smashed into the leading edge of his port wing, near
its tip, lifting a huge flap of the covering skin. Instantly, the nose
of the aircraft dipped and it started to spiral into a deadly spin.
Battling to regain control, Paterson 'confronted the reality of death
as never before. I instinctively half stood up within my harness,
threw my left foot onto the side of the cockpit and with my right
leg applying the full right rudder, heaved the control column as far
as it would go to the right.'[12] It took all Paterson's strength to hold
this position, but to his relief the aircraft levelled out.

Next it was the turn of No. 2 Bomber Wing led by 854 Squadron with 820 close behind. The CO of 854 Squadron – the same
man who had expressed such reservations about the balloons
before the mission – looked down at the balloons and, hoping for
the best, gave the order to attack. 'I could see a balloon cable,'
recalled one Avenger pilot following his plane, 'and I thought he
would go around it, but he didn't; to my horror he hit it, sheering
off most of his wing, like a hot knife through butter, then going
into a vicious one-wing spin . . . and blew up in front of my eyes
when he hit the ground.'[13]

Across the refinery the AA guns continued to blaze as explosions sent columns of orange flames hundreds of feet into the air.
Pulling out of the dive, the TAGs facing the rear had the best view.
'We had given it a really good plastering, the oil was on fire, there
was smoke everywhere,' said one.[14] But as the Avengers emerged

from the smoke in a thirty-mile arc from the refinery to the rendezvous they came under sustained attacks from Japanese fighters.
The Fireflies accounted for two more fighters, but the same problems recorded in Meridian I were emerging. Many of the British
fighters had been distracted by dogfighting at higher altitudes
over the target, despite superior numbers and weaker opposition.
Whole flights of British aircraft were attacking single Japanese
fighters, which 'although good fun from the fighter point of view,
is a dangerous policy for fighter escorts', said one Hellcat pilot.[15]
Other Japanese fighters were remaining at lower altitudes to pick
off the unprotected Avengers. 'It was total mayhem . . . these
fighters were coming at you from all directions. You were hammering away at your guns hoping you were going to hit them. You
didn't have time to be scared', recalled a TAG.[16]

In desperation, the Avenger pilots threw their tubby aircraft
around like single-seat fighters and tried to alert Ronnie Hay that
they needed more protection. But the single radio channel was
once again jammed with chatter and shouts, and he failed to hear
their calls. Hay also had his hands full. Circling over the target
area for the duration of a raid, he became a magnet for enemy flak
and fighters. He was trying to photograph the refinery at 10,000
feet when 'I soon had to change my mind as a Tojo was coming
for us. In shooting this one down, we descended to nought feet
and, attracted by the gunfire, an Oscar came along.'

Hay pushed the throttle to maximum and climbed until he
had a 1,500-foot height advantage. Then, accompanied by an 1836
Squadron Corsair, he attacked the Oscar, and a vigorous dogfight
ensued. After a series of steep turns 'the Jap settled down for a
moment, straight and level. My shells hit the pilot's cockpit, which
glowed with a dull red as the bullets slammed home, then he
rolled over and crashed into the trees',[17] recalled Hay's wingman.

Most of the battered Avengers were now making their way
back towards the coast, but the nightmare was continuing for Ian
Paterson, whose stricken plane had become separated from the

rest of the strike force and was only a few feet above the jungle canopy. While Paterson struggled to keep control, Bob Taylor climbed down from the turret to check on Tommy Gunn. He hadn't answered Taylor's calls over the intercom since the shell had hit their aircraft in the bombing run, and they now needed Gunn to navigate them back to the fleet. Crawling into the belly passage, Taylor was met with a horrific scene, with Gunn prostrate in a pool of blood in front of the rear-firing gun. The armoured shield on which he was lying had provided pathetic protection. Hot fragments of metal had spewed out from the exploding shell, lacerating the underside of the Avenger and ripping through Gunn's waist, hips and upper left leg.

Taylor carefully propped his crew mate up and settled him in a semi-sitting position. 'He was, miraculously, still conscious,' said Taylor, 'and together we did what we could with the sparse material available to staunch the blood flow from his wounds. I gave him a pain-killing injection and then hurriedly returned to the turret after reporting Tommy's condition to Pat.'[18]

Faced with this dire situation, unpleasant thoughts raced through Paterson's mind as he wrestled with the controls of the Avenger. He later said, 'mindful of the great fear we had in the Fleet Air Arm, that capture by the enemy would ultimately end in execution, it was a sore temptation to push the stick forward and end it all – we were now skimming the treetops, and I knew I did not have the strength to hold the wing up for the probable two-hour flight home.' But Taylor was having none of it. 'I think it's the instinct to live,' said Paterson. 'People say it's easy to drown and it's quite a nice death . . . but you do everything you can to survive. And on the way back Bob was very good and jollying me up and encouraging me to stay in the air.' Paterson forced the control stick as far as it could go to the right with his right forearm, grabbing the lower part of the instrument panel with his right hand and using his left hand and arm to support it. By also keeping his foot hard on the right rudder pedal, the Avenger motored on.

Like a hyena smelling blood, however, the ailing Avenger had attracted the attention of a circling Tojo, which made a number of attacking passes that Taylor tried to fend off using the turret gun. A bullet went clean through the turret missing him by inches, while Paterson was hit in the head by a piece of perspex from the canopy. Another Tojo joined in the attack, and it seemed only a matter of time before they'd get their quarry. But fortuitously another Avenger had spotted what was happening and dived in, shooting down one Tojo fifty feet above the treetops, before executing a tight 360-degree turn and fending off the other, helped by Taylor's gunnery.

Taylor crawled down from the turret again 'to attend Tommy and do what I could to ease his suffering. He was still clinging to consciousness and losing blood, but I managed to fashion a tourniquet and fit it to the extreme upper part of his left leg as a means of staunching the blood from one particularly open wound.'[19] They were now all alone once again, and with Gunn in such a bad way Taylor had to take over his duties and try to plot a course back to the fleet.

Climbing into the observer's cockpit, Taylor quickly realized they were flying in the wrong direction due to a faulty compass and used another to fix a new course for Paterson, before crawling back to comfort Gunn and give him a second morphine injection to ease his agony. Bearing in mind Taylor was not trained as an observer, the fact that he managed to pinpoint their position over unfamiliar terrain and under such stressful circumstances was impressive indeed. Paterson was under great physical and mental strain just keeping the aircraft airborne, and Taylor made regular calls over the intercom to keep his spirits up. He also managed to fix the VHF set, allowing them to get a bearing on the fleet to pinpoint their position and to radio through to *Victorious* that medical attention would be needed for Gunn as soon as they landed.

An hour later the fleet finally came into view. They had managed to fly the stricken Avenger right across the mountains of Sumatra and over the sea. Paterson looked down at his petrol gauge, uncomfortably near the zero mark. He suspected the hydraulics were damaged and the flaps might not go down. With broken steering controls to boot, he had few options left. But he knew Gunn would probably not survive ditching in the sea and he decided to attempt landing the battered Avenger on the flight deck.

The reassuringly familiar flat grey tops of the four carriers, positioned in a diamond formation and surrounded by the rest of the fleet, were now just a few miles away. Paterson lost height and headed for what he thought was *Victorious*, only to find it was her sister ship *Illustrious*. Down to his last teaspoon of petrol, he lined up on *Illustrious*, hoping she was steaming into the wind and would accept the crippled Avenger. He lowered his hook and dropped the undercarriage, only to discover the port wheel was jammed. Now less than a hundred feet from the flight deck, he was waved off by the batsman and flew down her starboard side past the island, looking across to his left and gesticulating with his hands for an emergency landing and hoping for a sympathetic response from the bridge. The Avenger was losing height rapidly. The wing stalled as Paterson made the first 180-degree turn, sending the aircraft plunging. With sweat pouring down his face, he managed to regain control. But flying downwind he would need one more turn before approaching *Illustrious'* flight deck into the wind.

As Paterson gingerly started to bank the aircraft, its wing stalled yet again. This time there was no height to play with. The aircraft hit the sea at about a hundred knots. 'I hit my face on the instrument panel and was knocked out cold. God knows how Bob and Tommy had fared – the former was in the observer's cockpit, unstrapped, and the latter lying on his back in the belly . . .'

Ian Paterson's watch stopped at 11.25. His Avenger had been airborne for four and half hours. It was the last plane to return from the strike and was almost an hour overdue.

He came to in the cockpit, dazed and confused. Whereas moments ago there'd been the throb of the engine and radio chatter, now there was silence except for the peaceful sound of the water gently breaking over the aircraft's nose and windscreen. With mild concussion, Paterson found it difficult to stay awake, but with the recurring thought that a helpless Tommy Gunn might be trapped in seven tons of slowly sinking aeroplane, he carefully took off his helmet, undid his safety harness and parachute straps, slid back the cockpit canopy and climbed out onto the wing.

To his amazement, Gunn had managed to climb out and was already bobbing about in the blue ocean, his wet brown hair stuck to his forehead. Still conscious, he was struggling to stay above the water, the salty waves from a fifteen-foot swell slapping against his face. Given his condition, it had taken a superhuman effort to get out. Paterson opened a hatch on the side of the Avenger, hoping the emergency dinghy would automatically pop out, but the aircraft was one of the older models, and the dinghy was in a package that had to be manually inflated using an oxygen bottle. When he tugged the cord the whole thing shot out of his hand and fell into the water a few feet away. He didn't have the strength to retrieve it and instead slipped into the water and swam over to help his friend. 'I reached Tommy to try and support him, only to realize how utterly spent I had become,' said Paterson. Neither man had inflated his life jacket. Wearing sodden flying overalls and with Gunn holding on to him tightly for support and reassurance, Paterson frantically trod water to prevent them both from going under.

Bob Taylor had also been knocked out by the crash and came round trapped in the sinking plane unable to open the canopy. Finding strength 'more than likely derived from desperation'[20] he finally prised it open, stepped onto the wing and quickly found and inflated the yellow dinghy, before pushing it to a grateful Paterson and swimming over to help support Gunn. But 'I wasn't able to get into the dinghy,' said Paterson. 'I was absolutely shagged. I had no energy at all. I could just about hang on.'

The three men struggled in the water for ten minutes as a destroyer, *Whelp*, launched a lifeboat. On reaching *Whelp*, they were pulled up onto the deck, where Taylor and Paterson stood dripping wet and were each handed a mug of steaming Bovril as Gunn was gently carried below. A few minutes later *Whelp* signalled *Victorious*, 'Regret to report the death of Sub. Lt. Gunn. Other two members of crew suffering from cut face and shock.'[21]

'It was Bob who told me that Tommy was dead,' said Paterson, 'but I think we both knew before we got onto the *Whelp* that he wouldn't make it. When you think how hard Bob had tried to kill the pain with the morphine and put on a tourniquet. He had a friend who was dying, desperately needing help, and Bob was giving it all he could. I was bitterly disappointed when I tried to save him in the water that I didn't manage to do so. So there was a sense of not only failure and disappointment, but also grief and numbness.' *Whelp*'s doctor confirmed there was little they could have done, so severe were Gunn's injuries. Paterson was taken to a vacant cabin, 'my clothes removed for drying, and, wrapped in a blanket, left alone with my thoughts', with Taylor receiving similar treatment.[22]

The crew of *Whelp*, which included a young lieutenant who would later become the Duke of Edinburgh, had been busy since the strike returned, rescuing two Avenger crews and a Corsair pilot who had ditched. A twenty-one-year-old TAG from 849 Squadron recalled later, 'as the ship's boat came alongside, Prince Philip was at the rail looking over. He welcomed us aboard and took us all down to his cabin, where he lent us towels to dry ourselves and arranged some clothing for us to wear. He had a framed photograph of his sweetheart [the future Queen] on the table in his cabin.'[23]

There were other similar tales of survival. Seven Avengers and two Corsairs ditched near the fleet, either because they ran out of fuel or were badly damaged and couldn't make the carriers.

Admiral Vian thought the relatively high proportion of ditched aircraft was 'a natural reflection of the resolve of aircrews to avoid becoming captive to the Japanese'.[24] But it was also a clear sign of aircraft that had been flown at the very edge of their operational limits. Many more aircraft crash-landed on the carrier decks. Heading back some pilots had called each other up on the radio for encouragement and support, one even asking how long it would be until they reached the fleet. Ronnie Hay, with good reason, wasn't impressed. 'It is about time that everybody know [sic] their emergency drill without having to talk about it like old women,' he said later. Hay held his men to high standards even, or rather especially, on such big missions.[25]

With the aircrews back and debriefed, individual carrier commanders assessed the damage. In only two days' flying *Illustrious* had lost 10 per cent of her fighter pilots and 8 per cent of her bomber crews. In terms of aircraft, there were 24 per cent fighters and 24 per cent bombers lost. Inevitably, some squadrons had suffered more than others. In the second strike alone 849 had lost six aircrew. Between the target and rendezvous ten out of the twelve aircraft in the squadron were shot down or damaged by flak and enemy fighters. One of the lucky few to make it back onto the flight deck unscathed admitted he 'nearly fainted with fear for the others. My legs were like jelly as I made my way to the Ops room.'[26] Remembering the worn-out faces of his aircrew in 849 Squadron, its CO later observed, 'it was a sad and rather silent group of young men who attended the debriefing'.

Over both strikes, eleven airmen from *Victorious* had been killed or were missing and twenty-one of her aircraft were either lost or damaged. 'This is by far the highest casualty rate to aircraft endured during the some dozen operations *Victorious* has carried out during the past ten months,' said the captain commanding the carrier.[27]

But as the bomber crews were debriefed in the carriers, outside the action was far from over. Japanese aircraft had been trying to locate the fleet all morning, with Seafires, Hellcats and Corsairs chasing off small, sporadic attacks. Just before midday the fleet was preparing to steam away from the Sumatran coast when a blob was detected on the radar. Approaching twenty-eight miles to the south were one Nakajima Ki-49 Helen heavy bomber and six Mitsubishi Ki-21 Sally bombers. At first it seemed the twin-engined aircraft were shaping up to launch torpedoes, but when they split into two groups and started individual attacks, it appeared they had a far more sinister plan. The British Pacific Fleet was being attacked by suicide pilots.

The fleet increased its speed to 30 knots and sheets of spray surged over their bows as the ships sliced through the waves. As the Japanese aircraft approached, the destroyers and cruisers opened up with their anti-aircraft guns. Flashes ran down the length of their hulls and shot from the clouds of spray and water. Moments later, the guns of the four carriers and *King George V* joined in, their booming rhythmic fire thundering over the sea. The mighty barrage shattered the already fragile nerves of Ian Paterson, huddling naked under a blanket in the *Whelp* in a state of shock. 'I was terrified, to be honest,' he remembered. 'I leaped out of bed . . . it's the reaction at what we had been through, and you felt that you'd reached your limit and here was more to come . . . it was Palembang all over again.'

Clouds of black smoke criss-crossed the grey sky following the course of the bombers. The air was now thick with shells, but the lumbering aircraft kept on coming, hugging the water, steady and resolute. The Japanese knew they were outnumbered and out-gunned, but by flying at deck level they massively increased the potential for hits by friendly fire on ships and aircraft. One Hellcat was damaged by an overenthusiastic gunner who continued firing until he received a blow on the head from a steel helmet 'swung with great force and determination' by the fleet gunnery officer.[28]

A Sally made a low run on *Illustrious* and smashed into the sea just a few hundred feet short. Its pilot was 'either killed or must have lost his nerve at the critical moment, otherwise he would certainly have crashed into *Illustrious*', commented an observer on the cruiser *Argonaut*.[29] The Seafires were in the thick of the action. They'd had a difficult time during the first strike, with little action and countless mechanical problems. Now their pilots were able to show what the plane could do in the air. Ken Ward, who was already airborne with other members of 894 Squadron – including its CO Jimmy Crossman – chronicled events in his diary immediately afterwards:

11.55 A patrol has been sent to intercept bogeys on the deck to the East. 'All airborne chickens stand by to repel attackers from the South-east!' On our toes now – though the CO doesn't hear it! We continue to circle at 400 feet.

11.57 Bursts of flak in the centre of the Fleet at 150 feet so we dive straight into it – don't ask me why! There are 2 Sallys in formation below at 2.00 p.m. Jimmy takes the far one, I take the Leader. Gyro to 'Sally', button to 'Fire', wait for the range to shorten: 600 yards – 500 – 400 – 300 – now. Blast! I missed 'cos my Starboard cannon jams. Just then Jimmy's target blows up in the air and I'm thrown off mine. Pulling her nose around, I close in again and wait while the Sally dives onto the *Illustrious* from 100 feet and soars up again. In the sight now and I press the button of the machine-guns. Pieces fly from the tail unit and the Sally dives. An accurate burst of pom-pom blows her Starboard wing in half and she hits the water with an enormous explosion. Nothing but red flame. Wizard! I take a look around and see flak on all sides coming at me from the carriers and *KGV*, and I decide I have been very foolish and climb out of it. There must be some more Sallys somewhere – I can see 4 burning now.

12.00 Ah! now there's one by the *KGV* so in I go again. 400 yards now, steady, fire! One short burst only and the Sally turns to Starboard. Her inner wing touches the water and she spins around and explodes. No one else seems to be firing at it – they're firing at me. Hell! Let me get out of here!

12.30 Nice landing with an obstinate machine. What a
morning! I guess I have two to my credit. I don't know. After
being debriefed and having had lunch, I rested on my bunk.
I felt I had earned it. I still had a twinge somewhere for
having killed numerous Japs. At 5.00 p.m. I was 'at readiness'
again and a signal came from the Admiral: 'The splendid
work of your fighters was admired by us all.' The ratings are
delirious with delight. Some of them are saving up their tots
of rum to give to the CO and me, it's amazing!

Ten minutes after the beginning of the raid, seven Japanese aircraft had been 'splashed'. British fighter pilots, including Ward,
had flown through a sky thick with shells to shoot them down just
yards from the carriers. According to Admiral Vian's official
report, 'with total disregard for safety they very courageously followed their targets into point-blank pom-pom range of the ships,
and in most cases shot down or crippled them'. A signal was
pinned to *Indefatigable*'s wardroom noticeboard that evening. It
read, 'L/Cdr. Crossman and S/Lt. Ward were outstanding in the
defence of the Fleet.'[30]

While there was no doubting the skill shown by the fleet's
fighters, the same couldn't be said of the Japanese airmen. British
commanders were surprised by their apparent ineptitude, and
wondered if they may have actually stumbled across the fleet by
accident rather than design. Tragically, the most serious damage
was caused in a friendly-fire incident when *Illustrious* was struck
by two shells fired from the cruiser *Euryalus*. Twelve men were
killed and twenty-one wounded. The attacks had shown up the
fleet's poor standard of anti-aircraft fire discipline and control.
Nevertheless, the inept Japanese attack 'did nothing but mystify
us', said the captain of *Indomitable*. 'If it had not been for the casualties and damage suffered by HMS *Illustrious* by our own ship's
gunfire this attack would have proved an entertaining interlude,'
he added.[31]

*

Overall, the two raids on the refineries had been far from entertaining for the aircrews. Thirty flyers had been killed or were
missing. A number were most likely now on the run in Sumatra,
possibly badly injured or prisoners of war in Japanese hands. Over
both missions 41 British aircraft were lost in 378 sorties. This
translated to a loss rate of 10.8 per cent, not far off the figure for
the most costly air raid of the entire war. That unfortunate record
had been set when 95 aircraft – 11.9 per cent of those dispatched
– were lost during an RAF night-time attack on Nuremberg in
March 1944.

Although Meridian I and II were daylight raids on a much
smaller scale, the losses do nevertheless provide a powerful barom-
eter of the impact the two strikes on Palembang had on the
fledgling British Pacific Fleet and its young crews. The numbers
may have been minute compared to the Bomber Command raid –
which lost 545 men – but this was the largest strike the FAA had
ever carried out, and it was soon to embark on much longer and
potentially more dangerous operations. Compared to the hit-and-
run raids they'd been used to, the intensity and violence experienced
over Palembang affected the young aircrew for months to come,
and worsened the twitch that would seriously affect some airmen
in the Pacific. It also highlighted how slender the fleet's resources
were.

But whereas the Nuremberg raid had been judged a failure,
the Palembang strikes seemed anything but. The Japanese general
in charge of the refineries admitted later that the attacks were carried out in a 'daring and efficient manner', adding that their impact
was 'infinitely greater' than the B-29 raid by the Americans the
previous August. 'I think that the low-level bombing tactics of the
naval planes contributed largely to the success of the raid. Targets
were found and bombs were well aimed,' he said.[32]

In his action report Ronnie Hay, who had experienced
dozens of missions in all theatres of the war, reckoned it was
'the most interesting and successful operation I know of', praising the accurate Avenger bombing in the 'face of maximum

discouragement'. The fighter escort, he added, 'proved itself against the most serious air opposition it has so far met'. Admiral Vian's assessment was that, in executing the plan, the squadrons had pushed the 'limit of human endeavour'.[33]

The British Avengers' impressive debut had exacted a price. On the ground almost 200 men were killed and 300 injured, mainly Japanese military personnel but also a handful of Sumatran civilians. Damage to both refineries was extensive. Over the following five months average monthly oil production was halved. Repairs were limited to plants producing aviation fuel and other essential products, and the most severely damaged installations were abandoned. One senior British commander said later, 'I consider Meridian achieved its object and dealt the Japanese oil industry in Sumatra a severe blow from which only a very partial recovery will be possible'.[34]

But while the Royal Navy had clearly hit the refineries hard, just how severe was this blow for the wider Japanese war effort? According to an unpublished War Office report written in 1946 for Major General Sir Harold Redman, chief of staff Allied Land Forces South East Asia, the facts suggest that actually the attacks 'did not seriously hinder Japanese operations'.[35] Indeed, in the months following the strikes, despite the Palembang refineries producing less oil overall production levels didn't drop by a great deal, as output was increased in other plants across Sumatra. Smaller 'field refineries' were also built in the jungle, which the Japanese hoped wouldn't attract further attacks. They had also accumulated large stocks of oil in Singapore, which helped make up the shortfall. All army and air force units were told to economize on fuel, and the only effect the reduction in oil production had was in hampering training. Just fifty days after the raids the plants at Palembang were restored to 80 per cent of their pre-bombing production capacity, and it was only the lack of oil tankers that forced production to be reduced to about half.

However, the report also looked at the wider strategic impact of the strikes. 'The raids had a great jitter-effect on the Japanese,' it concluded, and by striking Palembang, 'one of the most strategic points in the Southern Regions, on one hand meant a bold leap in the Allied tactics and on the other hand it caused undeniable irritation among Japanese military circles as well as the general public'. In other words, it was the symbolic and propaganda effect of the two Palembang strikes by the British Pacific Fleet that was perhaps most important. To the Japanese, 'this direct attack by the Allies against one of the most strategic points in Japanese-held territory was considered to indicate a stepping-up of tempo of Allied strategy'.

Crucially, the strike came when the Japanese were also feeling the pressure elsewhere. Oil supplies from the East Indies to Japan itself had been all but cut off by defeat in a series of actions in the Philippines; the Allied reoccupation of Burma was already well under way, and the previous November B-29s had begun bombing the Japanese home islands.

In Britain no public mention was initially made of the carriers' role in the strikes. A week later, however, Fraser signalled Vian, 'I am glad to say that the Admiralty have now agreed to publish the names of the carriers who have so gallantly taken part.' Even so, news of the strikes was barely picked up by the newspapers back home.[36]

Admiral Vian had initially considered a third strike on the refineries, and wasn't happy that the objective of completely incapacitating the refineries had not been achieved. But the effectiveness of another strike was questionable given the depleted strike force and exhausted young aircrews. Besides, it was out of the question anyway as the ships now only had enough oil left to reach Australia if they steamed there directly.

As the fleet began its two-week voyage to Australia, sitting in his cabin Vian knew Operation Meridian had had another effect. Crucially, it had shown Nimitz that the British Pacific Fleet was capable of carrying out American-style carrier strikes. Despite their losses, the crews and ships' companies held their heads high, knowing they now had a considerable notch in their belts. A total of fifty-five aircrew would later be decorated, including Ronnie Hay, who received a Distinguished Service Order to add to his collection of gongs, and Bob Taylor, who received a Distinguished Service Medal.

At eleven minutes past five on the afternoon of 29 January 1945, *Whelp* signalled *Victorious* with a simple message: 'Propose to bury late Sub-Lieut Gunn after dark today Monday unless you have any wishes to the contrary.' Fourteen minutes later *Victorious* signalled back, 'Reply . . . Your 1711. Thank you, concur.'[37]

After sunset the stokers deep in the boiler room of *Whelp* were ordered to reduce speed as a small group of figures quietly gathered in the darkness on the quarterdeck to say farewell to Tommy Gunn. Sewn into a white hammock, with weights attached to his feet, his body was laid on a flat timber catafalque supported by trestles and covered in a white ensign. Against the gentle hum of the ship's engines, Whelp's captain, Commander George Norfolk, used a dimmed torch to read aloud the burial service from the Anglican Book of Common Prayer. Ian Paterson and Bob Taylor looked on in 'confusion, loss and absolute despair. It was very simple. Very respectful,' said Paterson. Finally, the board was raised and their friend slipped from beneath the ensign and into the sea, committed to the deep for ever.

13

The body crashers

The Japanese airmen who had stumbled across the British Pacific
Fleet off the coast of Sumatra at the end of January 1945 were at
best outflown, at worst incompetent and either way largely impotent. If they had any premeditated objectives, they were not
achieved. For what appeared to be the first kamikaze attacks on
the fleet, the British had got off extremely lightly. The same
couldn't be said for the Americans, however. Four months before
the British struck Palembang in the two Meridian operations US
forces had begun the great struggle to retake the Philippines. This
mosaic of islands in the equatorial heat of the Far East were a crucial bridge between Japan's oil-rich conquered lands in south-east
Asia and the Japanese home islands. An Allied victory here would
up the pressure on the vast Japanese empire and further emphasize its isolation.

In the way were 400,000 Japanese troops. The American invasion was overseen by General Douglas MacArthur, who decided
an amphibious assault on the island of Leyte would allow him to
build airfields from which land planes could then be used to give
him control of the skies and assist in the liberation of the rest of
the archipelago. The operation was preceded by a series of mass
strikes by Nimitz's carrier boys.

In the middle of October 1944 the fighters and bombers of
Admiral William Halsey's fleet launched more than 2,500 sorties
against targets on various islands south of Japan. Over 500
Japanese aircraft were destroyed in three days. Nevertheless, the
Japanese navy's attempt to lure Halsey's ships into an elaborate

trap around Leyte Gulf almost succeeded. This would have been embarrassing for Halsey and resulted in serious losses – although probably not overall defeat – for MacArthur's landing troops. But the Japanese faltered at the critical moment and failed to press home their advantage. Instead, the Battle of Leyte Gulf ended with the Imperial Japanese Navy effectively destroyed. It had lost three battleships, four carriers, ten cruisers and nine destroyers.

Crucially for the Allies, their losses meant Japanese pilots were being rushed through training and straight into action with about a hundred hours' flying time and no combat experience. Many didn't even reach the carriers. A dearth of qualified instructors for trainee pilots' conversion to more powerful aircraft exacerbated the problem, and in the first quarter of 1944 alone 524 fighters were lost in training accidents. But from these ashes a phoenix rose which was to have a direct impact on the British fleet and its aircrews once they reached the Pacific.

On 19 October 1944 Yukio Seki, a handsome twenty-three-year-old naval academy graduate, sat down in front of Wing Commander Asaichi Tamai at Mabalacat airfield in the Philippines. Seki was the son of an antique dealer and had grown up in rural Japan. A promising sportsman at school, his parents' divorce had resulted in financial hardship. He was unable to attend high school and forced instead to join the navy in 1938. Four years later he applied to naval flying school, and by 1944 he had been made an instructor.

Seki had a passion for art and off duty enjoyed quietly sketching and drawing. He fell in love with the daughter of a family who lived near the flying school and they married in May 1944, but their happiness was short lived. In September Seki was posted to Formosa and then Luzon, the main island in the Philippines. Admiral Takijiro Onishi, who commanded the Japanese naval air forces on the islands, had agreed that attaching 500-pound bombs to fighter planes and diving them into targets would achieve more damage than conventional attacks. Initially, the concept was called *shimpu*, meaning 'divine wind', but it soon became better known by a name which would haunt thousands of American and British servicemen – kamikaze.

Onishi needed an experienced naval airman for the inaugural kamikaze attack, and Tamai asked Seki if he would agree to lead a unit of Zero fighters. Seki agreed, and the following day pilots of the 201 Air Group assembled before Onishi, who, described as 'pallid and troubled' by onlookers, told them, 'Japan is in grave danger. The salvation of your country is now beyond the powers of the ministers of state, or the general staff and lowly commanders like myself. Therefore, on behalf of your hundred million countrymen, I ask of you this sacrifice and pray for your success . . . You are already gods, without earthly desires. You are going to enter on a long sleep.'[1]

Onishi shook hands with the pilots and wished them luck. At 7.25 a.m. on 25 October 1944 Seki and his Shikishima unit of nine suicide aircraft took off. Almost three and a half hours later Seki flew his Zeke into the deck of the USS *St Lo*, an American escort carrier. The resulting fireball penetrated the flight deck and roared into the hangar below, where aircraft were being refuelled. More than one hundred men were killed. Seki had made history. He was branded a hero in the Japanese papers and posthumously promoted two ranks.[2]

Yet in reality Seki was something of a reluctant hero. He told a reporter off the record just before his final mission that the dwindling numbers of experienced airmen should not be squandered but used instead to train other pilots. Alive to his duty, however, he proceeded. In his final letter to his parents Seki acknowledged Japan was at the 'crossroads of defeat' but concluded, 'because Japan is an Imperial Domain, I shall carry out a body-crashing attack on an aircraft carrier to repay the Imperial Benevolence. I am resigned to do this.'[3]

Until Seki's raid, suicide attacks by the Japanese had been one-off improvised affairs when pilots knew their aircraft was so damaged that a return to base was out of the question. Now dedicated suicide units were formed. A torrent of pilot volunteers willing to sacrifice their lives came forward. Over the following months hundreds of airmen joined the Special Attack Units. Many cherished the chance to sacrifice their lives for the greater good. Others, privately, did not but volunteered out of honour. Whether they were enthusiastic or not was hardly the point. After a cautious beginning, the Japanese high command concluded that organized suicide attacks offered the best prospect of stopping the American forces, given conventional tactics against a far superior enemy had failed and led to huge losses. Hundreds of pilots, most with little experience, were rapidly trained and then shipped across to the Philippines for their kamikaze missions.

American casualties in the seas around the Philippines mounted as they were hit by wave after wave of kamikazes. Observers noted how the Japanese approached using the cover of returning US carrier aircraft to confuse the American radar operators. Some attacks were coordinated in their approach, with skilful use of cloud cover to evade defending American fighters, but in the final moments it was every man for himself.

Japanese tactics varied. Sometimes decoys were used to draw off American fighter patrols, with the remaining attackers splitting up into small groups at sea level, climbing at full power, before carrying out steep dives out of the sun from heights of up to 10,000 feet. Other pilots feigned torpedo attacks by approaching American ships at sea level, only pulling up at the last minute to 300–500 feet, turning and diving sharply. Some even attacked almost vertically, but for the less experienced pilots approaching the target using a shallow glide of around twenty degrees allowed adjustments to be made in the final moments to ensure a hit. The focus of the attack depended on the nature of the target. The sweet spot in a battleship or cruiser was the bridge; attacking destroyers and smaller ships, pilots aimed for the side of the hull; in carriers hitting the flight deck on the lift created the greatest chance of penetrating the hangar. US servicemen were faced with a terrifying death or horrific injury as thousands of tons of aviation fuel in the hangar could be ignited by a single aircraft smashing through the wooden flight deck.

Franklin, *Intrepid* and *Belleau Wood* were among the American carriers most badly damaged over the following weeks. Cruisers, destroyers and battleships were also all targeted. The bombs the kamikaze planes carried were relatively small. It was often the aviation fuel and ammunition 'cooking off' which actually caused the most damage and casualties.

An internal British Admiralty staff paper written in March 1945 confirmed that by employing kamikaze attacks the Japanese were indeed getting, in Admiral Fraser's words, 'more bang per plane with a less well trained pilot' than with conventional strikes.[4] Of the ninety-four suicide attacks carried out off the Philippines in October, four actually sank American ships while thirty more hit and damaged ships. 'The suicide attacks were more profitable to the Japanese than non-suicide attacks by a factor of the order 10', the report concluded.[5]

From 20 October 120,000 troops of MacArthur's Sixth Army battled to take Leyte in tropical rain and over difficult hilly terrain, often against skilful and defiant Japanese opposition. By the end of the year they had largely secured the island at the cost of more than 15,000 American casualties, with eventual Japanese dead numbering more than three times this. On 15 December MacArthur began the second phase of his campaign, and three weeks later his forces landed at Lingayen Gulf, halfway up Luzon, the largest island in the Philippines. This vast amphibious assault was again targeted by kamikazes. Among the armada of American ships supporting the landings was the battleship *New Mexico*. Admiral Fraser was aboard, keen to see the landings for himself and to evaluate how effective the American defence against suicide attacks was. His own British Pacific Fleet might have to confront the same spectre before long.

On the morning of 6 January 1945, accompanied by General Sir Herbert Lumsden, recently dispatched as Churchill's special representative to General MacArthur, Fraser watched from the ship's bridge as the Americans opened up their bombardment from battleships and cruisers. Fraser crossed over to the starboard side after being beckoned over by American Vice Admiral Jesse Oldendorf, an action which saved his life. Seconds later a Japanese plane smashed into the port wing of *New Mexico*'s bridge. Lumsden and the ship's captain were killed instantly, but among the fire, chaos and dead bodies, Fraser had escaped serious injury.

Fraser's experience had two consequences. Firstly, every man in the British Pacific Fleet now knew that, deskbound though he'd be, their commander-in-chief had been at the sharp end and knew personally what it was like to go through the unique and distinctly chilling experience of a kamikaze attack. Secondly, Fraser was able to report back to London first hand about kamikaze tactics and how the Americans defended themselves by saturating the air with anti-aircraft fire.

Lumsden's death shocked Churchill, coming as it did just twenty-four hours after he'd received a personal signal from Edward Wood, Earl of Halifax and Britain's ambassador in the States, reporting President Roosevelt's increasing concern about this new weapon. 'He was bothered about Japanese suicide aircraft attacks on their ships . . .' Wood told Churchill, 'which meant that they were constantly losing 40 or 50 American sailors for one Japanese and was not very sanguine about early end of either war.'[6]

Churchill turned to his friend and trusted scientific adviser, Professor Frederick Lindemann – an important influence on much of the prime minister's wartime thinking – to suggest ways the British Pacific Fleet could be protected from kamikaze attacks. Churchill was so concerned he considered sending a telegram to Roosevelt asking for help in trialling new weapons. Lindemann, who had become Lord Cherwell in 1941, drafted a note detailing possible solutions. These included the K rocket, which fired a curtain of mines to a height of 20,000 feet. Each mine consisted of a bomb suspended by 1,000 feet of wire from a parachute. The bomb was detonated by an aircraft snagging the wire. But First Sea Lord Andrew Cunningham immediately rejected Lindemann's idea, pointing out the limitations of a device which would need a thousand rockets to stop one suicide fighter and weighed eight tons. Churchill remained concerned about the threat the kamikazes posed to the British Pacific Fleet, however. 'It would be a pity if naval thoughts on this matter were not active,' he told Cunningham. 'Cannot a shell be made which casts out, like a star, obstructions or splinters in all directions? . . . Please give the utmost stimulus to all inquiries and set your best brains to finding a remedy for this great danger.'[7]

Cunningham replied that various ideas had been tested, including giant flame-throwers, guided missiles and flash weapons to distract the pilots. None, he concluded, was as effective as conventional anti-aircraft fire, adding, 'There is no doubt the first line of defence against suicide bombers or any other airborne attack is, and is likely to remain, an adequate number of well-directed fighter aircraft.' A secret memo based on information sent by British liaison officers stationed with the American fleet circulated by Admiral Fraser's staff in January 1945 agreed, stating that the kamikaze was 'the most dangerous form of air attack so far developed; its defeat will call for skilful fighter direction, backed up by resolute, accurate and well-distributed gun fire.'[8]

Fraser also had other issues to contend with. At the beginning of February 1945, as his carriers made their way to Australia fresh from the Palembang strikes, rumours continued to swirl on both sides of the Atlantic and in Australia that Admiral King resented the Royal Navy taking any part in the Pacific war, and believed that the British ships and men were not prepared, trained or equipped for it. To counter these notions, Admiral Fraser ensured reporters were briefed that there were no operational difficulties and the British Pacific Fleet would be ready for action. It was, he said, up to Admiral Nimitz what he wanted to do with the fleet, including whether it might be used to assist MacArthur's amphibious operations in the south-west Pacific.

Privately, however, he was getting frustrated and wrote to Nimitz requesting assurances his fleet would assist the US Fifth

Fleet in the invasion of Okinawa, a strategically crucial island just 350 miles south of the Japanese home islands, planned for 1 April 1945. Nimitz told reporters the British fleet would be used at the right time and in the best way to contribute to the success of the war against Japan. The reality was that Fraser and his fleet were pawns in an ongoing power struggle between Nimitz, MacArthur and King.

In the meantime the excitement in the fleet continued to grow. After a brief stop in the western Australian port of Fremantle, it sailed into Sydney Harbour on 10 February 1945, cheered by huge crowds of Australians waving union flags. For thousands of airmen and sailors, Sydney became a place of sanctuary and escape after long periods at sea. Each man was given a bag from the 'People of Australia' containing tinned pears, a Christmas pudding, a half-pound bar of Cadbury's Dairy Milk, boiled sweets, some shaving soap, a pencil and writing paper.

The men were ready for some much-needed rest and recuperation. 'There promised to be a very interesting lecture at 9.15 a.m. today,' wrote Ken Ward in his diary in *Indefatigable*. 'The Principal Medical Officer is speaking on "Australian Women: Where, When and How Often". He would have had a very attentive audience, had he given any such lecture. It turned out to be a buzz, and the gathering that had formed dispersed rapidly. Revenge is threatened to the perpetrator.'[9]

The people of Sydney donated £200,000 towards the building of the British Centre, a smart whitewashed prefabricated hostel and recreation centre. At its height, 6,000 meals were served daily and 1,200 beds provided each night. It had a sprung wooden dance floor. Three hundred women, taken from a voluntary roster of 63,000, attended each night as 'dance hostesses' and 4,000 Australians worked there.[10] Thousands of Australian families threw open their homes, providing food and lodging for men and officers. It was high summer, and the crews saw the country through a rainbow haze after weeks at sea.

Prince Philip, now second in command of *Whelp*, was roped

in to provide a touch of glamour at a press conference in Melbourne. 'Looking like a typical British naval officer with curling blonde beard and a cynical Cowardesque way of speech, he refused any attempt at a build-up of romantic background,' wrote one reporter. 'To the question, "Are you married?" The Prince responded with a fervent "God forbid."'[11]

The Australian government had, albeit reluctantly, allowed the British Pacific Fleet to use Sydney as its main base. New docks were built for the warships and their support vessels. Airfields were constructed for the squadrons. Over the coming months hundreds of ships arrived. The headquarters of the fleet was established above a motorcar showroom in Kings Cross, 'a rather sleazy district of Sydney, roughly equivalent to London's Soho'.[12] Wrens shipped over from the UK worked as cooks, clerks and teleprinter operators, and sorted the fleet's mail.

In addition to building up the fighting fleet, Fraser and his staff had to juggle the huge demands of assembling a fleet train from scratch. The Americans had declared that the British Pacific Fleet could only take part in operations if it was self-sufficient in provisions, ammunition and equipment. While oil would be shared from bulk stores with the USN, the Royal Navy would have to put in as much as it took out. From his headquarters in Melbourne, Rear Admiral Charles Daniel was responsible for ensuring the fleet train did its job. Supplies would need to be ferried to forward bases in the Admiralty Islands or on Leyte – once they'd been secured by the Americans – before being taken on to replenish the fleet in the operating area. With Fraser hoping that the British Pacific Fleet would have a strength of 100,000 men by July 1945, this was a massive task.

With the front line 4,000 miles away from Sydney, Fraser tried to illustrate the vast geographical and political challenge to the Admiralty back in Britain: 'The distances involved are similar to those of a fleet based in Alexandria, and with advanced anchorages in Gibraltar and the Azores, attacking the North American coast between Labrador and Nova Scotia,' he said.[13] Admiral Vian admitted, 'The distances were staggering to those of us accustomed to the conditions of the European War.'[14]

The fighting fleet would need to be supplied with everything from airmen, aircraft and ammunition to vegetables, beer and cigarettes while remaining at sea for months at a time. The Americans had perfected a logistical system using a series of forward bases which could be assembled or dismantled as quickly as the front ebbed and flowed. This meant they could keep up the pressure on Japanese forces by maintaining a modern, fully equipped fleet off the enemy's coastline.

The British promise to operate independently from the American fleet was an almighty scramble, and the Royal Navy had to learn on the hoof. The problems of physical distance and an immensely long supply chain were compounded by political complications, with Fraser and Daniel having to deal with London, Australia but also the Americans, under whose command the forward bases were. Much depended too on the war ending in Germany so that ships could be released. The fleet train could only grow as and when they became available, and when they did arrive, many of the ships were in a poor state of repair and totally unsuited for work in the heat of the tropics. Even so, by VJ Day the fleet train supplying the British units on the front line consisted of 125 ships crewed by more than 26,000 men. This included more than 20 victualling ships which constantly ferried food and clothing from Australia to the fleet. Each was capable of carrying a month's supply of food for 30,000 men, as well as clothes and mess gear for 10,000.[15] The fleet would consume millions of pounds of meat and vegetables. Supplies to canteens included 50,000,000 cigarettes and 800,000 razor blades every month.[16]

Replacement aircraft were sent from Britain. They often required refurbishment, having been exposed to sea spray and rain, or had been packed in pieces to be assembled from scratch. One of the main challenges was having the right piece arrive at the right place at the right time. Planners learned to think in terms of months and thousands of miles. Ammunition needed to have left Britain not less than three months before it was required.

This massive effort came at a price. The Australian government agreed to contribute more than £21,000,000 in the first six months of 1945 alone, including £10,000,000 on food, £2,000,000 on ships' maintenance and repairs, £250,000 on medical and dental equipment and £250,000 on clothing.[17] Supply requirements were worked out at 20 tons of food and 10 tons of general stores weekly for every 1,000 men afloat.[18] Supplies were stored in one of the largest naval and air depots in the world, covering more than 1,000,000 square feet and employing some 1,500 people.[19] All this diverted much-needed investment from Australian domestic affairs. Australians would have to sacrifice much and posters declared, DON'T LET THE NAVY DOWN.[20] But throughout 1945 supplies were hit by dock strikes and union disputes.

At the end of February 1945 Admiral Fraser received permission from the Americans to move the fleet towards the war zone, and on 7 March the British arrived at Manus, a wooded island in the Admiralty Islands recently captured by the US Navy, which had set about building a vast naval and air base, with living quarters for 150,000 men, fuel depots and repair shops. The British Pacific Fleet sat off Manus for over a week, crews and sailors wilting in the scorching heat and humidity while their destiny was discussed in air-conditioned offices on the other side of the world. Just two degrees from the equator, the conditions made a mockery of Churchill's promise in the House of Commons the previous September of a 'tropicalized' fleet. Finally, on 14 March, a signal from Admiral King arrived at the British Pacific Fleet's Sydney headquarters: 'You are to operate under Nimitz.' King had relented under pressure, helped no doubt, by Fraser's continued lobbying. However, King retained the right to transfer the British fleet to MacArthur's south-west Pacific command with just seven days' notice.

When it wasn't operating air strikes under Admiral Vian, the British Pacific Fleet would be commanded at sea by Vice Admiral

Sir Bernard Rawlings, a quiet, likeable man, who shunned publicity but shone as a tactician and politician. He had commanded in the Mediterranean during some of the fiercest fighting and had the experience required to balance the delicate political niceties of operating with the Americans in the field. Rawlings knew the Japanese better than most, having spent three years in Japan as a naval attaché. He set the tone immediately with Nimitz: 'It is with a feeling of great pride and pleasure that the British Pacific Fleet joins the US Naval Forces under your command.' Nimitz replied, 'The United States Pacific Fleet welcomes the British Carrier Task Force and attached units which will greatly add to our power to strike the enemy and will also show our unity of purpose in the war against Japan.'[21]

It was an historic moment. For the first time in the Second World War, the Royal Navy was working under the direct command of the Americans, although their orders were issued in the form of requests. Fraser agreed to adopt the American style of signalling and other operating procedures. Men had to learn new signal flags and pennants; commanding officers were given reams of paperwork to plough through. All British aircraft were repainted a deep royal blue. The traditional Fleet Air Arm roundel with its red circle was replaced by a blue and white circle in a white bar, which from a distance was intentionally difficult to distinguish from American aircraft markings. This was also to ensure the roundel was not mistaken for the red 'meatball' painted on Japanese planes, reducing the chance of friendly-fire incidents.

Four days later, the British Pacific Fleet, now Task Force 57, weighed anchor for the USN's advance base at Ulithi in the Caroline Islands to refuel. The massive lagoon, twenty miles long and six miles wide, was filled with more than 1,000 American warships and assault vessels of all kind, preparing for the invasion of Okinawa. There the squadron COs from all four British carriers gathered in *Indomitable*'s hot wardroom for one last conference. The familiar figure of Admiral Vian walked in. 'Stand up, the flying boys!' said Vian. 'I've a short message. No. Don't bother taking notes. It's only four words for you to take back to your air-crews. GET BLOODY STUCK IN! Any more questions? Right, and the best of luck to you.'[22]

Japan recognized that an American assault on Okinawa was a prelude to a major landing on the Japanese home islands. No attempt was made by the government to conceal from its people the grave situation they now faced, with one newspaper in Tokyo announcing that the loss of the island would leave Japan with no hope of turning the course of the war.[23] But if enough American blood was shed in the process of taking Okinawa, Japan's leaders believed President Roosevelt, bowing to public pressure, wouldn't have the stomach for an all-out invasion of Japan, and they could negotiate for peace. The Japanese were correct in their former assessment, but few realized at that stage just how mistaken they were in assuming the alternative to an invasion was a peace settlement.

The American Chiefs of Staff had sound strategic reasons for capturing Okinawa. It had a good natural harbour and would provide a platform to launch B-29 bombing raids on Japan. They still hoped a blockade and bombing would achieve victory, but if Japan did not surrender, Okinawa was only 350 miles from Kyushu – the southernmost of its four main islands – where Operation Olympic, the invasion of the Japanese home islands, was scheduled to commence the following October.

Sixty miles long and up to eighteen miles wide, Okinawa sits in the middle of the Ryukyu archipelago – a chain of more than one hundred islands strung out across 800 miles in a gentle curve from the south of Kyushu in Japan to the north-eastern tip of Formosa, off the coast of China. The Japanese had established airfields on many of the larger islands, which they used to move aircraft and supplies back and forth between Japan and Formosa. The Japanese were all too aware of the strategic importance of the Ryukyu Islands. Okinawa alone was defended by more than 80,000 troops and 20,000 conscript Okinawans. All the islands had been closed to outsiders for years, and intelligence was scarce as to the strength of their defences. The Americans took no chances. Saving only the D-Day invasion of Normandy, the landings on Okinawa – code name Operation Iceberg – were the greatest amphibious assault of the Second World War. Almost 300,000 soldiers, marines and logistics staff were embarked in more than 1,000 vessels for an invasion which would commence on 1 April 1945.

The crucial air support for the invasion was provided almost exclusively by carrier fighter cover from the US Navy's mighty Fifth Fleet, commanded at sea by Admiral Raymond Spruance, who reported to Nimitz back in Hawaii. Spearheading this was the battle-hardened Task Force 58, split into four task groups and comprising up to fifteen fast carriers with a striking power of 1,000 Avengers, Hellcats and Corsairs supported by battleships, cruisers and destroyers. Its commander, Rear Admiral Marc Mitscher, was a master of modern carrier fighting, and had fine-tuned the art of using his task groups separately or together, depending on the size of the operation.

The Japanese knew their air force was no match for that being amassed by the Allies. Their answer was the kamikaze. The Americans estimated that using conventional tactics a Japanese pilot might make two sorties only in his lifetime, with a 3 per cent chance of hitting a ship. In a suicide attack the chance of hitting a ship rose to 15–20 per cent with just one sortie.[24] Indeed one study reckoned it was up to ten times more profitable for the Japanese to use kamikaze strikes.[25] Japanese commanders knew too, by this point in the war, that their pilots had little chance of coming back alive, even when they used conventional attack methods. Utilized sparingly until now, the Okinawa operations saw a dramatic escalation in the use of this terrifying weapon.

Ahead of the American amphibious assault, on 18 March 1945 Mitscher's carrier boys swept over airfields on Kyushu. The Japanese quickly retaliated. The following day USS *Franklin* lost almost 800 of her crew when two bombs dropped in a low-level Japanese attack smashed through her wooden deck, blowing up in the hangar below and igniting tons of fuel in a huge fireball. The Americans knew they were open to attack on their exposed left flank – Formosa, 400 miles to the west, had numerous airfields and was used extensively to train suicide pilots – so they asked the British Pacific Fleet to 'neutralize' key airfields on the Sakishima Islands, which ran like stepping stones between Formosa and Okinawa, hoping the Japanese would then be prevented from staging reinforcements through the islands. The British Pacific Fleet's aircrews were expected to put the airstrips out of action and hunt down kamikazes in the air or on the ground. The fleet would, in effect, act as an independent force. The length of the operation would depend on how long the Americans took to capture Okinawa.

For the next eight weeks the intensity of operations at sea would test the FAA like never before.

At 06.30 on 23 March 1945 the British Pacific Fleet sailed out of Ulithi and steamed north for its 1,200-mile journey, led once again by the four carriers of the 1st Aircraft Carrier Squadron and a strike force of more than 200 aircraft. Mitscher sent a signal to Rawlings: 'Fifth Fleet welcomes Task Force 57 and wishes you good hunting.'[26]

For the first time the crews began to realize the huge scale of the Pacific. For day upon day they saw nothing but other ships, ocean and sky. A canvas of blues and greys. There was an unsettling vastness to it all. Giant clouds towering into the sky sat on the horizon like sentries, blushed pink by the setting sun. Intense tropical downpours developed in minutes, whipping the sea into a boiling swell. Just as quickly the skies would clear, turning the rainwater on the decks into clouds of steam. Flying fish sprang out of the sea alongside the ships, using their silvery fins to skim over the surface for fifty feet before plopping back into the water. Distant storms would flicker silently on the horizon. In the pitch black of the nights the wakes of the ships emitted a ghostly phosphorus glow as millions of microscopic plankton churned to the surface.

Aircrews were briefed. A few months before, most had never even heard of Okinawa, let alone the Sakishima Islands. In the wardroom in *Indefatigable* Ken Ward noted the reaction of his fellow flyers when the CO pointed to a map and said, "'Here is the group Sakishima Gunto in the left-hand corner. Here, in the right-hand corner, is the Japanese mainland, the island of Kyushu.' There was a most audible gasp from his audience, and looks of intermingled surprise and joy. Perhaps it was twitch too,' wrote Ward.[27] They were just 1,000 miles from Tokyo.

The two main targets were six airfields on the islands of Miyako and Ishigaki. From the air these were stunning little coral-ringed islands shaped like saucepans, fringed with pale blue lagoons and sandy white beaches – Robinson Crusoe territory. But this myth would soon be shattered. A mixture of flat plains, lagoons, mangrove swamps and hills covered in tropical rainforest, in reality the islands were little more than military outposts. Malaria was rife. In 1945 alone more than half of the 20,000 population of Ishigaki contracted the disease and almost 2,500 died.[28]

According to American air intelligence photos, the airfields, which were used by aircraft from both the Japanese army and navy, were heavily defended. The main airfield on Ishigaki was protected by one hundred light and heavy anti-aircraft guns, while Hirara airfield on Miyako had almost seventy. These airfields would need to be bombed up to four times a day, depending on photographic results from reconnaissance Hellcats. Fighters would patrol over the islands regularly to shoot down any Japanese aircraft that managed to take off and maintain combat air patrols over the fleet in case it was attacked.

On the evening of Sunday 25 March the crews received more detailed briefings. Maps, data and aerial photographs were pinned on boards. The latest 'gen' (flyers' argot for information) from intelligence photos showed anti-aircraft posts and revetments that were potential hiding places for planes. As usual, the ships' bars were open but there were few takers that evening. Instead, the crews drifted off to their cabins, wrote letters home and tried to get some sleep. As he went to bed, Ken Ward noted in his diary that the sea was looking 'very angry . . . all the time, we could feel the ship quivering from blows by the sea'.

Before dawn on Monday 26 March the British Pacific Fleet arrived in its first operating area, one hundred miles south of Miyako. The twenty-eight rapid notes of the 'Hands to flying stations' bugle call echoed through the PA system. Men ran down passages, up ladders and across decks. Myriad signal flags were hoisted. Orders were relayed through the speakers; aircraft were armed and fuelled in the hangars; buzzers, bells and further bugle calls issued instructions. Up on the bridge telephones rang and voice pipes sang with communications to other parts of the ship. All the while the soundtrack of the fleet went on – the rhythmic jolt of the screws powering the ships through the water, the high-pitched whirring of lifts and gun turrets, the roar of fans forcing fetid air through miles of pipes and the growl of aircraft engines.

Rather than a single mass strike Palembang-style, Admiral Vian planned a series of smaller raids. This first day's operations would begin with a sweep of the airfields by forty-eight Hellcats and Corsairs and be followed by a strike of twenty-four Avengers escorted by the same number of Corsairs. These two strikes would be supplemented by smaller sweeps throughout the day depending on enemy activity. Individual crews could expect two or three missions a day and to be airborne for as much as five or six hours in total and up to four and a half hours at a time. It would be physically shattering.

At sunset the fleet would withdraw south for the night, before repeating the process the following day. After two or three days it would sail 300 miles south to a prearranged patch of ocean to meet the fleet train, spend up to three days taking on fuel, spare aircraft and pilots, food, stores and post, before steaming north once again to repeat the strikes. Smaller escort carriers would provide replacement aircraft and protective air patrols so the front-line pilots could rest.

If there was any risk of enemy attack, the entire fleet would remain at action stations throughout the day's strike. All water-tight scuttles and doors would be sealed, creating particularly fetid conditions below decks. On the carriers the men working on the flight deck, in the island, and manning the sixteen 4.5-inch AA guns in their turrets and dozens of exposed smaller guns would don white flame-proof clothing, hoods and steel helmets. Every-one would remain in their positions. Meals, such as 'tiddly-oggies', which were rather like Cornish pasties and easy to eat quickly, were passed around.

The aircrews didn't know how the Japanese would react. But memories of Palembang still loomed large for Ian Paterson, who recalled, 'on that particular day before taking off I have never felt as absolutely . . . I can't describe it . . . I just felt like jelly . . . I was more scared to admit to anybody that I was scared than I was to go on with it. So it was a case of gritting one's teeth. But I didn't feel as though I had any strength at all.'[29]

Paterson's nerves were based on experience but, facing their first action, sprog pilots had fear of the unknown to cope with. As usual, a revolver and ammo were issued to each aircrew member before flying over enemy territory. These were handed back during non-operational periods. On the order 'Pilots, man your aircraft', the pilots strode out of the island and made their way across the slippery flight deck, climbing into their machines in the half-light of the Pacific morning.

'We did our own checks and then came the worst part, the waiting and time to wonder what lay ahead. That sinking feeling in the pit of the stomach knowing the many things which could go wrong,' one pilot said.[30] Over the loudspeakers, the flight deck parties were ordered to 'Stand clear of propellers' followed by

'Start up.' The aircraft signal flag – a red diamond on a white back-ground – was quickly hoisted and fluttered in the strong breeze.

Activity intensified. A few backfires, belching flames and the noise of powerful whirring props filled the air. The pilots felt the throbbing of the ship's engines intensify, the deck heeling as the massive carrier turned into the wind. The deck commander signalled for the first Corsair to rev its engine to maximum, then swung his green flag down to the go position. One by one the planes leaped forward, their tails quickly rising as they hurtled away.

Forty-five minutes later the outline of Miyako island appeared in the distance through the clouds, and their first target, Nobara airfield, 6,000 feet below, could be made out, its criss-cross white landing strips framed against the surrounding green fields like an asterisk. Pilots reported feeling twinges of fear, yet also the 'thirst for revenge' upon seeing their target as they recalled rumours of Japanese mistreatment and executions of their colleagues.[31] But revenge had to be tempered. The fighter pilots were reminded once again not to do more strafing sweeps over the airfields than was prudent – no matter how tempting.

Fighters flew in standard configurations as laid down in 'Naval Air Fighting Instructions', such as the finger formation, which comprised a flight of four aircraft spaced around 30 yards apart with the flight leader in front and his wingman set back on one side, but squadron commanders were encouraged to design and perfect their own formations for strafing runs. Ramrods exposed fighter pilots to moments of extreme violence. During the few seconds of a strafing run – when they faced the biggest danger – pilots reacted in different ways. Some fell into a silent, focused concentration. Others muttered obscenities, sang or shouted to release the pressure in their eardrums as they came out of the dive, jinking across the airfield to avoid the flak.

One Corsair pilot detailed his strafing technique after the mission. He carried out attacks in a 20–30-degree dive at 250 knots through mist and light rain, starting his run at 200 feet and ending up at 'zero height'. He opened fire on each target at about 400 yards, and 'released the tit' at 100; all together, his two-to-three-second bursts expended only 147 rounds from his six 0.5-inch guns. After the attack he left the airfield 'low on deck', and did not return a second time.[32]

Following the fighter sweeps, the Avengers of 849 Squadron approached, flying through thick white cumulus cloud, the twelve aircraft huddled up close together but barely able to see the wing-tip of the adjacent aeroplane. Deploying into line astern, one by one the dark blue Avengers dived down like swifts, each dropping two of its four 500-pound bombs on hangars and aircraft on Nobara. After a quick check that no one was missing, the strike headed for Miyara airfield on Ishigaki, flying below the low cloud base and braving heavy anti-aircraft fire to bomb the runways. Meanwhile, Fireflies from 1770 Squadron had knocked out gun positions with 20-mm cannon and 60-pound rockets.

The crews were gripped by a mixture of excitement, fear and adrenaline. Over Ishigaki airfield a shell smashed through the cockpit of a Hellcat, but despite a splinter of hot metal cleaving through his right leg, the twenty-two-year-old New Zealand pilot pressed home his attack, in searing pain and losing blood fast. He then ripped open his first-aid pack and injected himself with morphine, flying a hundred miles alone back to the fleet, before landing on *Indomitable*'s flight deck.[33]

This was the typhoon season. Hot and sunny conditions could quickly break down, with high winds and driving rain reducing visibility. All aircrew had been given the bearing for where the fleet would be on their return. However, they also carried a piece of card with a circle divided into twelve segments with a different Morse code letter in each. When the homing beacon was switched on, the radio transmitted the Morse code of the segment the aircraft was currently flying in. The Morse code letter would change when the aircraft flew into an adjacent sector. The pilot could then determine if he was flying towards his carrier or away from it, making the necessary adjustments to zigzag his way back to the fleet.

The main body of the fleet covered an area of about sixteen square miles. At its centre was a cruiser with the four carriers stationed in a diamond around it. The battleships *King George V* and *Howe* along with four cruisers circled the carriers 4,000 yards out. A circle of destroyers provided a final protective shield of anti-aircraft fire, and acted as couriers between the carriers – delivering replacement parts, post and the occasional senior officer. Destroyers nicknamed body snatchers were also stationed behind each carrier like faithful dogs at heel, ready to pick up downed aircrew.

Throughout the day the whole fleet wheeled and turned in and out of the wind, for the carriers to land on and fly off strikes and escorts. When strikes returned, the aircraft would break into a left-hand circuit around the fleet until each squadron saw its own carrier, which flashed recognition signals. Each carrier had its own airspace, allowing squadrons to break up into flights orbiting at its stern, before being called in turn to fly up the starboard side of the carrier in tight echelon to a 'break-up point' and into a final circuit to land.

With their limited range, rather than going on strikes the Sea-fires provided combat air patrols at different altitudes above the fleet, watching out for enemy aircraft. In *Indefatigable*, Ken Ward had woken at 05.15, and was airborne two and a half hours later, landing at 09.45 to refuel before another two-hour patrol at 10.50. Ward had been on the 'jack patrol', flying at fifty feet above the water to intercept any attackers who might approach beneath the radar cover. 'We fly in pairs, up and down on each side of a square – the fleet in the middle, 5 minutes one way then 5 minutes back again. The day was very hazy with cloud at 3,000 feet, making it very difficult to see the fleet,' he wrote in his diary.

By the end of the first day of the British Pacific Fleet's participation in Operation Iceberg, one Avenger from 854 Squadron from *Illustrious* had been shot down, its three crew being killed, and one Corsair had been downed while strafing Hirara airfield. A dozen Japanese aircraft had been destroyed on the ground by the fighters, and although a number of enemy aircraft appeared on the radar, none had attacked the fleet. In all likelihood they were 'snoopers', sizing up the opposition to report back to the commanders on Formosa.

The Avenger crews had watched with satisfaction as their armour-piercing bombs sank deep into the runways and exploded, sending up huge showers of coral and earth and leaving behind deep craters. The success of this first action in the Pacific boosted spirits and the FAA flyers eagerly anticipated further encounters but, returning to the airfields for more strikes over the following days, they found the Japanese had simply filled in the craters. With no night fighters available, there was little they could do. It was impossible to keep the airfields permanently out of action. Army staff, labourers and even young trainee Japanese pilots all pitched in to help repair the runways overnight.

The crews of the British Pacific Fleet began to liken their daily sorties to businessmen commuting to work. 'Day by day morale deteriorated as losses and crashes mounted just for the sake of displacing earth for it to be replaced in a matter of hours,' said one pilot.[34] But the job had to be done. The cycle continued. And the casualties mounted. By the end of day two Task Force 57 had lost nine aircrew and six aircraft in combat. Another eleven aircraft had been lost operationally – most of them Seafires, their fragile frames crumpling on the pitching carrier decks in the Pacific swell.

Some pilots said they had never seen a more eerie place than the Sakishima Islands. 'You never see the least sign of life,' one told a reporter. 'No smoke comes from the chimneys, no cattle graze in the fields, no trucks drive on the roadway, no people ever walk about. It gives you the creeps to fly over the islands.'[35]

While anti-aircraft fire was not always as intense as in the European war, commanders noted that 'a new and threatening menace' had emerged in the form of smokeless, trackless munitions. 'This is a major debit point for the aircrews and makes anti-flak counters almost impossible by direct retaliation . . . aircraft do not know they are being fired at until they are hit.'[36] On the few occasions tracer was used, it was disconcerting for the attacking pilots. The Japanese were also experts at setting flak traps, using dummy aircraft to attract the ramrod fighters. Once the pilots were committed to a strafing run, the defenders opened up with intense bursts of anti-aircraft fire. 'You started off full of gung ho, but you went down with some trepidation eventually. Those little pink balls come past your eyes, you became aware they were spot on. You were jinking all over the place to try and get away. And when they filled the runways in overnight it made you think, *What the hell is this all about?*' said a New Zealander Corsair pilot with 1830 Squadron.[37]

A third day of air strikes on 28 March was cancelled when Admiral Rawlings learned a typhoon was approaching. He wanted to ensure the fleet was replenished, back and ready to strike the islands by 1 April, when the Americans would begin their assault 250 miles away on Okinawa. So the warships sailed south-east, skirting the typhoon, to rendezvous with the fleet train.

Casualties were transferred to the hospital ship, which by international convention was clearly marked as such, keeping its lights on at night and staying away from the main fleet. Refuelling began. Admiral Spruance signalled Rawlings to congratulate him on the first strikes. In *Indefatigable* Ken Ward and other airmen sat down to watch a screening of *Show Business*, a musical rom-com. It was Good Friday. Life seemed almost bearable. But in a matter of hours their newly established routine would come to a shuddering and explosive end.

14

April fools

Easter Sunday, 1 April 1945. The Americans landed in force on Okinawa, halfway up the island on the west coast. There was little resistance, but after establishing a firm bridgehead and pushing inland, they came to a grinding halt in their advance towards Naha, the capital, checked by stiff opposition. In the air the Japanese were slow to react, but when they did their response was fierce.

Two hundred and fifty miles to the south-west the twenty-two ships of Task Force 57 were once again poised off the Sakishima archipelago, preparing to launch a second cycle of strikes against the islands' airfields, having returned from the fuelling area the previous morning. Admiral Rawlings knew that the American invasion of Okinawa increased the chance of his fleet being attacked, so he adopted a new tactic, deploying a cruiser and destroyer thirty miles to the west of the fleet as a radar picket. The picket scoured returning strikes for enemy aircraft. Every British plane had to be visually identified before it was allowed to continue to the fleet. Fighters patrolled overhead ready to react.

Bearing in mind the British ships' maximum anti-aircraft-gun range was eleven miles and enemy planes travelled at approximately five miles a minute, the window in which to react was tiny. The picket vessels tripled the fleet's response time. Returning aircraft not passing the picket were treated as the enemy. Each plane was also fitted with an 'identification friend or foe' beacon, or IFF, as an additional safeguard.

Rawlings was right to be cautious. The Japanese were fully

aware of the British Pacific Fleet, and goaded the Americans, suggesting its presence was evidence they didn't have the balls to fight the final battle without their old ally. 'Although the enemy has been saying he will fight the Pacific War single-handed, his inability to do so is seen in the fact that he has been aided by the British forces in the Okinawa operations,' Rear Admiral Etsuzo Kurihara told the Japanese press. 'The British Fleet is aiding the Americans to a considerable extent. Several British battleships, including *King George V*, and regular aircraft carriers and other auxiliary warships are engaged in the naval operations around the Okinawa islands. We may say that the combined Anglo-American fleets in their entire strength have come to the Pacific Ocean to fight this country.'[1]

The sun hadn't yet risen at 06.15 on 1 April as eight Seafires thundered down *Indefatigable*'s gloomy flight deck, past the shadowy shape of the island and up into the dawn sky to begin their overhead patrols. Twenty-five minutes later two dozen Corsairs and Hellcats from *Victorious* and *Indomitable* took off, disappearing towards Ishigaki for the opening ramrods of the day. It was a beautiful morning. Officers were having breakfast at their stations. There was even time for a brief Easter Holy Communion service in the admiral's cabin in *King George V*.

But at ten to seven the fleet's radar picked up a formation of unidentified bogeys seventy-five miles to the west, flying at 8,000 feet and closing fast at 210 knots. A group of about twenty aircraft from the Japanese First Air Fleet based in Formosa was about to launch a kamikaze attack on the British Pacific Fleet.

Admiral Vian immediately recalled the Corsairs and Hellcats en route to Ishigaki and launched more fighters to support the combat air patrols. A well-practised drill clicked into place, with the fighter control officers in the plotting rooms of the carriers following the enemy contacts on the radar, directing fighters towards them. Forty miles from the fleet the incoming raid split in half, a classic tactic which made the attack more difficult to deal with as it presented the British fighters with more widely spread targets. At the same moment the first Corsair pilots made contact, shouting, 'Tally ho!' over the radio and ripping into the enemy. One Zero was shot down by *Victorious*' Corsairs, and moments later the squadron commander of 1844 Hellcat Squadron closed in on an Oscar, recalling afterwards how 'he was flying out of killing range and I carefully fired a good long blast over his port wing. He very kindly obliged by executing a rather difficult turn to port, which enabled me to close and shoot this unhappy amateur down.'[2]

In the fighter direction room in *Indefatigable*'s island twenty-four-year-old John Robertson – who trained as an observer – watched the Japanese attack develop over the radar. Robertson had been a prisoner of war of the Vichy French in Tunisia after his Swordfish crash-landed in the Sahara while he was attempting to deliver a Tunisian secret agent carrying a bicycle and a suitcase containing two million francs. Robertson later escaped from a POW camp in a tunnelled 'blitz out', before being recaptured and then finally released when the camp was overrun by advancing Allied forces. But in a somewhat baffling decision, not entirely alien to the bureaucratic monster that was the wartime Royal Navy, this experienced second-seat observer had been posted to the British Pacific Fleet in 24 Wing – the collective term for 894 and 887 Seafire squadrons – despite it comprising solely single-seat Seafires. He had become a self-declared 'nursemaid' and un-official mentor to *Indefatigable*'s Seafire pilots, who nicknamed him Grandpa because he was a few years older than most of them and had a big bushy red beard.

The fighter direction room was tense, hushed and lit only by the bluish glow of the radar screens. With enemy aircraft ap-proaching, everyone had donned their protective hoods and suits. Robertson watched two ratings in the gloom in the centre of the room working behind a vast perspex plotting board marked with a series of concentric rings with the ship in the middle. Using wax pencils, they scribbled the shifting positions of the aircraft on the board – enemy in red, defenders in green, writing back to front so the information was legible to the fighter direction officer on the other side. Robertson observed, 'there was an eeriness about the way the coloured marks would appear on the transparent perspex as if by themselves'.[3]

The only sounds over the hum of the ventilation fans were the quiet voice of the fighter direction officer passing the airborne Seafires their courses to intercept the enemy and the loud intermittent fuzz over the radio as the pilots radioed back acknowledgements. All pilots had code names. Snippets of flying jargon could be heard. Bogeys were unidentified aircraft; those confirmed as hostile were called bandits; 'angels' signified their height in blocks of 1,000 feet. In the thick of the action a few thousand feet above, the pilots' voices were strained and tense.

The board began to show increasing numbers of enemy plots getting ever nearer. 'I didn't want to admit how scared I was,' said Robertson, 'but knowing you have a large fleet of aeroplanes approaching, many of whom will probably be kamikazes. They don't drop bombs that probably miss you, they hit you, and doing nothing, hanging around waiting, was petrifying.' The fleet went into a code red – an air raid was imminent. The Americans had worked out that a kamikaze had a 40–50-per-cent chance of hitting a ship once it had started its dive. It was only a matter of time before those odds were tested on the British ships. And even if a diving aircraft was hit head-on by flak, it could still continue on its course for up to 300 feet.

The last line of defence was the fleet's gunfire, which now opened up in a thunderous roar, peppering the surrounding skies with hundreds of explosions. The heaviest of the carriers' anti-aircraft batteries – the eight pairs of 4.5 inch guns built into the sides of the flight deck – engaged first, with flames flashing from their sixteen muzzles as they shot out fifty-five-pound high-explosive rounds at more than 2,300 feet per second. Depending on the elevation of their seventeen-foot barrels, the guns had a maximum range of almost eleven miles. Some shells were armed with a VT proximity fuse, one of the war's most effective inventions. A radio wave transmitted from inside the nose bounced back from the target and set off the explosive when it was about seventy feet away, negating the need for the round to actually hit the target. The new munitions had recently been delivered to the fleet at Admiral Fraser's request. However, bringing the large guns into action was not a split-second operation. They were controlled by fire control directors in the island, who used gunnery radar to locate and then lock onto the target, but couldn't fire until separate teams calculated and adjusted the settings for the fuses and for the guns themselves.

To John Robertson, standing inside the island, the big guns sounded like 'bombs exploding each time they fired. The ship's hull shuddered and vibrated, and everything that wasn't secure fell crashing to the decks. Several times I was certain we must have been hit as a particularly heavy blast seem to shake the whole ship.'[4]

Down in the near-forward 4.5-inch gun turret, fitted flush into the flight deck of *Indefatigable*, 17-year-old sailor Les Wills was part of the team tasked with keeping the twin barrels loaded. The conditions were hot, noisy, fast and furious, with the whole turret, itself weighing almost 40 tons, revolving at 15 degrees per second. Wills and his team had to collect the rounds from the magazine below via an electric lift and then carry them over to the gunlayers while dressed in thick protective overalls. It was demanding work which brought them near to the limits of physical endurance. Each brass shell weighed over 50 pounds; temperatures reached 40 degrees Celsius. The electric motors of the turret and the lifts whined constantly. Fans struggled to force in air to clear the smoke from the guns.

Wills was consumed by the 'noise of the guns and smell of the cordite. It was narcotic. It was raw.' Each gun was now firing up to

12 rounds a minute, the breech recoiling 18 inches with every shot and spitting out the shell case, which clattered to the deck before being pushed through a hole and dropping into the churning sea 40 feet below. Wills wore no earplugs and took an occasional blessed swig from a bucket of water when he could. The pace was frantic, and although they were sealed off from the action above, it was clear a big attack had started. 'We couldn't see a thing but we were firing so fast we knew there must be something going on up there,' said Wills.[5]

As the Japanese attackers came within range, the big guns were joined by the smaller rapid-fire Oerlikons and pom-poms mounted in the open at the sides of the flight deck and around the island. For the gunners this was both terrifying and exhilarating. One, hunched in his seat and crouched like a jockey, sang at the top of his voice, 'How we gonna keep 'em down on the farm?' to the rhythm of his gun, watching the little yellow tennis balls of tracer bubble up from its muzzle.[6]

Dogfights now littered the sky, which was filled with thick smoke, making the panorama of the battlefield even more disorienting. The fleet's fighters managed to shoot down four more Zekes, but some of the Japanese aircraft had penetrated the fighter screen and were closing in fast. An Oscar broke through the bursting flak, swooping low over *Indomitable* with its machines guns flashing. Bullets crackled and popped along the entire length of the flight deck, smashing the windscreen of the little truck used for towing aircraft and ripping through a group of running sailors, killing one and wounding six.

Another Zero dived towards *King George V*, whose gunnery officers barely had time to deploy its blistering firepower before its pilot made a last-second violent swerve away, exposing the meat-ball markings on its wings. His primary target was a carrier – the ultimate prize – but he was hotly pursued by 894 Squadron pilot Dickie Reynolds, twisting and turning in his Seafire *Merry Widow*, desperately trying to close in on his jinking quarry. Reynolds was still out of range and the angles were acute, but then with some sharp shooting he managed to pepper the root of the Zeke's port wing with cannon fire as it cut inside him. However, before he could get his aircraft into position to deliver the kill, the Zeke rolled onto its back and dived towards *Indefatigable*.

In the fighter direction room directly below, John Robertson suddenly got the urge to sneeze. It must have been the itchy material of the protective mask covering his nose and mouth. He ripped away the flap and leaned out of the doorway into the passage.

Reynolds flicked the *Merry Widow* into a steep dive and followed the Zero into the chain mail of flak from *Indefatigable*'s guns. He fired off another burst but to avoid crashing into the carrier was forced to break off his pursuit, pulling back on his stick. In the final seconds the Zeke shuddered and bounced, repeatedly pummelled by flak. The pilot may have already been dead. But he'd done his job, as the plane smashed into *Indefatigable*, causing an enormous ball of flame which covered the ship from stem to stern.

John Robertson came to, dazed, and looked around. He had been flung back into the fighter direction room by the explosion. The blue glow had disappeared, but the dogfights could still be heard on the radio and the ship's gunfire rumbled on outside. Someone muttered expletives in the darkness. A blackout screen was yanked away from a porthole and sunlight flooded in, catching the dust and smoke in its rays. In the passage outside a ruptured pipe hissed steam.

Robertson picked himself up and walked gingerly down the passage to the operations room, where he was greeted with a scene of carnage. A giant hole had been punched through the side of the island, its bent, jagged edges resembling a grotesque mouth. Black smoke poured in. The smell of burned oil and paint mingled with the sweet aroma of seared flesh and blood. Robertson peered out and saw the flight deck in flames and the bottom half of a body, its chest and head ripped off.

Charts, files and loose paper littered the room. Some nearby ratings were ordered to treat the wounded, but were frozen with shock and fear. 'Some of these youngsters had never been in battle before or been bombed or seen the results of that, and then suddenly the place they knew as home was torn apart,' said Robertson.

Armed with a 550-pound bomb, the Zeke had hit the ship at the junction of the flight deck and the island, exploding on impact, killing three officers and five ratings instantly. The ship's barber, who also acted as a messenger during action stations, said later 'the smell of dead flesh stayed there and in that part of the island till the day I left the ship'.[7]

A gunner near the island complained he couldn't see through his sight before realizing it was blocked with a sliver of human flesh. One air mechanic responded to an urgent call for stretcher bearers, a decision he soon regretted, as 'it meant picking up limbs and trying to match them to bodies . . . I didn't eat much for a couple of days'.[8]

The explosion had written off the flight deck sickbay, killing the ship's Canadian doctor. A makeshift replacement was set up in one of the messes, where five more men later died. Sixteen were injured in total. Although there was serious damage to the side of the island, the bridge itself had remained largely untouched. Steam and water rupturing from pipes had prevented bigger fires taking hold. Robertson ran up to report the damage to the commander of operations, who, to his surprise, burst out laughing. The observer's beard had been completely singed off by the heat of the blast after he'd removed his face flap to sneeze.

Black smoke belched from the island as fire parties with hoses battled to bring the flames under control. One man found his voice had become 'all high and squeaky. Every time I tried to speak I had to stop and try again. I suppose it was the shock.'[9] Splinters from the blast had peppered the ship. The crash barriers were bent and twisted. Remarkably, considering it appeared the kamikaze pilot had tried to fly down the ship's funnel in a near-vertical dive, the flight deck had largely withstood the impact, its steel-plated armour dented to a depth of just three inches over an area of about fifteen feet in diameter. After extinguishing the fires, chucking the remains of the Zeke over the side of the carrier and clearing up the debris, engineers used quick-drying cement and steel plates to patch up the hole. *Indefatigable* was able to fly off Seafires again after about forty-five minutes.

But while the attack's physical damage was largely superficial, its psychological impact was deeper. Until now it had been an airman's war. The violence had taken place hundreds of miles away, over the horizon and safely out of sight. For many of the ships' crews that there was even a war on at all was betrayed only by the battle-scarred aircraft returning from a strike or the names of the killed or missing airmen posted on the noticeboards. By comparison, their war had comprised days or even weeks of drudgery and routine. But the kamikazes had brought the front line to the fleet. The attack was a sudden shift from the mundane to the terrifying. The men didn't have the measured rhythm of continual combat that soldiers on a battlefield experience. 'It would almost have been better if it was in the heat of battle when the kamikazes came in. But when nothing happens and suddenly you're fighting them off, that seemed to make it more real,' said Robertson.

This was 360-degree warfare, directly affecting everyone, regardless of rank. 'The kamikazes didn't distinguish between the admiral or the boy sailor,' one seaman said. 'The skipper later joked with us it had been an Easter egg sent by Hirohito. But we felt we were all in it together.'[10] The effects of the attack lingered in other ways. For weeks afterwards some men reported seeing ghosts walking through flames on the flight deck.

In their squadron diary the pilots of 894 Squadron in *Indefatigable* gave their own unique account. 'APR 1 "ALL FOOLS DAY" and did we buy it! Early in the morning the Japs attacked with suicide – their first reaction . . . Diving from 2,000 ft, it hit the bottom of the island doing no mean rate of knots. SPLATTTTT!'[11]

As *Indefatigable* licked its wounds, the battle raged on in the skies above. Dickie Reynolds, still seething that he'd been unable to stop the kamikaze attack and looking to settle some scores, shot down a Zeke in two slick passes. Scanning the sky for more targets, Reynolds immediately engaged a second Zero, whose pilot tried to use its superb turning capabilities to outmanoeuvre Reynolds in a twisting dogfight. But the twenty-two-year-old was already too experienced to be lured in, and used a series of high-speed 'yo-yo' dives and climbs. By pulling up into a near-stall turn, he then reduced speed and banked steeply, cutting across the Zeke, using his remaining ammo as he did so. Within a couple of minutes Deadeye Dick had sent another victim crashing into the sea and become the Royal Navy's top-scoring Seafire pilot. Reynolds remarked to a squadron mate later that once the attacking aircraft had missed their targets, they were 'sitting ducks . . . they didn't know quite what to do'.[12]

The majority of the kamikaze pilots who attacked the British Pacific Fleet were young and inexperienced. However, aircraft flown by more experienced airmen often accompanied the suicide pilots to ensure they reached the fleet, but then hot-footed it back to Formosa. It is a myth that suicide planes only carried enough fuel for one-way trips. But if they couldn't find a target, unless they managed to make a sneaky escape in the heat of battle, most found themselves 'stooging' about at the mercy of greater numbers of allied aircraft flown by more experienced airmen.

Like a tropical storm, forty minutes after the attack developed, it had passed. The British Pacific Fleet had survived its first major kamikaze attack albeit with a bloody nose, and the fighter boys had shot down at least six Zekes without any losses from enemy gunfire. In the melee, however, the fleet's fighters had inevitably been exposed to friendly fire, as Ken Ward later recorded in his diary: 'My morning ride was rather a troubled one. The entire

Fleet at one point thought I was a low-flying Jap and hurled many shells towards me. I looked around for the enemy but there was no one . . . My Log Book records 4 separate attacks by Corsairs.'[13]

The ships' young gunners certainly had a difficult job. Admiral Rawlings later said that differentiating between his own aircraft and the enemy's became 'daily of more importance. With the suicide attack and, as is inevitable, with our own fighters pursuing the enemy tight on to the fleet's guns, there is only a matter of seconds in which to act.'[14] In the smoke and heat of battle decisions had to be made in seconds, and once one gunner started shooting, the rest tended to follow in a frenzy.

Air strikes on the Sakishima Islands resumed later on Easter Day while the clear-up continued. But the enemy had not finished. At 17.30 radar detected two aircraft, which were then spotted by the fleet's patrolling fighters. A game of cat and mouse ensued, with the Japanese flying into low cloud to avoid being drawn into a dogfight. All the fighters in the air were told to fly due west 'ten miles very low', which simply resulted in the radar screens becoming 'a milky way of bogeys'.[15] A few seconds later the Japanese aircraft burst out of the cloud towards the fleet, which responded by opening up with its guns.

One of the fighters levelled out 500 feet above the water, jinking and twisting in the bursting balls of flak, and dived towards *Victorious*, which scythed through the swell to starboard at more than 30 knots as the aircraft skimmed over the flight deck in a flash of sparks before spinning into the sea, detonating its bomb. Tons of water and bits of plane spewed into the air and drenched the ship. A list of target priorities for the suicide pilot was found on deck and promptly taken up to *Victorious*' captain, who remarked the 'only unmistakable feature of this document was its reek of cheap scent'.[16]

After more bombing and strafing missions over the islands the following day, the fleet retired to the fuelling area for forty-eight hours to lick its wounds, returning to start another cycle of air strikes as the sun rose on 6 April. Everything was continuing as routine until four enemy aircraft broke out of the cloud in the late afternoon and dived on the fleet. Covering fighters quickly inter- cepted and shot down one of the aircraft, but a Yokosuka D4Y Judy single-engined bomber dived on *Illustrious*, whose gunners responded quickly, shooting away its port wing and part of the tail before its starboard wing sliced through the radar mount just ten feet in front of the bridge. The plane spun into the sea and exploded.

The remains of the aircraft and the pilot showered onto the carrier's flight deck, and a yellow rubber dinghy landed on trans- mission aerials. Men climbed up and yanked it down before quickly posing with it for the ship's photographer. Rashers of flesh hung from a radar aerial. Don Cameron, a tough Kiwi Corsair pilot in 1833 Squadron who had just landed back on *Illustrious* after successfully shooting down a kamikaze, spotted a linen flying helmet near the door to the island with a rising sun painted on it. 'I was even more surprised on looking in the helmet to see the top of a skull about the size of an ashtray with little red veins forming a mosaic in the bone,' said Cameron, who promptly stuffed the trophy into his Mae West and reported for debriefing.[17]

After supper two days later, deep in the belly of *Illustrious*, Cameron and a number of other fighter boys gathered for a drink- ing session. In the gloomy light, with condensation continuously dripping from the pipes on the ceiling, bottles of gin, vodka and whisky were dug out. The drinks flowed. Someone then produced a brown eyeball 'looking for all the world like a tadpole', which they had found on the flight deck, and dropped it into the bottom of the vodka bottle. 'The motion of the ship induced the eye to circle endlessly around the bottle as it stared out at us,' said Cameron. Not to be outdone, he rose unsteadily to his feet and staggered off to his cabin, returning with 'my piece of skull in which we took great delight in stubbing cigarettes out'. Battlefield trophies are as old as battle itself, and although Cameron con- ceded years later that he was 'not exactly proud' of what he did, he also remained bullish: 'we were all very young, we hated the enemy, it was kill or be killed.'

Hatred of the Japanese was the prevailing attitude at the time. Although a few pilots in the fleet had a grudging respect for the skill of the kamikaze flyers – after all, hitting a ship at high speed when it was moving at a rate of knots and turning sharply was no mean feat and a technically difficult piece of flying – they were also imbued with a deep loathing for them. They were risking their lives on a daily basis against an enemy they couldn't understand and knew little about. The concept of kamikaze was alien to them. Of course there were one-off instances, which often led to posthumous awards, of Allied pilots pressing home an attack knowing full well it would almost certainly lead to their death. But these were spontaneous exploits rather than wholesale pre-planned actions by men who seemed to embrace the inevitability of death – an attitude apparently ingrained in the psyche of an entire nation.

No one knew this better than the men serving with the American fleet off Okinawa. On 6 April the Japanese launched the first of ten massive attacks they named *kikusui* – 'Floating Chrysanthemum'. Over the following 48 hours more than 650 aircraft, half of them suicide planes, targeted American Task Force 58. Almost 400 were shot down but many broke through, sinking 6 and damaging 20 ships. But the Americans got their revenge. On 7 April the Japanese launched a doomed attack using the world's largest battleship. *Yamato* only had enough fuel for a one-way journey and lacked air cover because the Japanese were keeping their planes back for kamikaze operations. Some 380 carrier planes of Task Force 58 had a field day, sinking *Yamato*, a cruiser and 4 destroyers in less than ninety minutes.

Vice Admiral Rawlings admitted he felt 'admiration' and 'envy' when he heard about the action, as his own aircraft of the British Pacific Fleet continued the daily drudgery of bombing the runways of the Sakishima Islands.[18] However, the Americans were impressed by the apparent ease with which the British armoured

20. Although it was a wonderful fighter to fly, the Seafire was too fragile for the rough and tumble of carrier life. Its success as a kamikaze hunter was marred by its high accident rate and limited range.

21. In contrast to the Seafire, the American-built Corsair had a stout undercarriage, making it better suited for carriers. Landing on deck was still challenging, yet Keith Quilter makes his inaugural deck landing look easy as the batsman signals him to cut the throttle.

22. Pilots of 1841 and 1842 squadrons gather on the flight deck of *Formidable* after their strikes on Tirpitz in northern Norway, August 1944.

23. The oil tanks at Pladjoe burn fiercely after the first of two daylight raids on Sumatran oil refineries by the FAA in January 1945.

24. While Admiral Ernest J. King, commander-in-chief of the United States Fleet (right), objected to the British involvement in the Pacific, on the frontline Admiral 'Bull' Halsey, commander of the US Third Fleet (left), welcomed it.

25. With his charming personality, Admiral Bruce Fraser was a popular leader across all ranks. His strong relationship with Admiral Nimitz was one of the most important factors in the British Fleet joining the Americans.

26. The BPF was commanded at sea by Vice Admiral Sir Bernard Rawlings, who shunned publicity but, on the whole, shone as a tactician and politician.

27. Admiral Sir Philip Vian commanded the flyers of the BPF. With a no-nonsense attitude and beetling blue eyes, Vian cut an imposing figure.

28. A US Navy Corsair fires its rockets on positions in Okinawa. In operations over mainland Japan, British combat losses were 48 per cent higher per sortie than those suffered by the Americans.

29. Initially one of Japan's most impressive aircraft, by 1945 the Mitsubishi Zero was no longer feared as a conventional fighter but still packed a punch as a suicide bomber.

30. 4 May 1945: a Zero captured just seconds before it crashed into the flight deck of *Formidable*, killing eight men and injuring forty-seven.

31. *Formidable* seconds later, just after it had been hit.
'It did not look possible that anyone could be alive in that inferno,'
said one onlooker.

32. An Avenger of the BPF flies over HMS *Indomitable* as it returns from a Sakishima attack.

33. Aircrew pored over target maps in the hours before their missions, working out the best way to inflict maximum damage while avoiding lethal anti-aircraft fire.

34. A sketch by Wally Stradwick. In overcrowded ships some aircrew had to sleep on beds out in corridors, but Wally and Keith Quilter wangled a large cabin in *Formidable*, with the bottom bunk doubling up as a sofa.

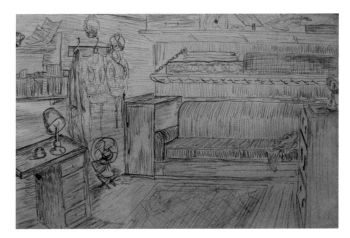

35. Admiral Fraser signs the Japanese Instrument of Surrender on board USS *Missouri* in Tokyo Bay.

36. Liberated prisoners of war, mostly British, after being discovered in a Japanese prison camp on Formosa by a Pacific Fleet mercy unit, 5 September 1945.

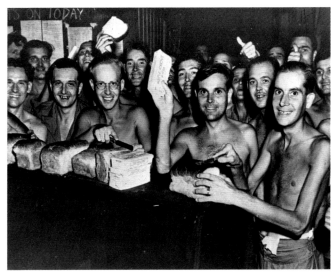

37. Keith Quilter on a visit to America, 2013.

38. Keith Quilter visits a squadron mate's grave at Yokohama Cemetery, 2012.

carriers withstood kamikaze attacks. According to one visiting US liaison officer, 'When a kamikaze hits a US carrier it means six months of repair at Pearl. When a kamikaze hits a Limey carrier it's just a case of "Sweepers, man your brooms."'[19]

This perception may have contributed to Admiral Spruance's next request: he signalled Rawlings with a request for British planes to attack northern Formosa, to try and stem the kamikaze attacks at source. His own vulnerable wooden-decked carriers were needed nearer Okinawa. Formosa was the responsibility of General MacArthur, but he considered an attack a waste of effort, much to the chagrin of Nimitz and his fleet, which was now getting a battering off Okinawa.

Seeing Spruance's request as a sign that the Americans were beginning to accept the British Pacific Fleet, Rawlings agreed despite the fact his aircrews were beginning to show signs of strain due to the intensity of operations. In strikes on 12 and 13 April waves of Avengers escorted by fighter patrols and supplemented with ramrod attacks pounded targets on Formosa, although low cloud and driving rain forced them to abandon attacks on some key airfields for railway stations, docks, shipping and factories. Flak was heavy but losses were light, and on the second day the fleet's fighters shot down sixteen enemy aircraft in combat for the loss of three British planes.

Rawlings was relieved losses had not been greater and told Vian later that he'd 'kept his fingers crossed throughout the operation'.[20] Although opposition had been weaker than expected, their attacks had certainly not gone unnoticed: 'the British task force has been attacking Formosa lately', wrote Admiral Matome Ugaki, commander of the Japanese navy's Fifth Air Fleet, in his diary on 13 April. 'They were indeed impertinent.'[21]

They were also very tired. Many of the pilots in *Illustrious'* Corsair squadrons had been operational without a break for over a year. The strain could be seen on their faces. The heat and intensity of the Sakishima strikes had brought everything to a head. Experienced pilots began to made mistakes.

Norman Hanson, 1833 Squadron CO, acknowledged, 'most of us began to suffer from off days; dreadful mornings when our normal relaxed attitude to flying was nowhere to be seen; days when the very thought of making low-level attacks was positive anathema'. They were becoming twitchy. 'To seek an early night's sleep just didn't seem to work,' said Hanson. 'One flew round the cabin, dodging the flak, practising a landing, for the first two hours; and if sleep eventually came, only three hours or so fitful rest remained before a shake from the duty boy.'[22] And so the cycle went on.

In eleven strike days, including the Palembang operations, *Illustrious*' three squadrons had lost eighteen aircrew. And the ship had been more badly damaged by the kamikaze attack than initially thought, with the outer hull and some of the frames cracked, and a main screw out of action. But with the Americans bogged down in bloody fighting in Okinawa, the fleet would need to continue striking hard at the islands whose names they had come to hate. New blood and fresh legs were needed. Luckily they were to hand. After months of frustration the *Formidable* boys were about to join the party and were determined to make up for lost time.

15

A formidable return

ROYAL NAVY TASK FORCE NEAR JAPAN – STRIKE AT RYUKYU IS., announced the headline on the front page of the *Sydney Morning Herald* on 31 March. 'A British task force on Monday and Tuesday attacked the Ryukyu Islands, between Japan and Formosa. The British Fleet has never before made such a long-range strike.'[1]

For the airmen in *Formidable* it had been somewhat galling to read reports about the fleet 'getting stuck in' when they were still 4,000 miles away. But now en route to join the fleet, Wally Stradwick's excitement was palpable. 'We should soon be joining the rest of the British Pacific Fleet whose exploits have hit the news for the last few days,' he wrote in his diary as the ship steamed north through the Pacific. 'Will a cheer ever go up when they see the old *Drydockable* arrive at last!'[2] *Formidable*'s squadrons carried out intense exercises while travelling. Both 1841 and 1842 had collected new Corsairs, and the 848 Squadron mechanics ensured its Avengers were ready for the rigours of front-line flying. The reality of preparing for operations focused minds. The ship and her crew were reaching fighting weight, or as near as they could get to it, bearing in mind they'd not seen action since the previous August.

Commanding officers worked their pilots hard. Tony Garland, CO of 1842 Squadron, had his pilots carry out regular dummy attacks on the ship while others acted as defenders, honing their skills in the sky. Garland's hard work extended to ensuring his squadron continued to bond in the wardroom. 'Judy had a gramophone and the most superb collection of big band 78s [records]. We would carry over our drinks and listen to them,' remembers

Keith Quilter.[3] Their journey was not altogether quiet in other ways. Action stations sounded when an 'enemy aircraft' was spotted in the late-afternoon sky. But the possible bandit was soon identified as the planet Venus, somewhat to the embarrassment of the spotter, and a rhyme circulated around the *Formidable* before the evening was out:

> Twinkle, twinkle, little star,
> We just thought the Japs were nigh,
> You're safe enough you're up so far,
> Four point fives can't shoot so high.[4]

On 14 April *Formidable* arrived at the refuelling area 300 miles south-east of Miyako, where she joined the rest of the British Pacific Fleet. For the aircrews and ship's company there was a feeling of anticipation and excitement at getting involved at last. They could clearly see the blackened island of *Indefatigable*. What would the kamikazes have in store for them?

Stradwick wrote to his younger sister Sheila: 'you would be surprised to know where we are now – and sister o' mine we are still going on. The squadron is pretty well up to strength in pilots at the moment and our aircraft are all on top line, ready for the next "do".' In a letter to his mother, he promised, 'I will definitely write as soon as I get some breathing space, things are rather busy right now . . . Still, don't worry about me, we'll be right on the ball . . . thanks for your prayers Mama – you deserve a lot yourself.'[5]

In the days before *Formidable*'s first strikes the squadron commanders and aircrew busied themselves with the usual flurry of briefings. Airmen who'd been on the operations over the islands felt they now knew the attacking runs like the backs of their hands and warned *Formidable*'s new pilots not to do more sweeps than were necessary on the ramrods, and to go in hard, low and fast. One pilot, who had excelled in leading *Indomitable*'s Hellcats and was shortly going home, advised new COs such as Tony Garland, 'if you want to live, never do more than one run on any target up here. If you do two they'll get the bead on you and that will be the end of you.'[6] Garland had been unwell with a fever, and when *Formidable* stopped in Leyte to refuel a few days before it joined the fleet, he had been confined to hospital. But 'I think he heard we were sailing the next day and discharged himself because he was so anxious to lead us into the next action. I have often wondered if he wasn't really fit to come back,' said Quilter.

On the eve of the first operations the maintenance teams were kept busy tinkering with engines, arming-up, cleaning cockpit covers and doing last-minute odd jobs. Corsairs were fitted with belly tanks to ensure they could carry out four-hour patrols over the fleet. Ramrod fighters had a 500-pound bomb attached under each wing to give them extra punch. Admiral Vian gave *Formidable*'s crews and company a pep talk, confirming the target was the Sakishima Islands and wishing them all the best of luck.

The following morning – Monday 16 April – the tenth day of strikes began. At 04.30, with the black Pacific skies yet to reveal the first smudge of dawn, the bugle strains of 'Hands to flying stations' came over the tannoy, permeating dreams and banishing sleep. Stewards gave the blinking, yawning aircrews a shake – 'It's four thirty, sir' – and a welcome cup of tea before filling their washbasins with warm water.

H hour was 06.30. In the morning gloom bells shrilled as Corsairs emerged on the lift from the hangar below with their wings still folded. Soon the deck was covered by strange, angular silhouettes. Following a briefing at 05.15 in the air ops room, pilots from 1841 Squadron walked from the island across the cold hard steel of the flight deck, buffeted by a strong sea breeze. A few minutes later eight Corsair engines burst into life and settled into a steady, rich growl.

The flight deck director, dressed in a yellow waistcoat and cap and armed with a torch wand, beckoned the first aircraft down the deck. On his order the Corsair unfolded its wings. The deck tilted as the ship turned into the wind. The director waved the chocks away, waited until the chock men were clear, then waved a green flag around his head. The lead pilot gave the thumbs up and opened the throttle. The Corsair thundered down and off the flight deck, momentarily disappearing out of sight below the bow before reappearing and climbing lazily into the gunmetal sky. In a blitz of noise and motion less than five minutes later all eight aircraft were forming up above the fleet to start their four-hour patrol. The scene was mirrored across the fleet as the Avengers thundered off the carriers, with Fireflies, Hellcats, Seafires and Corsairs providing patrols, escorts and ramrod strikes.

Wally Stradwick's Corsair was laden down with two 500-pound bombs and a belly tank full of fuel. 'I certainly didn't feel like a fighter,' wrote Stradwick, who experienced a few hairy seconds as his plane lumbered off *Formidable* and into the air. Following a 'rather dull' mission accompanying Avengers to their bombing runs on airfields over Ishigaki, Stradwick's landing was more eventful when he found he was unable to jettison an unused bomb and had to put down praying it didn't bounce off and explode. It dropped off as he taxied forward but didn't detonate, much to Stradwick's relief.

All the while the two battleships, the destroyers and cruisers continued their sentry duties. Unless the fleet was under enemy attack, away from the carriers the men led a somewhat tedious existence, although one officer in *King George V* reckoned the rest of the fleet were 'emotionally involved', particularly those who could watch the flying operations. 'Lookouts, gun crews and other upper-deck personnel watched the carrier operations intently, all urging struggling aircraft into the air and cheering on a damaged aircraft trying to land safely on its carrier.'[7]

As the day drew to a close, *Formidable*'s captain Philip Ruck-Keene breathed a sigh of relief knowing he had only one flight of four Corsairs still to return. This was led by the experienced Tony Garland, who was carrying out the last target combat air patrol of the day with another three aircraft from 1842 Squadron. But in the gloom of the evening only three dots appeared in the sky and brought the worse news possible. At around 18.20, with the dying embers of the sun casting long shadows over Ishigaki airfield,

Garland's Corsair had been hit by flak during a second strafing run, and his aircraft had crashed into the sea just offshore.

Garland's death reverberated through the steel walls of *Formidable*. He was a huge figure in the ship, but it was an especially bitter blow for the young pilots of 1842. The squadron was utterly thrown. Garland was a hero to them. 'Judy's place was difficult to fill as he was an inspirational leader and he'd been with us since the beginning,' said Chris Cartledge. 'It was a depressing time for us. His loss was keenly felt. He had been an exceptional and popular leader and we felt sadly weakened without him.'[8] Cartledge was shocked too because, in contrast to the *Tirpitz* missions, he had encountered little opposition in his initial runs over the Sakishima Islands. 'It was like a pleasant afternoon flying around in the sun. I didn't feel I was in any danger at all. I was surprised that anyone could not come back from it,' he said.[9] Now any thoughts that this might be a cushy job vanished.

Strikes continued over the following two days, with various dramas and incidents. Wally Stradwick was ordered to look for an Avenger pilot who had ditched his aircraft in the sea. Flying low over Miyako island, Stradwick wrote later, 'I could have been shot down with a bow and arrow, but I didn't see a sausage. The islands, from the air, look more like cemeteries, they're so damned inactive, but the craters on the runways seem to be filled in every night.'

To other airmen in the fleet, however, the islands really were cemeteries. Seven more had been killed on bombing or strafing runs in just two days. Unlike over Palembang, the fleet had not suffered dramatic losses, but there had been steady wastage of aircrews and aircraft. With no spares, the margins were tight. Rawlings and Vian decided to withdraw to Leyte to replenish and restock. The Americans would send over a task force to continue bombing the islands until the British fleet returned.

When the fleet arrived back at Leyte on 23 April, Vian and Rawlings took stock. The British Pacific Fleet had been at sea continuously for 32 days, longer than any British fleet since Nelson's

day. Over 12 strike days flying almost 2,500 sorties, it had lost 34
aircrew and almost double that number of aircraft. Three British
carriers had been hit by kamikazes, killing 19 men and seriously
injuring 17. By and large, the objective of keeping the airfields out
of action had been successful. It was, though, impossible to tell if
this had kept any kamikazes off the backs of the Americans. However, the fleet's fighters had destroyed or damaged 127 aircraft,
including 30 shot down in the air. Admiral Vian sent out a signal
that the last strikes were 'as good a three days operations as I have
seen'. High praise indeed, but privately there was much to concern
him.

Vian believed their losses were an 'unremunerative return' in
an operation offering little opportunity to inflict 'high losses on
the enemy'. Beyond hunting down potential kamikazes, there
was little chance for the fighter pilots to do what they were primarily trained for. Dogfights were rare, with Japanese air attacks
confined to small groups of kamikazes 'who split up 30 or 40 miles
from the fleet and in their approach through cloud formed
difficult targets'.[10]

Rawlings agreed. Despite his vast experience, this was like
nothing he'd been up against before. The use of suicide attacks
created new problems. 'Japanese attacks cannot be compared with
those of the German dive-bomber, whose pilot wished to live and
return to his base, and whose tactics were different anyway,' he
said. 'Whereas, even a deterrent fire would often be a contributory
cause to the dive-bomber dropping his bombs early or inaccu-
rately, the kamikaze is a menace until he is destroyed, hence early
vital hits are essential.' Rawlings believed there were 'special problems of the Pacific and Japanese forms of attack' and that at sea the
Japanese had 'shown more cunning than the Germans' in framing
their attacks to evade defence by directed fighters. He added,
'Against the Germans the battle was half won if a formation could
be intercepted, broken up and coordinated attack prevented.
Against the Japanese, the initial interception is no more than the
beginning of a series of individual encounters and the danger to

major units of the force is only passed when each and every aircraft has been shot down.'[11]

For the aircrew this was a dirty and frustrating operation. Vian acknowledged that attacks from dawn to dusk on airfields were 'difficult and costly' against targets which 'do not display their wares. The bombers are exposed to flak concentrated in the area of attack throughout their bombing runs, while ramrod sweeps are faced with dummy or unserviceable aircraft dispersed in revetments and other conspicuous places in centres of flak.'[12]

There were problems with the aircraft too. Despite good results hunting down kamikazes in the air, the small fuel tanks of the Seafires meant they couldn't carry out strikes over the islands and had to land on every two hours to refuel, and twenty-five had been lost or damaged beyond repair with four pilots killed in accidents. Even the normally buoyant line book of 894 squadron was sober: 'The whole tragedy of war is borne out to the full by our four losses during this operation, none of which were directly due to enemy action . . . everyone was feeling a "bit off", troops were working like slaves and there was little apparent reward. We had lost four pilots. There were rumours of Hellcats and disbanding.'[13]

With *Indomitable* soon to leave the front line taking its Hellcats with it and a second Seafire carrier, *Implacable*, due to join the fleet later in the year, there was no question of the Seafire squadrons being disbanded. Nevertheless, their poor operational performance and a lack of spare pilots and planes meant extra pressure on the pilots flying American types of aircraft. The Corsair and Hellcat pilots had been flying up to eight hours a day on hard seats in hot cabs, alternating between patrols over the fleet and attacking targets over the islands. They had flown on average forty-five hours – twice that of the Seafire pilots – during the operations so far.

Some squadrons were going home and at least half of those remaining would soon be due for relief, but before then there were more strikes on the Sakishima Islands to plan. In the stifling heat of Pedro Bay off Leyte kamikaze damage to the carriers was patched up and the fleet set about replenishing stores and replacing aircraft and crews. After a week it was time to resume operations. On the last evening before they left, some of Tony Garland's belongings which his friends had considered too fragile to send back to his family in Essex were auctioned off. They included his prized gramophone and some of the records. A memorial service was held on the quarterdeck. 'I think we shall miss Judy for quite a while,' wrote Wally Stradwick.

Garland's replacement Doug Parker, who had previously commanded 1845 Squadron, would now be leading the pilots of 1842 Squadron into action. He had big shoes to fill. He knew his pilots had been blooded, but what had happened was nothing compared with what was about to hit them.

16

Little yellow baskets

It had been an unfortunate moment for the British Pacific Fleet to leave the Sakishima Islands. The *kikusui* mass suicide attacks had continued against the American fleet off Okinawa, which was losing almost a ship a day, while on land the US advance had become bogged down in bitter fighting with daily casualty rates nearing 1,000 men.

The wooden flight decks of the American carriers were proving vulnerable. Kamikaze damage to the carriers *Intrepid* and *Enterprise* had forced Admiral Spruance to reorganize his forces, and he needed the British Pacific Fleet back on his left flank to minimize the kamikaze threat from Formosa. Despite this, Admiral King had requested that the British Pacific Fleet relocate to support the forthcoming Allied assault on Borneo. This was being resisted by Nimitz, Spruance and Rawlings, and rumours about their next destination swirled around the ships' companies.

Task Force 57 left Leyte harbour at 06.30 on May 1. To groans, catcalls and curses from the aircrews, the captains announced they were heading back to the Sakishima Islands. For the young aircrews of the British Pacific Fleet, the tempo of their war was increasing just as events in Europe were coming to a head. Mussolini had been caught attempting to cross the Swiss border and shot by Italian partisans. The following day, Wednesday 2 May, Ken Ward wrote in his diary, 'Almost the very first words I heard this morning, apart from the steward's brief, was the joyous news that Hitler is dead. No details are known of where or how killed, in fact British statesmen are said to be full of disbelief until the body is produced. Sensible, I suppose!'[1] In the same entry Ward noted more good news. He had been awarded a DSC for his part in the Palembang strikes three months before.

To the Americans' relief, the British air strikes resumed on 4 May, with almost fifty Avengers attacking targets, supported by the usual Fireflies, ramrod attacks and fighter escorts. It was a violent welcome back for the flyboys of Task Force 57. The anti-aircraft fire over the islands was accurate and heavy from the off, shooting down an Avenger on an early sweep. The 500-pound bombs, machine-gun fire and rockets had only a limited effect, and Rawlings knew the heavy guns of the battleships and cruisers would have a better chance of destroying the Japanese emplacements around the airfields. He was also conscious that, in the five months since the fleet was formed, his gunners had not been given a single opportunity to bombard land targets. For weeks they had been watching the planes leave the carriers to make their strikes over the islands, and were itching to show what they could do.

Rawlings therefore requested and received permission from the Americans to take his battleships and cruisers off the coast of Miyako. 'I particularly wished to bombard for the sake of the personnel concerned. Many of these are very young and untried . . . the effect on morale of ships of the bombarding force would be most beneficial,' he said later.[2] While Rawlings' decision was generally welcomed, it was also one hell of a gamble. The carriers and the rest of the fleet would be left alone thirty miles south while the bombarding force took up its position. Without the extra radar sets and heavy anti-aircraft screen provided by the battleships and cruisers, the carriers were exposed, and the fleet had almost certainly been spotted by a Japanese reconnaissance aircraft. Rawlings reasoned this was nothing unusual. His fleet had been spotted by snoopers several times over the previous few weeks without an attack always developing. It was certainly not, he concluded, a good enough reason to deny the crews of his battlewagons some morale-boosting action. But this decision was a major miscalculation by Rawlings and would have disastrous consequences.

At 10 a.m. on 4 May, under beautiful skies and in calm seas, the mighty battleships *King George V* and *Howe*, accompanied by a flotilla of ten cruisers and destroyers, parted company with the carriers and cruised majestically in line ahead at high speed towards Miyako. Soon Miyako's hills and its tiny adjacent islands appeared in the binoculars of the watchers on the ships' bridges. Just after midday, fourteen miles off the coast, a great boom rolled across the sea and echoed back off the land as *King George V* opened the bombardment, hurling salvos of one-ton shells landward. Seconds later plumes of black smoke and dust rose from behind a hill. Several more were fired before the cruisers, steaming ten miles off the shoreline, joined in at the scheduled time, hammering different targets around the island. Fighters buzzed overhead, spotting for the ship's guns and helping them hit their targets.

David Divine, a veteran war correspondent, was standing on the bridge of *King George V* with Rawlings, watching on in awe. But then something caught Divine's eye as the ship turned to start another bombardment run. Back out to sea, just visible above the horizon, he spotted a 'dirty great mushroom cloud of blue smoke'.[3] Rawlings had lost his gamble.

The first dots appeared on the carriers' radar almost an hour after the bombardment force left. Four small groups of bogeys, comprising twenty aircraft in all, were approaching fast from the west. Lacking its main artillery umbrella, Admiral Vian's exposed fleet huddled together for protection. Keeping the four carriers in their diamond formation, he positioned two destroyers at equal intervals between each carrier to ensure the most accurate arcs of fire.

The fleet was already at action stations and combat fighter patrols in the air were given vectors. White clouds dotted the sky, perfect kamikaze weather. Acting as decoys, one group of bandits sheered off and worked its way around from the south. The bait was swallowed hook, line and sinker, with Seafires immediately directed to intercept. Corsairs engaged another group, and enemy aircraft were soon splashed. But this allowed a small number to slip through.

On the flight deck in *Formidable* pilots and deck handling parties were moving eleven Avengers down the deck to make room for the morning strike, which was due to return any minute. The ship's loudspeakers announced Corsairs from *Victorious* had knocked down a Zeke seventy miles from the fleet. 'It was like listening to the commentary of a football match,' said one rating.[4] Everyone got on with his job but couldn't help looking up occasionally, nervously scanning the skies.

Without warning a single Zeke burst out of the clouds from astern. Over in *Victorious*, steaming parallel 2,000 yards away, one Corsair pilot stood on the quarterdeck and watched the plane dive straight for *Formidable*. 'I said, "That silly bugger is going to get shot at if he's not careful." I thought he was one of ours. Then I saw these puffs of smoke coming from his wings and I said, "That silly sod's firing."'[5]

Perched high up on the lookout above *Formidable*'s island, one nineteen-year-old rating spotted a 'brown blob' in the distance, shimmering through the heat from the ship's funnel. He initially thought it was a Seafire approaching to land, but when it flashed past the island with a loud roar, strafing the flight deck with its machine guns, he realized he was 'looking at the top of a Zero with its red circles on the fuselage'.[6]

The bugle command to repel aircraft was piped over the loudspeakers, prompting some men to sing along, 'There's a bomber overhead. There's a bomber overhead.' Captain Ruck-Keene put *Formidable* into a hard turn to starboard, watching the Zeke, whose pilot pulled out of his dive at the last second and climbed steeply away to starboard. An Australian war correspondent in *Formidable*, said later, 'The pilot was superb. As I watched from the flight deck of the British carrier, he threw the Zero into a vertical climb.'[7]

The ship's guns opened fire and desperately followed the aircraft as it pulled back round. Down on the flight deck men watched the yellows balls of tracer streaming up and tracking its flight. Still climbing, it momentarily disappeared from view behind the island before reappearing on the other side. Then the aircraft turned and it seemed to hang in the air before turning and diving again towards *Formidable*.

Those who could sprinted to the nearest hatch or the catwalk at the side of the deck, expecting to be blown to bits. Chain hand-rails clattered as men ran for their lives down ladders like mice scurrying into holes. Up on the lookout the sailor had nowhere to go, so he dived for the deck. 'I remember thinking, *I've been through the Blitz; we've had bombs, we've had incendiaries, we've had landmines thrown at us, but it's the first time I've had the bloody plane thrown at me as well.* You feel that it's aimed at you, especially when he looks around and you think, *Can he see me?*'[8]

Very little footage exists of kamikaze attacks on British ships, but one piece of shaky black and white film shot from another ship captured the last few seconds of the attack on *Formidable*. Taken abeam, it shows little more than the silhouette of the plane as it streaks in at an angle of about forty degrees towards the carrier, before pulling up at the last moment and banking. The film immediately cuts to another scene, starting with the final two seconds of the plane diving in again. And then 5,000 pounds of metal and wood moving at 300 mph just disappears into the flight deck in a flashing ball of flames, followed by masses of thick black smoke. A war correspondent watching from *Indefatigable* said, 'to think they were knowing they were going to their deaths like that was uncanny. You couldn't help thinking they were heroic but in a rather bad cause.'[9] One rating felt the ship 'jump out of the water' and a 'tremendous explosion and sheet of smoke and flames'.[10]

The pilot had released a 500- or 1,000-pound bomb just before impact. The nearest Avenger – all five tons of it – was blown over the side like a leaf in the breeze, and another burned fiercely. Shards of hot metal penetrated the steel walls of the island, and a splinter of armoured deck shot down through a number of lower decks to sever a steam pipe in the boiler room, sending plumes of white steam up through the funnel.

Flying at 6,000 feet above the fleet in his Corsair, Wally Stradwick witnessed 'one of our carriers appear to explode. I could only see the bows protruding from a colossal pall of black smoke in the centre of which was an ugly sheet of flame.'[11] The fleet held its breath, and those who could looked on from other ships in morbid fascination at *Formidable*'s plight. She looked finished. Men stood 'opened mouthed' on *Victorious*. 'I had never seen anything so horrifying or quite splendid too, in a way,' recalled one.[12]

Anthony Kimmins, a film director who had joined the navy at the outbreak of war and was now the fleet's press liaison officer, was in *Indomitable*, which had itself just been grazed by a kamikaze. He accounted later how

> We were just getting our breath back when a voice beside me said: 'God, look at Formy!' It was a ghastly sight. All you could see was the bare outline of her hull, and rising above it from stem to stern an enormous pall of black smoke, belching furiously as huge red tongues of flame shot upwards every time something else caught fire. And right amidships, a gigantic white fountain, as high-pressure steam screamed up into the sky. But the thing which almost took one's breath away was the fact that something else was screaming upwards too. More kamikazes were diving to attack and to our amazement tracers from 'Formy' were racing up to meet them. It did not look possible that anyone could be alive in that inferno, and yet – somehow or other – guns' crews, scorched and with their throats clogged, were still sticking to their job. Whether she was hit again or not we couldn't see. There was too much smoke and flame already. But she still held on. Her engines were still heaving over. Boilers had been put out of action, but those men down in the boiler and engine rooms were determined that she should keep her place with the fleet.[13]

Out of the black smoke rising from the ship, a tiny, single bright light flickered defiantly from the island. Captain Ruck-Keene had flashed a three-word signal by Aldis lamp to Admiral Vian, who was witnessing the whole thing from *Indomitable*: 'Little yellow bastard.' Heartened to see signs of life, Vian shot back a droll reply: 'Are you addressing me?' Ruck-Keene was a fighting man, made of the same metal as Vian, who was clearly relieved despite this being 'the most serious kamikaze attack we had yet suffered'.[14]

'This suicide boy couldn't have done a worse job in some ways,' wrote Wally Stradwick. 'He had hit the flight deck just abreast the island . . .' The main force of the blast was absorbed by the compartment in the island housing the air intelligence department. When the bomb exploded, the metal door and scuttle looking out onto the flight deck were blown in. Twenty-year-old Roy Beldam, the youngest member of 848 Squadron, had not been flying that morning and was on duty assisting the air operations officer. He was thrown off his feet by the explosion and came to moments later, dazed but uninjured. He ran over to another assistant, slumped over the desk by the scuttle, only to find the force of the explosion had blown the window in and his face had been obliterated. Most of the other men in the room were seriously injured by flying glass.

The captain's first priority was to steer the ship into a course which reduced the wind fanning the flames. Small fires had started in the hangar. Orange flames licked around the island. Its smart livery blistered and blackened. More worryingly, in addition to the grey smoke from the fires on the flight deck and the white steam from the burst pipe, thick black smoke was also bellowing from the funnel, suggesting an oil tank had been hit in the bowels of the ship.

Two hundred men dressed in the sinister-looking asbestos suits of firefighting parties emerged from below decks, dragging rubber hoses as thick as a man's forearm. The hoses pumped a mixture of water and animal blood from large tanks below decks. The blood reacted under high pressure with carbon dioxide to create a white foam which smelled foul but formed an effective blanket to smother flames fed by burning oil and aviation fuel and prevented oxygen from reigniting the fire. Within a few minutes what had once been gleaming aircraft were grotesque, tangled skeletons, dripping with thick white liquid.

The deck had been crowded with aircraft handling parties and crews when the kamikaze struck. Six men were killed immediately, burned or scythed down by flying debris. The most seriously injured were treated as they lay on the flight deck, and the first-aid post in the island was used as a triage centre before casualties were taken below deck. Most casualties were given morphine injections before having their wounds treated and many were bleeding heavily. The medical team went through more than 250 bottles of plasma and thousands of units of penicillin. A petty officer working as an aircraft handler had most of his legs blown away. He died three days later. Another man had to have his eye removed after shrapnel pierced his cornea.[15]

The sickbay and its small medical team – run by an elderly reservist doctor – was overwhelmed, its pokey confines totally unsuited to dealing with mass casualties, despite additional 'after-action helpers', men who had volunteered from the ship's company to carry out nursing duties, shake up dried plasma bottles, make beds and empty bedpans. Thirty-three men required beds but only sixteen cots were available. Some had to lie in corners and in the gangway. The sickbay was directly below pounding pom-pom guns. The fleet's surgeon commander arrived by destroyer some hours later and quickly took over from the reservist, who he thought 'too old for this type of war and too frail to stand the pace'.[16]

A makeshift operating theatre was set up in the laundry, with overflow wards in the warrant officers' mess and the officers' anteroom. However, the equipment left much to be desired. According to one journalist on the ship, 'scalpels were blunt, rusted and unusable'.[17] The American liaison officer aboard *Formidable* fetched some razor blades. Breaking one of them in two, he clasped one half in a pair of forceps, sterilized the instrument and handed it to the surgeon. 'Here's your scalpel,' he said. As each blade became blunt, another was inserted and sterilized. 'There's been a doctor in my family continuously for more than 150 years, but I bet even the first one didn't have to operate under these conditions,' the surgeon apparently said after he finished.[18]

Although a number of medical staff in *Formidable* were rightly decorated for their work in the aftermath of the attack, the surgeon's concerns in a private letter to a fellow doctor illustrated the continuing struggles the Royal Navy was having with Pacific warfare. 'You see the conception of carrier warfare out here is quite different to anything we have experienced before,' he wrote.

> When you are striking and you may strike for several days, you do not withdraw with your wounded – you've got to look after them and continue operating. Well this class of ship with sickbay is <u>useless</u>, except as a peacetime job, and even then it is only a rather dirty corridor . . . It's a tough war out here and we have been at sea continuously for nearly three months except for a short break to replenish stores at a harbour where it was not worth going ashore – just a place full of dead Japs and Malaria.[19]

At least a dozen men had received nasty burns after being engulfed by flaming aviation fuel when the kamikaze struck. Don Jupp, an Avenger pilot in 848 Squadron, was enveloped in flames as he sat in his cockpit on the flight deck, but managed to climb out, still burning, and was taken to the sickbay. Blue-eyed and dimpled with a broad dazzling smile, twenty-one-year-old Jupp, from Gloucestershire, was modest and quiet – the youngest pilot in the squadron – and had won a DSC for his actions during the *Tirpitz* strikes the previous August. He affectionately called Roy Beldam, his observer, Kid, and the two men had become close.

Jupp had second-degree burns covering 40 per cent of his body – from his waist up to his scalp, including his face, eyelids and hair. He had also been blinded by the flash of the explosion.

For the first thirty hours after he was injured, medical staff could do little but treat him with morphine and give him plasma infusions, before moving him to the makeshift theatre. There, he was swathed in bandages, his face covered with a mask treated with saline solution. Over the following days Beldam visited Jupp, keeping him company, reading to him to try and distract from the pain of his wounds. 'Not for long, but just to reassure him,' he said. 'I was struck by the extraordinary courage and patience with which he bore his pain. One evening, being examined by the doctor, he said quite quietly, "Doc, you never told me you had blue eyes." I realized he could see again.'[20]

Serious casualties needed to be transferred to the hospital ship. Two days later Jupp was one of thirty-three men moved to a cruiser by the extremely precarious means of a breeches buoy. Each man was placed on a makeshift stretcher and pulled across the open water between the two moving ships using a system of ropes and pulleys. 'He was in considerable pain when he left the ship because he shouted out loud, which, apart from for fun in the wardroom, I had never heard him do,' said Beldam. 'I went with him to the ship's side and we clasped hands. I said, "See you in Sydney," or something similar.'

Jupp was transferred to the hospital ship *Oxfordshire* but died ten days later of kidney failure, a common cause of death among severe burns victims. Overall, eight men were killed and forty-seven wounded in the attack on *Formidable*. The mental and physical scars to the men caused by the kamikaze would last far longer than those to the ship itself. Among chaotic scenes down in the boiler room one warrant officer had braved scorching steam to make emergency repairs to an oil tank ruptured by a piece of armoured deck – hence the black smoke pouring from the funnel – but the damage was not critical and the following day the ship was able to steam at full power.

Throughout the rest of the day the Japanese mounted further attacks, and the fleet's fighters shot down ten kamikazes and one high-flying aircraft, believed to be an escort plane which had been given the job of locating the fleet. This interception was one of the most important. A Canadian Corsair pilot took off from *Victorious* and climbed to 15,000 feet, where 'by sheer luck I spotted a small dot about 5,000 feet above us'. His combat report detailed the kill:

> I dropped my tank and gave full boost; climbed up and under enemy aircraft. At 300 yards aircraft started to turn to port, I fired a 1 sec. burst at about 30° and he straightened out and must have dropped his flaps and cut his throttle as I began to gain on him rapidly. I cut my throttle and fishtailed and had time to give him a 2 sec burst from astern at about 100 yards. He blew up in a terrific flash of flame and at the same time the bombs or drop tanks dropped loose from the wings. The aircraft then descended in pieces and burned on hitting the water. A parachute made free from the aircraft while it descended and was strafed, but there was only the harness attached when I had a closer look.[21]

Despite being hot and uncomfortable to live under, the armoured flight decks of the British carriers had prevented serious damage and meant *Formidable* could remain with the fleet. After the fires were extinguished, a hole in the flight deck two feet deep and wide was filled with quick-drying cement and covered with wood and steel plates. When it became clear the ship would live to fight another day, Ruck-Keene gripped the arm of the American liaison officer standing alongside and, shaking his fist, asked, 'What do you think of our bloody British flight decks now?'

'Sir', came the reply, 'they're a honey.'[22] By 17.00 *Formidable* was able to land on aircraft once again.

That evening the fleet retreated to the refuelling area to take on new aircraft and stores, and transfer casualties. Rawlings and Vian took stock of the day's events. Rawlings had been in a 'considerable state' when he realized the carrier fleet he'd left behind was under attack. 'He was very sober and very quiet about it, but you could see he was deeply moved by the whole thing,' said someone present.[23]

Vian admitted later that he was not 'sufficiently alive' to the possible consequences of the temporary absence of the radar and anti-aircraft capabilities of the battleships for his carrier fleet.[24] However, both men stood by their decision, which of course had been made without the benefit of hindsight. Rawlings said later, 'the bombardment was a very valuable tonic to the fleet . . . I felt this tonic was timely, as there is a tendency for the personnel of ships other than the carrier to become stale.'[25] Being at sea for weeks on end, the crews' morale was paramount. The battleship bombardment of land targets was still a strong part of the Royal Navy's DNA, despite the emergence of carrier warfare by 1945. Furthermore, the operation had indeed relieved boredom for the ships' gunners, and some damage was inflicted on the runways. The mission had also illustrated just how well the steel decks of the British carriers had withstood this new form of warfare.

The 4 May attacks on the British Pacific Fleet were the fringe of the fifth *kikusui* mass kamikaze raid on American shipping around Okinawa. This had involved more than 120 suicide aircraft in support of a counter-offensive by the Japanese army on the island. After two days this collapsed. Artillery and tanks had been smashed, and the Japanese 24th Division suffered 5,000 casualties.

A few days later Anthony Kimmins managed to get his account of the attack on the British fleet through to the BBC in London. In it he referred to Ruck-Keene's laconic signal, but watered it down to 'Little yellow baskets' for his domestic audience. 'Fortunately it just got through in time and was put over from the BBC on VE Day. I hope it reminded one or two people that we still had a packet of trouble to compete with in the Pacific,' he said afterwards.[26] But as people celebrated the end of the war in Europe, that packet of trouble showed no signs of disappearing.

*

At 3 p.m. on Tuesday 8 May 1945 Winston Churchill broadcast to the British nation. The war with Germany was at an end, he said. 'We may allow ourselves a brief period of rejoicing, but let us not forget for a moment the toil and efforts that lie ahead. Japan, with all her treachery and greed, remains unsubdued. The injury she has inflicted on Great Britain, the United States and other countries, and her detestable cruelties, call for justice and retribution. We must now devote all our strength and resources to the completion of our task, both at home and abroad.'

Churchill's reflective tone was at odds with the national outpouring of joy and celebration across Britain. The country burst into life. Drab war-weary villages, towns and cities were transformed with a rainbow of flags and bunting. In London crowds partied, waving flags and streamers. Smoke hung in the balmy May sky from countless bonfires burning effigies of Hitler. From 'Land of Hope and Glory' to 'Knees up, Mother Brown', the sounds of a nation letting off steam after six years of war resonated across Britain. There were occasional pockets of restraint. In Glasgow the city council flew flags at half-mast 'because there was still bloodshed in the Far East', but for the most part the day was one of rare indulgence and high spirits.[27]

Around the same time Churchill was being driven back to the Commons giving his famous victory sign to cheering crowds, 6,000 miles away in the Pacific one young Corsair pilot from New Zealand was decorating the inside of a 4.5-inch brass shell case after a heavy impromptu drinking session in the stuffy wardroom of *Victorious*. 'VE Day produced quite a result,' said a squadron mate who watched his friend sidle over to the shell case, which was used as an ashtray, before 'vomiting into this thing so he didn't make a mess in the wardroom'.[28] Twenty-four hours earlier, news of VE Day had reached the Pacific. 'We hear with rapturous delight that Germany surrendered today – unconditionally. The rest of the world will celebrate tomorrow (Victory Day) whilst we plod on here,' wrote Ken Ward in his diary on 7 May.[29]

Operations over the Sakishima Islands the following day were

cancelled due to bad weather and, although they were scheduled
to resume on 9 May, the combination of the recent battering by
the kamikazes and the news from Europe was a good enough
excuse for the flyboys to hit the bar that evening. The news from
Europe inspired mixed emotions in the servicemen stuck out in
the middle of the Pacific Ocean. While they were relieved that
their families were no longer in danger, they couldn't help feeling
their continuing efforts were being forgotten.

From *Formidable*, Chris Cartledge wrote home a few days
later,

> I am very glad to think that you are worried no longer by the
> various marks of the 'V' weapon. I must admit that I had to
> try very hard to work up any excitement over the surrender
> of Germany. I suppose everyone went mad with joy and
> relief, but they must have felt that it was not quite complete,
> it was not a clean sweep from war into peace. Most of those
> at home must have some relative connected with the BPF.
> I do hope we are being useful out here; it is the feeling that
> the Americans may be regarding us more as a liability than
> an asset that constantly undermines my morale.[30]

On 9 May seventy Avengers thundered off the decks of the carriers
of Task Force 57 to resume the pounding of the airfields across
Ishigaki and Miyako once again – the eighth series of strikes the
aircraft of the British Pacific Fleet had made on the islands. After
the news of VE Day everything seemed that little bit harder.
A journalist with the *Melbourne Argus* reported, 'There were no
victory celebrations for the men of this task force – we were carrying out another attack against the battered Japanese Sakishima
group.'[31]

That afternoon a small group of low-flying bogeys appeared on
the radar twenty-odd miles to the west of the fleet. Four Seafires
were vectored but allowed themselves to be drawn away by a
single Zero, which they splashed comprehensively. Unfortunately,
that left three Zekes powering towards the fleet. One kamikaze

dived through scattered cloud towards *Victorious* low on her starboard quarter. Despite being repeatedly hit, the aircraft smashed into the forward part of the flight deck, starting a fire which was quickly put out. Four crew were killed. A few moments later a second Zeke approached *Victorious* from astern, but the carrier wheeled hard, causing the Zero to skid across the flight deck through the deck park in a mass of sparks before sliding off into the sea.

Since the first kamikaze strike on *Formidable* five days before, extra precautions had been introduced, including a klaxon blast and a red flag which was waved from the platform next to the bridge to signify an imminent attack. This no doubt saved many lives. Keith Quilter was warming up his Corsair for a strike when he spotted the flag and 'ran for my life' seconds before the Zeke smashed into the flight deck. The only death on *Formidable* was that of Petty Officer George Hinkins, who had bravely stayed at his pom-pom, pushing his crew below the protective armour when the aircraft began its dive. Elsewhere, a first-aid party found a gunner wandering around the deck with one arm blown off at the elbow. 'Anybody got a cigarette?' he asked.[32]

Once again a combination of superb seamanship by *Formidable*'s captain and the armoured flight deck had prevented serious damage to the ship. However, eighteen aircraft were destroyed, many of which had been taken on board during the last replenishment just two days before. These aircraft could be replaced, but five new aircraft needed per carrier for every two-day strike period was unsustainable. Admiral Rawlings admitted, 'The Japanese seem to have suddenly made up their minds to increase the attacks on us. Their tactics are not too easy to deal with because we get such very short warnings due to their low approach.'[33]

The kamikaze attacks prompted debate and baffled some in the fleet. One pilot remarked, 'If they could get that close to the fleet, why didn't they just drop a bomb and go back again and live to fight another day?'[34] And for the flyers there was the nagging thought of what might happen if they were shot down. Although all the aircrews had been given some survival training, few men really seriously considered – openly at least – what they might do if this happened. The seas around the Sakishima Islands looked pretty enough, but within them lurked nasty surprises. All carrier flyers were issued with a copy of *Far Eastern Survival Land and Sea*. Airmen were warned, 'poisoning by fish occurs in all tropical waters and chiefly the Pacific, and comparatively close to the shore'. The really unpleasant fish were characterized by 'tough skin devoid of scales and may be covered with rough thorn-like spines, long plates or soft spines which give the appearance of hair'. A chance encounter could lead to a 'risk of violent vomiting and diarrhoea, with severe abdominal cramps. There is profound shock, convulsions with delirium, and stupor may precede death.'[35] The Japanese were rumoured to be brutal and even the fish in their sea seemed barbaric. If an airman could reach land, he was told to look out for edible fruit including the coconut, papaya and Chinese water chestnut.

Few in the fleet contemplated life as a POW. Fewer still had already actually experienced it. One exception was New Zealand Corsair pilot Don Cameron. His first experience as a POW had begun on 15 September 1943 when, as a raw twenty-one-year-old, he was shot down in his Seafire while covering the Allied landings at Salerno in southern Italy. Crash-landing on the beach after his cockpit hood and a two-inch chunk of his arm had been shot away, he was captured by German troops. He was told to dig a trench which he thought might be his grave but survived a night of heavy shelling by Royal Navy ships positioned offshore. A few days later, while being taken to a POW camp, Cameron leaped unseen from the back of a moving truck with an Italian-speaking American intelligence officer, escaped over Mount Vesuvius and hid in a cave for two days until being escorted down to a liberated village by a partisan. Cameron was transferred to flying Corsairs and initially joined 1833 Squadron, but was transferred to *Victorious* when *Illustrious* left the Sakishima Islands.

On the afternoon of 9 May 1945 Cameron took off from

Victorious to strafe a series of targets on Miyako. When his wing-man was shot down over the airfield in a ball of flame on their first run, Cameron, his blood up, returned alone, making three passes at full throttle. But as 'I streaked up the runway at nought feet and as I passed the hangars at the far end, there was a terrible bang and the aircraft seemed to jump sideways.'[36] Cameron sent out a Mayday call over his radio, slid his hood back, tightened his straps and ditched into the sea a few thousand feet off the coast. Inflating his dinghy, he climbed in and waited to be rescued, but as the light faded, so did his hopes. Just before dawn the following morning figures appeared on the beach a few hundred feet away. He was picked up by Japanese soldiers.

Less than a month before, three US Navy airmen had been shot down in their Avenger over Ishigaki and captured by Japanese sailors. Interrogated and tortured, two were beheaded and the third was beaten and stabbed to death with bayonets. It didn't bode well for Cameron.

Over the following days the Kiwi was tied up and kept in various huts, receiving the obligatory beatings from Japanese soldiers in between bouts of being offered cigarettes and food. His captivity wasn't made any easier by knowing the Royal Navy was so near. 'I sometimes found that my old mates were only a few thousand feet above me at times, as they went about their business of bombing and strafing.' Cameron was then transferred to Formosa and kept in a bamboo cage. Curled up in the fetal position, he pushed his face into the mud floor to protect his eyes as giggling school-children poked his head and rectum with sharp sticks through the bars. Later, after being imprisoned, he seized a chance to escape after an American air raid by climbing out of a light well in his cell and over the roof, and followed a river down to the coast. But sheltering in a garden for some rest, he felt warm liquid trickling onto his head and neck. He had unwittingly hidden in a lavatory. He was soon picked up again by soldiers and taken to Japan to await his fate.

17

Breaking point

Six weeks into Operation Iceberg there was no let-up for the US forces, who were still bogged down in heavy fighting on Okinawa. American soldiers and marines fought yard by yard in a bitter struggle to root out Japanese defenders entrenched in bunkers, caves and on hilltops. Despite superior US firepower, their losses were grim. Men experienced savage and bloody hand-to-hand combat. At times the Japanese sent over ten shells every minute. Added to the lead raining from the sky, tropical downpours rendered parts of the churned-up battlefield a muddy hell. It was a confused, frightening and violent experience. And yet Japanese losses were ten times worse.

Insufficient airfields had been captured to support land-based air cover for the US Tenth Army, so Admiral Mitscher's Fifth Fleet had no choice but to remain to provide air protection. Two further *kikusui* mass suicide attacks were launched, and on 11 May Mitscher was forced to move his flag to the carrier *Enterprise* after *Bunker Hill* was hit twice by kamikazes. A few days later *Enterprise* was hit and Mitscher had to decamp to the USS *Randolph*. In April and May 1945 alone 182 American ships were hit by kamikazes, more than the total number of ships hit over the previous five months.

Until a breakthrough came on Okinawa, the British Pacific Fleet would have to continue to batter away at the airfields of the Sakishima Islands 250 miles to the south-west to try to prevent the Japanese from sending further kamikazes. On 19 May its young airmen started their twentieth day of strikes since the campaign had started on 26 March. Writing home, Chris Cartledge made no secret of his desire to leave. 'I count up the days that have to pass before I'm relieved – then back to the UK like a streak of lightning, I reckon on Christmas at home myself – this may be wishful thinking.'[1]

It wasn't all doom and gloom – the men were young and it took a lot to get them down for long. They also knew theirs was largely a 'clean' war, not bogged down in the mud and rain of a battlefield. In a letter to his mother Wally Stradwick as usual put a cheery gloss on the situation. 'Well Mama, it still goes on, we fly and sweat, and then sweat some more. Boy when I think of all the second-line pilots stooging around England and the States! Still, the war can't last for ever and I am looking forward to the day when I can sink a pint of beer after laying my bowler hat on the table.'[2]

But non-stop operations in the middle of the Pacific Ocean, cooped up in a hot carrier with no escape, began to wear away at them. One senior British pilot who had been in front-line operations for eighteen months described the particular stresses for aircrew serving in the Pacific.

> At night we had to darken ship. All scuttles were shut. All deadlights were down . . . The ship was really closed up like a tin. So you can imagine thumping through the night at 25 knots, a wardroom of 120 people . . . produced a hot and humid atmosphere which wasn't really at all healthy. With all the noise and the rattle of a ship battling on you never knew what was going to happen next. It was all dark and black outside so you just knew you were going to the next flying-off position. And to try and get sleep and rest in all those conditions imposed an enormous strain on individuals. It's all right for the people who had a job to do driving the ship. At least they were doing their job. For aviators, whose air machines were in the hangar or on the deck, who were trying to get some form of relaxation from the tensions of flying

that day, in that sweaty and dreadful din. No one has yet attempted to describe . . . this almost amazing way that the human frame can stand this sort of treatment, day after day, week after week.[3]

The carriers were stuffed to capacity. At action stations working spaces were grossly congested. The carriers had been designed for the cooler climates of the Atlantic and the Mediterranean, not the tropical Pacific. The crews endured hot nights and scorching days, nicknaming the carriers 'steel coffins'. Cooling machines and evaporators worked flat out. The little ice available was often required to cool the developer in the photographic section to print the hundreds of images taken by reconnaissance aircraft. The ship's needs came before those of the crew, and fresh water was rationed and only available at certain times of the day. When the water was turned on, the cry went through the mess decks, 'Water's on!' The desalination plants seldom provided enough water. Many had to wash in seawater, which caused itchy rashes.

Wally Stradwick described the conditions in a letter home to his sister Sheila.

Remember what Mother is like when the weather is cold; always nattering about fires and things? Well I'm jolly sure she'd pass out in the heat we're experiencing. It's really chronic! Just khaki shorts, shirts and sandals and yet the perspiration keeps dropping off onto the deck until it forms a puddle in about fifteen minutes! Cruises in the beautiful tropics may be delightful, but in this man o' war in times like these, it just isn't my piece of cake at all. It isn't even much cooler when we're flying . . . Mother wouldn't get warm – she'd melt, all 4 feet 11 inches of her.[4]

Up on the flight deck, men working on the aircraft found them too hot to touch without using a wet rag or cotton waste. Writing to his parents, Chris Cartledge explained:

the Flight Deck absorbs and reflects and magnifies and con-
centrates all the sun's rays into the ship's interior where we try
to live useful lives. Trying to be efficient in such conditions is
a trial of patience and endurance, and a pilot who's been
flying has little to spare of these qualities. A cold bath is out
of the question because water that comes out of the cold tap
is too hot to put your hand in. There is a limited amount of
ice in the bar and we can stave off the heat temporarily by
drinking iced drinks and sitting under a fan.[5]

Men tried to sleep on the weather decks, but this was often
impracticable at sea. Officers found some respite by sleeping on
the breezy quarterdeck or even up on the flight deck. 'In the US
I had brought some sheets from Saks, on Fifth Avenue, which I'd
lay out on a camp bed on the quarterdeck. But even so, the heat
would melt the tar between the decking, smudging the sheets with
black,' said Keith Quilter in *Formidable*.[6]

In the cramped confines of the mess decks the humidity
encouraged plagues of insects. In one destroyer a sailor recorded
the resident population of cockroaches growing rapidly: 'the orig-
inals had all been black; now, with the tropical heat, we had three
varieties, black, brown and white. They were everywhere; a loaf
fresh from the galley was all right, but any of the bread ration kept
for breakfast would be full of burrows by the morning.' On hitting
the loaf with the flat of a knife, he found 'the multi-coloured cockroaches would swarm out onto the table'.[7]

Ratings assigned to carry sacks of flour up from the hold,
found sausages of dough formed on their perspiring backs. Down
in the boiler rooms the stokers – widely considered some of the
toughest men on the ships – toiled in sealed compartments which
could only be reached through a series of hatches and ladders.
Using a tin cup swinging from a hook at the bottom of the fan
trunking, they took it in turns to swig from a bucket of barley
water. A packet of rehydrating salt tablets was taped to an adjacent
pipe. According to research published in the *British Medical*

Journal just after the war, in certain spaces temperatures could reach an incredible 65 degrees Celsius. Not surprisingly, the heat had an impact on health. In an average month, of every 100 men in ships at sea with the British Pacific Fleet, 28.6 were being treated in the sickbays as outpatients and 4.6 were unfit for duty.[8]

By far the most common cause of ill health were skin complaints such as boils and fungus infections. Prickly heat, a rash of small raised red spots which causes excruciating stinging or prickling sensations on the skin, was universal in most ships, and the monthly incidence of heat exhaustion was one man in every twenty. Stuck in hot cabins for up to five hours at a time, for the airmen it was often just as uncomfortable in the skies above. One Corsair pilot developed dermatitis around his mouth from a perished rubber oxygen mask, and just a few weeks after arriving in the Pacific had lost all the skin under his arms and between his legs. 'It was not glamorous,' he said.[9] Medical staff made up large quantities of calamine lotion, which helped soothe the skin.

Scabies was another common complaint and was treated by giving the patient a hot bath, scrubbing the affected area and then applying tincture of benzyl benzoate. 'This would make the man jump a foot in the air, as it stung like blazes,' said one leading sick berth attendant on *Illustrious*.[10] Lice were treated with mercury ointment, while syphilis, a complaint that usually appeared a few weeks after leaving port, would clear up with an injection which used a derivate of arsenic.

Little wonder that, according to the report in the *British Medical Journal*, aircrew in one fleet carrier lost more than three times the number of flying days in three months in the Pacific than they did in a previous quarter operating off the coast of Norway. According to the study, work took longer to do and was not so well done as in cooler climates. Heavy operations, such as 'bombing-up' a wing of twenty-four aircraft, took half as long again as in home waters.[11]

Although Admiral Vian recognized many of his aircrew were at their operational limits and relieved some squadrons after the first half of Operation Iceberg at the end of April, there were insufficient pilots with enough experience coming through the system for the wholesale replacements of air groups. The Admiralty proposed capping front-line tours of duty at fifteen months, but this was considered too long by the fleet's surgeon commander, who told a friend in May 1945 that it 'will never work out here, with intensive type of operations undertaken, not a hope . . . The FAA has done more operations in the last three months than in the last two years put together.'[12]

The naval chiefs then agreed to adopt American-style tours of duty for squadrons of no more than six months in front-line operations. According to one medical officer in the British Pacific Fleet, the number of nervous breakdowns was 'remarkably few' because aircrews knew they would be relieved on time and 'not go soldiering on until they eventually "bought it", as was the previous belief held by the average Naval pilot'. In reality, however, many pilots already out in the Pacific were not relieved after six months and did soldier on. Ken Ward, for example, was in 894 Seafire Squadron in *Indefatigable* from 21 July 1944, and took part in the *Tirpitz* attacks, Palembang and Iceberg. He would fly right up until VJ Day on 15 August.

It was down to the medical officers and squadron commanders on the carriers to select individual flyers for relief, as they knew their operational background and how they were performing. Those airmen who had served the longest were normally the first to be relieved, although they were also the most needed given their experience, so they were often encouraged to stay or take up command duties in other squadrons. New pilots were slow to come through, and those who did were often rookies – some of whom could barely even deck-land. They were thrown straight into action without the chance to adjust to operational life at the sharp end. 'You got to know them as individuals and you soon knew whether they were much good or not in the air,' said Keith Quilter.

Many commanders advocated alcohol as a way to keep pilots

going, believing the 'threats and psychological pressures' could be negated with 'a few stiff whiskies'.[13] Even soused in alcohol, however, not everyone could take the pressure, and medical officers were trained to look out for signs of twitch. This was difficult. There were often no obvious symptoms, and for every man who admitted to twitch, there were many more who privately felt it but didn't say anything. Doctors identified 'trigger points'. Many aircrew, for instance, found it difficult to get sufficient sleep day or night. Worries about flying or going into battle were compounded by the constant noise of preparations, orders from loudspeakers and the ordinary life of the ship. This was of course impossible for medical officers to remedy.

The night before his maiden operation to attack the Sakishima Islands in May 1945 Val Bennett, who had joined *Indefatigable* with 1772 Squadron as a Firefly observer, had to sleep on a camp bed directly above the propeller screws because the ship was so crowded and there were no free cabins. 'I thought, *God! Tomorrow morning I'm going to be shot at by a Jap.* Why had I let myself into this? All the time the propellers were going, *thump, thump, thump.* The whole ship was jumping up and down and the vibration was terrific. There was a lot of apprehension,' said Bennett.[14]

Steps were taken to deal with flying stress. The Royal Naval Air Medical School was founded in Eastleigh in the spring of 1944. Training included a three-week course for all medical officers covering the theory of flight, medical aspects of safety equipment and the psychiatric care of aircrew. More than 150 MOs had passed through the school by the end of the war. In March 1945 an interview board was set up in Sydney for the purpose of assessing neuro-psychiatric cases in the British Pacific Fleet.[15]

But in reality there was no means of preventing flying stress except by the maintenance of morale, fixed and special extra periods of rest and leave, and limiting operational flying hours. No doctor could stop a nervous breakdown if a flyboy was overworked, tired and discontented. Besides, most men kept flying rather than admit they were scared. 'They all wanted to be in it.

I've seen them cry when they've not been taken on operations. And that was hell,' said one senior officer in *Indefatigable*.[16] Ian Paterson admitted, 'I just knew that I couldn't face my friends – if I had stopped somebody else would have had to do it. It was like that.'[17]

This fear of being found out could have tragic consequences. On 17 May 1945, coming back from a bomber escort trip, Ron Chambler and the other Corsairs in 1836 Squadron arrived in the landing circuit. Chambler was looking forward to a cold beer when he was horrified to see the plane two places in front of him hurtle down the flight deck of *Victorious*, miss all the wires, go clean over the barrier and explode amidst the deck park. Two men were killed and four injured. The twenty-one-year-old piloting the Corsair was killed immediately. 'He was a great friend of mine,' said Chambler. 'He always had problems deck landing but told me, in the strictest of confidence a few days before his incident, that he was now terrified of them but wanted to carry on. I was always struck with his adamant wish to carry on and [how he] could not bear the thought of leaving [his] friends in a sort of disgrace.'[18]

If stress did have a bearing on this pilot's death, he was not alone. In a report into the causes and effects of flying stress on aircrew, which the FAA published at the end of the war, anxiety was cited as the second-biggest cause of breakdowns behind lack of confidence, and either came about over time or was triggered by a bad accident or a series of nasty landings. 'Such a mental state [anxiety] makes a man more accident prone, and there must have been several cases, who were killed in aircraft accidents, not having reached the hands of the medical authorities in time to diagnose their condition,' concluded the report. The average time to rehabilitate those who resumed full flying duties was about four and a half months, but of 116 cases suffering from anxiety, only four resumed full flying duties.[19]

Most aircrew empathized with those affected. One observer in 1772 Firefly Squadron in *Indefatigable* said, 'We were very very sympathetic to aircrew who got twitch. Because it was a disease rather than a piece of cowardice . . . Lack of moral fibre was a sentence for cowardice but twitch is battle fatigue. The boundary between the two was very, very hazy.'[20] This sympathy was understandable. They were all going through the same thing. Landings became tricky affairs after long and tiring flights. The weather around the Sakishima Islands could turn in minutes, plunging the fleet into squally rain or thick banks of sea fog. 'The concentration could be tiring with only yourself to do the workload,' said Chambler.

> You constantly checked your instruments and that petrol gauge. You made sure you stayed in formation. You swivel-searched the sky for enemy planes. At 20,000 feet, on oxygen and in very cloudy conditions, it was easy to get lost or become disorientated. We'd had instances of this when radios had failed with sad results. I sometimes surveyed those endless waters of the Pacific and admired even more air pioneers like Amy Johnson who did so much with rather primitive planes and very basic navigation equipment.

The batsmen did their best to land pilots safely but there was only so much they could do, and they were as fatigued as the pilots. There was no such thing as a routine carrier landing. Aircraft with windscreens covered in oil, chunks of wing missing, only one wheel down or nursing ropey engines could sometimes make perfect landings. On other occasions a seemingly straightforward landing would end in disaster. Even after landing danger remained. It was not unusual for returned bombs to cartwheel up the deck or for an unspent rocket to go off with a magnificent whoosh when an arrester wire checked an aircraft.

The goofers' gallery was directly above the barrier and therefore perfect for observing crashes. A crowd gathered to watch most landings, and it was almost as popular a place to talk shop as the wardroom bar. Although open to all, it was mainly inhabited by off-duty aircrew. Out in the Pacific the hot weather made goofing particularly popular, the gallery's rails draped with brown or pasty shirtless bodies, providing a running commentary on each and every landing while also putting the world to rights about all things aviation.

A former pilot's account in a 1945 edition of *Flight* magazine described the scene: 'The main object of the types who frequent the "Goofers" is, of course, to watch the landings. This can be a much more twitch-making business than actually landing yourself . . . Each and every landing is closely watched and criticized.' Aircrew joked that any landing was a good one if 'you could walk away from it'. For those lucky enough to, 'the first thing the unfortunate pilot sees on stepping from his bedraggled aircraft is a row of his chums' faces peering down with gloating expressions – another member of the barrier club'.[21]

Keith Quilter was a regular goofer. 'If you were off flying duty you might see another flight come in and think, *God I thought they had better formation than that*, but it's only after they landed you realized one of them might have half his tail plane shot off.'

Accidents were not confined to the flight deck. On 18 May 1945, while the British Pacific Fleet was steaming to its refuelling area, *Formidable* suffered a serious fire in its hangar when the starboard guns on a Corsair were accidentally fired directly into the petrol tank of an Avenger sixty feet away. The huge explosion started a fire, fuelled by kerosene, ammo cooking off and the varnish used to preserve the fabric surfaces of aircraft, and was in danger of reaching 13,000 pounds of bombs. The rest of the fleet closed in, ready to pick up survivors if *Formidable* had to abandon ship, but once again the fire crews and the saltwater sprays brought the fire under control and there were no serious casualties. But the accident left *Formidable* battered and bruised, with only eleven serviceable Corsairs and two Avengers, and the morale of its men at a low ebb.

Looking for ways to boost morale, the Admiralty studied the success of the Americans in the Pacific, observing that particular care was taken to keep aircrew and ships' companies fit, both physically and mentally. 'Recreation, sun-bathing, a quality and variety of good books, ice cream and medicinal whisky (in otherwise dry ships) are freely used to this end,' concluded one report.[22] The Admiralty's director of naval equipment was asked to investigate, and even worked out the dimensions of a Wall's ice cream bar and estimated how much room would be needed to supply men with a regular ration. (The answer was two cubic inches, per man, per day.) He concluded that too much storage space would be occupied, so explored instead what equipment would be needed to make ice cream on board.[23]

Admiral Fraser knew that the American carriers tried to create the most pleasant environment for their crews as possible. Good food, the latest films and a regular mail delivery were all advocated for the British ships. More than 2,000 bags of mail were delivered to the British Pacific Fleet during Operation Iceberg, and post from the fleet to Britain and back again could take as little as twenty-five days, but fresh food was scarce and the men became fed up with rehydrated substitutes for weeks on end. 'I used to eat raw onions just for something fresh,' said one British Corsair pilot.[24]

Fraser pleaded with London for improved conditions for his men, citing American ways of raising morale, but Admiral Cunningham (based in London) cautioned being 'blinded by American lavishness', adding, 'I am sure that soda fountains, etc. are very good things in the right place, but we have done without them for some hundreds of years and I daresay can for another year or two.'[25] Admiral Cunningham's dismissive reply showed that the vast gulf between the pen-pushers in London and the front line in the Pacific was not just a geographical one.

The fleet's crews would just have to make do with what they had. When the ships were away from the front line, anything to take minds off routine was jumped upon. Deck hockey leagues were played on the flight deck, drawing big crowds. Nets were strung up in the lift wells, creating makeshift volleyball courts. To keep fit during long stretches at sea, all under-forties – 90 per cent of the crew – had to attend physical education classes on the flight deck before breakfast. A Royal Marine band would be on hand to oblige in another naval custom. 'Can you imagine a flight deck miles from anywhere in the Pacific Ocean covered with human males bending and stretching in their shorts at 6.30 in the morning to the tune of "Daisy, Daisy, give me your answer, do"?' said Chris Cartledge.[26]

A daily paper – the *Pacific Post* – was launched. Printed 4,000 miles away in Sydney, it was then transported to the ships of the British Pacific Fleet, and kept the men in touch with news from home. Drinking and bawdy songs around the piano continued to be an effective way to let off steam. In *Formidable* Wally Stradwick and Keith Quilter, who had become close friends and cabin mates, decided to lighten up the mood on the entire ship. 'Apart from flying and the damned watches we have to do, there is little else to occupy us, so whenever we've had the opportunity, Keith and I have been putting on programmes on the ship's radio system – you know – "Request Hour" and that sort of stuff,' wrote Stradwick in a letter home.[27]

Formidable had been kitted out with American speakers and record-playing equipment during a refit in Norfolk, Virginia in 1941. 'We had LPs and a good stock of records,' said Quilter. 'Training in the States we had got used to the jargon of DJs, which we didn't have in the UK. Officers and the crew would drop a chitty into our cabin and we'd try to play as many as we could when we were on air, which were then piped around the whole ship.' But Quilter was hauled up in front of the captain one day after a major in the Royal Marines requested the somewhat un-marine-like vaudeville classic 'How Come You Do Me Like You Do?' 'You feel screened from everyone in the studio and I made some comment about "our romantic major in the marines" which was piped all around the ship. I got hauled over the coals for being insubordinate and not giving him the status he deserved,' said Quilter.

*

Despite such distractions, the German capitulation, the new wave of kamikaze attacks, increasing numbers of accidents and the continuing drip of casualties served only to emphasize the slog that lay ahead. 'It's a dirty war; all war is dirty, this one particularly so,' wrote Chris Cartledge in a letter home on 16 May 1945. 'Judging by the fanatical methods of defence used by the Japs they do not intend to give in however hard pressed. Of course one cannot anticipate the reactions of a race so radically different from us. We can't apply our logic to them.'[28]

Many in the fleet felt they had been forgotten, a feeling not helped by scant UK press coverage of their war. One journalist had only been aboard *Indefatigable* for two weeks when he witnessed the 4 May kamikaze attack on *Formidable* and filed his report to his editor back in London. 'The *News Chronicle*'s treatment of my eye-witness accounts was the clearest of indications as to how much the Pacific war had become the half-forgotten war. Had these been German suicide planes attacking a British Fleet in the Atlantic, every front page in Fleet Street would have vied for the most lurid of headlines.' The first of his dispatches, severely cut, was tucked away under the drab headline JAP SUICIDE PLANES SENT INTO ACTION. Another shared equal space on page 3 with a domestic story headed HOSPITAL WARD CLOSED. NOT ENOUGH NURSES.[29]

Understandably, part of the reason for the lack of coverage was distance. The war in Japan simply didn't affect the everyday lives of Britons – except when one of their relatives was directly involved. However, the truth behind the scant news coverage, as always, was more complicated. Although many war correspondents were still in Europe, a number of experienced reporters from British and Australian newspapers were granted accreditation with the British Pacific Fleet. Admiral Fraser knew full well the power of the press and had a superb grasp of what made a good news story or picture. But the importance of keeping the world informed of its activities was not very high on the Royal Navy's list of priorities. In contrast with the lavish press facilities provided by the American navy, hacks posted to British ships had no means of transmitting copy at sea. And information wasn't always forthcoming. Moreover, owing to the strictly limited time during which transmission of press material was allowed, dispatches were often confined to 200 words, and there was no guarantee they would reach London the same day. Back in the newsrooms, stories were cobbled together from agency copy wired from the American Pacific Fleet headquarters in Guam.

Friction between reporters and Rawlings, who was suspicious of newspapermen, only made matters worse. Most reports were carefully balanced, but a small number of negative stories began to appear, criticizing Rawlings, which in turn made him resent the press even more. Things did slowly get better, but Anthony Kimmins, who was tasked with improving press relations for the fleet, admitted after the war, 'the problem of providing adequate naval information had been prepared far too late at the Admiralty'.[30]

In an attempt to get more colour for his story, a reporter from the *Sydney Morning Herald* joined Ian Paterson in his Avenger for a bombing mission over Ishigaki, sitting in the observer's cockpit. 'I think it was the only time he flew over the enemy coast. Although we explained how the intercom worked, I never heard a dicky bird from the time we took off to the time we landed. I was flying there thinking, *I wonder if I've got a dead journalist in the back*,' said Paterson.

By mid-May there were signs at last that the enemy was weakening. The kamikaze attacks on the fleet had tailed off and there were few aircraft on the Sakishima Islands to target. Although weeks of fighting remained before the Americans completed the capture of Okinawa, Admiral Spruance signalled Admiral Rawlings to say he could end operations on 25 May and return to Sydney. Better still, Admiral Halsey, who was about to resume command of the American task force, indicated to Rawlings he intended to integrate the British fleet into the summer air strikes over the Japanese mainland ahead of the invasion in October.

As the sun sank into the Pacific Ocean on 25 May, the British Pacific Fleet steamed south. Operation Iceberg was over. Task Force 57 had spent 62 days at sea with a break of 8 days for replenishment at Leyte. Just short of 5,000 sorties had been flown over 23 striking days, nearly 1,000 tons of bombs were dropped, 500,000 rounds of ammunition fired and 950 rockets released. Despite the fleet's young airmen shooting down 42 enemy aircraft, the majority kamikaze bombers – with 100 more claimed on the ground, it was difficult to assess with any real accuracy just how successful the mission had been in stemming the flow of kamikaze attacks on the Americans. Nevertheless, in a speech a few weeks later Nimitz was clear in his praise for the British, saying that the fleet 'took the Jap suiciders off the necks of our ships which had to stay anchored off Okinawa.'[31]

In a sense it was job done. One of Fraser's main aims during Operation Iceberg had been to ensure his fleet did enough to impress the Americans so that it was retained for the showdown over mainland Japan. But the damage suffered by the British fleet may have had a greater impact than the damage it caused. In May alone the British Pacific Fleet had lost 42 per cent of its original aircraft strength and 79 per cent of its Corsair establishment.[32] Overall, 41 British and commonwealth aircrew had been killed in action – around a tenth of the total aircrew in the fleet – the majority to anti-aircraft fire over the islands. A further 44 men were killed and 83 wounded in the kamikaze attacks. Every British carrier had been hit at least once by a kamikaze. The armoured carriers had proved their worth, and there is no doubt that without them the British Pacific Fleet would have been crippled.

Spilt blood and damaged steel were demonstrations of Britain's commitment to its ally in the common cause. Although its losses were dwarfed by the Americans' – almost 10,000 US Navy men had been killed or wounded by the time the Americans gained full control of Okinawa in late June – the proportionately heavy losses suffered by the Royal Navy proved to the Americans that Britain was happy to share the burden. Spruance signalled Admiral Rawlings to congratulate him on the 'fine work' and 'splendid spirit of co-operation' which 'typified the great tradition of the Royal Navy'.[33]

Most worrying for Admiral Vian, however, were the fleet's huge aircraft losses. A staggering 93 per cent of the 218 aircraft in the force had to be replaced, with losses caused by enemy action amounting to just 16 per cent.[34] Deck landing accidents, mainly to the fragile Seafire, were double this. The suicide attacks and the fire in *Formidable* had also contributed to significant damage. Nevertheless, while much of the damage could and should have been avoided, no one could accuse the British Pacific Fleet of not giving its all in a type of warfare the Royal Navy was totally unused to, even if it was something of a pyrrhic victory.

While most of the fleet sailed back to Sydney to prepare for operations off Japan in July, Rawlings headed to Guam, where Admiral Nimitz was piped aboard *King George V* to give a speech to more than 1,000 Royal Navy officers and men. Standing in brilliant sunshine below the battleship's 14-inch guns, Nimitz told the ship's company that their 'most efficiently performed' aid in the war against Japan had been appreciated by the American forces. He denied the 'idle gossip' circulating in the press that the US Navy didn't want the British fleet there and preferred to wage a 'private war' against the Japanese. 'I assure you that those statements are without foundation,' said Nimitz, attacking 'those who plant stories that tend to drive a wedge between the United Nations'.

During a news conference with American war correspondents in his cabin later on board the *King George V* Rawlings said, 'at the bottom of everybody's heart is the feeling that if the Americans and we stick together our children and grandchildren will not face another war like this. It seems that you Yanks eliminated all the old-fashioned Japanese pilots before we arrived on the scene, and all we've had to contend with are these last-ditch kamikaze people, and I can't say there's anything we learned from the way they handle their machines.'[35] American newspapers were now sitting up and taking notice of the British Pacific Fleet. The *New York Times* commented, 'American Naval Observers with the BPF agree that the spirit of aggressiveness of the men and aircraft is unsurpassed in ANY Navy. No one is more anxious to get into battle than these men. Their morale is immense.'[36]

But beneath the good news and the smiles Vian and Rawlings knew things would now only get more intense. Japanese resistance on Okinawa ended on 2 July 1945. There was now nothing in the way of the Allied forces and mainland Japan. The Allies had reached out to make peace but the Japanese government showed no sign of surrendering. The mighty Third Fleet of the US Navy would begin carrier strikes to soften up targets over Japan from mid-July, ahead of a full-blown invasion of Kyushu in October.

The flyboys of the British Pacific Fleet were now in Australia and finally had a chance to relax. Keith Quilter and Wally Stradwick spent ten days in the Blue Mountains, playing tennis, walking and climbing, and enjoying 'the full domestic life again'. Meanwhile damage to the ships was repaired and new stores taken on. Some squadrons re-equipped with brand new aircraft, and were refreshed with new aircrew.

In late June the British fleet prepared to sail from Sydney once again. The men on board had still not been told where the next operations would be, but few failed to guess their destination. 'We still haven't heard where the next trip is going to be,' jotted Stradwick in his diary. 'I wonder if we'll get the full – Japan.' In a matter of days Stradwick and the rest of the fleet's young airmen would indeed be getting the full. Only six weeks remained until peace would reign again but many wouldn't live to see that day. The final showdown of the Second World War was about to begin.

18

The absolute full

Considering the fierce reaction from the Japanese to Operation Iceberg, it was clear that missions over mainland Japan would be even more perilous. With Okinawa secure and planes able to operate from its airfields, the vast American Third Fleet, which comprised three carrier groups with some sixteen carriers, twelve hundred aircraft and more than one hundred cruisers and destroyers, began operations over the Japanese home islands on 10 July 1945. They tested and probed the Japanese defences by strafing airfields over the wide plains near Tokyo. Five days later the sea links between the islands of Honshu and Hokkaido were targeted, US planes sinking rail ferries and crippling coal supplies.

Hundreds of Japanese planes were destroyed on the ground as the Americans mounted 2,000 sorties a day, targeting inland shipping, freight and occasionally road transport. A force of battleships and cruisers pounded the Japan Ironworks in the coastal city of Kamaishi. B-29 Superfortress USAAF bombing raids were mounted, pulverizing Japanese towns and cities and reducing their wooden houses to ashes. The power of the heavy bombers was chilling. While carrier aircraft from the American Fifth Fleet had dropped just over 12,000 tons of bombs during the entire four-month Okinawa campaign, the Superforts delivered 30,000 tons in June alone.[1] The role of the carrier planes was as much psychological as military. Their presence off the Japanese coast meant nowhere was safe.

Despite this awesome display of firepower, the Japanese government refused to surrender. The Allies therefore had no option but to press ahead with the planned invasion of Kyushu, the southernmost of Japan's four home islands. Operation Olympic would commence in October 1945, to be followed by an invasion of Honshu and an assault on the plains around Tokyo in March 1946. Allied military planners predicted casualties for their own forces exceeding 100,000.

Throughout the summer of 1945 the Japanese military poured men into Kyushu. Civilians were mobilized. The entire nation would defend itself to the death, using the kamikazes that had been so effective in slowing the Americans down on Okinawa. Up to 10,000 aircraft were available for the defence of the home islands, at least half for suicide attacks against the invaders. Just how effective these would have been if the invasion had happened is impossible to say. Only after the war ended did it become clear how desperate the situation was within Japan. The Allied naval blockade meant there was little oil or food being imported. The population was starving. The navy was almost totally destroyed and the air force and army were on their knees. The country might have capitulated more easily than the Allied Chiefs of Staff believed, but of course not all this was known at the time.

No one wanted an invasion of Japan, least of all the Americans, but planning for it went on right up until the last day of the war. This meant a summer and autumn of softening-up targets, and for the first time American and British carrier-based aircraft would fly side by side to attack the heart of Japan, targeting airfields, shipping and factories in low-level daylight raids. For British naval aviation this was a remarkable turnaround. With 252 aircraft flying from four carriers, the striking power of the 1st Aircraft Carrier Squadron dwarfed the front-line air strength of the entire Fleet Air Arm in 1939. Gone were the old Stringbags and Skuas. Here was a naval air force 90 per cent manned by hostilities-only men who had volunteered and been trained in Britain, Canada and America in the last five years.

The British fleet was spearheaded by *Formidable*, *Victorious* and a new carrier, *Implacable*, which carried seventy-eight Avengers, Fireflies and Seafires piloted by largely young and inexperienced crews. *Indefatigable* made up the quadrumvirate when it arrived after completing repairs in Sydney, and the carriers were supported by a fleet of twenty-two cruisers, destroyers and the ever faithful *King George V*. On the morning of 16 July the British Pacific Fleet rendezvoused with the American Third Fleet, 200 miles off Japan's east coast. Even for Admiral Vian in *Formidable*, who had served with the Royal Navy across the world and seen it all, this was 'a mighty assemblage of naval power stretching out upon the ocean as far as the eye could reach ... the escort or screen of battleships, cruisers and destroyers would in themselves have formed a larger fleet than had ever been assembled elsewhere during the war'.[2]

The entire force would serve under Admiral William 'Bull' Halsey, a flamboyant, ebullient man with a love for publicity, who had vowed that one day he would ride Emperor Hirohito's white horse through the streets of Tokyo. Halsey was by no means an intellectual commander; his success came through a combination of colourful personality and surrounding himself with extremely able staff. While Halsey couldn't have been more different to Rawlings, they were set for a close working relationship when they met, together with Vian, in the American battleship *Missouri* on 16 July 1945. For political reasons, the British Pacific Fleet had become Task Force 37, while the American Third Fleet was code-named Task Force 38. In reality, the British fleet operated as a fourth task group alongside Halsey's three others, which were each of a similar size, made up of three carriers, two light carriers and an accompanying screen of ships.

The British Pacific Fleet would operate on the right-hand, northern flank of the task force. The groups were stationed abreast in a straight line twelve miles apart so aircraft could form up without fear of collision. At the centre of each task group were the carriers, with the battleships and cruisers in a circle two and a half miles out, with an outer ring of destroyers providing cover from air and submarine attacks. At predetermined times (every two hours during operating periods) the whole fleet turned into the wind together, flying off strikes and patrols and landing on incoming aircraft. Once the force flagship had completed this operation, her group turned out of the wind and continued on its course. The aim was for the other groups to turn at the same time, preserving the formation. If a task group hadn't landed on all its aircraft, it would have to play catch-up and hope it could steam around and join the rest of the force before it turned again two hours later.

To maximize the impact on the Japanese, Halsey intended the fleet to roam up and down the entire east coast of Japan, striking from different areas and changing targets regularly every few days. The Americans had several fleet trains hundreds of miles apart off the coast of Japan so their fleet could refuel and supply at will. The British group could only move at the speed of its single train with its slow tankers. The Royal Navy could now only marvel at what they had once considered lavish American planning. Little wonder Admiral Fraser remarked, 'the British Fleet is seldom spectacular, never really modern, but always sound'.[3] While Fraser's first two points were surely unfair, the latter was open to debate. Rawlings would have a number of hairy moments simply trying to keep up, and if it hadn't been for seasonal typhoons postponing some strikes, he would have probably failed.

Nevertheless, as the American and British aircraft flew over each other's ships in a recognition exercise a few hundred miles to the east of Tokyo on 16 July 1945, the most powerful navy ever assembled stretched out below, with hundreds of ships spread across 300 square miles of ocean. The aircrews found the site breathtaking. 'As soon as you got off the deck you could look around and see miles of bloody great ships, spread out. It was a wonderful sight,' said Val Bennett.[4] Halsey had told Rawlings and Vian that the objectives over the coming weeks were navy bases, airfields, shipping, transport and factories. The first strikes would begin the following day.

In *Formidable* Philip Ruck-Keene invited the COs of his two Corsair squadrons for a drink and to brief them about the upcoming operations. He had decided 1842 Squadron would lead the first attack, followed by twelve Corsairs from 1841 two hours later. That night the flight commanders pored over target maps and planned their attacks. The anticipation of going on a strike was certainly worse than doing it. Once they got in the air, the fear went. Up in his cabin in the island Admiral Vian was struggling to sleep. 'During the night before the next series of operations I wondered, *Could we make good?*'[5] Only time would tell.

Although there was no real sign the fighting might soon end, as they prepared for their first operations over mainland Japan many of the British airmen couldn't help thinking about life after the war. Some crews were due to be relieved soon and would go home at last. After six years of war, what might the future hold? They weren't dyed-in-the-wool servicemen, but neither did they have jobs to go back to. Some had still been at school when the war broke out and had left early to join up. How could they know what to expect in Civvy Street when they'd never been there?

In a letter home Wally Stradwick confided to his mother, 'It certainly looks as if post-war life and the post-war world isn't going to be honey and roses for several years. Personally, when I'm released from the Navy, I can't imagine what the routine will be.' Stradwick joked he might 'have to marry a barmaid or something after I turn down all the jobs I won't be offered. Bad thing I suppose to sound cynical – but there you are. Or rather, there I am.'[6]

Letters from home boosted morale, and writing them allowed men to unburden themselves. Stradwick, for example, sought reassurance from his mother she would visit the doctor about a health scare she had confided to him. But it was hard to communicate on delicate matters from 6,000 miles away and with a month's delay. He longed to hear from his younger brother Gerald, knowing he was fighting in the jungles of Burma with the commandos. Letters didn't always bring good news of course. Tales of death, affairs and illness unravelled over months. A few words could sap a man's morale as instantly as it could boost it. Often on the surface letters seemed to contain little of face value. But sometimes it was simply the contact that counted. 'Thank you for all your letters. You must know how much they are enjoyed and looked forward to,' Chris Cartledge told his parents.[7]

As the first strikes over Japan neared, the briefings intensified. Topics ranged from fleet manoeuvres to methods of approach, strafing techniques and strategy. It was all becoming very real. Countless anxieties emerged. 'I thought about dying a lot and what would happen to my mother if I did die. Also, wondered what I would actually do if I was ever in a dogfight,' remembers Cartledge.[8] Val Bennett had finally been given a bed in a cabin after its previous owner was killed when the guns of an Avenger with its wings folded were accidentally fired, sending 0.5-inch bullets through the flight deck. 'These bullets went down through four decks, and into the stomach of some poor observer in 1770. I got his bed, and there was me lying there looking at bloody great holes in the ceiling trying to sleep,' said Bennett.[9]

Unlike the previous strikes over Palembang and the Sakishima Islands, there would not be an overall British air commander. Instead, strikes made up of squadrons or flights were tasked individual targets across Japan by the Americans. Flight commanders would decide how they would attack and what methods would be used. Once again, it was the art of strafing which fell under the spotlight. Many of the targets would be aircraft on the ground and effective strafing would be critical. One commander stressed the importance to his pilots of split-second timing with low-level attacks. Pilots were reminded to consider the effectiveness of their own fire and their vulnerability to flak.

According to one Admiralty briefing, enemy fire could be considered as belonging to three categories: fire from the target during the approach, fire from the target pulling out, and fire from other guns nearby. In a 5-per-cent dive firing at 400 feet, the zone of fire was about 12 by 144 feet. 'A nearly horizontal attack is most effective in silencing (temporarily) an enemy who seeks cover and most lethal to a determined enemy who continues firing,' dictated one briefing. If firing opened at 1,000 yards in an attack along the deck, then the pilot had about 5 seconds in which to hit the target. This changed to 2.7 seconds attacking in a 30-per-cent dive and just 1.5 seconds in a 60-per-cent dive. The steeper the dive the less time for strafing. A shallow dive provided a better chance of hitting the target, and this was the tactic therefore favoured by many pilots.[10]

Crews practised strafing when the weather permitted and towed drogues so the ship's anti-aircraft gunners could improve their skills. A number of more powerful 40-mm anti-aircraft guns had been fitted to the carriers in Sydney, beefing up their defences against kamikaze attacks, which were expected to be heavy. Lectures were given about Japanese geography and the weather. Cloud and rain could close in at any time. Crews needed to be aware of winds, morning fog and air masses, warned one lecturer. 'Refusing to comment himself on the question of volcanoes, he admitted to the possibility of typhoons,' joked the 1841 Squadron diary.[11]

Aircrews would have to be hotter than ever on recognition signals in case they lost the fleet in bad weather. All flights would once again come back via pickets to winkle out enemy intruders. Maintenance crews worked hard getting the aircraft into top shape. Ken Ward completed a painting on his Seafire *Minerva*, the goddess of lightning. 'Looks really good!' he wrote in his diary.[12]

Stradwick wrote to his sister Sheila, 'I don't know if the papers at home are giving out much gen on the Fleet Air Arm, but we've been getting around sister – and I mean getting around.' He was able to attend Mass with a visiting chaplain before chatting with him over a bottle of beer in the wardroom. His faith was important. Knowing what was coming up, he signed off to his sister, 'say a prayer for me, especially this time'. On 14 July he wrote again to Sheila to wish her a happy birthday. 'I am writing now because the last post for a while will be going shortly, and we have been at sea for quite a time now, and the fun will be starting very soon . . . I trust that our Dear Mama has been seeing the Doc? Look after her. Will write as soon as poss. Your loving brother, Wally.'[13]

At 06.30 on 17 July 1945 sixteen Corsairs of 1842 Squadron roared off the flight deck of *Formidable* – steaming approximately 200 miles east-north-east of Tokyo – quickly formed up and headed towards Japan in four flights of four. Their mission was to strike airfields at Matsushima and Sendai on the east coast of Japan. A blanket of thick heavy cloud hung at 500 feet. Visibility was poor. Flying at less than fifty feet above the water, within minutes the enemy coast appeared in the haze. Bright tracers zipped through the murk from a lighthouse, hitting one Corsair in its drop tank, which was promptly jettisoned by the pilot who was just thankful he'd not gone up in a ball of flame. The lighthouse keepers watched the dark blue aircraft of the Royal Navy flash past and make land-fall. For the first time in the Second World War the roundels of British aircraft were flying over mainland Japan.

Less than five minutes later they swooped down over the rooftops and attacked Matsushima airfield, aiming 500-pound bombs into hangars, workshops and barrack blocks, and machine-gunning aircraft. The flak was heavy and intense. The figures in the lighthouse had clearly been on the radio.

'The Japs were ready for us and greeted us with a barrage of anti-aircraft fire,' said Chris Cartledge, who flew low and hard over the airfield firing his six 0.5-inch Browning machine guns into a line of parked aircraft. As he turned and lined up a hangar there was a huge bang and his Corsair jumped. 'I had to use full right rudder to keep straight and pull hard on the stick to stop it from diving.' Cartledge radioed his squadron mates to say he was returning to the fleet as 'I would have been a lame duck if I had tried to keep up with the rest of the squadron' and headed alone back out to sea.[14]

About half an hour later, after a tiring climb holding right rudder to 5,000 feet, he was relieved to see the tell tale white wakes of the fleet come into sight. Assuming his hydraulics had been damaged and he might not be able to jettison his extra fuel tank or lower the flaps and arrester hook for landing, Cartledge wisely decided a deck landing would 'probably be disastrous' so decided to bail out over the fleet. But when he pulled the lever to release the hood it had jammed shut. 'I was trapped. I remember looking down on the *Formidable* and thinking quite calmly, *This is it*. I had always noticed this unreal feeling while flying. There was no sense of speed through the air or height above ground or sea. It seemed more as if one was just sitting on a cushion with tiny objects on earth moving slowly below. This pleasant and artificial feeling of security kept me from panicking in what was clearly a life-threatening situation,' said Cartledge.

He radioed *Formidable* to say he would risk a deck landing. The carrier began to turn into the wind as he dropped to circle. On the deck of the carrier bells rang as the barriers were raised. 'Prepare for emergency landing,' piped out from the speakers. Fire crews ran to their positions, readied their equipment, watched and waited. The vultures gathered on goofers' gallery.

Cartledge made his final approach only to be greeted by the batsman waving him around again as the ship started to go into a turn. He then received a signal that the carrier was too far out of position and he would have to wait until it turned into the wind again. He was losing his cool and becoming frantic. He circled the ship and tried again to pull back the canopy, letting go of the stick so that he could twist round and get both hands on the hood to give it a good shove. 'Several times I did this, losing height each time until, giving it one more go, I felt a sudden and very powerful braking sensation.'

Cartledge's Corsair had smashed into the sea. According to one eye-witness, it 'went in off the bows and close to the ship, cartwheeled about four times and went in'.[15] Seconds later the boy from Richmond was floating among the waves watching the last section of his aircraft's wing disappear below the surface twenty yards away. The impact had snapped all his parachute and seat

straps, knocked off the aircraft's hood and thrown him clear with
nothing more than cuts and bruises on his chin, forehead and
shin. 'Miraculous! Ever since that day I have felt I have been given
an extra life, and I still find it wonderful,' says Cartledge, who was
picked up by a destroyer.[16] Two more pilots from 1842 ditched and
were rescued from the sea after being hit by flak and limping back
to the fleet. It was a tough baptism of fire over Japan, but no one
had been killed.

Two hours later Richard Bigg-Wither, CO of 1841 Squadron,
led a formation of nine Corsairs up through thick cloud and
appeared 'about ten miles north of the target – a stroke of genius
so far as most of us were concerned', said one pilot. Achieving
complete surprise, 'we went down to the field, picked our targets
and, while the CO circled, went in and dropped the eggs'.[17] All
the pilots landed on safely a few hours later. During the flight the
pilots he led were reminded once again why they regarded their
CO with such affection. 'Biggy was a pretty casual chap. Instead of
weaving around over enemy territory, he would not bother until
the Japs opened up with anti-aircraft fire, upon which, still in a
seemingly unhurried way, he'd call, "Break, chaps," in his pukka
voice, and the squadron would turn madly in all directions before
reforming but then weaving en route to our target area,' said one.[18]

The other carriers had been having an equally eventful day.
Corsairs from 1834 Squadron on *Victorious* flew right across
Japan to strafe and bomb Niigata airfield on the west coast of
Honshu. 'We were all keen to get on with the job but couldn't help
having reservations,' said one pilot. 'I recall spasms of apprehension as we flew over mainland Japan for the first time. As you flew
over the small towns you sensed a feeling of brooding hate.'[19] After
1834 landed back on safely almost three hours later, a relieved
Vian signalled, 'Very glad to hear your Corsairs got to Niigata in
such unfavourable cloud conditions and left their mark.' Many of
the squadrons were straight up again minutes later for combat air
patrols. Some pilots flew more than six hours in total.

Val Bennett and his pilot Pete Kingston had also flown their first mission over Japan in one of *Indefatigable*'s Fireflies. 'Flying over mainland Japan. I remember being horrified and fascinated by the idea of all these little yellow men down there.' The airmen knew very little about the Japanese. It was a world unknown.

The new boys from *Implacable* had been in action too, with seven Fireflies strafing airfields near Tokyo, although twelve Seafires, now fitted with drop fuel tanks enabling them to carry out strafing missions, were thwarted by foul weather. In total, the fleet had flown seventy-eight offensive sorties and no crew had been lost. Vian could afford to be quietly relieved.

The following morning the men were roused from their bunks once again and a series of strikes was flown off. On *Formidable* Keith Quilter and Wally Stradwick climbed into their Corsairs just before 14.00 for the fleet's fifth ramrod of the day. It would be their first strike over the Japanese mainland. The new CO of 1842, Doug Parker, would lead the first flight of four, and Quilter the second. The weather had 'clamped down hard' once again, with squally showers and strong winds. Everything on deck was soaked. 'It was still raining and hardly anyone was about, covers were still on and some parachutes were soaking in the inadequate storage place on the island,' noted the 1841 Squadron diary.

Nerves were not helped by the fact their targets kept being changed because of bad weather. Admiral Halsey turned the fleet south to search for better conditions, and at last 1842 was told to attack two airfields on the flat plains of a peninsula east of Tokyo, striking the fighter aerodrome at Choshi and a medium-bomber base at Katori. There was little time to brief the aircrews and the strikes had to be launched immediately because the entire fleet was turning into the wind to launch and recover aircraft.

With coughs and flashes of flame the Corsairs snarled into life and one by one roared off the wet flight deck, slowly climbing into the grey sky, each laden down with two 500-pound bombs and a 90-gallon fuel tank. Before long, the two flights were barrelling towards Japan in a tight V formation. Perhaps conscious of the hot reception his squadron had received the previous day, Parker was keen to surprise the Japanese gunners. He ordered Quilter and Stradwick to keep their two sections of two aircraft at treetop height while he took his flight up to draw fire from the airfield's AA gunners by dive-bombing from 8,000 feet. 'All you have to do is keep an eye on me,' Parker told Quilter. 'They'll be looking up at me and won't see you.' It was a nice idea in theory, but 'the silly bugger went above the clouds. We ended up over this aerodrome and weren't in a good attack position,' remembers Quilter.[20]

Quilter and Stradwick came in over the airfield low and very fast, line abreast with their two wingmen either side. But without the element of surprise they were totally exposed. It was too late to pull out now. They had no choice but to press home the attack and pray. Ripping across the airfield at 300 knots, Quilter emptied his six Brownings into aircraft and hangars and felt the usual jolt as he released his bombs, before quickly glancing over both shoulders to check on his other pilots. All four Corsairs were still flying abreast at high speed just twenty feet above the deck, but a thin trail of white smoke streamed from the nose of Stradwick's aircraft.

'He didn't look right and I radioed and said, "Are you all right, Wally?" But he didn't answer,' said Quilter, who desperately repeated the question. He could see the hunched outline of his friend through his canopy but there was no movement. As the three Corsairs pulled up and away, 'His nose just dropped and he ploughed straight into the ground in a great big ball of flames.' Stradwick's aircraft skidded across a field and came to a halt, its scattered remains burning furiously.

Landing on *Formidable* an hour later, Quilter was debriefed and made his way back to the cabin. The empty top bunk yawned at him. Quilter sat down, feeling numb and lost. He began the task of sorting through the few belongings which needed to be sent back to Stradwick's family in Cato Road, Clapham. In the desk drawer he found his friend's small leather-bound brown diary. It fell open to where the neat, loopy handwriting suddenly stopped. The last entry had been made on 14 July 1945, four days before.

> We have been at sea for some time now, and for the last week have known where we are next striking – the absolute full, apart from getting out and saying 'Hallo' to the yellow baskets.
>
> I don't know if it is a particular fault of this Air Arm or not, but we have been on the ship so long, with long periods between ops, that I feel the full twitch over this coming 'do'. The whole thing hinges on strafing. God knows I'm just as scared as anybody flying on any op, but that disappears once the fun starts. However, I like the idea of fighting with brains and skill. Air to air fighting is the ideal. You have to use both whether the odds are for or against you. Strafing on the other hand, in its present form of diving over defended (strong or weak) airfields, etc., is another matter. My argument is that you can use your brains and still, in choosing and executing the approach, attack and get away, but no matter how well you are acquainted with the AA defences and their positions, at the vital moment when you are down over the target in full view of the defenders, I maintain that the odds are pretty high that some, maybe only one gunner, has a near enough no-deflection shot on you. Hence, at the only time that matters, your life depends to a very great extent on absolute luck. All that comprises the one fact that gives us the jolly old twinge of twitch. However, we shall force on.

Walter Stradwick, twenty-two, was the first British forces airman to be shot down and killed over mainland Japan. His death shook up 1842 Squadron. He was one of its original members. A few days later Philip Ruck-Keene wrote a personal condolence letter to Stradwick's mother, praising her son for his 'fine and daring attack'. The letter is blotted and stained, tatty and well thumbed, testament to a mother's need to read over again Ruck-Keene's words describing her son's last moments: 'he went into a shallow dive and crashed in a small field. The aircraft appeared to blow up and was immediately enveloped in a large sheet of flame. His speed in crashing must have been between 200 and 300 knots and there is no doubt that if he was not already dead he must have died immediately.'[21] It was scant consolation, but Stradwick was awarded a posthumous mention in dispatches for his work.

Quilter was lucky not to have bought it himself in a second strafing run after the attack on Choshi, when a 20-mm shell hit his fuselage and blew a hole 'you could put your head through' out the other side. 'Shrapnel actually went right through the rod which connected the stick to the elevators. I was in this steep dive at the time, so if it had severed the rod I would never have pulled out of the dive. You lived on a hair breadth,' said Quilter.

As if they didn't need reminding, Stradwick's death high-lighted too the odds fighter pilots faced in strafing attacks. 'You never knew each time you took off whether you were coming back or not. You had to get yourself in a mindset – which not every-body, but most did – where you didn't allow yourself to think that way, otherwise you would get the twitch,' said Quilter.

> There was another chap on the squadron who got the twitch. He had worked out all the averages and said, 'Oh well, I'm the last guy on my course who is still alive, I must be next.' But actually you had to believe that those averages don't actually apply. Your chances of being shot are just the same on your very first operational flight as your very last. Psychology in the way people's minds work is infinitely variable, so some people could accept that way of looking at it while others got captured by this idea, 'I am the last guy on my flight or course,' or, 'I must be next – my number is up.'

At this point in the war aircrews were looking somewhat eccentric as they clambered out of their hot, cramped cabins wearing a variety of clothing culled from America, Ceylon, the RAF and the navy. None of the carriers had facilities for hanging flying clothing, and gear rapidly deteriorated as it was more often than not left in a damp bundle in some odd corner. Some aircrew wore Australian jungle-green lightweight flying overalls with just underpants beneath. Another admitted flying in his pyjamas on one mission and managed to prang his Corsair landing on *Victorious* when his silk scarf blew up over his head.

Anti-gravity suits filled with water were tested, the theory being they would help counter the tendency of pilots to black out momentarily as they exited steep dives or turns. But the suits were cumbersome and impracticable, and were soon ditched. Besides, the pilots had become used to the grey fuzzy sheen which briefly enveloped their eyesight. It lasted seconds and had no serious impact on their health.

Much of the flyers' equipment, such as sunglasses and shark repellent, had to be bought in Australia owing to a delay in supplies from Britain. Shark repellent did little to reassure crews. Sitting in his Corsair on the deck waiting to take off one afternoon, one Corsair pilot looked down and saw a 'huge shark idly swimming by. A few moments later on take-off I almost bent the throttle I was so anxious to get safely off', he said.[22]

With the fleet now more than 4,000 miles from Australia, the supply of fresh fruit and vegetables had dwindled to 'such an infinitesimal dribble that it was quite ineffectual', according to one medical officer, who reckoned the lack of fresh food contributed directly to the increase in men seeking medical treatment for boils, carbuncles and other skin complaints. 'When one has been weeks at sea without sight of land, even the issue of a few apples or oranges, which have not been seen for some time, had a remarkable effect psychologically', he wrote in a report.[23]

On operational days a running buffet was introduced at the captain's dining table. Aircrews being debriefed could pick from a buffet in the cabin next door, with food such as sausage rolls, bread and butter, canned fruit and cheese laid out for them. Doctors advised that 'under the nervous tension of operational

flying' the food available should be 'easily digestible and sufficiently palatable to attract the rather queasy appetite'. They also
advocated high-energy food such as dates and raisins.

After replenishing with fuel, two more days' strikes were carried
out, with a record 416 sorties flown by British aircraft on 24 July,
hitting airfields, radar stations, small shipping and dockyards. It
was crucial no Japanese transport remained, even if there was little
fuel left to power it. Meanwhile, American carrier planes began
the final destruction of the heavy units of the Imperial Japanese
Navy, which were lying camouflaged at its naval base at Kure on
the Seto Inland Sea between the islands of Honshu, Kyushu and
Shikoku.

Frustratingly for Rawlings and Vian, the Americans refused
to allocate British aircrews larger shipping targets. Halsey wanted
to ruin the Japanese navy, primarily as revenge for Pearl Harbor,
but later admitted 'we forestalled a possible post-war claim by
Britain that she had delivered even a part of the final blow that
demolished the Japanese fleet'. But although denied the chance to
take part in missions against major naval targets, British pilots
were attacking with ever-increasing venom.

Arthur Hudson, an RAF armourer who had been captured in
the Dutch East Indies in 1942 and been sent to a POW camp at
Shimonoseki, Japan, watched in awe as two Corsairs came
'screaming in across the sea' to attack a harbour, their white Royal
Navy roundels standing proud against sleek blue fuselages as they
'blew it to bits'. The following day three more raked the harbour
again, killing a number of Japanese and inadvertently injuring one
POW. 'This is how accurate these lads were,' said Hudson.[24]

Indefatigable was also having fun after finally joining the fleet
on 20 July, its Seafire crews rejuvenated by the arrival of a new
wing commander – Buster Hallett, one of the most experienced
pilots in the Fleet Air Arm, who like Ronnie Hay was small in
stature but large in personality. 'I have always known what he

looked like, he's the big boy in the FAA, but I could not believe the size of him when I saw him. He gives me the impression of being able to live comfortably in a Seafire. He is that little. I think I like him,' wrote Ken Ward in his diary. Hallett was a key figure in getting ninety-gallon belly tanks fitted to the Seafires, and although the planes were still limited by their range and delicate undercarriages, over the final days Hallett led a series of aggressive strikes over Japan, flying in his distinctive silver-painted Seafire.

While there was scant air opposition, ground flak remained deadly. Flying over Japan could be deceptive. It was easy to become seduced by the mosaic of pretty rice fields, green terraced hills and pretty wooded valleys. This all changed when raiders reached an airfield. 'I have never seen quite so much 20-mm and 40-mm flak,' said the CO of 880 Seafire Squadron in *Implacable*. 'The general sensation of being over Japan was one of foreboding, deep fear. We had heard tales of what the locals did to airmen who got hacked down. We got in and out as quickly as we could,' he added.[25]

The lack of air opposition was frustrating: 'when you have trained to be a fighter pilot your greatest ambition is to shoot down an enemy aircraft'. However, 'We soon found out ground attack was much more dangerous and chancy without the feeling that you were pitting your hard-earned skill against an adversary you could see,' said Keith Quilter. He was about to find out just how true that was.

19

The final onslaught

The little town of Owase, on the south-east coast of Honshu, is a typical Japanese fishing town. It sits on a bay backed by a plain three miles wide, which gently rises from the harbour front, until two miles back a horseshoe of hills covered in thick mixed woodland steeply rises for 1,000 feet. Warblers, brown bears and monkeys live among the cedar and fir trees, drinking from opal-green freshwater lakes. Behind this is another range of higher hills and mountains, the menacing outline of their black serrated summits permanently kissed by wisps of low cloud. The bay itself, flanked by more steep-sided woodland, widens into the Pacific Ocean and is guarded by a handful of little islands. A five-mile long inlet with high wooded hills on both sides runs into the side of the bay from the north.

Its relatively deep natural harbour and steep hills on three sides made Owase an attractive location for the Japanese Imperial Navy to anchor some of its minor ships, now largely inactive due to the threat from the Allies. Approximately a quarter of a mile from the quayside a 600-foot harbour wall ran across the bay's mouth. Larger vessels could anchor on the inside of this wall, their commanders knowing they were well protected against attack from the sea. Anti-aircraft guns were positioned and concentrated into a narrow field of fire, so that attacking aircraft faced a barrage of flak.

The Japanese reasoned a successful air attack approaching from over the land was unlikely. Also the harbour was too small a target for the big B-29s, and Avengers were not nimble enough for the confined airspace. Even the pilot of a single-seat fighter would have to dive steeply down the hills at treetop height and across the rooftops of the town, releasing his bomb three seconds before he flew over his target, in the hope he could skip it across 350 feet of water to slam into the ship's hull. This would require skilful airmanship and a ton of luck.

As the sun rose over the bay on the morning of 28 July 1945 there were at least four ships dotted around Owase harbour. The biggest and most visible from the air, anchored on the inside of the harbour wall, was *CD 45*, a 750-ton 150-foot Kaibokan Class frigate. Powered by two 1,900-horsepower diesel engines, it was by no means a large vessel, with a crew of around 136. But with two 120-mm guns fore and aft and six 20-mm guns, it packed enough punch to send up a shell at 3,000 mph that would smash a nasty hole in a Corsair zooming over at 50 feet.

At 04.15 three flights of Corsairs from 1842 Squadron had taken off from *Formidable* in the gloomy dawn sky for ramrods against targets on the Inland Sea. An hour later, as the flights neared the Japanese coast flying at 10,000 feet, Doug Parker looked down to his left and spotted the frigate in the harbour. It wasn't their primary target but seemed too good an opportunity to ignore. Parker radioed Keith Quilter to take his flight down.

Quilter pushed the control stick forward and took his Corsair into a long diving 180-degree turn to the port. His plan of attack was to bring the four fighters in over the hills landside from the west and to attack the target in two sections, flying fast and low, using the element of surprise to reduce any anti-aircraft fire. It was a gamble, reasoned Quilter, but he was convinced it was the only way to get a good clean shot at the ship.

With the 2,000 horses of each Pratt & Whitney engine pulling the four Corsairs through the air at 250 knots, the pilots adopted well-practised attack tactics as they straightened out from their final turn, with the outside planes cutting in behind in a scissors manoeuvre to confuse any targeting AA batteries.

Quilter led the flight with his wingman, while New Zealander

Ian Stirling attacked in the second section one hundred feet behind. With Owase dead ahead, Quilter glanced down to check the 500-pound bomb under each wing was fused and the six Browning 0.5-inch machine guns were armed. He was now flying at 350 knots at a height of just 50 feet, the treetops skidding below in a blur. He flew down the final hill, flattened out over the glinting grey rooftops of Owase and headed for the black outline of the frigate. Quilter released his bombs just as he reached the shoreline, felt the aircraft lift a touch as the frigate flashed underneath and then used his rudder bar and control stick to weave and skid the aircraft a few feet above the waves towards the open sea of the Pacific.

'I just aimed to chuck the bomb straight on,' said Quilter.[1] It worked. Behind him a pillar of white water gushed one hundred feet into the sky just as Stirling and his wingman flew over, dropping their bombs with deafening roars and huge explosions.

In the ship below, Saito Shuuji had been busy washing his face thinking about the day ahead when an emergency announcement was made: 'Prepare for naval air combat.' Several approaching specks could be seen in the sky. 'Missiles came shooting towards us,' recalled Shuuji. 'Several direct hits later, and there was mass chaos with some men fighting back and others responsible for moving the injured to safety,' he added.[2]

Captain Iwata had been among the first to be hit and was covered in blood. 'I rushed towards him to ask him if he was OK and to take him to safety. However, despite his pain and filled with the immense feeling of duty and responsibility, he calmly instructed me to ignore him, rescue the injured and then come for the dead. I urged him to allow me to help him to safety, but he would not allow it. "Leave me until last," he said and with that he made no attempt to get off the boat.'

People in Owase ran to the nearest shelter. One boy took refuge in an air raid shelter his father had made near a bamboo grove. 'The ripe crops of sweet potato were in full bloom in the fields. Watching from the entrance of the shelter, I could see cartridge shells landing in the sweet potato fields,' he said.[3]

It was only as he reached the open sea that Quilter realized the attack hadn't gone quite as smoothly as he'd hoped. Stirling had ditched in Owase bay after his aircraft was hit by intense anti-aircraft fire and was now scrambling into his dinghy under fire from some Japanese who were taking pot shots at him from a few hundred feet away on the shore.

'One of the guys called up and said Ian had ditched after being hit by anti-aircraft fire,' said Quilter, who now needed to check on Stirling's position but couldn't risk flying back over the town. 'As we came down for the attack I had spotted out of the corner of my eye a side creek. So I stayed down at sea level and went around using the creek to approach the bay from the side without being seen.'

Quilter barrelled his Corsair up along the coast before cutting in again and flying low and fast down the creek back towards the main bay. Breathing quickly through his oxygen mask, his eyes narrowed and flicked all around the sky, keeping a sharp lookout for flak or enemy fighters. But there seemed to be nothing more than wooded hills above him and the odd trawler below.

Then, without warning, his engine cut out.

'There must have been an AA battery among the trawlers or fishing boats, as it just stopped dead,' said Quilter. Too low to bail out he had no other option but to ditch. In a matter of seconds he needed to make a series of decisions which would either save his life or kill him. With the water rapidly approaching, he yanked the lever to release the spare fuel tank, closed the throttle and gently pulled the stick back for a three-point landing, bracing himself by locking his arms against the side of the canopy as his Corsair glided down into the bay a mile from the harbour he had just attacked.

The Corsair planed across the water, tipped onto its nose momentarily in a shower of spray, slammed back down and came to a halt. There was silence except for the ticking of the rapidly cooling engine and the splash of water. Quilter slid back the hood, climbed out onto a wing and inflated his yellow dinghy. He jumped in and 'paddled like mad towards the open sea'. He was less than a mile from Japan, 'feeling very alone and vulnerable'.

As Quilter and Stirling contemplated life in a Japanese POW camp a well-oiled drill was under way. Ever since his fleet started operating in the Pacific, Admiral Vian had been especially keen to ensure the best possible efforts were made to rescue his downed aircrew, and Admiral Halsey had reassured him use would be made of the numerous Allied submarines roaming up and down the coast of Japan. The Lifeguard League system was proactive. More than a dozen submarines were stationed off the coast of areas being attacked by carrier planes. Their locations were known to the airmen, who could communicate with the submarines via secure radio channels.

It had been a routine morning for the eighty-strong crew of the USS *Scabbardfish*, a 300-foot Balao Class submarine, until Commander 'Pop' Gunn received a report via VHF radio of 'two pilots down in Owase Wan'. Gunn ordered his crew to head for Owase at 'flank speed'. Thirty-one minutes later *Scabbardfish* neared the coast. According to the action report written immediately afterwards, the lookouts spotted 'one raft inside mouth of bay. Sighted puffs of ACK-ACK, but all on far side of first range of hills. Air cover said they would strafe the beach to cover us.'[4]

The sunshine was now beating down hard as Quilter continued to paddle furiously. The little wooden paddles were proving useless against the Pacific swell. Green hills rose either side of the bay for about two miles until they reached the open sea. 'It reminded me of Falmouth Harbour,' said Quilter. Looking back he could see flak from the shore batteries targeting the fighters overhead. The waterfront of Owase town was clearly visible. Ian

Stirling, who was half a mile closer to Owase, felt pellets of lead plop into the water all around him.

Quilter was making little headway and knew it was only a matter of time before the Japanese sent out a boat but was determined to keep paddling until he was picked up. Perhaps the Corsairs above would keep them off for a while yet. Just when he thought things couldn't get any worse, looking out towards the mouth of the bay, Quilter saw a 'black sinister-looking thing' appear on the horizon. 'I assumed it was a Japanese sub which used this harbour and it was coming back into port.' He immediately chucked his revolver over the side of the boat. Survival was about capitulation, not conflict. 'I just thought, *Oh God now I'm for it*. What could I do?'

As the black shape got closer he saw figures. And then he recognized the white hats and uniforms. There was no mistake. They were US Navy Gobs – US Navy slang for ordinary seamen. 'I could see they were Yanks and I just thought, *Thank God for that*. It's an American submarine. It was huge!' The men hauled Quilter up on board, who introduced himself. 'We've got ourselves a goddamn Limey,' was their first reaction, to grins all round. 'I then said, "Well my mate's just a little bit further up in the bay, so if you don't mind getting him too . . ."'

Quilter was sent below while *Scabbardfish* headed further into Owase bay to pick up Stirling, before it motored out at flank speed into the safety of the Pacific Ocean. The American Corsair pilots of *Scabbardfish*'s combat air patrol received permission from Gunn to attack the frigate, scoring two more direct hits. Down below, Stirling and Quilter were given shots of whiskey by the captain and issued with American navy trousers, shirts, socks and boots. 'I had a freshwater shower. It was wonderful after weeks of saltwater on *Formy*,' said Quilter.

For him and Stirling the war was over. They would spend the next three weeks on the submarine, and the Japanese surrendered before they were returned to their carrier.

*

The Americans launched some of their biggest strikes that day, flying over 250 sorties. At the end of the day Admiral Halsey signalled, 'Mark well the 28 July. To Dumbos and Lifeguard, to CAP and the men of the surface team, to the valiant British force on the right flank, well done. For the great flying fighters who fought it out over Japan to a smashing victory I have no words that I can add to the glory of the factual record they wrote with their courage, their blood and lives.'

Following a strike on 30 July, over the next week the fleets refuelled and tried to dodge the typhoons which were now plaguing the region, creating driving rain, huge swells and giant waves.

With at least a dozen men shot down in the last two weeks of July alone, the shortage of first-line FAA aircrew remained critical. By the late autumn, when Operation Olympic was due to start, it was hoped the 1st Aircraft Carrier Squadron would be supported by two reserve air groups operating from escort carriers, with 500 serviceable aircraft in Australia. Naval bases in Ceylon were expected to make up the shortfall in numbers eventually, but pilots were still being sent straight into operations without any refresher flying, often with deadly consequences. A number of American-built Royal Navy escort carriers were already in the Pacific – some being used in the air train ferrying replacement aircraft up from Australia to the fleet, others engaged in getting new pilots 'oven ready'.

With the war all but over in most theatres, pilots with a minimum of 500 flying hours were asked to volunteer to make up the shortfall in numbers. In June 1945 twenty-four pilots from the Royal Australian Air Force were transferred, taking a drop in rank to join the Royal Navy. Between them they had experienced action across North Africa, Europe and the Far East and had in many cases had been decorated. A number of naval air bases were also established in Australia. One of the largest was at RNAS Schofields, where some of the most experienced naval pilots were tasked with training flyers before they went into the operational area. The instructors included Dickie Reynolds, whose good looks and louche demeanour made him a magnet for journalists wanting glamour in their reports.

While the fleet battled the typhoons, diplomatic attempts to navigate a clear passage to peace were also struggling. Tokyo was eager for a settlement, but its terms were deemed unacceptable by the Allied powers. The Japanese leadership assumed an American invasion was inevitable but hoped it could negotiate conditions knowing the Americans would dearly like to avoid the casualties that would mean. That there might be a third way even more dramatic and terrible was beyond their comprehension.

Down in *Scabbardfish* Keith Quilter and Ian Stirling were enjoying their new life as submariners. With the vessel continuing its mission to rescue other downed airmen, they knew it would be some time yet before they were returned to *Formidable*. It had been ten days since their dramatic rescue, and the ship had now become something of a club for ditched aviators as they had been joined by a number of American fighter pilots also rescued off the coast of Japan. 'Us airmen used to tease the crew, asking if they could do a slow roll in the submarine for us,' said Quilter.

Conditions were cramped but luxurious compared to a British carrier, with fresh food, air conditioning and even a little library, where Quilter tucked into *The Nine Tailors*, a 1934 mystery novel by Dorothy L. Sayers. Quilter also got permission to listen to the submarine's radio, tuning into American forces broadcasts, and on 7 August 1945 heard news of the most extraordinary event of the Second World War. An American B-29 Superfortress called *Enola Gay* had dropped an atomic bomb on the Japanese city of Hiroshima. 'The report said we had dropped an atom bomb, but no one in the ship believed me, so I put the loudspeakers on,' said Quilter. 'None of us knew anything about atomic warfare, but it seemed incredible that one bomb could do all this damage.'

Back on the ships of the British Pacific Fleet cruising off the east coast of Japan, men hearing the news were equally confused and amazed. 'Incredible news this morning about just one bomb dropped by the Yanks on a Japanese city on Sunday last,' wrote Ken Ward in his diary. (In fact it was the day before.) 'It is a new bomb – an atomic bomb – 2,000 times more explosive power than any bomb yet used in the War. It seems colossal devastation results from this bomb. Why are we hitting Japan and sinking junks?'[5] The following day Ward found out more details: 'The city was Hiroshima. The Americans claim that all living matter was wiped out within a radius of 10 miles. Any person later entering the area is killed too! The crew of the Superfortress were 10 miles away at 30,000 feet but felt it strongly. They say it weighed 100 pounds. It seems too unbelievable. And barbarous!' But the news was almost universally welcomed by the men of the British Pacific Fleet, who knew that maybe, just maybe, peace was on the horizon.

In the meantime the airstrikes continued. On 9 August, as a second atom bomb was dropped over Nagasaki, 750 miles to the north-east the British Pacific Fleet's aircraft roared off the flight decks for their first set of missions in almost two weeks. Throughout the day ten individual and four combined strikes were launched, with more than 400 sorties hitting targets on the east coast of Honshu in one of the most intensive and successful days' flying for the fleet. It was also the most costly: six aircrew were killed, most by anti-aircraft fire while carrying out low-level raids despite being advised by commanders to 'take it easy' bearing in mind the war might be so near its end.

During one ramrod Hammy Gray, the senior pilot of *Formidable*'s 1841 Squadron, was leading two flights of four Corsairs over Onagawa Bay, thirty miles up the coast from Sendai. Gray was a most unlikely warrior – boyish and plump, with a dimpled, smiling face and an easy-going quality. He was extremely popular. But in the air the Canadian was known by his boss Bigg-Wither as a hunter who had already shown skill and bravery in attacking

Japanese ships in low-level point-blank attacks. 'He just didn't like them,' said Bigg-Wither.[6]

Gray led his flight down in a fast dive from 10,000 feet towards the land and then out into the steep-sided bay. But roaring down through ravines and across the open stretch of water, they were met by furious flak and machine-gun fire from four ships. Gray's aircraft was almost immediately hit, and one of his bombs shot clean off. Pressing home his attack, he released his second bomb almost on top of a ship, before his now-flaming Corsair flipped sharply onto its back and dived into the water one hundred feet beyond.

'There goes Gray,' one of the other pilots shouted over the radio.[7]

Gray's bomb struck home, penetrating the engine room of the escort ship *Amakusa*, which blew up, killing seventy-one crew, before sinking. The other three pilots headed towards the open sea, not quite comprehending that their senior pilot was dead, but returned to make two more sweeps over the bay, until their guns were scorched and spent. They flew back to *Formidable*, leaving Onagawa Bay in smoke and flames.

Gray was only the second Fleet Air Arm pilot in the war to be awarded the Victoria Cross, but Bigg-Wither was angry.

> I wondered why we were being asked to continue attacking after this enormous bomb had been dropped. It seemed pretty clear to everybody that the Japs couldn't withstand that for very long . . . I was most surprised when we did those last two days' operations . . . I rather resented it because in those two days I not only lost my senior pilot Hammy Gray, but two other pilots – one Canadian and one British – and I just thought it was unnecessary to go on.[8]

Further strikes took place the following day, with Admiral Nimitz keen to ensure the Third Fleet continued to attack. The USSR had only declared war on Japan on 8 August and was now advancing into the Japanese puppet state of Manchukuo. One Corsair, an

Avenger and two Fireflies were lost in 372 sorties. During one of these strikes the Firefly belonging to Ian Darby, a New Zealand observer, was hit by flak at 5,000 feet and his pilot, Burn O'Neil, managed to invert the machine so they could both literally drop out. 'We wondered what reception they were going to get when they got down,' said Val Bennett, as he looked on from his Firefly.[9] They landed safely and ditched their revolvers. 'We decided as a matter of circumspection that we would take what the Japs hurled out,' said Darby later. 'There was nothing we could do and no point attempting this gung-ho James Bond stuff, so we were quite happy to let it evolve at the time and see what happened.'[10]

Captured and beaten up, they were placed in solitary confine- ment. Darby had long conversations in Morse code via the piping with a British Royal Navy Avenger pilot in 828 Squadron who had been shot down and was in the neighbouring cell. 'We became very quick and adept at this, and we were rattling these messages off no trouble at all through this pipe,' remembers Darby. They were soon transferred to Omori POW camp near Tokyo, where more than 375 mainly American, British and Dutch prisoners were being held. Knowing the war was about to end, discipline among the Japanese guards broke down. They hated flyers and some were determined to exact personal revenge.

> We were the dreadful people and we knew we were going to get the chop if things turned nasty. We had reports the Ameri- cans were coming in to take us away. That evening some of the Japanese guards revolted, came into our hut with this Japanese sword hoping to give us the death blow. Burn and I stood on either side of this door prepared to belt them as they came through. But fortunately there was a Japanese official who leaned up and grabbed hold of the sword with his hand.

The renegade guards ran out of the camp and were never seen again, but for Darby 'that was quite frightening. That chap cer- tainly saved us. Mind you, Burn and I would have dealt with one or two of them, but not the lot.'

Conditions in the camp were frightful, with the prisoners surviving on handfuls of rice and water. 'I had a dose of the skidders for twenty-four hours, during which time I went twenty-seven times. I could almost fill in a logbook with the number of times I went,' said Darby. In the last few days before the camp was liberated two weeks later, low-flying American aircraft dropped forty-four-gallon metal drums packed with medical aid and food, which would bounce through the camp at high speed, smashing through the hut walls. Despite these provisions Darby lost more than two and a half stone.

Darby saw first-hand the state of Tokyo.

I couldn't believe the damage that was done . . . there was nothing left but concrete reinforced buildings, and very few of them. The whole lot was just gone, and that's the mess they [the Americans] made of it. They kept bombing and rebombing it, and they were determined to wreck Tokyo, which they did, lock stock and barrel. According to people in our hut, bodies [of Japanese people] were still being washed up until shortly before we came into their camp . . . still being washed up from the tide.

After the strikes of 10 August the majority of the British Pacific Fleet departed for Sydney for planned replenishment in order to return in time to take part in the early stages of Operation Olympic. They didn't know that those strikes would be their last. No one could deny that the airmen of the British Pacific Fleet had risen to the task. In eight days of operations off the coast of Japan Royal Navy fighters flew 1,172 sorties – 121 more than during the twenty-four days of Operation Iceberg. Aircraft losses per sortie were three times those of the missions over the Sakishima Islands, illustrating the greater offensive effort and the more intense flak over the Japanese mainland. Thirty-two airmen had been killed, an average of four per strike day.

The Royal Navy's airmen had pulled their weight with the

American task groups, with almost identical figures for the number of enemy aircraft destroyed per sortie. However, British combat losses were 48 per cent higher per sortie than those suffered by the Americans. This was a testament to the FAA's offensive spirit but also demonstrates one effect of the smaller numbers of aircraft used by the British in each ramrod or bombing sweep compared to the US Navy, which often left the British horribly exposed – as Wally Stradwick found out so tragically. The Americans may have attacked more heavily defended targets, but, unlike 90 per cent of the British Pacific Fleet aircraft, their planes were armed with rockets and had flak-busting bombs.[11]

The most heavily defended airfield in Japan had over 180 guns of all kinds. However, average fighter losses in strikes against airfields defended by over 70 guns were actually less than those sustained in strikes against airfields defended by 30–70 guns. This was because ramrods against larger airfields tended to be made up of formations of at least 34 fighters carrying out combined strikes. Losses by smaller sweeps of 7–16 aircraft against airfields less well defended were 57 per cent higher than those of fighters in combined strikes. In other words, combined strikes with greater numbers of aircraft compensated for the greater risk of flak experienced on heavily defended airfields.[12]

With the end in sight, a British token force remained, comprising *Indefatigable*, *King George V*, two cruisers and ten destroyers. On Sunday 12 August Ken Ward wrote in his diary, 'We awoke to the news that the Allied powers have accepted Japan's offer of surrender. So we think the War is over when the Captain announced it. What excitement!' But it was short-lived. Some Japanese wanted to fight on. There was deadlock between some members of the Japanese military, the cabinet and the emperor. To the outside world Japan remained silent, so the strikes continued. On 14 August Ken Ward noted, 'We had a briefing at 5.45 p.m. for a strike tomorrow on Tokyo and we think it disgusting to put lives at risk at this time. Our small strike could make no difference to the issue.'

Val Bennett agreed. His squadron, 1772, found ground fire lethal in low-level daylight bombing raids. 'They were pretty hot because they had plenty of practice and plenty of ammunition. If you were visible above the rooftops they would have you.' In the last ten days of operations over Japan 1772 Squadron lost four crews out of twelve. 'If it had gone on another month our chances would have been pretty small. You could see where that was heading.' Bennett and his fellow airmen were not impressed. 'We didn't discuss it a lot, but I made a drawing of the captain, in a diving attitude, in the squadron line book, saying, "I shall continue strike," looking like he was dropping a bomb. It wasn't him though, was it? It was us that were bloody well being sent to strike. We couldn't really see the point of going on. We were just waiting for it to stop . . . but I suppose he had to.'

Bennett was understandably peeved but there was no question of not carrying on. At 04.00 on 15 August 1945, *Indefatigable* launched a combined strike of six Avengers, eight Seafires and four Fireflies. After little enemy air action and with peace only hours away, crews were told to strafe airfields but once again not to do anything that would unduly endanger their lives. However, for the first time in weeks, they were ambushed by a group of about twelve Zekes over Tokyo Bay, sparking off the last dogfight of the Second World War. 'It was the only day I saw a Japanese fighter,' said Bennett. 'We were just about to go into the dive and I looked up and could see wings flashing and we could hear them saying, "Look out," over the radio.'

Pete Kingston, Bennett's pilot, took the Firefly into a steep dive to strafe an airfield, but 'there was a hell of a bang, and Pete's windscreen had blown off – jettisoned itself'. Fireflies had been known to lose their canopies, and just at this critical moment it was a British design defect rather than a Japanese shell that looked like it could put a messy end to Bennett and Kingston's war. 'It made a hell of a roar and Pete and I could hardly hear each other.

We pulled out of the dive and headed home. Not a very brilliant operation,' said Bennett.

A vicious melee had broken out. The Seafire pilots flew skilfully, shooting down four Zeros, with four more probables, but Freddie Hockley, a pilot in 887 Squadron, failed to hear a warning because his radio had broken, and was shot down from behind, bailing out over Tokyo Bay and parachuting safely down. Hockley landed in rural farmland on the Chiba Peninsula east of Tokyo. The noise of his Seafire crashing and the pillar of black smoke alerted locals, who accepted his offer of cigarettes and chocolate from his escape kit. Shortly afterwards, he was taken to a local school and handed over to a Japanese army unit. After being blindfolded and beaten, Hockley was taken to the house of a local landowner, where the regimental commander was billeted. The landowner's wife took pity on Hockley and gave him a kimono, while he showed her a locket with a picture of his sweetheart inside.

At noon the Emperor's recorded reading of the Imperial Rescript on the Termination of the War was broadcast to the nation. The Second World War was over. One of the soldiers listening rang divisional HQ to ask what should be done with Hockley. 'Finish with him in the mountains tonight,' came the reply.[13] Hockley was taken to regimental headquarters, where another officer ordered ten soldiers to dig a makeshift grave half a mile away. After initially hoping he would be treated well, Hockley must have guessed now that he had little time to live.

Between 8.30 and 9 p.m. that evening, as it was getting dark, Hockley was led away by a handful of Japanese soldiers. He was blindfolded with a small towel, his hands tied lightly in front of him, and made to stand with his back to the freshly dug hole. Standing just a few feet away, Lieutenant Masazo Fujino raised his revolver and fired two shots into Hockley's chest. But Hockley didn't fall. Fujino fired again and Hockley collapsed into the hole. 'He was still moving. He seemed to be in much pain, therefore I borrowed a sword . . . and stabbed him in the back,' admitted Fujino later.

It was a tragic end for the last Allied airman shot down in the war. Two years later two men were hanged after a British military tribunal. Hockley was not the only airman from the British Pacific Fleet to be executed by the Japanese. In the months following the end of the war, it emerged that nine aircrew who had been shot down over Palembang the previous January had been killed in similar ways. There was some good news, however: Don Cameron had survived a grim few weeks in captivity after being shot down over Ishigaki, and was soon reunited with his squadron mates in *Victorious*.

Over the following weeks the flyers turned aid workers, flying numerous missions over Japan to identify POW camps and drop supplies. By now, *Indefatigable* had been at sea for six weeks and there was little left in its stores. Nevertheless, fifteen canvas bags were filled with everything from half-empty tubes of toothpaste to tinned food, cigarettes and medicine from the sickbay and dropped by parachute on Yokkaichi camp, south of Tokyo, where prisoners had painted 'PW' in large white letters on a roof.

'The prisoners gathered outside their huts, waving exuberantly,' said Roy Hawkes, flying his Avenger over the camp. On the beach they had drawn 'YANKS 196 BR 25 DU 75' in the sand – their numbers by nationality.[14] Hawkes flew back over the camp, opening the bomb-bay doors to allow his observer to release the bags. 'It was very moving to see all these chaps,' agreed Val Bennett, who flew such missions in his Firefly. 'I was conscious we were finally doing something which we felt was saving lives and optimistic. One had the burden of the worry of survival lifted off and it was now a pleasure to fly, knowing that one was going to come back.' The aircraft swung out to sea and watched the parachutes open. Some fell short into the sea, and immediately figures from the beach waded out to retrieve them. Down in the camp Fred Baumeister, a Dutchman who had been a prisoner of war since March 1942, scribbled in his diary, 'August 29, 1945 – Allied planes flew over our camp. 12 packages Red Cross stuff dropped, enough for 2 days; afterwards more packages will be dropped (coming from the British battleship "the Indefatigable").'15

An observer in 820 Squadron penned a personal letter and included it in a drop, attached to a makeshift parachute made from a pair of old pajamas. The men in the camp sent a reply:

1 September 1945

FROM EX-POW YOKKAICHI L/Cpl. G. Rochester
Northumberland Fusiliers

Dear John,

I wish to thank you and all on board for everything you have done for us in the past few days, the first day we saw the British Navy overhead we went absolutely mad, and we were scared in case you missed us. You men have no idea how we felt when we knew the Navy was here, because we have been looking for you every day for the past three and a half years, but we always knew some day that you would win this war.

The food you gave us has done wonders for everyone, we are all looking much better so we shall be fit and well by the time we reach 'Good Old England' which, we hope, will be very soon.

You sure made the Yanks look with your fine air display, they sure got a big kick out of it, we have 200 in this camp against 25 British so we have had a hard time of it keeping the old flag flying but we won through the day you men arrived.

I wish you could have seen the men get mobile on the cigs and all the other food, everybody was talking between big mouthfuls of peaches and crackers and cheese, and it did not take long to finish off the lot. I hope that you did not run short in the messes but we thank you from the bottom of our hearts.

We looked for you all day yesterday but you never came and we were very disappointed. I hope that you have not moved as we want to see you all again as often as possible. We had food, cigs and clothing dropped by a B-29 yesterday and he promised to come again today, it is a big day for the camp as we have a lot to square up with these heathens.

We are all at a dead loss as to how to send these letters but we are expecting Red Cross Delegates today so hope to send them through to you.

I have more letters to write so I will close by wishing you and the ship all the best.

G. Rochester.

PS The Japs have left us alone.

PPS Cheerio: Good Luck and a Happy Reunion Soon! [16]

On 2 September in Tokyo Bay American sailors crammed every vantage point on board the battleship USS *Missouri* to watch history being made. Down on the ship's deck a dark green baize tablecloth had been laid over a metal trestle table where the documents that would end a war in which at least sixty million people had died were about to be signed.

At just before 9 a.m. local time a small launch came alongside the ship, and the Japanese foreign minister, old and lame, dressed in formal morning coat and top hat, limped on board, followed by military representatives. They waited patiently in front of the gathered rows of American admirals and generals, national representatives from other Allied countries, press photographers and film cameras.

At 09.02 General MacArthur came on deck with Admirals Nimitz and Halsey, and made a short speech before instructing the Japanese to sign the surrender document and doing the same. Admiral Fraser then signed on behalf of the United Kingdom, followed by representatives from other key Allied countries. It was a well stage-managed event oozing with American power, in which, ironically, the British had once again played a symbolic supporting role, with *King George V* providing the wooden chairs which the signatories used.

Twenty minutes later, as the ceremony drew to a close, a massive fly-past comprising hundreds of American carrier aircraft rumbled overhead. Two dozen British aircraft from *Indefatigable* had been scheduled to join them, but, in a further twist of irony, a US Navy Hellcat making an emergency landing on the carrier two hours before had smashed into the barriers, grounding all British aircraft.

Over the following weeks the flyboys contemplated life in a peaceful world. Where just a few weeks ago aircraft had been thundering off to reap violence and destruction, peace now reigned on the flight deck, with the gentle sound of willow on leather from cricket bats, near-naked bodies enjoying the sunshine, and shouts and cheers from men splashing in the canvas swimming pools.

On 19 September 1945 *Formidable* sailed into Sydney. Chris Cartledge, who had been in Australia on leave since his accident in July, wrote to his parents after being reunited with the rest of 1842 squadron:

> I was very glad to welcome the squadron back and stood in the Botanic Gardens in Sydney Harbour as the BPF sailed in. I found a lot of new faces on board and several old ones missing. Considering the small amount of operations our squadron has taken part in it has not been very lucky. Of the eighteen original pilots represented in the first squadron photograph only six remained in the squadron and altogether nine are alive. The total losses since it formed up are fifteen. I hope they weren't wasted; sometimes I feel they were, for we achieved so little and were so entirely out of date. I suppose it's no use being morbid about it, but one shouldn't forget otherwise what little we did achieve we will definitely be wasted.[17]

For many it was finally time to go home. There were farewell parties. In Sydney harbour in December, the flight deck in *Formidable* was turned into a floodlit dance floor, with a restaurant and funfair transforming the hangar. Dancers were lifted aboard on a giant platform using the ship's crane. The electricians attached a giant flashing red heart with a white arrow to the funnel. A few weeks earlier, Keith Quilter, who had spent three weeks on *Scabbardfish* and was sent back to Sydney when the war ended, had climbed aboard *Victorious* for the six-week journey back to Britain. As the Australian coastline disappeared, Quilter quietly made his way alone to the quarterdeck, where he had spent so many hours on *Formidable* watching the frothing wake and wondering where they would be going next. 'As I looked out at the wake and I thought about Wally and Ted and all the others who we'd lost, it suddenly dawned on me I knew where we were going. The war *was* over. I had got myself into a certain mindset but now, finally, I could relax and let go.'

Epilogue

The British Pacific Fleet was formed as part of a diplomatic gesture to prove Britain's commitment to the Allied cause in the final months of the Second World War. It was a force intended chiefly to refute any claim that Britain was only fighting in the east to regain its empire, while the US was left to finish off Japan. By the time the Royal Navy reached the Pacific in 1945, Allied command of the sea was pretty much complete. The military focus had shifted to the projection of naval power to first combat Japanese kamikaze attacks and then strike targets across Japan in order to weaken its defences ahead of invasion.

No one challenges the thesis that the Americans could have secured the Pacific alone, but it was nevertheless a momentous achievement for the British Pacific Fleet even to be there, given that less than a year before it had not existed. The financial cost of the campaign was, in Admiral Fraser's word, 'colossal', but in the circumstances prevailing at the time its creation was understandable and indeed politically necessary.[1] As he signed the surrender document in Tokyo Bay Fraser held his head high, knowing that British forces had been fighting alongside the Americans until the very end. Politically, it was job done.

But what was its military contribution? The strikes by the Fleet Air Arm on the Palembang oil refineries in January 1945 had had some effect on oil production. The operations also allowed the Royal Navy to prove that its aircraft could strike at targets hundreds of miles inland, in a new type of warfare the Americans had taken three years to perfect. But the so-called jitter effect the raids had on the Japanese military and people was even greater. The success of the strikes over the jungles of Sumatra paved the way for British participation in Operation Iceberg, the BPF taking its place on the left flank of the mighty American Fifth Fleet and pounding the Sakishima Islands for two months in the spring of 1945.

Admiral Nimitz, probably the most successful admiral of the Second World War, was not in the habit of paying lip service to anyone, and chose his words carefully when he told the gathered press in early June 1945 that the British Pacific Fleet had helped keep 'the Jap suiciders off the necks of our ships which had to stay anchored off Okinawa' – not just by hunting down the kamikazes but also by sharing the terror through kamikaze attacks on its own carriers.

Admiral Fraser, for his part, wanted the British to be there at the end and not consigned to some backwater. Bearing in mind figures such as Admiral King had tried to limit its involvement, the BPF had been in a difficult position. But on VJ Day Fraser could feel justly proud that his airmen had flown over the Japanese home islands. Indeed the operations over mainland Japan were the FAA's most polished performance of the war – striking blow for blow with the Americans in an intensity of operations never before attempted or experienced.

During its short life a total of 105 airmen from the British Pacific Fleet were killed in enemy action across 36 strike days, 20 per cent of all FAA crew killed worldwide in 1945.[2] At least 10 were executed by the Japanese after being shot down, but the vast majority were killed by anti-aircraft fire as they carried out strafing runs and bombing raids.

There can be no doubt that the British Pacific Fleet was a somewhat ragtag affair assembled in a mad scramble. The refuelling situation was at times only a pendulum swing away from bringing the whole fleet to a grinding halt. Yet despite this, at the sharp end, on the decks of the carriers and in the cabs of the planes flying sortie after sortie against kamikazes and over enemy territory, the bravery and skill of the men involved cannot be questioned. The campaign was often neither glamorous nor particularly thrilling, but the airmen's esprit de corps and willingness to get the job done remained until the end. While never challenging US hegemony, Fraser's fleet had also gained American respect.

Until the final days of the war there was a genuine belief that the British Pacific Fleet would be contributing even greater numbers of men and machines to the final battle for Japan. How its airmen would have fared can only be conjectured, but we do know many young and inexperienced rookies would have replaced battle-hardened pilots like those of 1842 Squadron before Operation Olympic began. Despite the unimaginable horrors for those on the receiving end, most of the aircrew and ships' companies approved of America's decision to drop two atomic bombs. It shortened the war and preserved the lives of thousands more, including those who might otherwise have been killed in continued missions over Japan. Fraser himself admitted that when the war ended his fleet had yet to achieve 'the overall efficiency' which would have been needed for Operation Olympic.[3] He also knew the plan for the British Pacific Fleet to field a larger fleet alongside the Americans – including eight carriers and four battleships – would have been severely tested by its continuing inability to secure enough refuelling ships.

The end of the Second World War did not signal the immediate end of the British Pacific Fleet. By the end of September 1945 its carriers had helped repatriate more than 24,000 POWs and internees from Japan. Just as important was the reoccupation of British territories, and a task force of light carriers and other ships was assembled. A small detachment sailed into Hong Kong harbour and oversaw the peaceful surrender of the Japanese in the colony on 16 September 1945. Other ships repatriated POWs from across the Far East, including Korea and Formosa.

But the great fleet broke up soon after. While the BPF had succeeded as a tool in building an alliance with the USA in the final months of the war, its longer-term legacy in history is harder to define. Many of the lessons and practices adopted from the American fleet were forgotten, opportunities missed. America emerged from the Second World War as a superpower and an industrial powerhouse. Britain meanwhile was tired, battered and broke.

At the very top levels of government the entente soured. In May 1945, in the first general election for ten years, Winston Churchill was swept from power by a new Labour government. President Roosevelt had died the previous April and was replaced by Harry Truman. Any sentiments based on the US and UK's shared experiences in the Pacific were brushed aside when, just a week after the end of the war, the American Congress abruptly shut the door on Lend-Lease, leaving Britain with a bill of millions. The British government had to return Lend-Lease aircraft, buy them in dollars or destroy them.

Around 1,000 Avengers and Corsairs which had formed the strike force of the Royal Navy's most powerful fighting fleet in history were taken out to sea on carriers and dumped over the side, where they lie today on the seabed off the Australian coast. Britain agreed to a new multi-billion-pound loan from America, knowing that without it its post-war regeneration would be impossible. Relations between the two countries might have soured further had it not been for the growing threat of the Soviet Union and the realization that America needed to retain close ties with its old ally across the Atlantic.

Nevertheless, the Pacific campaign changed naval warfare for ever, with battleships as the centre of fleets being replaced by carrier task forces operating far from home and able to launch air strikes deep into enemy territory. When communist North Korean forces crossed the 38th Parallel on 25 June 1950, British carriers with FAA planes (albeit British types, which once again struggled to perform as well as the American aircraft) fought alongside the US Navy, with many of the same faces present who had worked together five years before. There were echoes too in 1982 of the logistical challenges faced in the Pacific by the Royal Navy, when it sailed across the Atlantic to liberate the Falkland Islands.

But the men of the British Pacific Fleet were not thinking about such legacies when they returned home in 1945. When Keith Quilter arrived back in Portsmouth Harbour on a rainy November morning he faced an uncertain future in a war-weary Britain. He loved flying, but not enough to sign up for a permanent commission in the more restricted environs of a peacetime navy. Quilter considered applying to become an airline pilot, but figured that as a pilot of single-engined fighters he wouldn't stand a chance against the RAF pilots who had flown multi-engined bombers and were now being demobbed in their hundreds.

So, like many others returning, Quilter picked up where he had left off five years before, resuming his aeronautical studies at de Havilland's Aeronautical Technical School in Hatfield. He married in 1952 and spent the next thirty years working in the aircraft industry, helping to negotiate contracts during Britain's golden age of jet aviation. He stayed in touch with Nancy and they became lifelong friends.

Val Bennett also returned to de Havilland, working with Rolls-Royce before launching his own successful business, selling miniature bronze wildfowl across the world.

Chris Cartledge arrived home in Richmond, welcomed by his mother 'doing a little dance' in the front garden.[4] His love of art had blossomed during his time in the FAA. Using an ex-servicemen's grant he took a national diploma course in painting and design at Goldsmiths College School of Art with a view to becoming an artist. However, after meeting his wife Dorothy, also a student, marriage and children required a more reliable career at the family's metal merchant business in the City, and he only resumed painting and music full time when he retired.

Ken Ward and Roy Hawkes became teachers, while Roy Beldam read law at Oxford and was called to the bar in 1950. He went on to become one of Britain's leading High Court judges, holding a string of senior positions including Lord Justice of Appeal and Chairman of the Law Commission.

Unlike the flyers of the Battle of Britain or Bomber Command, the aircrew of the FAA and especially the British Pacific Fleet were largely uncelebrated. Some joined ship or FAA associations but many chose to close that chapter of their lives. But the memories of war were never far away. Keith Quilter was driving his car a few years after the war when another vehicle backfired 'and I was immediately taken back to the skies over Japan'.[5]

A few weeks after he arrived back in the UK, Quilter was awarded a DSC for his 'offensive spirit' in operations over Japan. But the recognition felt rather hollow, having lost his best friend in one such mission. He understood too the grief that Wally Stradwick's mother would be going through and, knowing her son's last prophetic words before he was killed had been written down in his diary, couldn't bring himself to return it to her. Over the following years he carefully looked after the diary but had a nagging need to return it to its rightful owners.

In 2012 Quilter returned to Japan. Flying over the coast for the first time in sixty-seven years, as the plane began its descent to Tokyo airport his pencil momentarily hovered over the de-embarkation card asking passengers if there was any reason why they might be refused entry. Quilter visited Owase Bay, where he was shot down in 1945. Standing on the town's harbour looking out towards the sea, the memories of that early-morning attack flooded back. Chartering a fishing vessel, he soon identified the area where he had ditched his Corsair, a dark blob on the boat's sonar providing a tantalizing suggestion as to its final resting place.

Before returning home he had one final duty. Quilter made his way to the Commonwealth War Graves cemetery in Yokohama, Japan's second-largest city, which sits on Tokyo Bay. Constructed by the Australian War Graves Group after the Second World War, it is a peaceful oasis in a bustling metropolis, surrounded on all sides by a thick belt of trees. Pretty flowers sit at the bases of 1,555 gravestones, carefully positioned in neat rows. Tightly clasping a wreath of poppies, Quilter walked across the manicured lawns until he reached one particular grave. Bending down, he carefully laid the wreath. 'I've never forgotten you, Wally,' he said quietly.[6]

Soon after he arrived back in Britain Quilter received a call out of the blue from Wally Stradwick's great-niece Becky. After carefully keeping it safe for so many years, Quilter was finally able to give his friend's diary back to the family. He could sleep soundly at last.

Acknowledgements

I couldn't have written this book without the expertise, support and kindness of many people. Firstly, to the former airmen and sailors of the British Pacific Fleet, who were always willing to spare their time and remained patient and courteous, answering my various questions via letter, email and on the phone.

Keith Quilter's remarkable story was not only the trigger for the book but formed the basis of a wonderful friendship. Accompanying him back to Japan after sixty-seven years was an honour, and we both appreciated the kindness shown by Andy Edney, the defence attaché of the British embassy in Tokyo, and his team.

Both Keith and Chris Cartledge took time to read through various drafts of the book, pointing out glaring errors and offering advice. Any errors that do remain are, of course, entirely my own. Seventy years after leaving the congregation at St Vincent 'clawing for the note which wasn't forthcoming', I was proud to have Chris playing the church organ so beautifully at my wedding.

I've been lucky enough to use a number of private diaries, letters and memoirs. My thanks to Ken Ward's son Martin and his family, and to Wally Stradwick's great-niece Becky and her family. The book would not have been possible without these vital documents.

Many wives, families and companions of veterans kept me fed and watered in my various enjoyable visits around the country. Thank you to Joyce Hawkes, Mary-Ann Bennett, Liz Beldam, and Ken Ward's companion Joyce. I am also grateful to Steve Kerridge, Freddie Hockley's nephew, not only for sparing the time to talk to me about his uncle, but also for his generous hospitality in putting me up for the night at his guesthouse in Norfolk.

I was provided with vital background information by Wendy Larkin – whose remarkable father Buster Hallett deserves a book of his own – and Polly Thellusson, with whom I spent a wonderful few hours at the National Arboretum, where she shared some personal insights into her father. Thanks also to Felicity Winch, Mike Draper of the Fleet Air Arm Officers' Association and Ann Richards, Honorary Reunion Secretary of the HMS *Indefatigable* Association, who were able to track down veterans for me to interview.

My thanks to Harry Wallop, who introduced me to Veronique Baxter at David Higham. Veronique and her assistant Laura West were a pillar of strength and made it all happen. Many thanks too to Georgina Morley at Macmillan, for taking a leap of faith in going for the idea, and Zennor Compton and Fraser Crichton for their brilliant and patient editing, turning what was a very rough and unready first draft into something rather more palatable. I appreciate the time spared by Miwako Harty and Lis van Lynden for translating various documents.

Many hours researching this book were spent in various archives. I was lucky enough to have some wonderful guidance from the late Rod Suddaby at the Imperial War Museum. The staff at the National Archives in Kew were always on hand to provide advice. Barbara Gilbert, Catherine Cooper and Rachael Casey at the Fleet Air Arm Museum have been patient and professional. A visit to the museum archive is a treat.

This book was a labour of love, researched and written mainly at weekends or late into the evenings. In addition to the wonderful support from my family, finally my gratitude must go to my wife Jo, who provided not just support but also injected wisdom and clarity into my often overloaded brain. Writing a book is by its very nature a selfish act. Jo's patience rarely faltered, despite most other things at home taking second preference for so long. I promise I'll get on and paint those shelves now, darling.

Bibliography

Unpublished Primary Sources

Interviews

The following people were interviewed by the author on various dates between 2010 and 2014, either in person, on the phone or by written correspondence:

Roy Beldam, Denys Belham, Val Bennett, Chris Cartledge,
Ron Chambler, Ian Darby, Bob Glading, Roy Hawkes, Albert Hughes,
Bill Jones, John Maybank, Ian Paterson, T.G.V. Percy, Keith Quilter,
Vin Redding, Ray Richards, Norman (Dickie) Richardson, John
Robertson, Jack Routley, Philip Rowell, Gordon Showell, Don Taylor,
Polly Thellusson (née Vian), Brian Ryley, Ron Tovey, Ken Ward,
David (Bim) Wells, Johnnie Wells, Nancy Welbourn (née Parker),
Les Wills

Diaries, memoirs and letters

Baumeister, F.W., personal diary, 1941–46
Cartledge, Chris, letters, 1942–45
—— *My War*
Hawkes, Roy, memoirs
Paterson, Ian, and Taylor, Bob, *Palembang: A Day to Remember*
Stradwick, Wally, letters, 1945
—— personal diary
Ward, Ken, personal diary

Archives

Fleet Air Arm Museum, Yeovilton
Imperial War Museum, London
The National Archives and Records Administration, Washington, D.C.
The National Library of Australia, Canberra
The National Archives, Kew

Secondary Sources

Adey, Peter, *Aerial Life: Spaces, Mobilities, Affects*, Wiley-Blackwell, Oxford,
    2010
Abbott Rose, Lisle, *Power at Sea, Volume 2: The Breaking Storm,*
    1919–1945, University of Missouri Press, Columbia, 2006
Anon., *The Fleet Air Arm Songbook*, Barnard George Printers, London
Anon., *When a Sailor Learns to Fly,* Fleet Air Arm/HMSO, London, 1943
Axell, Albert, and Kase, Hideaki, *Kamikaze: Japan's Suicide Gods*,
    Longman, London, 2002
Barber, Mark, *Royal Naval Air Service Pilot 1914–18*, Osprey, Oxford, 2010
Bishop, Patrick, *Target Tirpitz*, Harper Press, London, 2012
Brooke, Geoffrey, *Alarm Starboard!: A Remarkable True Story of the War*,
    Pen & Sword Maritime, Barnsley, 2004
Brooks, Waite, *The British Pacific Fleet in World War II: An Eyewitness
    Account*, AuthorHouse, Bloomington, IN, 2013
Brown, David, *Carrier Fighters*, Purnell Book Services Ltd, London, 1975
Brown, Captain Eric 'Winkle', *Wings of the Navy: Testing British and US
    Carrier Aircraft*, Hikoki Publications, China, 2013
Churchill, Winston S., *Never Give In! The Best of Winston Churchill's
    Speeches*, Hyperion, New York, 2004
Crosley, Mike, *They Gave Me a Seafire*, Airlife Publishing, Shrewsbury,
    1986
Darling, Kev, *Supermarine Merlin Seafire*, Warpaint Books Ltd, Bletchley,
    2000
Eadon, Stuart, *Kamikaze*, Crecy Books, Manchester, 1995
—— *Sakishima: The Story of the British Pacific Fleet*, Crecy Books,
    Manchester, 1995
Foster DSO DSC*, David R., *Wings Over the Sea*, Harrap Press,
    Canterbury, 1990

Gardiner, Juliet, *Wartime: Britain 1939–1945*, Headline, London, 2004

Guinn, Gilbert S. and Bennett, G. H., *British Naval Aviation in World War Two: The US Navy and Anglo-American Relations*, Tauris Academic Studies, London, 2007

Goldstein, M., and Dillon, Katherine V. (eds), *Fading Victory: The Diary of Admiral Matome Ugaki 1941—1945*, trans. Masataka Chihaya, Naval Institute Press, Annapolis, MD, 1991

Hadley, Dunstan, *Barracuda Pilot*, Airlife Publishing, Shrewsbury, 1992

Hobbs, David, *The British Pacific Fleet*, Seaforth Publishing, Barnsley, 2011

Hanson, Norman, *Carrier Pilot*, Patrick Stephens, Cambridge, 1979

Hastings, Max, *All Hell Let Loose: The World At War, 1939–1945*, HarperPress, London, 2011

—— *Nemesis: The Battle for Japan, 1944–45*, Harper Perennial, London, 2007

Heffer DSC RNZNVR, Lt (A) Francis Bentinck, *From Cow Bells to Bell Bottoms: Wartime Experiences,* Canrig Publishing, 1998

Humble, Richard, *Fraser of North Cape*, Routledge and Kegan Paul, 1983

Judd DSC, Donald, *Avenger from the Sky*, William Kimber & Co. Ltd, London, 1985

Key, Teddy, *The Friendly Squadron: 1772 Naval Air Squadron: 1944–1945*, Square One Publications, Upton-upon-Severn, 1997

Kimmins, Anthony, *Half Time*, William Heinemann, London, 1947

Lavery, Brian, *Hostilities Only: Training the Wartime Royal Navy*, National Maritime Museum, Greenwich, 2004

MacIntyre, Donald, *Aircraft Carrier: The Majestic Weapon*, Macdonald and Co., London, 1968

Masters, A. O. 'Cappy', *Memoirs of a Reluctant Batsman*, Janus Publishing, Cambridge, 1996

McCart, Neil, *The Illustrious and Implacable Classes of Aircraft Carrier: 1940–1969*, Fan Publications, Cheltenham, 2000

Ministry of Defence Naval Historical Branch, *Okinawa Battle Summary: No. 47 March–June 1945 Operation Iceberg*, 1949

—— *War With Japan Volume VI*, 1995

Moynihan, Michael, *War Correspondent*, Pen & Sword, Barnsley, 1994

The Naval Review, London

Pearcy, Arthur, *Lend-Lease Aircraft in World War II*, Airlife Publishing, Shrewsbury, 1996

Poolman, Kenneth, *Illustrious*, William Kimber & Co. Ltd, London, 1955

Preston, Anthony, *Aircraft Carriers*, Bison Books, London, 1982

Potter, E. B., *Nimitz*, Naval Institute Press, Annapolis, MD, 2008

Robb-Webb, Jon, *The British Pacific Fleet: Experience and Legacy, 1944–50*, Joint Services Command and Staff College and King's College London/Ashgate, Farnham, 2013

Robertson, John, *Trapped in Tunisia: Troubled by Bears and Other Events*, Twin Eagles Publishing, Sechelt, BC, 2012

Rosher, Harold, *In the Royal Naval Air Service, Being the War Letters of the Late Harold Rosher to His Family*, Pickle Partners Publishing, 2013

Vian, Sir Philip, *Action This Day*, Frederick Muller Ltd, London, 1960

War in the Air: Aerial Wonders of Our Time, The Amalgamated Press Ltd, London

Seedie's List of Fleet Air Arm Awards 1939–1969, Ripley Registers, 1990

Soward, Stuart E., *A Formidable Hero: Lt R. H. Gray, VC, DSC, RCNVR*, Canav Books, Toronto, 1987

Stafrace, Charles, *Vought F4U Corsair*, Warpaint Books, Bletchley, 2009

Sturtivant ISO, Ray, with Burrow, Mick, *Fleet Air Arm Aircraft 1939–1945*, Air-Britain, Tonbridge, 1995

Thomas, Andrew, *Royal Navy Aces of World War 2*, Osprey, Oxford, 2007

Wardroom Officers of HM Aircraft Carrier *Formidable*, *A Formidable Commission*, Seeley Service & Co., London, 1947

Willmott, H. P., *Grave of a Dozen Schemes*, Airlife Publishing, Shrewsbury, 1996

Winton, John, *Find, Fix and Strike*, B. T. Batsford, London, 1980

—— *The Forgotten Fleet*, Michael Joseph, London, 1969

Wragg, David, *Fleet Air Arm Handbook 1939–1945*, Sutton Publishing, Stroud, 2001

Notes and References

Where a source is cited several times within the text of a chapter, the full reference is given in the first note only, with subsequent references using a short form.

Abbreviations used in the notes

FAAM Fleet Air Arm Museum
IWM   Imperial War Museum
NID   Naval Intelligence Division
TNA   The National Archives of the UK government

Prologue

1 Juliet Gardiner, *Wartime: Britain 1939–1945*, Headline (2004), p.567
2 *Daily Mail*, 8 May 1945, p.1
3 Ken Ward, unpublished diary
4 Wardroom Officers of HM Aircraft Carrier *Formidable*, *A Formidable Commission*, Seeley Service & Co. (1947), p.78
5 Geoffrey Brooke, *Alarm Starboard!: A Remarkable True Story of the War at Sea*, Pen & Sword Maritime (2004), p.254
6 *A Formidable Commission*, pp.78–9

Introduction

1 Interview with author
2 John Winton, *The Forgotten Fleet*, Michael Joseph (1969), p.96
3 John Winton, *Find, Fix and Strike*, B. T. Batsford (1980), p.146

4 Letter from Philip Ruck-Keene to the mother of Walter Stradwick, 15 August 1945
5 Norman Hanson, *Carrier Pilot*, Patrick Stephens (1979), p.98
6 Ian Paterson, interview with author

1. Flying sailors

1 Interview with Roy Gibbs, IWM Sound Archive 28359
2 John Winton, *Find, Fix and Strike*, B. T. Batsford (1980), p.1
3 Winston Churchill quoted in Mark Barber, *Royal Naval Air Service Pilot 1914-18*, Osprey Publishing (2010), p.8
4 Letter from Harold Rosher to his mother, 15 March 1915; *In the Royal Naval Air Service, Being the War Letters of the Late Harold Rosher to His Family*, Pickle Partners Publishing (2013)
5 Anthony Preston, *Aircraft Carriers*, Gallery Books (1990), p.17
6 Washington Treaty/aircraft statistics from Donald MacIntyre, *Aircraft Carrier: The Majestic Weapon*, Macdonald and Co. (1968), pp.27–9
7 Lisle Abbott Rose, *Power at Sea*, Vol. II, University of Missouri Press (2006), p.70

2. They were like gods

1 John Winton, *Find, Fix and Strike*, B. T. Batsford (1980), pp.2–3
2 Statistics from FAAM, Yeovilton
3 David Brown, *Carrier Fighters*, Purnell Book Services Ltd (1975), pp.31–9
4 Winton, *Find, Fix and Strike*, p.62
5 TNA, ADM 167/124
6 Winton, *Find, Fix and Strike*, p.63
7 House of Commons debate, 3 November 1943, Hansard
8 *Flight*, No. 1832 Vol. XLV, 3 February 1944, p.116
9 TNA ADM 167/124
10 Cyril Price, IWM Sound Archive 28775
11 Interview with author
12 'Model Flying', *The Air League Bulletin*, No. 56 (1926) p.16, quoted in Peter Adey, *Aerial Life: Spaces, Mobilities, Affects*, Wiley-Blackwell (2010), p.50
13 Roy Beldam, interview with author
14 Val Bennett, interview with author

15 Capt. J. Laurence Pritchard, 'Sky Trails Across the World', in *War in the Air, Aerial Wonders of Our Time*, The Amalgamated Press Ltd (1936), p.250

16 Ibid. p.249

17 Chris Cartledge, *My War*, unpublished memoir

18 Chris Cartledge, interview with author

19 W. T. Stradwick, unpublished diary

20 Don Taylor, interview with author

21 *When a Sailor Learns to Fly*, Fleet Air Arm/HMSO (1943), p.23, quoted in Gilbert S. Guinn and G. H. Bennett, *British Naval Aviation in World War Two: The US Navy and Anglo-American Relations*, Tauris (2007), p.32

22 TNA, Air 2/4981

3. Wakey-wakey, rise and shine, show a leg

1 W. T. Stradwick, unpublished diary

2 Mike Crosley, *They Gave Me a Seafire*, Airlife Publishing (1986), p.27

3 Bob Glading, email exchange with author

4 Chris Cartledge, letter January 1942

5 Chris Cartledge, letter February 1942

6 As told to the author in an interview. The airman wished to remain anonymous.

7 Dunstan Hadley, *Barracuda Pilot*, Airlife Publishing (1992), p.23

8 Frank Stolvin-Bradford, IWM Sound Archive 28938

9 Roy Beldam, interview with author

10 As told to the author in an interview. The airman wished to remain anonymous.

11 Interview with Roy Gibbs, IWM Sound Archive 28359

12 Glading, email exchange

13 Chris Cartledge, letter February 1942

14 Chris Cartledge, interview with author

15 Eric Rickman, IWM Sound Archive 28735

16 Chris Cartledge, *My War*, unpublished memoir

17 Ibid.

18 A killicks was a single fouled anchor sewn on the left arm, which denoted the wearer was a (temporary acting) leading naval airman.

19 Chris Cartledge, letter May 1942

20 John Dickson, IWM Sound Archive 32297

21 TNA, ADM 261/12

22 Cartledge, *My War*
23 Chris Cartledge, letter May 1942
24 Chris Cartledge, letter June 1942
25 Chris Cartledge, letter May 1942
26 TNA, AIR 2/4981
27 TNA, ADM 1/17286

4. Bags of food and lights and girls

1 Keith Quilter, interview with author
 2 W. T. Stradwick, unpublished diary
 3 Ron Chambler, email exchange with author
 4 Private Papers of Sub-Lieutenant P. J. H. Cann RNVR, IWM 4658
 5 TNA, ADM 261/12
 6 *Flight: The Magazine of the US Naval Air Station, Grosse Ile*, March
    1943, US Navy, p.11
 7 Chambler, email exchange with author
 8 TNA, ADM 261/12
 9 Ibid.
10 Ibid.
11 Ibid.
12 Cann, IWM 4658
13 Ray Richards, email exchange with author
14 Cann, IWM 4658
15 Ibid.

5. Wings

1 Private Papers of Sub-Lt P. J. H. Cann RNVR, IWM 4658
 2 Ibid.
 3 W. T. Stradwick, unpublished diary
 4 Chris Cartledge, letter August 1942
 5 Ken Ward, unpublished diary
 6 Chris Cartledge, letter October 1942
 7 TNA, ADM 1/21186
 8 Ron Chambler, email exchange with author
 9 John Dickson, IWM Sound Archive 32297
10 Keith Quilter, interview with author
11 Chambler, email exchange with author

12 Gordon Showell, interview with author
13 Cann, IWM 4658
14 Ibid. Tragically she never did see her son again. The following summer Peter Cann was killed in an air accident in America just weeks before his squadron was due back in England. He was twenty-two.
15 Lt (A) Francis Bentinck Heffer, DSC RNZNVR, *From Cow Bells to Bell Bottoms: Wartime Experiences,* Canrig Publishing (1998), p.67
16 House of Commons debate, 17 March 1943, Hansard

6. They don't know what they want . . .

1 *Flight*, No. 1780 Vol. XLIII, 4 February 1943, p.109
2 Captain Eric 'Winkle' Brown, *Wings of the Navy: Testing British and US Carrier Aircraft*, Hikoki Publications (2013), p.136
3 Ken Ward, unpublished diary
4 TNA, AVIA 6/14566
5 *The Fleet Air Arm Songbook*, Barnard George Printers, p.3
6 *Flight Deck*, Vol. II No. 1, September 1945, Director of Naval Air Warfare and Flying Training, Naval Staff, Admiralty, printed by the Adelphi Press Ltd
7 Chris Cartledge, letter February 1942
8 House of Commons debate, 17 March 1943, Hansard
9 TNA, ADM 116/5534
10 Ron Chambler, email exchange with author
11 Keith Quilter, interview with author
12 Gordon Showell, interview with author
13 Charles Stafrace, *Vought F4U Corsair*, Warpaint Books Ltd (2009), p.1
14 Ian Paterson, interview with author
15 Eric Rickman, IWM Sound Archive 28735
16 A copy of which is in the IWM archives.
17 Roy Hawkes, interview with author
18 TNA, ADM 17286
19 Denys Belham, interview with author
20 John Dickson, IWM Sound Archive 32297

7. Flat-hatters

1 Ken Ward, unpublished diary
2 Philip Rowell, email to author

3 An extract taken from a eulogy read by Admiral Sir Raymond Lygo at Reynolds' funeral, shown to the author by Philip Rowell.

4 'Obituary: Commander Dickie Reynolds', *Daily Telegraph*, 4 July 2000

5 W. T. Stradwick, unpublished diary

6 Keith Quilter, interview with author

7 Gordon Showell, interview with author

8 *Flat-Hatting Sense*, Training Division, Bureau of Aeronautics, US Navy, US government, August 1943, p.1

9 Chris Cartledge, *My War*, unpublished memoir

10 Ray Richards, email to author

11 Lt Cdr D. C. E. F. Gibson, RN, *Straight from the Horse's Mouth*, quoted in Michael Whitby, 2014, *'Navy Blue Fighter Pilot': The Wartime Naval Aviation Career of Lieutenant Donald J. Sheppard, DSC, RCNVR*, available at: http://www.vintagewings.ca/VintageNews/Stories/tabid/116/articleType/ArticleView/articleId/468/Navy-Blue-Fighter-Pilot-Episode-One.aspx

12 Ibid.

13 Cartledge, *My War*

14 Cartledge, letter April 1944

15 Ibid.

16 Chris Cartledge, interview with author

17 Cartledge, letter April 1944

18 Cutting from an uncited newspaper in the 1841 Squadron diary, a copy of which was shared with the author by Keith Quilter.

19 Ibid.

20 Chris Cartledge, letter May 1944

21 Nancy Welbourn, interview with author

22 1841 Squadron diary, FAAM

23 Cartledge, *My War*

24 Ward, unpublished diary

25 Eric Rickman, IWM Sound Archive 28735

26 1841 Squadron diary, FAAM

8. Blooded

1 Keith Quilter, interview with author

2 W. T. Stradwick, unpublished diary

3 1841 Squadron diary, FAAM

4 Patrick Bishop, *Target Tirpitz*, Harper Press (2012), p.xxv

5 Sir Philip Vian, *Action This Day*, Frederick Muller Ltd (1960), p.210

6 An extract taken from a eulogy read by Admiral Sir Raymond Lygo at Reynolds' funeral, shown to the author by Philip Rowell.

7 Chris Cartledge, letter August 1944

8 Roy Hawkes, unpublished memoir

9 Chris Cartledge, *My War*, unpublished memoir

10 Ibid.

11 From an unnamed newspaper report, included in the 1841 Squadron line book, FAAM

12 German damage reports from: www.bismarck-class.dk/*Tirpitz*/history/tiropergoodwood.html

13 Stuart E. Soward, *A Formidable Hero, Lt R. H. Gray, VC DSC RCNVR*, Canav Books (1987), p.66

14 Hawkes, unpublished memoir

15 Chris Cartledge, interview with author

16 Cutting from the *Daily Sketch*, 6 September 1944, included in 1841 Squadron line book, FAAM

9. Flat tops

1 Chris Cartledge, letters September 1943

2 Cyril Price, IWM Sound Archive 28775

3 Norman Hanson, *Carrier Pilot*, Patrick Stephens (1979), p.118

4 TNA, DSIR 23/16187

5 Ray Richards, email exchange with author

6 Bob Glading, email exchange with author

7 TNA, ADM 1/21186

8 Take-offs were rarely as dangerous, although aircraft always risked dropping into the sea after leaving the deck, not a happy prospect for the crew with 27,000 tons of carrier bearing down. Steam-powered catapults could launch aircraft into the air, but being 'squirted off' was time-consuming and cumbersome, and rarely used.

9 *The Fleet Air Arm Songbook*, Barnard George Printers, p.3

10 Chris Cartledge, letter October 1944

11 Hanson, *Carrier Pilot*, p.146

12 Ron Tovey, interview with author

13 Les Wills, interview with author

14 Ken Ward, unpublished diary

15 Val Bennett, interview with author

16 Keith Quilter, interview with author

17 W. T. Stradwick, unpublished diary

18 Chris Cartledge, *My War*, unpublished memoir
19 *Flight Deck*, Vol. I No. 7, February 1945, Director of Naval Air Warfare and Flying Training, Naval Staff, Admiralty, printed by the Adelphi Press Ltd
20 *The Fleet Air Arm Songbook*, p.35

10. An enterprise of the first magnitude

1 'Bold Raid on Sumatra', *The Age*, 29 August 1944, Melbourne
2 Unless otherwise stated all quotes from *Official Minutes of the Octagon Conference*, from declassified papers released by the Joint History Office, Washington D.C., 2003.
3 John Gunther, *Roosevelt in Retrospect: A Profile in History*, quoted in John Winton, *The Forgotten Fleet*, Michael Joseph (1969), p.35
4 Jon Robb-Webb, *The British Pacific Fleet: Experience and Legacy, 1944–50*, Joint Services Command and Staff College and King's College London/Ashgate (2013), p.40
5 E. B. Potter, *Nimitz*, quoted in Robb-Webb, *The British Pacific Fleet*, p.40
6 H. P. Willmott, *Grave of a Dozen Schemes*, Airlife (1996), p.134, quoting State Department, (No. 7859) *Foreign Relations of the United States: Near East, South East, Africa and Far East, 1944*, US Government Printing Office, Washington D.C. (1965), 5:254–7
7 Ibid. 177–80
8 House of Commons debate, 28 September 1944, Hansard
9 Private Papers of Lt Cdr V. A. Cox RNVR, IWM 19000
10 *Sydney Morning Herald*, 12 December 1944, p.2, National Library of Australia
11 Richard Humble, *Fraser of North Cape*, Routledge and Kegan Paul (1983), p.252, quoting letter of Commander Charles Sheppard to author, 2 April 1978
12 David R. Foster, DSO DSC', *Wings Over the Sea*, Harrap Press (1990), p.175
13 Ronald Cuthbert Hay, IWM Sound Archive 13856
14 Denys Belham, interview with author
15 Chris Cartledge, letter February 1945
16 Ken Ward, unpublished diary
17 TNA, ADM 116/5302
18 Keith Quilter, interview with author

19 Betty Nesbit, 'British Fleet goes into action in Pacific', *Australian Women's Weekly*, 14 April 1945
20 Hay, IWM Sound Archive 13856

11. The balloons go up

1 TNA, ADM 199/188
2 Ken Ward, unpublished diary
3 *Flight Deck*, Vol. I No. 7, February 1945, Director of Naval Air Warfare and Flying Training, Naval Staff, Admiralty, printed by the Adelphi Press Ltd, p.214
4 House of Commons debate, 28 January 1944, Hansard
5 Memoir of 1839 Pilot, FAAM
6 Roy Hawkes, unpublished memoir
7 TNA, ADM 199/555
8 TNA, WO 208/1553
9 Donald Judd DSC, *Avenger from the Sky*, William Kimber & Co. Ltd (1985), p.165
10 Ibid., p.165
11 Lt (A) Francis Bentinck Heffer, DSC RNZNVR, *From Cow Bells to Bell Bottoms: Wartime Experiences*, Canrig Publishing (1998)
12 Hawkes, unpublished memoir
13 Norman Hanson, *Carrier Pilot*, Patrick Stephens (1979), p.195
14 Hawkes, unpublished memoir
15 Many of the details of the Palembang mission in the next two chapters are from official contemporaneous action reports filed at TNA, WO 203/4770 and TNA, ADM 1/24281.
16 Major Hideaki Inayama, *Royal Air Force Flying Review*, Vol. XV, No. 8. 1959, Royal Air Force Air Force Review Ltd
17 Ray Richards, email to author
18 Hanson, *Carrier Pilot*, p.197
19 Judd, *Avenger from the Sky*, p.166
20 Interview with Roy Gibbs, IWM Sound Archive 28359
21 Hanson, *Carrier Pilot*, p.198
22 William Fenwick-Smith, IWM Sound Archive 27756
23 TNA, WO 203/4770
24 Hawkes, unpublished memoir
25 Gibbs, IWM Sound Archives 28359
26 Denys Belham, interview with author
27 Roy Hawkes, interview with author

28 Ibid.
29 Inayama, *Royal Air Force Flying Review*
30 Belham, interview with author
31 Kenneth Poolman, *Illustrious*, William Kimber & Co. Ltd (1955), p.221

12. The jitter effect

1 Ronald Cuthbert Hay, IWM Sound Archive 13856
2 Supplement to the *London Gazette* 39191/1803, 3 April 1951, HMSO
3 Signal from Admiral Vian to the carriers, 17.21, 25 January 1945, FAAM
4 TNA,WO 203 4770
5 Ibid.
6 Ibid.
7 Eric Rickman, IWM Sound Archive 28735
8 Roy Gibbs, IWM Sound Archive 28359
9 Ken Ward, unpublished diary
10 Ian Paterson, interview with author
11 Ian Paterson and Bob Taylor, *Palembang: A Day to Remember*, unpublished
12 Ibid.
13 Rickman, IWM Sound Archive 28735
14 Gibbs, IWM Sound Archive 28359
15 TNA, WO 203 4770
16 Gibbs, IWM 28359
17 Michael Whitby, 2014, 'A Gallant Young Fighter Pilot': The Second World War Flying Career of Lieutenant Donald J. Sheppard, DSC, RCNVR, available at: http://www.vintagewings.ca/VintageNews/ Stories/tabid/116/articleType/ArticleView/articleId/471/Navy-Blue-Fighter-Pilot-Episode-Two.aspx
18 Paterson and Taylor, *Palembang: A Day to Remember*
19 Ibid.
20 Ibid.
21 Signal from *Whelp* to *Victorious*, 11.54, 29 January 1945, FAAM
22 Paterson and Taylor, *Palembang: A Day to Remember*
23 David Smith, 'Veteran tells of day Philip saved his life', *Observer*, 14 August 2005
24 Supplement to the *London Gazette* 39191/1803, 3 April 1951, HMSO
25 TNA, WO 203 4770

26 Donald Judd DSC, *Avenger from the Sky*, William Kimber & Co. Ltd (1985), p.172

27 TNA, WO 203 4770

28 Waite Brooks, *The British Pacific Fleet in World War II: An Eyewitness Account*, AuthorHouse (2013), p.87

29 TNA, WO 203 4770

30 Ken Ward, unpublished diary

31 TNA, WO 203 4770

32 NID 02477/47 quoted in J. D. Brown, notes for the unpublished naval staff History, *The Development of British Naval Aviation 1919–1945, Volume III, The Fleet Air Arm in the Indian and Pacific Oceans*, as quoted from David Hobbs, *The British Pacific Fleet*, Seaforth Publishing (2011), p.102

33 Supplement to the *London Gazette* 39191/1803, 3 April 1951, HMSO

34 Ibid.

35 TNA, WO 208/1686

36 Signal from FOCA to BPF in Company, 11.22, 4 February 1945, FAAM

37 Signal from *Victorious* to *Whelp*, 17.11, 29 January 1945, FAAM

13. The body crashers

1 Albert Axell and Hideaki Kase, *Kamikaze: Japan's Suicide Gods*, Longman (2002), p.49

2 It is not absolutely certain that it was Seki who dived into the *St Lo*. However, many historians believe him to be the most likely pilot.

3 Axell and Kase, *Kamikaze: Japan's Suicide Gods*, p.51

4 TNA, ADM 199/118

5 TNA, ADM 219/263

6 TNA, FO/954/7B

7 TNA, PREM 3/12/2

8 TNA, ADM 1/17242

9 Ken Ward, unpublished diary

10 Wardroom Officers of HM Aircraft Carrier *Formidable*, *A Formidable Commission*, Seeley Service & Co. (1947), p.55

11 Helen Seager, 'Greek Prince As Royal Navy Officer', *Argus*, 12 June 1945, Melbourne

12 Private Papers of Lt Cdr V. A. Cox RNVR, IWM 19000

13 TNA, ADM 199/118

14 Sir Philip Vian, *Action This Day*, Frederick Muller Ltd (1960), p.170

15 'Fleet Train. Largest ever run. Navy's Pacific Supply Line', *West Australian*, 4 June 1945

16 G. Kingsford Smith, 'Britain's floating base in the Pacific', *Sydney Morning Herald*, 20 April 1945

17 'How Australia will aid Pacific Fleet', *Sydney Morning Herald*, 16 December 1944

18 'Fleet's Support', *West Australian*, 13 December 1944

19 'Fleet Train', *West Australian*, 4 June 1945

20 *Western Mail*, 18 January 1945, p.26

21 TNA, ADM 199/555

22 Norman Hanson, *Carrier Pilot*, Patrick Stephens (1979), p.216

23 TNA, HW 28/125

24 TNA, ADM1/17242

25 TNA, ADM 219/263

26 TNA, ADM 199/555

27 Ward, unpublished diary

28 http://shimanosanpo.com/churajima01/kohama00/rekishinen_02.htm, translated by Bill Gordon

29 Ian Paterson, interview with author

30 Ron Chambler, conversation with author

31 Ibid.

32 'Report by Air Group Leader – Narratives of Strike Leaders' and LT D.J. Sheppard, RCNVR, 'Report by Leader of Strike CHARLIE Escort and MIYAKO CAP, 7th April', 14 April 1945, TNA, ADM 199/595. Both reports as quoted in Michael Whitby, 2014, *A Gallant Young Fighter Pilot': The Second World War Flying Career of Lieutenant Donald J. Sheppard, DSC, RCNVR*. Available at: http://www. vintagewings.ca/VintageNews/Stories/tabid/116/articleType/ ArticleView/articleId/475/Navy-Blue-Fighter-Pilot-Episode-Three-Until-the-Bitter-End.aspx

33 Many of the details of the Iceberg operations in the next three chapters are from official contemporaneous action reports filed at TNA, ADM 199/595.

34 Donald Judd DSC, *Avenger from the Sky*, William Kimber & Co. Ltd (1985), p.184

35 'Island probe for Japanese suicide pilots', *Darwin Army News*, 27 May 1945, p.6

36 TNA, ADM 199/595

37 John Maybank, interview with author

14. April fools

1 Albert Axell and Hideaki Kase, *Kamikaze: Japan's Suicide Gods*, Longman (2002), p.184
2 TNA, ADM 199/595
3 John Robertson, interview with author
4 John Robertson, *Trapped in Tunisia: Troubled by Bears and Other Events*, Twin Eagles Publishing (2012), p.63
5 Les Wills, interview with author
6 Stuart Eadon, *Sakishima*, Crecy Books (1995), p.173
7 Stuart Eadon, *Kamikaze: The Story of the British Pacific Fleet*, Crecy Books (1995), p.243
8 Eadon, *Sakishima*, p.178
9 Ibid., p.179
10 Wills, interview with author
11 894 Squadron line book, FAAM
12 An extract taken from a eulogy by Ray Lygo at Dickie Reynolds' funeral, shown to the author by Philip Rowell.
13 Ken Ward, unpublished diary
14 TNA, ADM 199/555
15 TNA, ADM 199/595
16 Ibid.
17 A. O. 'Cappy' Masters, *Memoirs of a Reluctant Batsman*, Janus Publishing (1996), pp.257–8
18 TNA, ADM 199/555
19 This quote is widely attributed in various published sources to a US liaison officer in *Indefatigable*, but no name is given.
20 Sir Philip Vian, *Action This Day*, Frederick Muller Ltd (1960), p.179
21 Donald M. Goldstein and Katherine V. Dillon (eds), Masataka Chihaya (trans.), *Fading Victory: The Diary of Admiral Matome Ugaki 1941–1945*, Naval Institute Press (1991), p.583
22 Norman Hanson, *Carrier Pilot*, Patrick Stephens (1979), pp.218 and 233.

15. A formidable return

1 *Sydney Morning Herald*, 31 March 1945, p.1
2 W. T. Stradwick, unpublished diary
3 Keith Quilter, interview with author
4 Wardroom Officers of HM Aircraft Carrier *Formidable*, *A Formidable Commission*, Seeley Service & Co. (1947), p.52

5 W. T. Stradwick, letter April 1945

6 Richard Lovelace Bigg-Wither, IWM Sound Archive 12175

7 Waite Brooks, *The British Pacific Fleet in World War II: An Eyewitness Account*, AuthorHouse (2013), p.158

8 Chris Cartledge, *My War*, unpublished memoir

9 Chris Cartledge, interview with author

10 TNA, ADM 199/555

11 TNA, ADM 199/590

12 TNA, ADM 199/555

13 894 Squadron line book, FAAM

16. Little yellow baskets

1 Ken Ward, unpublished diary

2 TNA, ADM 199/555

3 John Winton, *The Forgotten Fleet*, Michael Joseph (1969), p.141

4 Ron Tovey, interview with author

5 John Maybank, interview with author

6 Tovey, interview with author

7 Denis Warner, 'Steel Decks Spared Lives, And So Did Razor Blades', *New York Times* Online, published 9 May 1995

8 Tovey, interview with author

9 Michael Moynihan, IWM Sound Archive 15122

10 Tovey, interview with author

11 W. T. Stradwick, unpublished diary

12 Maybank, interview with author

13 Capt. Anthony Kimmins, RN, '*Formidable*: The Story you did not hear', *Evening Standard*, 1945

14 Sir Philip Vian, *Action This Day*, Frederick Muller Ltd (1960), p.185

15 TNA, ADM 1/18694

16 TNA, ADM 261/12

17 Warner, 'Steel Decks'

18 Ibid.

19 TNA, ADM 261/12

20 Roy Beldam, interview with author.

21 Lt D. J. Sheppard, 'Naval Aircraft Combat Report', 4 May 1945. DHH ADM 199/842

22 Geoffrey Brooke, *Alarm Starboard!: A Remarkable True Story of the War at Sea*, Pen & Sword Maritime (2004), p.250

23 Winton, *The Forgotten Fleet*, p.141

24 Vian, *Action this Day*, p.185

25 TNA, ADM 199/555

26 Anthony Kimmins, *Half Time*, William Heinemann (1947), pp.270–1

27 Juliet Gardiner, *Wartime: Britain 1939–1945*, Headline (2004), p.577

28 Maybank, interview with author

29 Ward, unpublished diary

30 Chris Cartledge, letters May 1945

31 John Loughlin, 'VE Day with British Task Force', *Argus*, 16 May 1945, Melbourne

32 John Loughlin, 'Task Force Tales', *Argus*, 16 June 1945, Melbourne

33 The Fraser Papers, National Maritime Museum, MS83/158, File 23

34 Richard Lovelace Bigg-Wither, IWM 12175

35 TNA, ADM 261/12

36 A. O. 'Cappy' Masters, *Memoirs of a Reluctant Batsman*, Janus Publishing (1996), pp.260–4

17. Breaking point

1 Chris Cartledge, letter May 1945

 2 W. T. Stradwick, letter May 1945

 3 Ronald Cuthbert Hay, IWM 13856

 4 W. T. Stradwick, letter April 1945

 5 Chris Cartledge, letter February 1945

 6 Keith Quilter, interview with author

 7 Stuart Eadon, *Kamikaze: The Story of the British Pacific Fleet*, Crecy Books (1995), p.196

 8 F. P. Ellis, 'Environmental Factors Influencing Health and Efficiency in Warships', *British Medical Journal*, Vol. 1, No. 4551, 27 March 1948, p.588–90

 9 John Maybank, interview with author

10 Private papers of K. Morris, IWM 12597, p.34

11 Ellis, 'Environmental Factors', p.591

12 TNA, ADM 261/12

13 Hay, IWM 13856

14 Val Bennett, interview with author

15 TNA, ADM 261/12

16 John Robertson, interview with author

17 Ian Paterson, interview with author

18 Ron Chambler, email exchange with author

19 TNA, ADM 1/21186

20 Desmond Gilbert John Wilkey, IWM Sound Archive 14150
21 'The Goofers' Platform', *Flight*, Vol. L, No. 1967, 5 September 1946, p.237
22 TNA, ADM 1/18646
23 TNA, ADM 1/17191
24 Gordon Showell, interview with author
25 MS83/158, File 23, CinC Operational Correspondence with Flag Officers, letters First Sea Lord to CinC, 19 January 1945, quoted in Jon Robb-Webb, *The British Pacific Fleet: Experience and Legacy 1944–50*, Joint Services Command and Staff College and King's College London/Ashgate (2013), p.123
26 Chris Cartledge, interview with author
27 Stradwick, letter May 1945
28 Chris Cartledge, letter May 1945
29 Michael Moynihan, *War Correspondent*, Pen & Sword (1994), p.155
30 Anthony Kimmins, *Half Time*, William Heinemann (1947), p.280
31 'Nimitz visits British Pacific Fleet', *Chicago Daily Tribune*, 1 June 1945
32 TNA, ADM 199/1745
33 TNA, ADM 199/555
34 TNA, ADM 1/17499
35 'British Task Force in Pacific Is Happy to Aid US, Admiral Says', *Port Arthur News*, 31 May 1945; 'Nimitz's Tribute to Worth of British Pacific Fleet', *Mercury*, 1 June 1945, Hobart
36 David Hobbs, *The British Pacific Fleet*, Seaforth Publishing (2011), p.198

18. The absolute full

1 Commander Air Force Pacific Fleet, *Analysis of Air Operations Okinawa Carrier Operations March–June*, 28 September 1945, kindly shown to author by Ms Wendy Larken, daughter of Nigel 'Buster' Hallett.
2 Sir Philip Vian, *Action This Day*, Frederick Muller Ltd (1960), p.195
3 TNA, ADM 199/118
4 Val Bennett, interview with author
5 Vian, *Action This Day*, p.195
6 W. T. Stradwick, letter May 1945
7 Chris Cartledge, letter May 1945
8 Chris Cartledge, interview with author
9 Bennett, interview with author

10 TNA, ADM 219/176
11 1841 Squadron diary, FAAM
12 Ken Ward, unpublished diary
13 W. T. Stradwick, letter June 1945
14 Chris Cartledge, *My War*, unpublished memoir
15 1841 Squadron diary
16 Cartledge, *My War*
17 1841 Squadron diary
18 Bob Glading, email to author
19 Ron Chambler, email to author
20 Keith Quilter, interview with author
21 Letter from Phillip Ruck-Keene to Walter Stradwick's mother, 28 September 1945
22 Glading, email to author
23 TNA, ADM 261/12
24 Arthur Hudson, IWM Sound Archive 13923
25 John Winton, *The Forgotten Fleet*, Michael Joseph (1969), p.322

19. The final onslaught

1 Keith Quilter, interview with author
2 This account was shown to author in Owase during a trip to Japan with Keith Quilter in 2012, by an anonymous local historian. It was translated from an article first published in June 1979 in local newspapers *Nonkai Nichinichi Shimbun* and *Kisei Shimbun* in Owase. Saito Shuuji passed away soon after the article was published and Captain Iwata died around 1980.
3 Ibid.
4 'Report of War Patrol Number Five. USS *Scabbardfish* (SS397)', US Submarine War Patrol Reports, 1941–1945, US National Archives and Records Administration. Publication Number: M1752. Declassified 1992
5 Ken Ward, unpublished diary
6 Richard Lovelace Bigg-Wither, IWM 12175
7 Stuart E. Soward, *A Formidable Hero, Lt R. H. Gray, VC DSC RCNVR*, Canav Books (1987), p.137
8 Bigg-Wither, IWM 12175
9 Val Bennett, interview with author
10 Ian Darby, interview with author
11 TNA, ADM 119/118

12 Ibid.
13 TNA, WO 235/1021. Some details of the incident are from an author interview with Steven Kerridge, Freddie Hockley's nephew.
14 Roy Hawkes, unpublished memoir
15 Diary of F. W. Baumeister 1941–6, courtesy of Irene Kusnadi-Baumeister, daughter of F. W. Baumeister
16 Letter courtesy of Roy Hawkes
17 Chris Cartledge, letter September 1945

Epilogue

1 TNA, ADM 118/119
2 Based on an overall casualty figure for 1945 of 514, supplied to author by the FAAM on 16 November 2012.
3 TNA, ADM 199/118
4 Chris Cartledge, *My War*, unpublished memoir
5 Keith Quilter, interview with author
6 As witnessed by the author, who accompanied Quilter to Japan in 2012.

Index

Admiralty:
  birth of naval aviation and 16–17
  briefing on categories of enemy fire 308–9
  British naval aviation on eve of Second
      World War, responsibility for state
      of 25–6
  British Pacific Fleet command and 174
  condolence letters and 9
  development of aircraft carrier and 23–4
  dimensions of Pacific war and 231
  FAA aircraft and 99, 105–6, 113
  FAA comes under control of 17, 61
  FAA organization, commissions Lord
      Evershed to investigate 29–30
  FAA recruitment and 30, 44–5, 48, 76
  FAA training and 51, 52, 53, 61, 68, 73, 76,
      77, 113
  First World War and 20
  inter-service squabbling over role of FAA
      and 22
  morale on aircraft carriers, studies ways to
      boost 295–6
  Meridian, Operation and 221
  outbreak of Second World War and 36
  paper on efficiency of kamikaze
      attacks 227
  press relations 299
  proposes capping front-line tours of duty at
      fifteen months 291
  RAF and 22
  Singapore, attempts to protect 14
  Tirpitz, KMS attacks and 138
  Y (Youth) Scheme 30
Admiralty Islands 231, 233
Admiralty Manual of Seamanship (Volume
    One) 52
aerodrome dummy deck landings
    (Addls) 131–2
Africa, HMS 16
Afrika Korps 127

Air League 32
Air Ministry 22, 25, 61, 68, 102, 138
Air Sea Rescue 41
Air Training Corps 29, 47
aircraft:
  American *see under individual aircraft*
      name
  biplanes 16, 18, 20, 27, 33, 34, 35, 62, 76,
      103, 113
  birth of naval aviation and 16–26
  bombers and fighters 100–1 *see also under*
      individual aircraft name
  bombs 6, 7, 102, 107–8, 111–12, 140, 143,
      144, 145, 148, 150, 185, 193, 224,
      242, 253, 263, 264, 270, 273, 300,
      310, 313, 322
  British *see under individual aircraft name*
  carrier *see* aircraft carriers; carrier flying
      and under individual aircraft name
  engines 18–19, 20, 25, 30, 40, 62, 75, 76,
      86, 101, 102, 103, 107, 108, 109,
      111, 112, 115, 121, 321, 344
  Fleet Air Arm (FAA) and *see* Fleet Air
      Arm (FAA)
  First World War 16, 19, 20, 23, 27–8, 33,
      34, 38, 100–14
  Japanese *see under individual aircraft name*
  machine guns 3, 18, 20, 54, 90, 103, 107,
      111, 112, 146, 149, 158, 177, 188,
      194, 217, 251, 270, 272, 310, 314,
      322, 329
  monoplanes 27, 28, 62, 83, 85, 86, 102,
      113
  'pusher' planes 19, 33
  seaplanes 17, 19
  Second World War 100–14
  speeds of 3, 6, 8, 20–1, 27–8, 64, 86, 88,
      90, 101, 102, 103, 104, 107, 108,
      109, 111, 112, 117, 143, 145, 154,
      194, 208, 273

aircraft *(cont.)*
    torpedoes 14, 15, 19, 21, 25, 27, 28, 41,
        100, 104, 111, 113, 138, 139, 140,
        141, 216, 226
aircraft carriers:
    alcohol/drinking on 160–1, 163–4, 291–2
    batsman (deck landing control officer) 153,
        154, 155, 157, 212, 311
    chapels on 159
    commander of flying ('Wings') 152–3, 157,
        191
    conditions onboard, attempts to
        improve 295–7
    cooks/diet 160, 317–18
    daily routine 161
    early 16, 19–24
    entertainment on 135, 159, 195, 245, 296,
        297
    FAA–RN–RNVR rivalry on 164–5
    first American 24
    first British 20–1, 23–4
    first custom-made 23–4
    first Japanese 23
    first landing on 19–21
    first take-offs from 16, 19, 20
    flight deck 152–3
    goofers' gallery 104, 294–5, 311
    hangars
        British carrier 17, 20, 24, 25, 101, 110,
            137, 142, 144, 146, 154, 155, 159,
            161–2, 239, 263, 295, 310, 339
        Corsair and 107, 108, 110, 137
        FAA training and 74, 78, 81
        US carrier 24, 226–7, 237
    hours flown by aircrew 10, 126, 140, 164,
        212, 239, 263, 264, 267, 290, 292,
        312
    Illustrious Class 25, 49, 175
    Implacable Class 25, 49, 175
    island 23–4, 110, 157–8, 162, 212, 240,
        247, 248, 250, 251, 252–4, 255, 257,
        262, 272, 273, 275, 276
    landings, deck 10
        accidents 21, 64–5, 104, 121–2, 131–3,
            156, 293, 294, 295, 301
        British carrier 21, 31, 101, 104, 109,
            110, 112, 131–3, 152–7, 165,
            192, 212, 218, 242, 260, 264,
            293, 294, 301, 306, 311, 314,
            317, 338
        training 64–5, 66, 68, 73, 75, 85, 89,
            115, 131–3
        types of aircraft and 101, 104, 109, 110,
            112

    US carrier 338
    life on 142, 152–60, 287–90
    maintenance crew 161, 233, 263, 309
    morale on 150, 183, 244, 270, 280, 282,
        292, 295–6, 302, 307, 308
    numbers of American/British/Japanese 24,
        98, 106
    operations *see under individual battle,*
        operation or place name
    officers onboard 153, 158, 160–1, 162, 164
    ratings onboard 160–1, 162
    sleeping accommodation 158–60
    tobacco ration 160
    wardroom 135, 148, 149, 162–3, 165, 178,
        190, 202, 203, 205, 206, 218, 234,
        238, 261, 278, 281, 287, 294, 309
    watches 161
    see also carrier flying *and under individual*
        carrier name
Akagi, IJN 24, 49
Alexander, A. V. 99, 105–6, 174
Alexandria, Egypt 36, 231
Algeciras, Spain 181
Allied Land Forces South East Asia 220
Altagaard airfield, Norway 146
Altmark, KMS 182
Amakusa, IJN 330
Andes, HMS 70
anti-aircraft fire ('ack-ack'):
    American 228
    British 3, 40, 41, 59, 246, 249, 251, 252,
        256, 259, 260
    German 105, 143, 145, 146, 147, 148, 149
    Iceberg, Operation, and 238, 239, 241, 242,
        243, 244–5, 265, 267
    Japanese 6, 8, 183, 188, 189, 193, 194, 195,
        198, 199, 200, 205, 207–8, 209, 215,
        216, 217, 218, 238, 239, 241, 242,
        243, 244–5, 265, 267, 308, 309, 310,
        312, 314, 315, 319, 320, 321
    Japanese mainland attacks and 308, 309,
        310, 312, 314, 315, 319, 320, 321,
        323, 324, 328, 329, 330, 331, 332,
        341
    kamikaze attacks, as defence against 228,
        229, 249, 251, 252, 256, 259, 260,
        265, 267
    Meridian, Operation, and 183, 188, 189,
        193, 194, 195, 198, 199, 200, 205,
        207–8, 209, 215, 216, 217, 218
    strafing tactics and 120, 141
    Taranto raid and 41
    Tirpitz, KMS, attacks and 143, 145, 146,
        147, 148, 149

Argonaut, HMS 217
Argus, HMS 131–2
Ark Royal, HMS 25, 49, 176, 177
ARP (Air Raid Precautions) 37, 41
atomic bombs 7, 8, 12, 327–8, 342
'A25' (pilots' unofficial drinking song) 157
Australia 14, 48, 173, 174–5, 176, 221, 229,
    230–3, 278, 292, 297, 298, 299, 302,
    305, 309, 317, 326–7, 331, 338–9, 343,
    345
Avro 504 34
Avro Lancaster 150
Azores 231

Bader, Douglas 30
Balao Class submarine 324
Balfour Committee, 1923 22
'Balls-Up' (FAA drinking song) 165
Barbican Plaza Hotel, New York City 128
Barin airfield, Florida 88
barrage balloons 41, 189, 193, 197, 198, 199,
    200, 204–5, 207, 208
Baumeister, Fred 335–6
Bay of Bengal 166
Beatty, Admiral 20
Beldam, Roy 33–4, 275, 277, 278, 344
Belleau Wood, USS 227
Ben-my-Chree, HMS 19–20
Bennett, Val 34, 39, 40, 46, 57, 163, 292, 306,
    308, 312–13, 330, 333–4, 335, 344
Bigg-Wither, Richard 'Biggy' 127–8, 312,
    328–9
biplanes 16, 18, 20, 27, 33, 34, 35, 62, 76, 103,
    113
Bismarck, KMS 28, 77, 105, 138, 177
Blackburn Skua 16, 28, 102, 119, 121–2,
    304
Blohm & Voss 138 (reconnaissance
    aircraft) 141
Boeing B-29 Superfortress 184, 189, 219, 221,
    235, 303, 320, 327, 328, 337
Boeing Stearman 76
Borneo 176, 269
Brewster Buffalo 116
Bristol Perseus 102
British Centre, Sydney 230–3
British Expeditionary Force (BEF) 17
British Pacific Fleet (BPF) 7, 227
    attempts to protect from kamikaze
        attacks 228–9, 230
    birth of 11, 173–6, 177, 182, 183, 340
    commanders *see under individual*
        commander name
    cooperation with American forces 9–10,

    170–1, 175–6, 229–30, 232, 234–5,
      301, 306, 331–2, 343
    financial cost of 340
    Iceberg, Operation and, 234–302, 303, 331,
      341
    ignorance about/uncelebrated 11–12,
      298–9, 302, 345
    importance to war effort of 11, 340–3
    Japanese mainland attacks and 6, 8, 13,
      303–39
    legacy of 342–3
    men return home 344–6
    Meridian, Operation, and 8, 176–7, 183,
      184–202, 203–22, 223, 229, 239,
      240, 260, 265, 270, 291, 308, 335,
      340
    Olympic, Operation, and 326, 331, 342
    renamed 'Task Force 37' 305–6
    renamed 'Task Force 57' 234, 237, 244,
      246, 269, 270, 282, 300–1
    role in Pacific war, Churchill negotiates 11,
      168–75
    strength/size of 2, 7, 231, 300–1
    Sydney base 173, 175, 230–3, 278, 292,
      297, 299, 301, 302, 305, 309, 331,
      338–9
    'Task Force 63' code name 185, 189
    see also under individual area, battle,
      operation and vessel name
Browning machine guns 3, 107, 177, 194, 310,
    314, 322
Brunswick, Maine, U.S. 123, 124, 128, 129, 134
Burma 2, 7, 170, 186, 221, 307
Bunker Hill, USS 286

Cameron, Don 257–8, 284–5, 335
Canada 175
    FAA airmen from 43, 86, 149, 279, 304,
      328–9
    FAA training in 60–1, 68, 71–2, 75, 85,
      86–9, 94, 95, 103, 113, 115, 118, 125
Caroline Islands 98, 234–5, 237
carrier flying:
    accidents 10, 18–19, 27, 66, 89, 104, 108,
      109, 117, 118–19, 121–5, 132–3,
      136–7, 156–7, 224, 267, 293, 295,
      298, 301, 308, 338
    aircraft 100–13 *see also* aircraft *and under*
      individual aircraft name
    bailing out 19, 88, 311, 323, 334
    batsman (deck landing control officer) 153,
      154, 155, 157, 212, 311
    commander of flying ('Wings') 152–3, 157,
      191

carrier flying (*cont.*)
  dive-bombing 28, 48, 49, 102, 108, 113, 116, 126, 139, 141, 143, 144, 147–8, 167, 185, 197, 199–200, 266, 314
  friendly-fire incidents 216, 218, 234, 255–6
  hangars
    British carrier 17, 20, 24, 25, 101, 110, 137, 142, 144, 146, 154, 155, 159, 161–2, 239, 263, 295, 310, 339
    Corsair and 107, 108, 110, 137
    FAA training and 74, 78, 81
    US carrier 24, 226–7, 237
  hours flown by aircrew 10, 126, 140, 164, 212, 239, 263, 264, 267, 290, 292, 312
  landings, deck 10
    accidents 21, 64–5, 104, 121–2, 131–3, 156, 293, 294, 295, 301
    British carrier 21, 31, 101, 104, 109, 110, 112, 131–3, 152–7, 165, 192, 212, 218, 242, 260, 264, 293, 294, 301, 306, 311, 314, 317, 338
    training 64–5, 66, 68, 73, 75, 85, 89, 115, 131–3
    types of aircraft and 101, 104, 109, 110, 112
    US carrier 338
  maintenance crew 161, 233, 263, 309
  morale and 150, 183, 244, 270, 280, 282, 292, 295–6, 302, 307, 308
  navigation 10, 30, 52, 54, 61, 62, 68, 73, 89, 100, 102, 112, 126, 140, 210, 294, 327
  observers 30
    Iceberg, Operation, and 292, 293–4, 299
    Japanese mainland attacks and 330
    Japanese POW camps and 335, 336
    kamikaze attacks and 226, 277
    Meridian, Operation, and 199, 206, 211, 212, 216–17
    separation from other members of aircrew 190–1
    Tirpitz, KMS, attacks and 143
    training/recruitment of 45, 46, 52, 53, 54, 61, 75, 248
    types of aircraft and 100, 101, 102, 112
    US 302
  operations *see under individual operation and place or battle name*
  ramrods (aggressive low-level sweeps):
    Japanese mainland attacks and 313,
      321, 328, 332
    Operation Iceberg and 241, 245, 247, 259, 262, 263, 264, 267, 270
    Operation Meridian and 185, 190, 192, 194, 195–6, 205, 207
  strafing attacks
    Japanese mainland attacks and 6, 8, 303, 308, 309, 312–16, 324, 333, 341
    kamikaze attacks and 272
    Operation Iceberg and 241–2, 243, 245, 256, 265, 285
    Operation Meridian and 185, 194, 195
    Tirpitz attacks and 141, 143, 148
    training 90, 116, 119, 120
  tactics 3, 8, 29, 89–90, 120, 163, 185, 197, 219, 221, 226, 236, 246, 247–8, 266, 283, 309, 321
  take-offs 10, 86, 103, 110, 112, 115, 121, 192, 317
  'twitch' 10, 89, 131, 156, 219, 238, 260, 292, 294, 295, 315, 316
Cartledge, Chris:
  accidents 121–2, 181, 310–12, 338
  Addls 131–2
  arrival back in UK, July 1944 136
  childhood and family 37–9, 41
  deaths of colleagues, on 105, 265
  DSC, awarded 150
  1842 Squadron, joins 126–7
  end of war and 282, 338, 344
  FAA fighter school, Yeovilton, time at 118
  Gibraltar, time on 181
  letters from family and friends, on 308
  life on aircraft carrier, on 142, 152, 158, 159, 163, 289, 297
  mainland Japan attacks, role in 308, 310–12
  New York City, in 129
  outbreak of war and 37–9
  reading and politics 41–2, 56, 158
  Sakishima Islands attacks, role in 265, 282, 287, 288–9, 297, 298
  Tirpitz, KMS, joins attacks upon 142, 143, 144, 145–6, 150, 265
  training, FAA 53–4, 56, 58, 60, 61, 63, 65, 67, 68, 86, 87–9, 105, 118, 121–2
  volunteers to the FAA 42
Cartledge, Reginald 38
CD 45, IJN 321
Ceylon 166, 173, 175, 176, 177–80, 181, 184, 316, 326
Chamberlain, Neville 37

Chambler, Ron 293, 294
Chance Vought Corsair 116, 159, 178, 261,
    284, 290, 293, 295, 296, 345
  accidents 108, 109, 124, 155–6
  appearance of 9, 109
  bombs 107–8, 140, 144
  carrier fighter, adapted as a 109–10
  deck landings 109, 110, 132–3, 136, 155–6
  design 107–10
  dumping of Lend-Lease aircraft off the
      Australian coast at end of war 343
  early models, difficulty with 109
  engine 107, 108, 109, 111, 121, 321
  FAA Corsair squadrons formed 110–11,
      125, 136
  fighter, effectiveness as 109, 111
  Goodwood, Operation, and 166
  guns 107, 177
  Iceberg, Operation, and 236, 239, 241–2,
      243, 245, 247, 248, 256, 257, 259,
      261, 263–4, 265, 267, 272, 274, 279,
      281, 283
  Japanese mainland attacks and 306–7, 310,
      311, 312, 313, 314, 317, 318, 321,
      323, 324, 325, 328, 329–30
  kamikaze attacks and 247, 248, 256, 272,
      274, 279, 283, 295
  losses of British Pacific Fleet 300
  Meridian, Operation, and 185, 188, 190,
      191, 192, 193, 194, 195, 196, 197,
      198, 201, 202, 204, 205, 206, 209,
      214, 215–16
  nicknames 9, 111
  Pangkalan Brandan oilfields attack and 180
  pilot training and 116, 121, 124, 125,
      127–8, 154, 155–6
  range/fuel tank 109
  speed 107, 108, 109, 111, 144, 194, 321
  Tirpitz, KMS, attacks and 137, 140, 141,
      142, 143, 144, 145, 146, 147, 148,
      150
  turbocharger 108
  wings 107, 108, 109, 110, 111, 112
Charger, USS 110, 132
'chasing tails' 118
Chesapeake Bay, Washington 132
chief petty officers (CPOs) 54–5, 56–7
China 13, 28, 235
Choshi, Japan 313–16
Churchill, Winston 1, 11, 17, 40, 97, 99, 106,
      130, 137, 138, 168–71, 172–3, 174, 227,
      228, 229, 233, 281, 343
Cobham, Sir Alan 34–5, 52
Combined Chiefs of Staff, Allied 97, 172

Commonwealth War Graves cemetery,
    Yokohama 345
Coral Sea, Battle of, 1942 48–9
Cossack, HMS 181–2
Courageous, HMS 24
Crossman, Jimmy 217–18
Cunningham, Andrew, First Sea Lord 25–6,
    228–9, 296

Daedalus, HMS 51
Daily Mail 1
Daily Sketch 150
Daniel, Rear Admiral Charles 231, 232
Darby, Ian 330, 331
de Havilland Aeronautical Technical College,
    Hatfield, Hertfordshire 36, 39, 47, 344
de Havilland Tiger Moth 62, 64, 76
de Havilland, Geoffrey 33
'death letters' 190
Distinguished Service Cross (DSC) 150, 177,
    222, 270, 277, 345
Distinguished Service Order (DSO) 222
Distinguished Service Medal (DSM) 222
Divine, David 271
dogfights:
  Corsair and 108, 180
  FAA training and 89
  future FAA pilots observe as teenage
      boys 33, 38, 42, 43
  Hellcats and 180
  Iceberg, Operation, and 251, 252, 255, 256
  Japanese mainland attacks and 308, 333
  kamikaze attacks and 266
  last few weeks of war 8, 10
  last of Second World War 333
  Meridian, Operation, and 197, 198, 201,
      204, 207, 209
  Pangkalan Brandan attacks and 180
  Sea Hurricane and 103
  training and 118
Dornier 18 (flying boat) 102
Downfall, Operation, 1945 169
Dunning, Commander Edwin Harris 20–1, 32
Duke of York, HMS 141, 173
Dutch East Indies 168, 318
Dutch government-in-exile, London 14

Eagle, HMS 43
Earhart, Amelia 32
East Indies 14, 15, 168, 221, 318
Eden, Anthony 186
Eglinton, Northern Ireland, FAA station
    at 115, 136
Eisenhower, General 174

Elizabeth, Queen 214
Emmahaven, Sumatra 166
Enola Gay 327
Enterprise, USS 24, 49, 269, 286
Errol air station, Dundee 121
Esmonde, Lieutenant Commander Eugene
    105
Essex, USS 132
Euryalus, HMS 218
Evershed, Raymond Evershed, 1st
    Baron 29–30

Fairey Albacore 16, 138
Fairey Barracuda 137, 139–40, 141, 142, 143,
    144, 146, 147, 148, 166
Fairey Firefly 2
    Iceberg, Operation, and 242, 264, 270, 292,
        293–4
    Japanese mainland attacks and 305, 313,
        330, 333, 335
    Meridian, Operation, and 185, 188, 196,
        197, 198, 200, 204, 205, 206, 207,
        209
    Tirpitz, KMS, attacks and 141, 143
Fairey Fulmar 103, 110
Fairey Swordfish (Stringbag) 43, 206, 304
    Bismarck, KMS, sinking and 28, 77, 104–5
    FAA and 27, 104–5
    North African campaign and 248
    replacement of 111, 113, 139–40, 206
    Scharnhorst, KMS/*Gneisenau*, KMS, attacks
        and 105
    Taranto raid and 41, 77, 104–5
Falklands conflict (1982) 343
Far Eastern Survival Land and Sea 284
Farman 33
First World War, 1914–18 7, 17–21, 23, 31, 33,
    34, 38, 62–3, 65, 83, 106, 173
flat-hatting 116–18, 121
Fleet Air Arm (FAA) 7, 13, 16, 22, 26, 27, 29,
    40–1, 52
    aircraft 16, 22–6, 27–8, 30, 49, 62–4, 99,
        100–14 *see also under individual*
        aircraft name
    Americanization of British airmen 9–10,
        77–8, 80–2, 136
    call-ups to 51–60
    carriers and *see* aircraft carriers
    casualties/losses
        deck landing accidents 156–7, 301
        Goodwood, Operation 180
        Iceberg, Operation 243, 245, 253, 259,
            260, 266, 267, 276–8, 280, 300,
            301

Japanese mainland attacks 8–9, 314–16,
    326, 328, 329–30, 331–2
    kamikaze attacks 5, 167–8, 227, 228,
        237, 276–8, 280, 300, 301
    Meridian, Operation 195, 196, 201–2,
        212–15, 216–17, 219, 260
    Pangkalan Brandan attacks 180
    Tirpitz, KMS, attacks 146, 147, 149
    total losses, Second World War 27, 28,
        125, 341
    training 113–14, 133, 136–7
commanders *see under individual*
    commander name
commissions, reception of 61, 94–5
cooperation with US Navy 343
flat-hatting and 117–22
friendships between pilots 122–3
Iceberg, Operation, and 8, 234–302, 303,
    331, 341
Goodwood, Operation, and 139–51, 166,
    180
Japanese mainland attacks, 1945
    and 303–39
Mediterranean campaign, 1940–5
    and 40–1, 96
Meridian, Operation, and 8, 176–7, 183,
    184–202, 203–22, 223, 229, 239,
    240, 260, 265, 270, 291, 308, 335,
    340
Norwegian campaign, 1940 and 27, 40,
    119, 176, 290
Olympic, Operation, and 326, 331, 342
Pangkalan Brandan strikes, 1945 and 180
Taranto raid, 1940 and 41
inter-service squabbling over role of,
    1918–39 21–3, 26
naval convoys, escorting of, 1940–5 40–1,
    96, 103, 113, 137, 138, 177
Towers Scheme and 68–9, 70, 73, 75–6, 82,
    83, 91, 94, 116, 120, 125
personal weapons of pilots 191
POW camps, identification of and supply
    drops to mainland Japanese 335–7
psychological effects of Pacific war on men
    of 5, 10, 88–9, 131, 156–7, 211,
    219, 238, 240, 254, 259, 260, 278,
    287–93, 295, 296, 315, 316
recruitment of pilots 7, 29–51, 326–7
squadrons 125 *see also* Fleet Air Arm
    squadrons
stations *see under individual station or*
    location name
size/strength of 16–26, 27–8, 49, 137
tactics 119, 120

Tirpitz, KMS, attacks, 1944 and 137–51,
166, 187, 265, 277, 291
training in North America 9–10, 68–9,
70–135 *see also under individual
location and training school name*
training in UK 51–69 *see also under
individual location and training
school name*
uniform 52–3, 61, 73, 77, 85, 316–17
wings, reception of 94–5, 103, 115
Fleet Air Arm squadrons 125
805 Squadron 127
820 Squadron 199, 202, 336
826 Squadron 137
828 Squadron 137, 330
848 Squadron 261, 275
849 Squadron 193, 199, 206, 208, 214, 215,
242
854 Squadron 199, 208, 243
857 Squadron 193, 198, 199, 202
880 Squadron 319
887 Squadron 139, 248, 334
894 Squadron 2–3, 139, 141, 217, 249, 251,
254–5, 267
1770 Squadron 242
1772 Squadron 292, 293–4, 333
1830 Squadron 110, 185, 196, 245
1833 Squadron 155, 159, 185, 190, 191–2,
257, 260, 284
1834 Squadron 185, 312
1836 Squadron 185, 209, 293
1841 squadron 127–8, 131, 132–3, 137,
143, 146, 147, 149, 156, 261, 263,
309, 312, 313, 328
1842 Squadron 125–6, 129, 132, 133,
134–5, 136–7, 139, 146, 147, 150,
163, 261, 264, 265, 268, 310, 313,
315–16, 321, 342
1844 Squadron 198
1845 Squadron 268
Fletcher, Rear Admiral Frank J. 48
Flight 29, 100, 295
Flight Deck 164–5, 186
Force X-Ray 192–3, 194, 196. 205
formations, flying:
FAA training and 116, 117–18, 120, 123,
127–8
Japanese mainland attacks and 306, 312,
313, 332
Operation Iceberg and 241, 247, 249, 266,
271
Operation Meridian and 193, 198, 200,
207, 212, 217
Tirpitz, KMS, attacks and 145

Formidable, HMS 113, 164, 168, 173, 260, 282
condolence letters from captain of 9
end of war and 338–9
1st Aircraft Carrier Squadron, formation of
and 7
Gibraltar, delayed at 181
hangar fire 295, 301
Iceberg, Operation, and 261–5, 272–7, 278,
279, 283
Japanese mainland attacks and 304, 305,
306–7, 310, 311, 313, 314, 321, 325,
327, 328, 329
kamikaze attacks on 3–5, 272–7, 278, 279,
283, 298, 301
living conditions on 289, 295, 297
padre in 159
size and design of 25
Tirpitz, KMS, attacks and 137, 138, 141,
142, 144, 146–7, 148, 149
Formosa 224, 235, 237, 244, 247, 255, 259,
261, 269, 285, 342
Franklin, USS 227
Fraser, Admiral Bruce:
Australian government, relations
with 174–5
commander-in-chief of British Pacific
Fleet 173–6
contribution of British Pacific Fleet to
Pacific War and 175–6, 182, 229–
30, 232, 233, 234, 341, 342
financial cost of British Pacific Fleet
campaign, on 340
Iceberg, Operation, and 300
Japanese mainland attacks and 306
Japanese surrender and 337
kamikaze attacks, experiences 227–8
leadership qualities 174, 182
living conditions on carriers, lobbies for
improved 296
logistical challenges of Pacific War
and 231, 232, 250
Meridian, Operation, and 176, 182, 183,
184, 221
press and 298
Royal Navy career 173–4
US commanders, relations with 175–6,
182, 229–30, 232, 233, 234, 341, 342
French, John 143, 146, 147
friendly-fire incidents 216, 218, 234, 255–6
Fujino, Lieutenant Masazo 334
Furious, HMS 20–1, 24, 110, 139, 141

Garland, Tony 126–7, 143, 145, 148, 150, 181,
261–3, 264–5, 268

George VI, King 1
Gibraltar 36, 181, 231
Gibson, Lieutenant Commander
       Donald 119–20
Gilbert Islands 98
Glorious, HMS 24, 173–4
Gloster Sea Gladiator 103
Gneisenau, KMS 105, 106, 119
Goodwood, Operation (1944) 139, 166, 180
Gotha G.V. 31
Grand Fleet Aircraft Committee 20
Granville, Edgar 99, 106
Gray, Hammy 149, 328–9
Great Marianas Turkey Shoot *see* Philippine
       Sea, Battle of
Grosse Isle, Quebec, Canada 72–82, 83, 84
Grumman Avenger 180, 236
       deck landings and 132, 156
       design 111–13
       dumping of Lend-Lease aircraft off
              Australian coast at end of war 343
       friendly-fire accidents and 295, 308
       Iceberg, Operation, and 239, 242, 243, 244,
              259, 261, 264, 265, 270, 272, 273,
              277, 282, 285, 299
       Japanese mainland attacks and 320–1, 330,
              333, 335
       kamikaze attacks and 2, 273–4, 277
       Meridian, Operation, and 185, 188, 190,
              191, 192, 193, 196, 197, 198, 199,
              200, 201, 202, 203, 204, 205, 206, 207–12,
              213, 214, 219–20
       replaces Barracuda in the Pacific 140
Grumman Hellcat 338
       Battle of the Philippine Sea and 167
       deck landing accidents 156
       design 111
       Goodwood, Operation, and 166
       Iceberg, Operation, and 236, 238, 239, 242,
              247, 248, 262, 264, 267
       Meridian, Operation, and 185, 187, 188,
              197, 198, 202, 204, 206, 209, 215,
              216
       Pangkalan Brandan attacks and 180
       Royal Navy/FAA and 111
       Tirpitz, KMS, attacks and 141, 143, 144
       US Navy use as standard carrier
              fighter 111
Grumman Wildcat 111, 121, 123, 125, 127,
       129
Guam 14, 168, 299, 301
Gunn, Commander 'Pop' 324
Gunn, Tommy 206–7, 210, 211, 212, 213–14,
       222

Haberfield, Jack 202
Halifax, Edward Wood, Earl of 228
Hallett, Buster 318–19
Halsey, Admiral William:
       Battle of Leyte Gulf and 223–4
       British commanders, relations with 299–
              300, 305, 324
       character 305
       Japanese mainland attacks and 305, 306,
              313, 318, 324, 326
       Japanese surrender and 337
Hanson, Norman 155–6, 159, 191–2, 197, 198,
       201–2, 204, 260
Harvard monoplane 85–6, 88, 90, 114, 121
Hawaii 14, 176, 236
Hawker Hurricane 27, 31, 118, 121
Hawker Sea Hurricane 103
Hawkes, Roy 142–3, 149–50, 191, 193, 198–
       200, 335, 344
Hay, Major Ronnie:
       'air admiral' role 177
       appearance and character 177–8, 318
       DSO 222
       FAA career 176–7
       Operation Meridian and 176–8, 182–3,
              193, 196, 197, 198, 203, 204, 205,
              207, 209, 215, 219–20
       Vian and 182–3
'hedge-hopping' 118–19
Heinkel bombers 57, 176
Hermes, HMS 23–4
Hinkins, Petty Officer George 3–4, 5, 283
Hirohito, Emperor 13, 254, 305, 334
Hiroshima, Japan 8, 12, 327–8
Hitler, Adolf 137, 138, 269–70, 281
Hockley, Freddie 334–5
Hokkaido Island, Japan 303
Home Guard 47, 58
Hong Kong 14, 342
Honshu Island, Japan 303, 304, 312, 318,
       320–6, 328
Hood, HMS 138
Hopkins, Harry 171–2
Hornet, USS 49
Hosho, IJN 23, 24
Howe, HMS 243, 271
Hudson, Arthur 318
Hull, Cordell 171, 172

Iceberg, Operation (1945) 8, 235–302, 303,
       331, 341
Illustrious, HMS 166, 168, 180
       British Pacific Fleet formation and 173
       commissioning of 25

1st Aircraft Carrier Squadron formation
 and 7
Iceberg, Operation, and 243, 257–8, 259,
 260, 284
kamikaze attacks and 257–8
living conditions on 159, 290
Meridian, Operation, and 185, 190, 191–2,
 193, 202, 204, 205, 212, 215, 216–
 17, 218, 260
Taranto raid and 41
Implacable, HMS 7, 25, 267, 304–5, 313, 319
Inayama, Hideaki 195, 201
Indefatigable, HMS:
 British Pacific Fleet formation and 168,
 173
 design 25
 1st Aircraft Carrier Squadron formation
 and 7
 Iceberg, Operation, and 238, 243, 245, 247,
 248–51, 252–5, 262, 273, 292
 Japanese mainland attacks and 305, 313–
 14, 318–19, 332, 333
 Japanese surrender and 332, 338
 kamikaze attacks on 2–3, 248–51, 252–5,
 273, 298
 length of tours for airmen on 291, 292
 living conditions in 160, 161, 162, 163,
 179–80, 190, 205–6, 245, 291, 292
 Meridian, Operation, and 186, 190, 191,
 193, 205–6, 218
 pilot stress on 291, 292, 293–4
 POW camps, role in identification of and
 provision of relief for 335, 336
 Sydney base, arrives at 230
 Tirpitz, KMS, attacks and 141–3, 147,
 148
India 177, 186
Indian Ocean 97, 125, 166, 168, 177–8, 179
Indomitable, HMS:
 British Pacific Fleet formation and 168,
 173
 design 25
 1st Aircraft Carrier Squadron formation
 and 7
 first raids on Japanese targets in Bay of
 Bengal and Sumatra 166–7
 Iceberg, Operation, and 234–5, 242, 247,
 251, 262, 267, 274–5
 kamikaze attacks and 251, 274–5
 Meridian, Operation, and 187, 192, 193,
 202, 203, 218
 Pangkalan Brandan attacks and 180
Indonesia 15
Inskip airfield, Lancashire 121

Inskip, Sir Thomas 26
Intrepid, USS 227, 269
Ishigaki Island, Japan 238–45, 247, 264–5, 282,
 285, 299, 335
Italy 40, 181
 Allied invasion of, 1943 96, 139, 284
 Mussolini killed, 1945 269
 Taranto raid, 1940 and 41, 104–5
 Tripartite Pact, signs, 1940 13
 US, declares war on, 1941 15
 Washington Treaty (1922) and 23
Iwata, Captain 322

Jackson, Lieutenant Commander P. B. 77
James, Lieutenant David 140–1
Japan Ironworks, Kamaishi 303
Japan:
 airmen, ineptitude of 218, 223, 224
 Allied raids on mainland, 1945 6, 8, 13,
 299–302, 303–39
 birth of naval aviation in 23, 24
 isolation in the 1930s 13
 'jitter-effect' of Palembang attack
 on 220–1, 340–1
 Okinawa, Allied invasion of and, 1945 8,
 235–302, 303, 331, 341
 Palembang, Sumatra, reaction to British
 attacks on oil installations at, 1945
 8, 176–7, 183, 184–202, 203–22,
 223, 229, 239, 240, 260, 265, 270,
 291, 308, 335, 340
 Pearl Harbor, attack on, 1941 6, 14, 15–16,
 24, 28, 41, 49, 68, 176, 318
 planned Allied invasion of 169–73
 surrender, 1945 334
 Tripartite Pact, 1940 13–14
 war, 1940–2, success of 13–16
Japanese Army Air Force, Imperial 19, 195–7
 *see also under individual operation and
 battle name*
Japanese High Command, Imperial 15, 99, 226
Japanese Naval Air Service, Imperial 23 *see
 also under individual operation and
 battle name*
Japanese Navy, Imperial 23, 24, 224, 247, 259,
 318 *see also under individual operation
 and battle name*
Japanese Navy Air Force (JNAF) 28–9 *see also
 under individual operation and battle
 name*
Jerome, Jenny 130
'jitter-effect' of Palembang attack on
 Japan 220–1, 340–1
John, Casper 110

Johnson, Amy 32, 294
Jupp, Don 277–8

K rocket 228–9
Käfjord, Norway 139, 143, 145–6
Kaga, IJN 24, 49
kamikaze attacks:
    Allied planned invasion of Japan and 8,
        304
    birth of 2–5, 216–17, 223–7
    British carriers withstand better than U.S.
        carriers 258–9
    British Pacific Fleet, attacks on 3–5, 8,
        216–17, 246–60, 266–7, 271–84,
        298, 299
    British Pacific Fleet's hunting of 8, 237,
        267, 269, 300, 341–2
    Churchill's concern about 228–9
    defence against 228–9, 249–50, 283, 309
    experience of being under attack by 10–11,
        227–8
    footage of attacks on British ships 273–4
    Iceberg, Operation, and 6–7, 8, 236–7,
        246–60, 266–7, 273–84, 298, 299
    kikusui mass suicide attacks 258, 269, 280,
        286
    numbers of 8, 304
    psychological effect of attacks 254–5
    repairs of damage done by 267–8
    respect for 258
    Special Attack Units 226
    success of 227–8, 236, 249
    tactics 226–7
    weather and 271
    willingness of pilots 225–6
Katori, Japan 313
Kawasaki Ki-45 (Nick) 196–7
Kimmins, Anthony 274, 280, 299
King George V, HMS 180, 216, 217, 243, 247,
    251, 264, 271, 301, 305, 332, 337
King, Admiral Ernest J. 170, 171, 172, 175,
    176, 229, 230, 233, 269, 341
Kingston, Pete 312–13, 333–4
Komerine, River 184, 185
Königsberg, KMS 102
Korean War, 1950–3 343
Kure, Seto Inland Sea 318, 321
Kurihara, Rear Admiral Etsuzo 247
Kyushu, Japan 235, 236–7, 238, 302, 304,
    318

landings, deck:
    accidents 21, 64–5, 104, 121–2, 131–3, 156,
        293, 294, 295, 301

British carrier 21, 31, 101, 104, 109, 110,
    112, 131–3, 152–7, 165, 192, 212,
    218, 242, 260, 264, 293, 294, 301,
    306, 311, 314, 317, 338
    training 64–5, 66, 68, 73, 75, 85, 89, 115,
        131–3
    types of aircraft and 101, 104, 109, 110,
        112
    US carrier 338
Langfjord, Norway 143, 144, 145
Langley, USS 24
League of Nations 13
Lee-on-Solent, Royal Navy airbase on 51, 54
Lend-Lease agreement, 1942 106, 111, 343
letters, morale and 307–8
Lewiston, US 124, 125
Lexington, USS 24, 48–9
Leyte, Philippines 168, 223, 227, 231, 263, 265,
    267, 269, 300
Leyte Gulf, Battle of, 1944 223–4
Lifeguard League system, The 324
Lindemann, Professor Frederick 228–9
Lingayen Gulf, Philippines 227
Link Trainer 65–6, 86
Liscome Bay, USS 98
Luftwaffe 42, 97, 138
Lumsden, General Sir Herbert 227, 228
Luzon, Philippines 15, 224, 227
Lyttelton, Oliver 106

Mabalacat airfield, Philippines 224
MacArthur, General Douglas:
    British Pacific Fleet and 176, 229, 230, 233
    Formosa, considers attack on 259
    Japanese surrender and 337
    Leyte assault and 223, 224, 227
    New Guinea fighting and 99, 168
McClean, Francis 16–17
Mackinnon, Lachlan 143
malaria 15, 187, 238, 277
Malay Peninsula 14
Malaya 14, 97, 168, 169
Malaysia 15
Malta 40–1, 96, 103, 110, 116, 177
Manchukuo 329–30
Manchuria 13
Manus Island 233
Mariana Islands 98, 99
Marshall Islands 98, 125
Martlet fighter *see* Grumman Wildcat
Matsushima airfield, Japan 310
Melbourne Argus 282
Meridian I, Operation (24 January 1945)
    184–203, 205, 209, 219–22, 223

Meridian II, Operation (29 January
1945) 184–5, 203–22, 223
Messerschmitt Bf '109' 102
Miami, US Naval air station at 116, 119, 120,
125, 129
Midway, Battle of, 1942 49
Miles Magister (monoplane) 62
Missouri, USS 305, 337
Mitscher, Rear Admiral Marc 236, 237,
286
Mitsubishi 3, 4, 23
Mitsubishi Ki-21 (Sally) 216, 217
Mitsubishi Zero (Zeke) 105
Battle of the Philippine Sea and 167
Iceberg, Operation, and 248, 251, 252,
253–4, 255, 272–3, 282–3
Japanese mainland attacks and 333, 334
kamikaze missions 3, 4, 225, 251–2, 253,
254, 255, 272–3, 282–3
Miyako Islands, Japan 238–45, 262, 265, 270,
271, 282, 285
monoplanes 27, 28, 62, 83, 85, 86, 102, 113
Moore, Admiral 141
morale 150, 183, 244, 270, 280, 282, 292,
295–6, 302, 307, 308
Musi, River, India 184, 185, 200
Mussolini, Benito 269

Nabob, HMS 141
Nagasaki 8, 12, 328
Nakajima Ki-43 Hayabusa (Oscar) 187–8, 209,
248, 251
Nakajima Ki-44 Shoki (Tojo) 188, 195, 196,
198, 203, 209, 211
Nakajima Ki-49 Donryu (Helen) 216
Naval Air Factory, US 76
Naval Air Factory N3N (biplane) 76
naval air power, birth of 16–26
Nazi Party 13–14, 37, 47, 138, 169, 170
Netheravon, Wiltshire 68
New Brunswick, Canada 71–2
New Guinea 48, 49, 99, 168
New Mexico, USS 227–8
New York, US 128–31, 133–5, 136
New York Times 302
New Zealand:
BPF and 175
FAA airmen from 43, 58, 76, 78, 95, 166,
190, 202, 242, 245, 281, 284, 321–2,
330
News Chronicle 298
Nieuport Scout (biplane) 18
Niigata airfield, Japan 312

Nimitz, Admiral:
British Pacific Fleet contribution to Pacific
War, on 301, 341
British Pacific Fleet commanders, relations
with 175–6, 221, 229–30, 233, 234,
269, 300, 301, 341
Iceberg, Operation, and 229–30, 233, 234,
236, 259
Japanese mainland attacks and 329
Japanese surrender and 337
Leyte invasion and 223
Meridian, Operation, and 176, 221
Octagon Conference, Quebec (1944)
and 171
Philippines recapture and 168, 223
Norfolk, Commander George 222
North American Texan 116
Norway:
Altmark boarded in fjord in, 1940 182,
290
FAA actions in, 1940 27, 40, 102, 113, 119,
176, 290
Königsberg, KMS, sunk off (1940) 102
Scharnhorst, KMS, sunk off North Cape of,
1943 173, 176,
Tirpitz, KMS, attacked off coast of
(1944) 137–8, 139, 140–1, 144, 148,
150–1
Nuremberg, bombing of, 1944 219

Octagon Conference 168–72
O'Neil, Burn 330
Okinawa, Japan:
British Pacific Fleet aircraft attack airfields
of Sakishima Islands in support of
US invasion of 234–45, 246–60,
286
British Pacific Fleet becomes involved in
fight for 229–30, 234–8
kamikaze's used to defend 6–7, 8, 269, 280,
304
Nimitz on British Pacific Fleet's
contribution to taking of 260, 300,
341
secured by US forces 299, 300–1, 302,
303
tonnage of Allied bombs dropped on 303
US invasion and capture of (Operation
Iceberg) 6–7, 8, 230, 234–45,
246–60, 286
Oldendorf, Vice Admiral Jesse 228
Olivier, Laurence 30
Olympic, Operation (plan for invasion of
Japan, 1945) 235, 304, 326, 331, 342

Onagawa Bay, Japan 328, 329
Onishi, Admiral Takijiro 224, 225
Oscar *see* Nakajima Ki-43 Hayabusa
Owase, Honshu 320–5, 345
Oxfordshire, HMHS 278
Ozawa, Admiral Jizaburo 167

Pacific Ocean 2, 6, 247, 282, 287, 297, 300,
    320, 325 *see also under individual place*
    and area name
Pacific Post 297
Padang, Sumatra 166
Palembang, Sumatra 176–7, 183, 184–202,
    203–22, 223, 229, 239, 240, 260, 265,
    270, 291, 308, 335, 340
Palembang Balloon Corps 193
Palembang Defence Corps 189
Pangkalan Brandan, Sumatra 180
Parker, Alice 129, 130
Parker, Doug 268, 313–14, 321
Parker, Nancy 130–1, 133–4, 135
Parker, Raeburn Hughes 129–30
Paterson, Ian 112, 113, 114, 206–14, 216, 222,
    240–1, 293, 299
Pearl Harbor, attack on, 1941 6, 14, 15–16, 24,
    28, 41, 49, 68, 176, 318
Pensacola, Florida 72, 83–6, 88, 89, 90, 91–3,
    115, 116, 129, 148
Personnel Dispatch Centre, Moncton, New
    Brunswick 71–2
Philip, HRH Prince 214, 230–1
Philippine Sea, Battle of the, 1944 167–8
Philippines 14, 15, 168, 176, 221, 223, 224,
    225, 226, 227
Pladjoe refinery, Sumatra 185
Port Moresby, New Guinea 48, 49
Portman, Ted 129, 130–1, 133–4, 339
Portsmouth 19, 51, 57, 59, 124
Pound, Sir Dudley, First Sea Lord 137, 138
POWs *see* prisoners of war
PQ17 (convoy) 138
Prince of Wales, HMS 14, 138
prisoners of war (POWs) 219, 318
    British Pacific Fleet repatriate 342
    escapees 140–1, 248, 284, 285
    FAA hunt for Japanese 10, 330, 335–7
    FAA pilots fear being taken as a 9, 186–7,
        283–4, 324
    FAA training for being taken as 187,
        284
    German camps 38, 140, 284
    gooly chits and 190
    Japanese treatment of 9, 186–7, 285,
        330–1

psychological effects of Pacific war 5, 10, 88–9,
    131, 156–7, 211, 219, 238, 240, 254, 259,
    260, 278, 287–93, 295, 296, 315, 316
'pusher' planes 19, 33

Quebec, Canada:
    Grosse Isle, FAA training at 68, 72–82, 83,
        84
    Quadrant conference at (1943) 97
    Octagon Conference at (1944) 168–72
Queen Elizabeth, RMS 70
Queen Mary, RMS 70, 71
Quilter, Keith:
    Australia, leave in 302
    childhood 31, 32–3, 35–6
    De Havilland Aeronautical College,
        attends 36, 37, 39, 40
    death of Wally Stradwick and 314–15, 316,
        345–6
    deck landings 154
    ditches in sea off Japan 323–5
    DSC, awarded 345
    end of war and 339
    'forgotten fleet', on 7, 11, 12
    Gibraltar, time in 181
    goofer 295
    Japanese mainland strikes and 313,
        314–16, 319, 321–2, 323, 324–5,
        345
    Joins 1842 Squadron 129
    on life onboard carrier 163, 297
    Nancy Parker and 130–1, 133–4, 135
    on new recruits 291
    Operation Iceberg and 261–2, 263, 283, 289
    return to England at end of war 344, 345
    returns to Japan (2012) 345–6
    on rivalry between Royal Navy and
        FAA 164
    Scabbardfish, USS, time on 325, 327, 339
    Tirpitz, KMS, strikes and 142, 143, 145,
        147, 148, 149, 150
    training, FAA 61, 70, 71, 74, 76, 78, 92–3,
        108, 116, 119, 130–1, 132, 133–4,
        135, 136–7

Rabaul, New Britain 48
Rabey, Sylvester 'Syl' 123–5
radio discipline 204
radio operator *see* TAG (telegraphist air
    gunner)
Rajah, HMS 134–5, 136
ramrods (aggressive low-level sweeps):
    Iceberg, Operation, and 241, 245, 247, 259,
        262, 263, 264, 267, 270

Japanese mainland attacks and 313, 321,
    328, 332
  Meridian, Operation, and 185, 190, 192,
    194, 195–6, 205, 207
Randolph, USS 286
'rat-racing' 118
Ravager, HMS 132
Rawlings, Vice Admiral Sir Bernard:
  Borneo, resists British Pacific Fleet
    relocation to support Allied assault
    on 269
  British Pacific Fleet commander 233–4,
    237
  character 234
  Iceberg, Operation, and 245, 246–7, 256,
    258, 259, 265–7, 270, 271, 279–80,
    283, 299–302
  Japanese mainland attacks and 299–300, 305
  kamikaze attacks and 246–7, 279–80, 283,
    301–2
  press, relations with 299, 301–2
  US commanders, relations with 259,
    299–300, 301–2, 305, 318
Red Cross 336, 337
Redman, Major General Sir Harold 220
Repulse, HMS 14
Reynolds, Richard 115, 141, 251–2, 255, 327
Richardson, Ralph 30
Robertson, John 248–9, 250, 252–4
Roosevelt, Franklin D. 15, 97, 168, 169–70,
  171, 172, 228, 235, 343
Rosoman, Leonard 112–13
Royal Air Force (RAF) 27, 219, 344
  FAA breaks away from and returns to
    Royal Navy control 26
  FAA compared to 16, 27, 29, 30
  FAA foundation and 21–2
  FAA under control of 21–2
  recruitment 29, 30, 41, 44, 47, 49, 68
  Tirpitz, KMS, attacks 138, 150–1, 178
  training 61–3, 68, 69, 71–2, 73, 76, 120–1
Royal Aircraft Factory FE2B 33
Royal Arthur, HMS 61
Royal Australian Air Force (RAAF) 326–7
Royal Canadian Air Force (RCAF) 86
Royal Flying Corps (RFC) 17, 21, 34, 38, 106
Royal Marines (RM) 16, 22, 176, 297
Royal Naval Air Medical School 292
Royal Naval Air Service (RNAS) 17–21, 23,
  106, 326–7
Royal Naval Volunteer Reserve (RNVR) 27,
  29, 95, 115, 139, 164–5
Royal Navy 2–5
  'air admiral' role and 177

Air Branch 26
aircraft used by 9, 99, 100–14 *see also*
    under individual aircraft name
bases *see under individual base name*
British Pacific Fleet *see* British Pacific Fleet
bureaucracy within 248
carriers *see* aircraft carriers *and under*
    individual carrier name
comes under direct command of U.S. in
    Pacific 234
cooperation with US in Pacific war 9–10,
    175–6, 229–30, 232, 234–5, 300– 1,
    306, 331–2
Eastern Fleet 166–7
1st Aircraft Carrier Squadron 7, 180–3,
    237, 304, 326
Fleet Air Arm (FAA) and *see* Fleet Air
    Arm (FAA)
Force Z 14
Home Fleet 138, 173
intelligence 188
new type of warfare for 183
operations *see under individual operation*
    name
RAF and, friction between 69
recruitment 29, 43–5
role in Pacific war, Churchill
    negotiates 168–75
Royal Marines (RM) *see* Royal Marines
    (RM)
Royal Naval Air Service (RNAS) and *see*
    Royal Naval Air Service (RNAS)
Royal Naval Volunteer Reserve (RNVR)
    and *see* Royal Naval Volunteer
    Reserve (RNVR)
strength of Pacific strike force 343
Towers Scheme and 68–9
training of airmen 9–10, 51–135
Royal New Zealand Air Force (RNZAF) 111
Ruck-Keene, Philip 9, 137, 140, 164, 264, 272,
  275, 279, 280, 306–7, 315–16
Russia 15, 96, 103, 113, 138, 150
Ryukyu Islands, Japan 235–6, 238, 261

St Eugene, Quebec 68
St Lo, USS 225
St Vincent, HMS 52–62, 68, 105, 122
Saipan, Mariana Islands 168
Sakishima Islands, Japan:
  aircraft losses per sortie 331
  British Pacific Fleet aircraft attack 240–5,
    246, 256–60, 263–7, 269, 270–1,
    281–2, 284
  British Pacific Fleet sails towards 237–40

Sakishima Islands, Japan *(cont.)*
  plans for attacks on 249–40
  US asks British Pacific Fleet to 'neutralize'
    key airfields on 237, 285, 286–9,
    292, 294, 299, 308, 341
Samson, Lieutenant Charles R. 16–17, 18, 32
San Pedro Bay, Philippines 267–8
Saratoga, USS 24
Scabbardfish, USS 324–5, 327
Scapa Flow, Orkney 137, 141
Scharnhorst, KMS 105, 106, 119, 173–4
Schofields, RNAS 326–7
seaplanes 17, 19
Second World War 1, 13
  Arctic convoys, 1941–5 96, 103, 113, 137
  atomic bombs dropped on Japan, 1945 7,
    8, 12, 327–8, 342
  Battle of Britain, 1940 38–9, 114, 121, 177,
    344
  Blitz, 1940 42–3, 47, 273
  D-Day, 1944 97, 113, 133, 169, 236
  Italy, Allied invasion of, 1943 139
  Japanese surrender, 1945 334, 337–8,
    340
  Mediterranean conflict, 1940–5 40–1, 96,
    103, 104, 110, 139, 234
  North Africa campaign, 1940–3 40, 41, 96,
    127, 181, 248
  Norway campaign, 1940 27, 40, 119, 176,
    290
  outbreak of, 1939 16, 27, 36–7
  Pacific war, 1941–5 *see under individual
    area, battle or operation name*
  Phoney War, 1939–40 37
  V weapons 136, 282
  VE Day, 1945 1–2, 7, 280, 281, 282
  VJ Day, 1945 111, 113, 125, 232, 291,
    341
Seki, Yukio 224, 225
Sendai airfield, Japan 310, 328
Service Flying Training School (SFTS),
    Kingston, Canada 68, 72, 86–9, 94,
    95, 115
Ship with Wings (film) 30–1
Shoho, IJN 48
Shokaku, IJN 49
Short S.27 (biplane) 16
Shuuji, Saito 322
Sicily 40–1, 96
Sinclair, Archibald 49
Singapore 14, 15, 189, 220
Skybird 32
Skybird League 32–3
Smuts, General J. C. 21

Society of Model Aeronautical Engineers 32
Soengei Gerong refinery, Sumatra 176, 184,
    185, 204, 207–9, 219, 220–1, 340
Sopwith Camel 31, 38
Sopwith Pup 20, 23
Soryu, IJN 49
South China Sea 14
Spartan NP-1 76
Spruance, Admiral Raymond 167, 236, 245,
    259, 269, 299, 301
Sri Lanka *see* Ceylon
Stirling, Ian 321–2, 323–5, 327
Stolvin-Bradford, Frank 57
Stradwick, Gerald 95, 307
Stradwick, Sheila 42, 95, 262, 288, 309–10
Stradwick, Wally:
  Australia, leave in 302
  death 314–16, 332, 339, 345–6
  FAA selection and 45–6, 47–8, 49
  FAA training 51, 52, 55, 56, 61, 70, 71,
    72, 74, 75, 78–81, 82, 85, 91–2,
    95–6, 98, 115–16, 117–18, 119, 121,
    122–5
  Gibraltar, time in 181
  on life onboard carriers 163, 288, 297
  Japanese mainland, operations over 307,
    309–10, 313, 314–16, 332
  Iceberg, Operation, and 261, 262, 264, 265,
    268, 274, 275, 286, 288, 297
  joins 1842 Squadron 125, 127, 128–9,
    133–4
  outbreak of war and 42–3
  return to London, July, 1944 136, 137
  Tirpitz, KMS, attacks and 141, 142, 146–8,
    149
strafing attacks:
  British Pacific Fleet deaths and 341
  FAA training and 90, 116, 119, 120
  Iceberg, Operation, and 241–2, 243, 245,
    256, 265, 285
  Japanese 272
  Japanese mainland attacks, 1945 6, 8, 303,
    308, 309, 312, 313, 315, 316, 324,
    333
  Meridian, Operation, and 185, 194, 195
  odds of death faced by pilots in 316
  techniques 90, 116, 119, 120, 241–2, 309,
    313, 315
  Tirpitz, KMS, attacks 141, 143, 148
Stringbag *see* Fairey Swordfish
Stringer, Joan 79
Sumatra 8, 97, 166, 169, 176, 180, 183, 184,
    185, 186, 187, 192, 194, 206, 211, 216,
    219, 220, 223, 341

Supermarine Seafire:
  Allied landings in Italy and 284, 291
  deck landings/deck landing accidents 104,
    132, 156, 301
  design 103–4, 156
  faults as naval aircraft 104, 156
  Iceberg, Operation, and 243, 244, 247, 248,
    249, 251–2, 254, 255, 264, 267,
    271–2, 282, 291
  Japanese mainland attacks and 305, 309,
    313, 318–19, 333, 334
  kamikaze attacks and 2, 3
  Meridian, Operation, and 185, 186, 205,
    215, 217, 291
  Tirpitz, KMS, attacks and 139, 141, 291
  training in 115, 121–2, 132
Supermarine Spitfire 27, 103, 107
Supermarine Walrus 127, 187
Sydney, BPF base at 173, 175, 230–3, 278, 292,
  297, 299, 301, 302, 305, 309, 331, 338–9
Sydney Morning Herald 174, 261, 299

TAGs (telegraphist air gunner) 30, 61, 190–1,
  206, 208, 209, 214
Taiho, IJN 168
Talangbetotoe airfield, Sumatra 195, 201
Tallboy bombs 150
Tamai, Wing Commander Asaichi 224, 225
Tarantula, HMS 173
Tarawa 98
Taylor, Bob 206, 207, 210, 211, 213–14, 222
Thailand 14
Thornberry, Eddie 142, 147
Thornberry, Joe 147
Tiger Moth *see* de Havilland Tiger Moth
Tinian 168
Tirpitz 97, 137–51, 166, 187, 265, 277, 291
Tojo *see* Nakajima Ki-44 Shoki
Tokyo, Japan 14, 235, 238, 310
  Allied air attacks near 303, 306, 313
  Allied air attacks on 331–4
  Japanese sign surrender in 337, 340
  planned Allied invasion of Japan and 304,
    305
  POW camps near 330, 335
  Quilter returns to, 2012 345
Tokyo Bay, Japan 333, 334, 337, 340, 345
Towers Scheme 68–9, 70, 73, 75–6, 82, 83, 91,
  94, 116, 120, 125
Towers, Admiral John H. 68, 69
Trincomalee, Royal Navy base at, Ceylon 173,
  179, 180–1, 183, 184
Tritton, Mike 110
Truman, Harry 343

Trumpeter, HMS 141
Tungsten, Operation, 1944 139
Tuxedo Park, New York 129–31, 133
'twitch' 10
  deck landings and 131, 156, 295
  Japanese mainland attacks and 315
  meaning of 89
  medical officers and 292
  odds of death faced by pilots and 316
  Operation Iceberg and 238, 260, 292, 294,
    295
  Operation Meridian and 219
  sympathy for those suffering from 294
  'trigger points' 292

U-boats 17–18, 70, 138, 141
Ugaki, Admiral Matome 259
Ulithi, Caroline Islands 234–5, 237
United Kingdom:
  birth of naval aviation and 16–26
  Far East empire, loss of 14–15
  First World War and *see* First World War
  Parliament 22, 35, 100
  role in Pacific war, Churchill negotiates 11,
    168–75
  Second World War and *see* Second World
    War
  see also under individual operation and
    armed force name
United States of America:
  assumes strategic responsibility for
    Pacific 48
  atomic bombs dropped by 7, 8, 12, 327–8,
    342
  attacks Japanese mainland 303–39
  British pilots trained in by US forces 9–10,
    68–9, 70–135
  British role in Pacific war negotiated
    with 169–73
  Combined Chiefs of Staff 97, 172
  dominance of Pacific war 6–7, 9–10, 11
  entry into Second World War 14–16
  state of naval aviation on outbreak of war,
    1939 22–3
  see also under individual operation and
    armed force name
US Air Force (USAF) 106–7
US Army 80
  V Amphibious Corps 98
  Sixth Army 227
  Eighth Army 286
US Army Air Forces (USAAF) 176, 184, 303
US Marines 6, 98, 109, 125
US Navy 233, 325, 332, 338

US Navy (cont.)
    advance through Pacific 97–9
    'air admiral' role and 177
    bases see under individual base name
    Bureau of Aeronautics 22–3, 68
    Central Pacific Force/Fifth Fleet 98, 125,
        172, 229–30, 236, 286, 303, 341
    cooperation with British 9–10, 170–1,
        175–6, 229–30, 232, 234–5, 301,
        306, 331–2, 343
    entry into war 14–16
    'Task Force 58' 98, 167, 236, 258
    naval aviation, birth of 22–3
    operations see under individual area and
        operation name
    Pacific Fleet 11, 15–16, 49, 168
    Pacific conflict, dominance of 6–7, 9–10,
        11
    Third Fleet (Task Force 38) 302, 303, 305,
        329
    Towers Scheme/FAA training and 68–9,
        72, 73, 76, 77, 78, 94, 96, 117, 119,
        120, 125, 132
    USAF, separation from 106
US Navy Air Corps 73
USSR see Russia

VE Day (1945) 1–2, 7, 280, 281, 282
Vian, Admiral Sir Philip:
    appearance and character 182–3
    commander of 1st Aircraft Carrier
        Squadron 181–3, 233, 234–5
    distances in Pacific War, on 231–2
    Japanese mainland attacks and 305, 306,
        307, 312, 313, 318, 324
    Operation Iceberg and 239, 247, 259, 263,
        265, 266, 267, 271, 275, 279, 280,
        290–1, 301, 302
    Operation Meridian and 183, 184, 185,
        192, 203, 205, 215, 218, 220, 221
    Royal Navy career 181–2
Vickers machine gun 20
Victoria Cross 105, 329
Victorious, HMS 293
    British Pacific Fleet formation and 168,
        173, 177, 178, 180
    commissioning of 25
    end of war and 339
    1st Aircraft Carrier Squadron, formation of
        and 7
    Goodwood, Operation, and 166–7

Iceberg, Operation, and 247, 248, 256, 272,
        274, 279, 281, 283, 284–5
    Japanese mainland attacks and 304, 312,
        317, 335
    kamikaze attacks and 4, 5, 247, 248, 256,
        272, 274, 283
    Meridian, Operation, and 185, 187, 193,
        204, 206, 211, 212, 214, 215, 222
    Pangkalan Brandan oilfields attack and 180
    Tirpitz, KMS, attacks and 138, 139
VJ Day (1945) 111, 113, 125, 232, 291, 341
VT proximity fuse 250
Vultee Valiant 85

WAAF see Women's Auxiliary Air Force
Walker, Gordon 'Doc' 148, 149
War in the Air 31
War Office 220
Ward, Dorothy 1–2, 5
Ward, Ken:
    atomic bombs, reaction to dropping of 328
    FAA training 88, 103, 115, 132
    friendly-fire incidents 256
    Hitler's death, reaction to 269–70
    Iceberg, Operation, and 230, 238, 239, 243,
        245
    Japanese mainland attacks, role in 309, 319
    kamikaze attacks and 2–3, 217–18, 255–6
    length of service 291
    life onboard a carrier, on 162, 179–80, 183,
        186, 206
    post-war life 344
    surrender of Japanese, reaction to 332–3
    on VE Day 281
Washington Treaty (1922) 23, 24
Wells, Johnnie 91–2, 117–18
Whelp, HMS 214, 216, 222, 230–1
Wheway, Derek 124–5, 137
Wills, Les 250–1
Winant, John 171
'Wings' (commander of flying) 152–3, 157, 191
Winton, John 29
Women's Auxiliary Air Force (WAAF) 181

Yamato, IJN 49, 258
Yoke, Force 205
Yokosuka dive-bombers 167, 257
Yorktown, USS 24, 48, 49

Zeppelins 17, 18, 20, 21, 31
Zuikaku, IJN 49